Social Canada in the Millennium

*Reform Imperatives
and Restructuring Principles*

Thomas J. Courchene

The Social
Policy Challenge 4

John Richards
and
William G. Watson,
Series Co-Editors

C.D. Howe Institute

C.D. Howe Institute publications are available from:
Renouf Publishing Company Limited, 1294 Algoma Road,
Ottawa, Ontario K1B 3W8; phone (613) 741-4333; fax (613) 741-5439

and from Renouf's stores at:
71½ Sparks Street, Ottawa (613) 238-8985
211 Yonge Street, Toronto (416) 363-3171

For trade book orders, please contact:
McGraw-Hill Ryerson Limited, 300 Water Street,
Whitby, Ontario L1N 9B6; phone (416) 430-5050

Institute publications are also available in microform from:
Micromedia Limited, 165 Hôtel de Ville, Place du Portage, Phase II,
Hull, Quebec J8X 3X2

This book is printed on recycled, acid-free paper.

Cover design by Leroux Design Inc.
Printed in Canada by Kromar Printing Ltd.,
Winnipeg, Manitoba, September 1994.

for Margie

Contents

Tables

Figures

Appendix Figure

Thematic Tableaux

Members of the C.D. Howe Institute

Foreword

This volume is the fourth in the C.D. Howe Institute's "The Social Policy Challenge," one of the most ambitious series of publications in its history. The 14 studies in the series range from workfare to pensions, from unemployment insurance (UI) to workers' compensation, from housing to aboriginal concerns.

The publication of this series is a daunting task not just for its scope, but also for the urgency and importance of the issues it addresses. Canada needs to modernize its basic social programs — programs that were conceived in an era of economic growth and expanding benefits for the recipients of ever-multiplying public services.

After nine years of Progressive Conservative government in Ottawa, Canadians began 1994 with a new, Liberal government in the early days of its mandate. Even though the Conservatives were driven from office — indeed, almost out of Parliament entirely — many of the cuts and clawbacks of social benefits they initiated are unlikely to be reversed by the Liberals. For example, the Conservatives were roundly criticized when, in 1992, they eliminated UI benefits for people who voluntarily quit their jobs, yet the Liberal Party platform outlined in the "red book" released at the beginning of the election campaign made no mention of the issue. Instead, it promised a full re-evaluation of programs:

> [I]f we want to have a country that works, we have to measure whether specific government programs actually deliver results over time. Whether it is in health care or regional development, we think it is important to measure the long-term outcomes and consequences of our policies and programs.[1]

Like many other Canadians, I believe the time is right for a wholesale re-examination of this country's social policies. There are several reasons why.

First, Canada's fiscal situation remains perilous: despite a healthy economic expansion, the federal deficit is expected to come in around $40 billion this year. So high a deficit means Canada's debt will continue to grow more quickly than its economic output, which in turn means the ratio of debt to gross domestic product (GDP) will keep on rising, as it has without exception since 1977. Even under fairly optimistic economic projections, the federal debt-to-

---

1 Liberal Party of Canada, *Creating Opportunity: The Liberal Plan for Canada* (Ottawa, 1993), p. 12.

GDP ratio is virtually certain to continue rising past mid-decade from today's 73 percent mark.[2] With still higher debt-to-GDP ratios, interest payments will consume an even greater share of public budgets, and the country's finance ministers will remain at the mercy of swings in interest rates. We do not necessarily have to reduce the debt ratio — though our children would appreciate it if we did — but we must stop it from growing. Expenditures on social programs are such an important part of public spending that a re-evaluation of how they work simply must be part of the solution.

Second, Canada is at a crossroads. The phrase is, of course, a rhetorician's reflex. Hardly a year goes by without someone's publishing a volume with that title. And to some extent the cliché is always appropriate: modern democracies make policy decisions almost daily, so they are continually at a crossroads. Still, the next few years will be especially pivotal for Canada, since one item on the agenda is a renegotiation of fiscal federalism — the arrangements by which Ottawa and the provinces share responsibility for public expenditures and levying and collecting taxes. At the meeting of First Ministers in December 1993 — the first held during the new Chrétien government's term — the participants promised unanimously to overhaul federal and provincial taxation as well as social programs. Although no specific proposals were put forward, it was clear that everything was on the table for discussion. No doubt, the tone of cooperation was in response to widespread public disapproval of governments' inability to work together.

Moreover, Canadians, even of the middle-of-the-road variety, are no longer willing to finance the apparently unending expansion of the welfare state into more and more marginal activities. The electorate's shift to the right — witness the dramatic rise in popularity of the Reform Party — is strong evidence that many Canadians think taxes are too high. Even the federal New Democratic Party, in announcing its election platform last year, promised to increase social spending by only $500 million, a mere drop in the ocean of a $160 billion federal budget.

Third, there is increasing concern that many of the programs Canadian governments have put in place over the years may not be good for the people they are supposed to help. Within the academic community, it is now respectable to speak of "transfer dependency," a concept for which Thomas Courchene, the author of this volume, was widely criticized when he introduced it into the Canadian debate in the 1970s. Many politicians and commentators, including Frank McKenna, Clyde Wells, and Bernard Valcourt, now agree that policies that were introduced for very good short-term reasons have created harmful

---

2 See William B.P. Robson, *Digging Holes and Hitting Walls: Canada's Fiscal Prospects in the Mid-1990s*, C.D. Howe Institute Commentary 56 (Toronto: C.D. Howe Institute, January 1994).

long-term incentives. For example, many Canadians have changed their life-styles to conform to the rules of the UI system. When, in a widely publicized case, a single mother in Toronto decided to give up her $41,000-a-year job to go on welfare, other regions of the country were brought face to face with the possibility — whatever the merits of this case — that transfer dependency may no longer be a problem exclusive to the Atlantic region.

Finally, Bill Clinton's election to the US presidency likely presages a rethinking of much social policy in that country and is bound to have spillover effects in Canada. US policy concerns are invariably reflected here, particularly with a Democrat in the White House and a Liberal government in Ottawa. Clinton regards himself as a "new Democrat," and his promise to reform welfare by offering "a hand up, not a handout" made him attractive to many middle-class Americans. In the long run, Clinton's chief effect on political life in this country may be to legitimize a rethinking of the Canadian welfare state that would have been *un*thinkable had the Republicans or Progressive Conservatives remained in power. If only Richard Nixon could go to China, perhaps only the Liberals can redesign Canada's social policies in ways that take their lead from a "new Democrat" US president.

Canadians and their governments thus are likely to be preoccupied with social policy over the next few years. It is with this in mind that the C.D. Howe Institute has decided to undertake this in-depth examination of social programs. In choosing the co-editors of the series — John Richards, Associate Professor of Business Administration at Simon Fraser University, and William Watson, Associate Professor of Economics, McGill University — I sought to bring a balance of views to the Institute's work. John Richards was a member of Allan Blakeney's New Democratic government in Saskatchewan in the early 1970s. William Watson terms himself "a member of the beleaguered cultural minority, the Canadian right." Although both are experts in the field of economics, neither had previously concentrated his formidable energies in the social policy area, and I felt they would bring a fresh view to some of the same old policy conundrums.

Readers will note that each volume will contain differing, at times oppos-ing, views as to whether a particular social program works as intended, needs fixing, or should be left alone. If the conclusion is that a program does need modernizing, the authors will recommend necessary reforms and ways to bring them about.

The C.D. Howe Institute's aim in presenting this series is to raise the level of public debate on issues of national interest by presenting diverse points of view — whether or not it agrees with them — in publications that are well researched and well grounded. The Institute hopes that, in so doing, it will give

Canadians much to think about, including the information they require to exercise their responsibilities as citizens.

The analysis and opinions presented in the study are the responsibility of the author and do not necessarily reflect the views of the Institute's members or Board of Directors.

Thomas E. Kierans
President and
Chief Executive Officer

Preface

This is the fourth volume in the Institute's series on social policy. It is unique in that it is the only volume authored by a single person. But this is appropriate, since the author himself is unique.

Tom Courchene is a native of Saskatchewan who made his way east by stages: from the University of Saskatchewan, to Princeton University (PhD. 1967), to the University of Western Ontario in London. While Professor of Economics at Western, he was chairman of the Ontario Economic Council from 1982 to 1985. Currently, he is the Jarislowsky-Deutsch Professor of Economic and Financial Policy at Queen's University, Kingston. This observation point allows him to keep tabs on the contrapuntal evolution of two of his main loves: Canada's federal government, which, despite his ex-prairie boy's decentralism, he so obviously regards as the country's axis; and the vibrantly distinct society downriver from Kingston in Quebec, which, because of his heritage, commands his fascination.

Like the country he so obviously cherishes, Courchene is a fascinating mix of talents and interests. He is an economist with a heart, a subspecies that, despite what many think, actually does exist. His professional credentials are impeccable. A past president of the Canadian Economics Association, he was trained in the intellectually rigorous neoclassical school of economics. Throughout his academic career, he has applied the analytical techniques he learned at Princeton and later at the University of Chicago to a wide variety of Canadian problems, ranging from interprovincial transfers to international trade to the macroeconomic policies of the Bank of Canada. The implacable logic of the economist's model persuaded him that the apparently perpetual relative poverty of Canada's poorer provinces may well be the result of a policy of generous federal transfers; these, he contends, encourage people not to move to other regions of Canada, where they might do better. As commonplace as this idea may seem in the 1990s, it was controversial in the 1970s when he first popularized it.

It was also in the 1970s that Courchene applied his impressive knowledge of monetary economics to the Bank of Canada's conduct of macroeconomic policy. He wrote the first two classic volumes in a C.D. Howe Institute series on the Bank, which, after Courchene moved on to still other interests, was carried on, first, by Peter Howitt, Courchene's former colleague at Western, and, most recently, by the Institute's William Robson and another Westerner, David Laidler, who last year shared the inaugural Doug Purvis Memorial Prize for economic policy analysis. Among those "other interests" were Canada's equalization system and its social policy. The interest in equalization led to another classic book, *Equalization Payments: Past, Present and Future*, written for the Ontario Economic Council in 1984. It is unlikely that, outside the federal Department of Finance, any Canadian knows more about Canada's equalization program than Tom Courchene. His growing interest in social policy bore fruit in yet another influential book, *Social Policy in the 1990s: Agenda for Reform*, published by this Institute in 1987.

All of the books that have been mentioned, as well as many more that have not — for there is much truth to the common saying among his colleagues that Courchene writes as prolifically as most people read — are characterized by two overriding qualities: hard-headedness and soft-heartedness. Courchene sees the world with the clear, unblinking focus that is modern economics' most compelling attribute: if you pay people who live in poor regions, they may stay there; if you provide generous unemployment insurance (UI), don't be surprised if unemployment rates rise; if you compensate provinces for the deficient revenue-raising capacity of their tax systems, they may re-jig their taxes so as to get the most money possible; if the money markets can figure out the rules the Bank of Canada is using to try to influence interest rates, the rules will have to be changed. These are facts of life — Courchene the hard-headed economist says. People do maximize, and if we ignore that fact we are simply fooling ourselves. Unsentimental analysis of this sort is the economist's stock in trade and, of course, it is what often gives economists a sometimes deserved reputation for being cold, hard-hearted, uncaring.

But anyone who knows Tom Courchene or has read his work knows there is more to the man — and the economist — than hard-headed analysis. As his writing plainly shows, he cares deeply about his country and about the effects that economic policies have on real people. *Has* the Bank of Canada's pursuit of an independent Canadian monetary policy needlessly worsened many Canadians' lives over the past few years? How *do* we adapt economic policies to Canada's apparently increased vulnerability to international trade? *Is* there a way of helping the less fortunate among us that does not also penalize them for helping themselves? What *is* the best way to redistribute money among the different regions of Canada, a task the polls show most Canadians still think is important? Finding the right answers to questions like these can make people — real, living, breathing people — better off. It is this endeavor that motivates Courchene.

Both these aspects of Courchene's writing — his hard-headedness and his soft-heartedness — are apparent in *Social Canada in the Millennium*. This book forms the linchpin of the Institute's social policy series. It is a book that we feel will be as important and influential as the others cited above.

Social Canada in the Millennium comes in essentially three parts. The first — which is actually Parts I to V, Chapters 1 to 8 — is Courchene's analysis of where Canadian social policy is today, how it got there, and what the future holds for it if we do not adapt it to changed circumstances. Courchene's bottom line is that "the status quo is...unsustainable and that a failure to undertake a comprehensive rethinking and reworking of Social Canada could well lead to a spiraling downward of many of our postwar achievements on the social policy front," a conclusion that establishes a sense of urgency for the prescriptive analysis that follows.

The eight introductory chapters are vintage Courchene, a rich loam of thought-provoking insights, impressions, charts, tables, and *obiter dicta*. He moves from

- interprovincial disparities — how they are like the gold standard system and why they are worse than Australia's interstate disparities;
- to the federal government's role in social policy, including the UI system, with all its problems, the retirement income system and its sometimes perverse interaction with provincial supplements to retirees' incomes, and family benefits, to say nothing about: the dubious wisdom of extending the government's monopoly over the school system to include universal day care;
- to a profile of "fiscal federalism," the many ways in which Ottawa moves money to the provinces, including equalization, Established Programs Financing (EPF), and the Canada Assistance Plan;
- to how the provinces spend on social policy and why their health care, welfare, workers' compensation, and education systems — including (a bold proposition for a professor) their universities — are in need of reform;
- to why the status quo in these matters has such tremendous inertial power, which Courchene thinks derives from the influence of vested interests, the regional "trump" in Canadian policy matters, evident now in the stalling of the Liberal government's social policy round while Quebec's politics work themselves out, and the new role of the courts and the Charter of Rights and Freedoms in determining social policies;
- to the federation's recent experience with the fiscal crunch and the offloading of deficits; and, finally,
- to the effects of globalization and the changing structure of the Canadian economy on Canadian social policy.

Taken all at once, it's a breath-taking ride.

This enthralling, encyclopedic exposition could stand as a book of its own. But, in *Social Canada in the Millennium*, it serves mainly as an introduction to the second two parts of the discussion. The first of these (Chapters 9 and 10) provides what Courchene sees as the main options for reform. Chapter 9 describes initiatives that are already under way in four provinces: Quebec, Ontario, New Brunswick, and Newfoundland. Courchene has always argued that a main advantage of the federal system of government is that it allows for a wide range of constructive experimentation, with Saskatchewan's initiatives with hospital and health care in the 1940s and 1950s being the prototypical examples. His Chapter 9 demonstrates that, in the 1990s as well, many of the most interesting ideas in social policy are being tried at the provincial level. Chapter 10 provides, as he says, a wide-ranging and fairly comprehensive (though not exhaustive) list. The reader who is pressed for time and who can only afford a few nibbles from the rich menu that Courchene has served up in his book would be best advised to try Tables 38 through 41, which compile a range of options for the retirement income system (Table 38), for UI (Table 39), for welfare (Table 40), and for federal-provincial fiscal transfers (Table 41). These options are presented and described with much discussion but minimal editorial content from the author and comprise a template of possible changes in our social policy system. Readers who want a guide to policy packages that are possible and internally consistent will be very well served by Chapter 10.

Finally, in Chapter 11, Courchene presents his own preferred blueprint for Social Canada in the year 2000 and beyond. The operational principles that underlie this blueprint are, first, that "social policy reform must begin 'from the bottom up' — that is , by focusing on individual Canadians and their social infrastructure needs". This implies that "the structure of federal-provincial transfers should be derivative, not determining." In other words, we should aim for what might be called functional federalism. Whatever federal-provincial structure will best serve individual Canadians is the structure we should aim for: "jurisdictional in-fighting cannot be allowed to stand in the way of designing a system appropriate to the needs of Canadians," a sentiment shared by almost all Canadians.

As a sampling of a few of the boldest strokes in this blueprint, Courchene would:

- *for unemployment insurance*, establish a uniform qualifying period of 30 weeks, with each week of benefits requiring three weeks of previous work;
- *for children*, abolish the Canada Assistance Plan and use the funds to provide a "low-income, anti-poverty, refundable tax credit (unlike the existing tax credit for children, which is middle income";
- *for welfare*, have the provinces focus welfare on adults, principally through an active labor market policy, emphasizing training and job placement along Swedish lines, *if* that is what provinces decide they want;

- *for minimum wages*, reduce or even abolish them — the goal of social welfare policy should be to guarantee an adequate income; wage subsidies and tax credits do this; minimum wages, which can keep people out of work, do not;
- *for postsecondary education*, the cash component of EPF should be turned into a voucher that students can take to the postsecondary institution of their choice, including universities, community colleges, private sector training institutes, and accredited industry-run apprenticeship or certification programs;
- *for training*, allow the provinces to exercise constitutional paramountcy, if they wish, so as to establish a "single window" for trainees and to improve the coordination of education, which the provinces do largely run, and training;
- *for health care*, replace the federal cash transfer with tax room for the provinces, equalized for the poor provinces, and abolish the *Canada Health Act*, since, as the "federal authorities must recognize...medicare remains a sacred trust because the provinces and their citizens deem it to be so";
- *for the retirement income system*, establish a negative income tax for the elderly by rolling old age security and Guaranteed Income supplements into a single Guaranteed Income Supplement and begin to think about doing away with the Canada Pension Plan;
- *for the constitutional division of powers*, if delivering good social policy requires some asymmetry across provinces, as it has in the past, find some way of finessing this problem, since it is citizens who should be served, not constitutional lawyers.

These are bold proposals and obviously not everyone — possibly not anyone — will agree with them. But the current social policy debate will benefit most from concreteness and least from the comfortable, woolly generalities that so far have dominated it. This book brings ample concreteness to the job — both by laying an encyclopedic foundation for the debate and by delivering a bold blueprint for what the finished structure should look like. For this, whether we agree with Courchene or not, he deserves our gratitude. And lest anyone underestimate the importance of the task that lies before us, his final paragraph reminds us that

> Canada will, in the millennium, be largely defined by its social infrastructure both in its own right and because an appropriate social infrastructure will be an integral part of competitiveness in the new global economic order....To be a Canadian in the next century must, among other things, mean that all citizens have access to a social infrastructure that allows them full opportunity to develop and enhance their skills and human capital in order that they

be full participants in the Canadian and global societies. This is what the social policy blueprint is all about. And this is why we have to succeed in rethinking and reworking Social Canada for the millennium.

If we do succeed, it will be because of contributions such as *Social Policy in the Millennium*. The Institute is proud to publish this work.

Thomas E. Kierans
John Richards
William Watson

Acknowledgments

Much of this book is in the nature of intellectual intermediation — namely, the drawing on the ideas of others and integrating them into a consistent and, I hope, unified treatise on Canadian social policy. Even a cursory glance at the references reveals the degree of my indebtedness. Thus, at the most general level, I want to express my appreciation to the Canadian policy community for their creative and insightful analyses.

By way of personal acknowledgments, my greatest debt is to Tom Kierans. Not only can he take credit for initiating the project, but his urging and encouragement led to my embedding the analysis of social policy within a much broader framework of societal forces and issues. It is also a pleasure to acknowledge the contributions of my colleagues at Queen's University: Keith Banting, Tom Kent, Arthur Kroeger, Judy Maxwell, Lisa Powell, and Hugh Segal, among others. Special thanks go to Art Stewart for our frequent discussions on virtually all aspects of the book. Colleagues outside Queen's whose ideas have had an important influence on my thinking in the social policy area include Bob Young at the University of Western Ontario, Richard Simeon at the University of Toronto, Paul Boothe and Ken Norrie at the University of Alberta, the federal government's Russell Robinson and Dick Zuker, Richard Lipsey at Simon Fraser University, and Marcel Côté at Secor. It is with special pleasure that I recognize the contribution of my daughter, Teresa Chandler, of the Economics Research Department of the Toronto-Dominion Bank, both for her valuable comments and suggestions and for converting some of the tabular data into figures.

Bill Watson, as co-editor of the C.D. Howe Institute's "The Social Policy Challenge" series, provided a chapter-by-chapter and often line-by-line critique of the penultimate draft. I am also grateful for comments and suggestions from David Brown, John Richards, Bill Robson, and Daniel Schwanen. Beyond this, the C.D. Howe Institute organized two pre-publication conferences — one for analysts and one for journalists — that provided valuable insight. In particular, the commentaries by Fred Gorbet and Jack Mintz, among others, led to important additions to the text. In this context, I would also like to thank Angela Ferrante, Monique Cormier, and the rest of the C.D. Howe crew for mounting these conferences. Every author should be so lucky!

Sharon Alton of Queen's School of Policy Studies coordinated the production of several drafts. Most important of all, however, was her always cheerful demeanor. At the C.D. Howe Institute, many thanks to Barry Norris and Brenda Palmer for seeing the manuscript through to its published form.

I wish also to express my appreciation to the Federalism Research Centre of the Australian National University for providing me with support and facilities to put the finishing touches on the book.

Finally, by far my most important source of ideas, encouragement, and counsel came from the countless hours of discussion with Margie Courchene. It is an honor and a privilege to dedicate this volume to her.

TJC
Canberra
July 1994

Part I

Introduction and Overview

Chapter 1

Introduction and Overview

The role of *Social Canada in the Millennium* is to describe, to evaluate, and, ultimately, to redesign Canada's social policy infrastructure. However, given that the manner in which we Canadians decide to rework our social envelope will be one of the defining characteristics of our nation in the twenty-first century, redesigning Social Canada is tantamount to redefining Canada. It cannot be otherwise, since this is the inherent nature of a social infrastructure — a seamless web where the social, political, economic, and regional threads lead here, there, and literally everywhere. But this is a two-way street. One cannot address the needs and challenges on the social policy front apart from the manner in which our economy and society are themselves undergoing transformation. Thus, forces such as globalization, the knowledge/information revolution, and the fiscal reality must of necessity inform the process of social policy restructuring. It is within this broader, interactive, and evolving context that the ensuing analysis of Social Canada will proceed.

It is true, of course, that at the most basic of levels Canadians may well associate social policy with the design and delivery of specific programs, such as health care, education, welfare, unemployment insurance, old age security, and the like. Yet, once one scratches the financial and analytic surface of these programs, the linkages become very apparent. Overarching, and critical to the well-being of most of these individual social programs, is the federal-provincial transfer system — Established Programs Financing (EPF), the Canada Assistance Plan (CAP), and equalization — which is, in effect, the set of social programs for the provinces. But embedded in this federal-provincial transfer system is an incredibly complex set of incentives and principles that reflect and articulate the political, economic, and redistributive underpinnings and, indeed, the values relating to the manner in which we Canadians have elected to approach not only our east-west social contract but also the way we practice federalism. This catapults social policy front and center into the politics of Canadian nationhood — issues relating to interregional or interprovincial equity and even the role of social policy as an indispensable part of the "glue" that binds us together as a nation.

Beyond these easily identifiable but very far-reaching financial linkages, there is also a set of emerging forces that at the same time redefine and constrain the role and scope of the social envelope. Some of these forces are the result of our own collective decisions. The Canadian Charter of Rights and Freedoms has brought the courts and the judiciary to the social policy table as a key player in several critical areas. Likewise, our collective decision at both levels of government to live beyond our means in terms of the debt/deficit excesses is reverberating with potentially explosive results on the future of Social Canada. Compounding this, in the eyes of many Canadians, was our decision to enter the Canada-US Free Trade Agreement (FTA) and then the North American Free Trade Agreement (NAFTA), so that the new challenge is whether Social Canada can remain a distinctive, made-in-Canada, collective choice or whether North American economic determinism will not only homogenize continental social policy, but Americanize it as well.

But not all the forces impinging on Social Canada are of our own making. The world is in the throes of one of its truly epic transformations, which, in this monograph, I shall encapsule in the terms "globalization" and the "knowledge/information revolution." In effect, this new revolution likely will do for human capital what the industrial revolution did for physical capital. This has immediate and dramatic impacts on one's conception of social policy — with knowledge progressively at the cutting edge of international competitiveness, aspects of social policy now become indistinguishable from economic policy. This is not without its own set of challenges, since the middle class in a knowledge world must include the likes of technologists, para-professionals, information analysts, and so on. While we do well at the upper (professional) end, we fail rather miserably, as do all Anglo-American societies, in such areas as technologists and apprenticeships. Social policy holds the key to offsetting the ongoing polarization of incomes and, consequently, to rebuilding the middle class.

The challenges to the social envelope inherent in globalization are equally problematical. Among many other issues, it is forcing us to reconcile our long-standing focus on east-west redistribution with the reality that our trading system is increasingly north-south.

Of necessity, all of these threads must interact with the basic values that Canadians bring to bear on the design and implementation of the social envelope. Intriguingly, this was *not* the case when much of the current infrastructure was put in place, basically in the 1950s and 1960s. Essentially, this was an era when Canada was basking in the luxury of resource rents and growing productivity, operating behind significant tariff walls and participating in a global economy that was not only tranquil but ever-expanding. As I have argued elsewhere (Courchene 1987, 7), this "sustained and unparalleled economic expansion, by bringing automatic increases in tax revenues or fiscal dividends, rendered social policy expansion almost costless in political terms." Although the Canadian social contract underwent a veritable explosion during these years, the apparent declining political and economic price of social policy in this environment of plenty meant that politicians no longer had to strive to sort out the tradeoffs between equity on the one hand and growth, liberty, and justice on the other. Indeed, the tradeoffs were deemed by our authorities to be so negligible that Canada embarked on major programs whose legislative intent was to interrupt the processes of natural and national economic adjustment — for example, the regional aspects of the unemployment insurance (UI) program. As Hugh Heclo (1984, 397–399) noted, in a comment that transcends the Canadian experience:

> After a generation or more of expansion, the democratic welfare states had produced a policy system that was admirably attuned to — and presumed — continuous economic growth. Politically it was a low cost system whose operation generated minimum conflict and maximum, if somewhat passive, support. Economically, it was in rough harmony with conventional thinking about fiscal management. Socially, it avoided raising difficult questions about social values. Commitments on the welfare state rose as commitment to it fell.

Heclo then adds (ibid.):

> more and more social policy was assumed to be aimed exclusively at solving social problems: any investment in confronting, debating and resolving po-litical problems (Who is losing and gaining? What are the implications for personal liberty? What rights are owned by whom? Is it worth it?) could be minimized.

This was the heyday of Social Canada — social policy could be and was designed and implemented without much (if any) reference to economic Canada.

However, virtually all aspects of the environment that led to this conception of our social infrastructure are now history. Sustained economic growth is no longer the norm. Except for the past couple of years, productivity has been flat for much of the period since the mid-1970s' energy shocks. Unemployment hovers frustratingly in the double-digit range. Resource rents have evaporated. The tariff walls have gone, a process hastened no doubt by the FTA and the NAFTA, but inevitable in any event. And the world economy is anything but tranquil as economies everywhere have restructured.

All of this is obviously important in its own right, especially since it undermines the viability of the status quo on the social policy front. However, it also has important implications relating to the interaction between social policy and Canadian values. One hears and reads that our traditional commitment to a generous social contract is wearing thin. This may well be true, but my hunch is that, to the extent that Canadians are harboring concerns with respect to the social envelope, these concerns attach more to particular programs than to a desire to abandon the notion of a "sharing community," to use Peter Leslie's (1993) term. Yet the former is surely beginning to impinge on the latter, which in turn heightens the imperative of social policy reform. The key point at issue here is that the societal changes alluded to above imply that the prism through which our values must be filtered has altered dramatically. Even an unswerving commitment to a sharing community will lead to a quite different social infrastructure in a context where the price of sharing is very low (as in the 1950s) than in a context where the tradeoffs between sharing and other societal goals and values have become increasingly acute.

It is in this sense that reworking Social Canada is tantamount to rethinking Canada. One example will suffice. For most of our history, we made our way in the world of nations as a resource-based economy and society. Yet, in an era in which human capital will likely dominate resource capital, we have no choice, despite our generous resource endowment, but to make the transition toward a knowledge-based economy and society. Indeed, the design of an appropriate social and socio-economic infrastructure not only holds the key to maintaining our position in the pecking order of nations, it will also be the bridge to this new era.

Initially, this book was intended to be a rather straightforward updating of my 1987 C.D. Howe Institute monograph *Social Policy in the 1990s*. While most, if not all, of the analytical content of the earlier monograph still applies (although not all is carried forward to the present volume), the scope and the context are, not surprisingly, quite different largely because the environment within which social policy must be reworked is now markedly different, despite the passing of only a half-dozen years or so.

Most important of all, the perspective is quite different. There is a sense of urgency in what follows that was not present in the earlier book — urgency in the sense that the status quo is obviously unsustainable and that a failure to undertake a comprehensive rethinking and reworking of Social Canada could well lead to a spiraling downward of many of our postwar achievements on the social policy front. Moreover, whereas the earlier volume was largely efficiency- and incentive-oriented, the ensuing analysis is rooted far more in a political economy framework. In addition, as befits a knowledge era, there is much more emphasis in the present monograph on targeting social policy reform around the needs of, and challenges facing, individual Canadians and much less emphasis on adhering to the jurisdictional and institutional structures and processes that have dominated the old social policy paradigm. Indeed, several of the themes or subthemes of the following analysis derive from this last observation. For example, I shall argue that, this time around, social policy restructuring must be a bottom-up process — in other words, a process centered on and sensitive to the needs of those who may have to fall back on the social policy support system. Among the implications of adopting this perspective is that the federal-provincial transfer system must become "derivative," not once again "determining." In other words, fiscal federalism must accommodate what makes socio-economic sense from the perspective of individual Canadians: it cannot march to its traditional drummer and once again limit what is both possible or desirable in terms of the new social policy paradigm. If there is a "mission statement" that carries throughout the entire analysis, it would be along the following lines: the role of Social Canada is to provide full opportunity for all Canadians to develop and enhance their skills and human capital so that they can become full citizens in the emerging Canadian and global society. In short, the time has come for the surpluses of the federal system to filter down to individual Canadians rather than being pre-empted by governments.

Now that I have broached aspects of the analysis that follows, it is appropriate to detail the outline of the book.

Outline of the Analysis

The structure of the analysis differs from most public policy treatises in that few, if any, of the chapters are self-contained — all represent essential building blocks leading to the development of a blueprint for the new Social Canada that appears in the final chapter. For illustrative purposes, consider the equalization program. The details of this program are presented in Chapter 4 as part of the description and evaluation of the status quo as it relates to fiscal federalism. While the chapter includes some options for reform, the analysis remains incomplete because it is only in later chapters (such as Chapter 7 on deficit shifting and Chapter 8 on globalization and the information revolution) that new and relevant perspectives are brought to bear on the role that equalization ought to play in the restructured social envelope. And it is only as part of the new blueprint for Social Canada (Chapter 11) that the new and markedly different proposal for equalization takes final shape and form.

What this means is that the analysis accumulates, layer by layer, as it were, as new factors or forces are introduced and as social policy progressively interfaces with the full reality of the new societal order. I recognize that this approach has drawbacks — as already noted, the major section on equalization in Chapter 4 does not incorporate the full equalization proposal that appears as part of the new social policy blueprint. The potential upside of this approach is that it drives home the message that what is appropriate in terms of Canada's new social policy infrastructure cannot be determined by focusing solely on the internal operations of the social envelope. One can, of course, derive operational principles at this level, but these principles must be filtered through the full set of realities that will characterize Canadian society in the millennium. The point here is not so much to defend the approach that follows, but to apprise the reader of the manner in which the analysis is structured.

In more detail, the content of the analysis is as follows. Part III focuses on the federal government's presence in the social policy area. Chapter 3 describes and evaluates Ottawa's role in delivering direct programs to Canadians — for example, old age security, pensions, UI, and day care. Chapter 4 then turns attention to fiscal federalism or the federal-provincial financial interface — EPF, CAP, and equalization.

Part IV, which consists of a single lengthy chapter, details provincial government presence in the social policy arena. Programs coming under review and assessment include health, education, welfare, workers' compensation, and training. The inclusion of training under the provincial umbrella is admittedly arbitrary — the rationale has to do with its close links with other provincial responsibilities such as postsecondary education and welfare.

With Part V, "The Political Economy of Social Policy Reform," begins the "layering process" alluded to earlier, where new perspectives are brought to bear on the analysis of the status quo undertaken in Parts III and IV. Chapter 6, focuses on why the social envelope has not evolved when wholesale restructuring was the order of the day in the private sector. The analysis deals in turn with the role of vested interests, the "capture" theory of federalism, the role of the courts, and the existence of public sector monopolies and sinecures. The framework for much of the analysis is adapted from the recent macro growth literature with its emphasis on positive feedbacks and path dependence and, more generally, the concept of Schumpeterian "creative destruction." The chapter ends on an optimistic note in that it focuses on a set of forces that may serve to overwhelm this evolutionary gridlock.

Chapter 7 addresses "federal offloading" or "deficit shifting." The issues here are potentially explosive — the EPF freeze, the 28-cent-dollar sharing for Ontario under CAP compared with 50-50 sharing for the have-not provinces, and the ceiling on equalization. The analysis presents both a provincial and federal perspective on this paring of the growth of federal-provincial transfers. However, the overarching issue here is the impact of the debt and deficit burdens on the future of Social Canada and, in particular, the reality that the new social order will have to be redesigned within a context of fiscal restraint, if not fiscal constraint.

The final and probably most important bit of layering is the subject matter of Chapter 8 — globalization and the knowledge/information revolution. In terms of globalization, developments such as the internationalization of production, the shift from an east-west to a north-south trading axis, and the fact that comparative advantage is becoming more a regional than a national characteristic all have a major influence on what is appropriate for the future of Social Canada. In terms of the informatics revolution, now the fact that knowledge is at the cutting edge of competitiveness implies that aspects of social policy become progressively indistinguishable from economic policy. Moreover, in a human-capital and skills-formation era, the east-west social contract has to begin to privilege "people" rather than "place." Until this point in the analysis, one could probably mount a case that a straightforward cost-cutting exercise on the social policy front represented a viable alternative to the status quo. Not so once globalization and the information/knowledge revolution are layered into the analysis: a restructured social envelope is essential to our future economic competitiveness and well-being.

With the mandate for reform and restructuring now established, Part VI, "Reform and Restructuring: Initiatives and Options," directs attention to reform initiatives and options. Chapter 9 details and evaluates a selective set of recent provincial initiatives and/or proposals as well as the social policy reform initiatives contained in the 1994 federal budget. Chapter 10 then provides a summary to this point in the analysis. The core of this chapter is a series of tables that present a rather comprehensive range of options with respect to UI, welfare, the retirement-income subsystem and the constellation of federal-provincial transfers. This serves as a convenient menu of reform options from which readers can select their own preferred future for Canada's social policy infrastructure.

The final chapter presents my blueprint for the evolution of Canada's social envelope. The chapter begins by drawing together the restructuring imperatives and the restructuring principles that underpin the analysis in the previous chapters. With this as backdrop, I then proceed to develop a 13-point blueprint for a renewed Social Canada. After focusing on the implications of the blueprint for various issues (such as the division of powers and the fiscal imperative), some concluding observations complete the chapter and the book.

The analysis of rethinking and reworking Social Canada begins with a focus on provincial economic disparities. The rationale for this as the launch point has to do with the fact that, whereas the origins of the typical European welfare state are found in the interplay of national or class politics, the origins of the Canadian welfare state arise largely in the context of the pursuit of interregional or interprovincial equity. In an important sense, therefore, as go the fortunes of the various provinces, so goes Social Canada. Thus, the first issue to be addressed is the following: what are the economic fortunes and prospects of the various provinces and provincial economies and with what likely impact for the evolution and future of Social Canada? To this I now turn.

Part II

Provincial Economic Disparities and the Transfer System

Chapter 2

Economic Underpinnings of Social Canada:
The Viability of the Provincial Economies

The purpose of this opening substantive chapter is to focus on Canada's economic and socio-economic prospects from the perspective of the viability of the individual provincial economies. As already noted, one rationale for this vantage point is that, unlike the typical European welfare state, which had its origins in national class politics, the Canadian welfare state arose not so much as part of an inclusive national social contract among citizens but as a way of addressing interregional and interprovincial equity (Banting 1992). That is, the emergence of our welfare state was grounded in "fiscal federalism" rather than "class politics" or, alternatively, fiscal federalism emerged in large measure to accommodate the development of the Canadian welfare state since much of what Canadians hold near and dear in terms of social policy falls under the constitutional responsibility of the provinces. Thus, from Chapter 5, the provinces collectively spent $100 billion in fiscal year 1990/91 on health, social services and education. Setting aside the social insurance (contributory) programs such as unemployment insurance (UI), the Canada Pension Plan and Quebec Pension Plan, and workers' compensation, provincial *direct* spending on social programs exceeds federal *direct* spending, although the shares become more clouded if one includes Ottawa's indirect spending (the federal-provincial transfers) in any comparison. In any event, the economic status of the various provinces and, in particular, their respective income, employment and transfer environments become critical variables in terms of such issues as the ability to sustain "national standards" in the social policy arena.

This provincial focus is, however, important for several other reasons. For example, among the observations arising in the context of the Chapter 8 discussion of globalization are that

- increasingly, Canada should no longer be viewed as a single east-west economy, but as a series of north-south cross-border economies and, relatedly,

- comparative advantage is more and more appropriately viewed as a regional, or in some cases a provincial, rather than a national phenomenon. What this means is that we will eventually have to balance our internal goals of interprovincial and interpersonal equity with the challenges relating to regaining comparative advantage and international competitiveness. To understand the implications of this tradeoff requires, among other factors, an appreciation of the existing economic situation of the various provinces.

Undoubtedly, however, the most controversial rationale has to do with the fact that an important part of what makes the status quo on the social policy front unsustainable relates to the impacts it has had on the various provincial economies. Thus, in what follows I shall introduce concepts such as "transfer dependency" and the related notion of a "policy-induced equilibrium."

A final rationale is that a knowledge and understanding of provincial disparities is essential in terms of framing proposals for a new Social Canada. For example, a dramatic change to the UI system would have different impacts across the provinces. How much of the resulting added pressure on welfare or social assistance should be borne (at least in the short term) by the federal government and how much by the provinces?

Hence, Social Canada is so inextricably linked with provincial economic prospects, with the nature of interprovincial adjustment, and with the overarching set of interpersonal and interprovincial transfers that understanding the latter is essential to rethinking and restructuring our social envelope. Accordingly, most of this chapter is devoted to detailing selected aspects of the various provincial economies.

The analysis begins with a comparison across provinces of alternative definitions of income per capita — gross domestic production, personal income, personal disposable income, and so on. The evidence will reveal large and persistent disparities. This leads rather naturally to a discussion of the various potential adjustment mechanisms and, in particular, why they have failed to ameliorate these long-standing provincial disparities. Part of the answer relates to the complex manner in which the overall transfer system (both interprovincial and federal-provincial) has interacted with the various provincial economies. In turn, this leads to assessing what I refer to as a triad of dysfunctions — transfer dependency, policy-induced equilibria, and intergovernmental gaming.

The final sections of the chapter broaden the analysis to include the national as well as the provincial perspective in terms of a set of economic indicators including tax rates and deficit/debt ratios.

The concluding section will draw out those observations and implications, often in the form of a series of bullets, that are relevant to rethinking and reworking Social Canada.

Provincial Economic Disparities

Per Capita GDPs

The most commonly used measure for focusing on provincial economic disparities is the provincial equivalent of gross domestic product, which will be designated by *GDP*. To facilitate cross-province comparisons, these income data will be presented in per capita terms. Thus, *GDP/P* refers to gross provincial or domestic product per person. One obvious approach would be to present the dollar value by province for these per capita income data. However, the approach adopted here is to express per capita income as a percent of the national average (or all-province average). If, as is the case, Prince Edward Island has a value for *GDP/P* that is 64 percent of the all-province average, then the entry for PEI will be 0.64.

With this as backdrop, I now turn to the provincial income comparisons for 1991, which appear in Table 1. The data for gross domestic product per person appear in column 1. Prince Edward Island and Newfoundland have per capita gross provincial products just under two-thirds of the national average. Alberta's *GDP/P* is 115 percent of the national average. In order to facilitate assessing the degree or extent of the disparities, the last row in the table presents what is referred to as a high/low ratio. In terms of *GDP/P*, the high province is Alberta and the low province is PEI and the resulting high/low ratio is 180 percent. That is, Alberta's income per capita is 180 percent of that of PEI.

At this point one could simply conclude that substantial income disparities do exist and move on to other aspects of the analysis (and some readers may wish to do so, since the analysis that follows is quite technical). However, the rest of Table 1 is designed to probe a bit deeper and to focus not only on some of the reasons these disparities are so large but also on the manner in which the transfer system ameliorates these earned-income disparities.

Toward this end, the first four columns "decompose" *GDP/P* into its components. Prior to approaching this decomposition in words, it is convenient to cast it in notational terms:

$$\frac{GDP}{P} \equiv \frac{GDP}{E} \bullet \frac{E}{LF} \bullet \frac{LF}{P} \, , \tag{1}$$

where

Table 1: *Provincial Income Disparities, 1991*
(relative to the national average)

	GDP/P (1)	E/LF (2)	LF/P (3)	GDP/E (4)	PY/P (5)	PDI/GDP (6)	PDI/P (7)	PDI'/P (8)	AHE^a (9)	Transfers to Persons: Wages and Salaries	
										Absolute (10)	Relative^b (11)
Newfoundland	0.65	0.91	0.83	0.87	0.76	1.25	0.81	0.83	0.92	0.57	2.21
Prince Edward Island	0.64	0.92	0.96	0.72	0.76	1.25	0.79	0.81	0.80	0.48	1.87
Nova Scotia	0.78	0.98	0.92	0.87	0.83	1.09	0.85	0.85	0.92	0.34	1.32
New Brunswick	0.76	0.96	0.88	0.88	0.80	1.10	0.83	0.84	0.87	0.39	1.53
Quebec	0.91	0.98	0.97	0.96	0.94	1.01	0.92	0.93	0.96	0.30	1.18
Ontario	1.09	1.01	1.04	1.04	1.10	1.00	1.09	1.09	1.04	0.21	0.83
Manitoba	0.86	1.02	0.97	0.87	0.86	1.06	0.91	0.92	0.90	0.29	1.15
Saskatchewan	0.80	1.03	0.96	0.82	0.82	1.06	0.82	0.86	0.91	0.36	1.41
Alberta	1.15	1.02	1.06	1.06	1.01	0.88	1.01	1.03	1.01	0.20	0.81
British Columbia	1.05	1.00	1.01	1.03	1.04	1.00	1.04	1.06	1.05	0.25	0.98
Canada	1.00	1.00	1.00	1.00	1.00	1.00	1.00	1.00	1.00	0.26	1.00
High/Low	1.80	1.13	1.28	1.47	1.45	1.42	1.38	1.35	1.31	N/A	2.73

Notes:

The product of columns (2), (3), and (4) may not equal column (1) because figures have been rounded to two decimal places.

PDI' equals PDI after the allocation of the federal deficit across provinces (by provincial shares of federal taxation).

^a AHE equals average hourly earnings (fixed-weighted).

^b The relatives in column (11) are not identical to those that would derive from column (10), because the calculations in (11) are based on four rather than two decimal places.

Source: Statistics Canada, *Provincial Economic Accounts: Annual Estimates, 1981–1991*, cat.13-213.

GDP/P =   gross domestic (provincial) product per capita;

E/LF =   the employment rate, where E is employment and LF is the labor force. This equals unity minus the unemployment rate. This is column (2) of Table 1.

LF/P =   the labor force as a proportion of total population. As a technical aside, this is the product of the participation rate, LF/LFA (where LFA is the labor force age population) and the dependency ratio, LFA/P (where the difference between LFA and P relates to those not of labor force age, that is, children and elderly). This is column (3) of Table 1.

GDP/E =   gross provincial product per employed person, E, which is calculated as a residual. This appears as column (4) of Table 1.

Thus, column (1) (GDP/P) is the product of columns (2) through (4) of Table 1.

To facilitate the interpretation of this decomposition, it is convenient to focus on a particular province, say Prince Edward Island. Statistically, the product of the figures in columns 2 through 4 equals the 0.64 figure in column 1— that is, $0.64 = 0.92 \times 0.96 \times 0.72$. Thus, whereas income per employed worker in PEI (column 4) is 72 percent of the national average, GDP/P is only 64 percent of the national average. (Note that one way to view GDP/E is that it is a proxy measure for provincial productivity.) Why is PEI closer to the national average in terms of productivity (GDP/E) than it is in terms of income per capita, GDP/P? The answer is that Prince Edward Island's employment rate (E/LF) is also less than the national average (that is, 92 percent) and so is Prince Edward Island's ratio of its labor force to its total population $(LF/P$ in column [3]).

What is particularly striking about these data is that for *all five provinces east of Ontario*, the value for each and every entry in columns (2) through (4) is less than unity — that is, below the national average. Thus, the reason Newfoundland or PEI has a low per capita income (column (1)) is not only that its income per employed person is low, but also that it has a lower-than-average employment rate and a lower-than-average ratio of labor force to total population.

Turning in somewhat more detail to the disparities in income per employed person $(GDP/E$ in column [4]), Prince Edward Island holds down the bottom rung with 72 percent of the national average. Saskatchewan is next lowest with 82 percent and then Manitoba and the rest of Atlantic Canada fall in the 87–88 percent range. On the upside, Alberta records a value of GDP/E that is 106 percent of the national average. Hence, it is clear that the disparities in income per employed person are much less than the disparities in income per capita. The high/low ratio (Alberta and PEI for column [4]) is 1.47, which is much lower than the 1.80 for column (1). Indeed, given that PEI is really an outlier in terms of column (4), the high/low ratio would fall to 1.29 were one to use Saskatchewan as the low end, or roughly 40 percent of the GDP/P high/low ratio.

The reason for this magnification of disparities as one moves from GDP/E to GDP/P has already been alluded to. It is not that the disparities in E/LF and LF/P are all that startling — their high/low ratios are 1.13 and 1.28, respectively.[1] Rather, it is because of the particular *distribution across provinces* of the values of E/LF and LF/P. Those provinces with low values for GDP/E tend also to have low values for E/LF and LF/P, and vice versa. For example, British Columbia, Ontario and Alberta have values of unity or greater for all of the entries in columns (2) through (4). This automatically means that the disparities associated with per capita GDPs across provinces will exceed those associated with GDP/E.

This is probably the appropriate point in the analysis of Table 1 to direct attention to column (9), the provincial relatives for AHE (average hourly earnings). Except for New Brunswick, the relatives for AHE for the remaining six "have-not" provinces[2] are at least as large as (and in most cases quite a bit larger than) the relatives for GDP/E. For example, Nova Scotia's wages from column (9) are 92 percent of the national average, whereas its income per employed person in column (4) is only 87 percent. If one assumes that GDP/E is a reasonable approximation for productivity, this means that, relatively speaking, wages are higher than productivity for most low-income provinces. This observation will accord well with the later analysis of the role of the transfer system on regional disparities. To anticipate this analysis somewhat, part of the argument will be that transfers keep wages up, which, in the face of lower productivity, keep unemployment rates up, which, in turn, more or less guarantee the relative income results described above.

---

1   As an aside, the high/low ratio for E/LF is small because it is expressed in terms of *employment rates*, instead of *unemployment rates*. Were one to use the latter, the high/low ratio would obviously be very much higher — well over 2.00 for example. However, the methodology of equation (1) calls for the use of employment rates.

2   I follow established convention here by referring to the seven provinces that qualify for equalization as the "have-not" provinces. These equalization-receiving provinces include all provinces except Ontario, Alberta, and British Columbia. These three provinces are typically referred to as the "have" provinces.

Personal- and Disposable-Income Disparities

The remainder of Table 1 brings the operations of the transfer system, in one way or another, into the comparison of provincial relatives. Column (5) presents the personal income per capita (PY/P) averages. From the national accounts methodology, transfers to persons, whether provincial or federal, do not enter GDP — that is, they do not enter the *GDP/P* data in column (1) — but they are a component of personal income. Not surprisingly, therefore, the column (5) figures reveal a *much reduced* degree of provincial disparity than do the column (1) figures. Newfoundland and Prince Edward Island are now at 76 percent of the national average (compared with 65 and 64 percent for *GDP/P*). Moreover, Ontario is now the "top" province, largely because much of the Alberta resource rents accrue to the province or to corporations and, therefore, do not flow through to personal income.

Personal disposable income (*PDI*) is perhaps the most appropriate comparative aggregate in terms of how the tax-transfer system operates to convert GDP into income in the hands of persons. Specifically, *PDI* equals that portion of GDP that accrues to persons plus transfers and subsidies to persons minus personal taxes. In identity terms, we can write

$$\frac{PDI}{P} \equiv \frac{PDI}{GDP} \bullet \frac{GDP}{P} . \tag{2}$$

In terms of Table 1, this means that column (7) equals the product of columns (6) and (1).

The data for *PDI/GDP* (column 6) reveal that the interplay of the tax-transfer system is such that Prince Edward Island and Newfoundland benefit by about 25 percent (relative to the national average) and Nova Scotia and New Brunswick benefit by roughly 10 percent. What this implies is that *PDI/P* (column [7]) is distributed much more equally than *GDP/P* — the high-low ratio falls by more than half from 1.80 to 1.38. From about 65 percent of the national average in terms of *GDP/P*, Newfoundland and Prince Edward Island now record ratios for *PDI/P* in the 80 percent range. Note that Alberta has the lowest *PDI/GDP* ratio (0.88) largely because, as already noted, the resource rents accrue not to persons but to government and corporations. Thus, while Alberta records the highest value for *GDP/P*, its value for *PDI/P* is roughly at the national average value (1.01).

The column (8) data, *PDI'/P*, incorporate the fact that the federal government is running a deficit for 1991 in the neighborhood of $30 billion on a national accounts basis. *PDI'* is defined as *PDI less* the amount of taxes by province that would be necessary to balance the federal budget, where the provincial shares of Ottawa's revenue are calculated from Table 6 of Statistics Canada's *Provincial Economic Accounts; Annual Estimates, 1981–1991.*[3] The results indicate a further narrowing of regional disparities — Prince Edward Island now has 81 percent of the national average and the high/low ratio falls further to 1.35. This reduction in provincial disparities as one moves from column (1) to column (8) is cast in graphical terms in Figure 1.

The narrowing of disparities from *GDP/P* through to *PDI'* reflects the operations of the transfer system. That after-transfer income should be distributed more equally than *GDP/P*, whether across individuals or across provinces, is hardly surprising. Indeed, this is one of the principal rationales for transfers and this rationale is not challenged in the analysis in this and later chapters. What can and will be addressed and challenged, however, is the magnitude of these transfers and the nature of the incentives embedded within the individual transfer programs as well as within the entire transfer system.

To conclude this discussion of interprovincial transfers, column (10) of Table 1 presents the absolute value of the ratio of transfers to persons (federal and provincial) to wages and salaries, while column (11) converts this to a relative measure. In absolute value, this ratio runs from 57 percent in Newfoundland to 20 percent in Alberta, with Newfoundland recording 221 percent of the national average in relative terms (column [11]). Figure 2 presents a graphical version of the data in column (11). Note that, in terms of column (11), Saskatchewan, at 141 percent of the national average, ranks above Nova Scotia in terms of this measure of transfer dependency. From a position in the first half of the 1980s, when it joined the "have" provinces (in terms of being ineligible for equalization), Saskatchewan now appears to be entrenched as an enduring member of the "have-not" provinces, thanks in part to falling energy and grain prices.

The Persistence of Regional Disparities

Table 1 is a snapshot in time — 1991. As such, it contains no direct information about the *persistence* of regional disparities. Fortunately, we can draw upon a recent study by the Canadian Labour Market and Productivity Centre (CLMPC 1990). Table 2, reproduced from this article, presents the trends in regional disparities for the Atlantic region. The data for GDP per capita reveal a closing of the disparity gap — 59.2 percent of the national average in 1966 to 67.8 percent in 1988. Calculations for 1991 indicate that the Atlantic region's relative

---

3 The shares are as follows: Newfoundland (.0127); Prince Edward Island (.0033); Nova Scotia (.0304); New Brunswick (.0209); Quebec (.2173); Ontario (.4383); Manitoba (.0308); Saskatchewan (.0263); Alberta (.0965); and British Columbia (.1236).

Figure 1: *Provincial Income Disparities, 1991*
(relative to the national average)

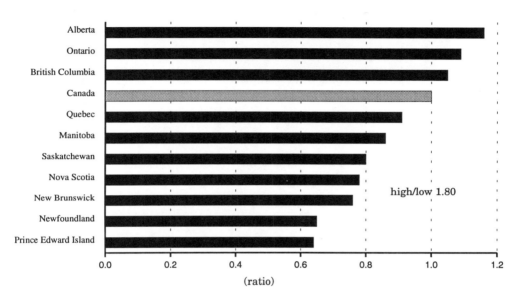

A. *GDP per Person* (GDP/P)

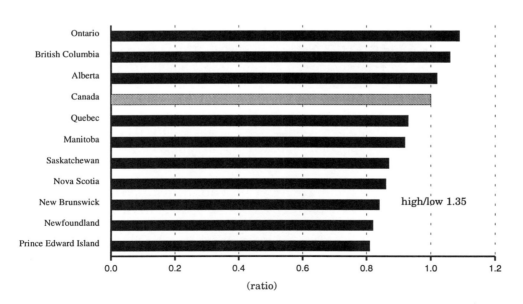

B. *Personal Disposable Income per Person* (PDI'/P)

Source: Statistics Canada, *Provincial Economic Accounts: Annual Estimates, 1981–1991*, cat. 13-213.

Figure 2: ***Transfers to Persons as a Share of Wages and Salaries, 1991***
                (relative to the national average)

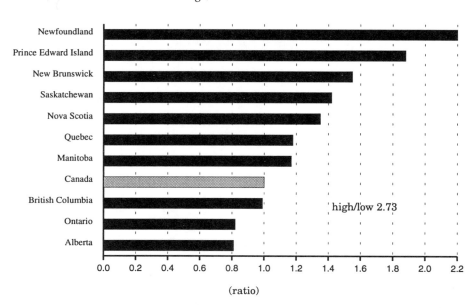

Source: Statistics Canada, *Provincial Economic Accounts: Annual Estimates, 1981–1991*, cat. 13-213.

disparity has been further reduced to 73 percent — although part of this may reflect the very distressed state of the Ontario economy in 1991. Commenting on the sources of the 1988 disparities, the CLMPC notes:

> In 1988, per capita GDP in Atlantic Canada was 67.8 percent of the national average...This 32.2 percentage gap was due about equally to lower productiv-ity levels in Atlantic Canada at 82.3 percent of the national average [nominal GDP per employed person in Table 2] and to the fact that the share of the working age population employed was 83.6 percent of the national average. Regional differences in age structure and average weekly hours played only a minimal role in accounting for regional income differences (1990, p. 29).

Note that the methodology underlying Table 2 differs a bit from that in Table 1. The latter focuses on E/LF and LF/P whereas the CLMPC approach uses E/LFA and LFA/P, where LFA is the labor force age population. This leads to a somewhat different interpretation of the roles played by the unemployment rate, the participation rate, and the dependency rate in terms of the sources of provincial disparity. Combining the results in Tables 1 and 2, what this essen-tially means is that the participation rate, LF/LFA, is really behind the low ratios in column (3) of Table 1. There is no "correct" way of presenting this.

Table 2: ***Trends in Determinants of***
Per Capita GDP in Atlantic Canada, 1966–88
(percentage of national average)

	1966	1973	1981	1988
Nominal per capita GDP	59.2	62.0	58.1	67.8
Nominal GDP per employed person	72.7	76.3	73.2	82.3
Employment/working age population ratio	86.3	85.6	82.6	83.6
Working age population/total population ratio	94.5	95.0	96.0	98.4
Actual average weekly hours	—	100.6	100.3	101.1
Nominal wages and salaries per employed person	76.3	79.4[a]	80.9	82.2

[a] This number is for 1975.
Source: CLMPC 1990, 29.

This comment aside, the CLMPC article goes on to point out that discretionary federal governmental expenditure policies contributed significantly to the reduction of income disparities in Atlantic Canada:

A rough estimate of the contribution [of federal government expenditure to the reduction in regional disparity] can be made by assuming that per capita federal expenditures on transfers to governments, transfers to persons, and goods and services increased over the 1961–88 period at the national rate, not the actual rate of increased expenditures in Atlantic Canada. Per capita GDP in 1988 would then have been $14,550 rather than $15,769, or 62.7 percent of the national average, instead of the actual 67.8 percent. By this calculation, increased federal expenditure would have directly accounted for 4.9 percent of the 8.6 percentage point improvement in Atlantic Canada's relative income position. The contribution of the federal government to the reduction in income disparities would be even greater when the indirect effects are factored into the analysis. (CLMPC 1990, 36.)

The article concludes:

While successful in reducing income disparities, the federal government spending has not been successful in lowering regional unemployment disparities. Atlantic Canada's unemployment rate is now much higher relative to the national average than it was in the 1960s and 1970s.

It appears to be relatively easy for the federal government to redistribute expenditure towards the poorer regions. Provincial governments are provided with equalization payments and other forms of assistance; national social programs which favor the poorer regions such as UI are developed; and procurement policy is used to purchase goods and services. Since the 1960s, all three of these policy tools have been used to support income levels and foster economic activity in Atlantic Canada.

It appears to be much more difficult for the government to create employment opportunities in underdeveloped regions. Subsidies to businesses to establish new industry may often be ineffective while direct government job creation may in many cases offer limited possibilities for long-term employment. This suggests that the government has had much less control over the job creation process than the income generation process. (Ibid.)

Readers will no doubt have different interpretations of these findings. One message could be that the federal government need only put more funds into the Atlantic region in order to ameliorate further the regional disparities. However, it would seem difficult to maintain this perspective in light of Tables 1 and 2. The role of transfers in the Atlantic provinces, and more recently in Saskatchewan, is already well above the national average. Indeed, for two provinces, Newfoundland and Prince Edward Island, personal income exceeds GDP for 1991. Moreover, not only has transfer growth leveled off since 1991 (especially in terms of transfers to provinces) but, given the depths of the recent recession as well as the deficit levels, Canadians' "taste" for the existing degree of interregional transfers is arguably diminishing. The position that I take on this issue is not all that different from the observations of Assar Lindbeck (1993, 9) on the Swedish economy:

[T]he traditional welfare state, chiefly designed to provide economic security and to wipe out poverty, may after a while turn into a "transfer state" with free-for-all redistributions to various groups of citizens at the expense of the general taxpayer. Politically determined redistribution may, in this context, largely become a complicated system of tax and transfer lotteries, which are often loaded in favor of politically powerful groups. As these redistributions may severely hurt the national economy, "the general interest" of society simply cannot be regarded as the sum of uncoordinated special interests.

However, prior to focusing on my preferred interpretation of these data — namely, that magnitude of and incentives within the transfers to persons and government are serving to jam up the processes of adjustment in the Canadian economy — it is instructive to direct attention to two further, related, background items, one factual and the other conceptual. The former relates to the collapse of the Ontario economy while the latter approaches the interregional transfer system from a "macro" framework. I shall deal with each in turn.

Figure 3: *General Assistance Recipients under the Canada Assistance Plan, fiscal years 1970/71 to 1991/92*
(as a percentage of provincial population)

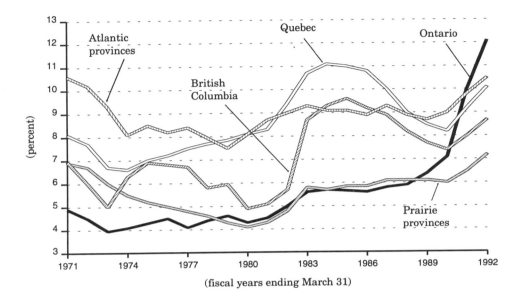

(fiscal years ending March 31)

Source: Hobson and St-Hilaire 1993, 132.

Ontario in Recession

Given that Tables 1 and 2 have been cast in terms of "relatives" or "percentages of the national average," this provides little or no information on the "absolute" position of the various provinces. The most important aspect here, in terms of fiscal federalism and the transfer system, is the degree to which Ontario has been ravaged by the 1990s' recession. This deterioration is effectively captured in Figure 3, which presents the number of Canada Assistance Plan (CAP) or welfare recipients as a percentage of the relevant provincial/regional populations. Until the late 1980s, Ontario either had the lowest ratio or was just above the ratio for the Prairie provinces. In the past few years, Ontario's recipients mushroomed and this province now leads the pack by quite a margin.

To be sure, some of the increase in Ontario's CAP recipients relates to the manner in which the province chose to enrich social assistance benefits. Nonetheless much of the spike in Figure 3 is recession induced. In terms of Tables 1 and 2, this represents a new perspective to the challenge — the ability of the "rich" provinces to sustain the existing level of transfers and/or interprovincial redistribution is no longer guaranteed, particularly if Ontario's decline is, as one suspects, structural as well as cyclical. Figure 4 presents an overview of

Figure 4:   *Employment Recovery after Two Recessions*

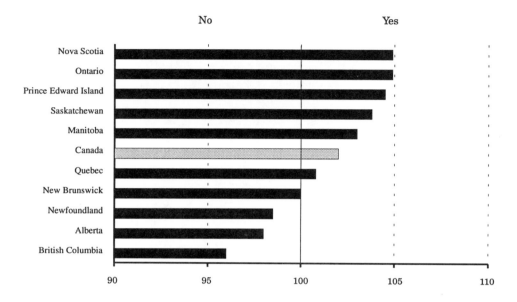

A.. *1980s' Recession:*
Employment Recovered Four Years Later?

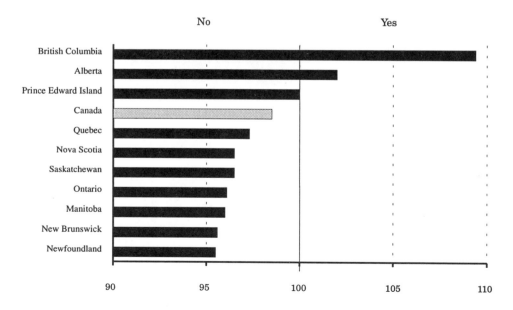

B. *1990s' Recession:*
Employment Recovered Four Years Later?

Sources: Statistics Canada; Toronto-Dominion Bank, Department of Economic Research.

employment recovery relating to the last two recessions. British Columbia, and to a lesser extent Alberta, largely escaped the 1990s' recession. Not so for Ontario. This is in sharp contrast to the pattern of the provincial employment recovery relating to the 1980s' recession (the lower panel of Figure 4). In the recession of the early 1980s, the West was ravaged by the collapse in commodity prices and Ontario rebounded quickly thanks to the auto boom. The story in Figure 4 will lend support to the claim (in Chapter 8) to the effect that Canada is no longer a single east-west economy but a series of north-south cross-border economies that do not have synchronous economic cycles.

This is not intended to be a lament for Ontario. After all, on a per capita basis the contribution of Alberta to the system of interregional transfers has on occasion far exceeded that of Ontario. However, because Ontario has so many more "per capitas," as it were, this province remains the key player in the transfer process.

But this is not the end of the story. In 1990, Ottawa introduced the "cap" on CAP, which limited the growth in CAP transfers to the three "have" provinces to 5 percent per year. In terms of Figure 3, whereas the seven have-not provinces retrieve 50 percent of their social assistance expenditures in terms of CAP transfers, the ratio for Ontario has fallen to 28 percent (with smaller declines for Alberta and British Columbia). This adds yet a further dimension to the earlier picture — namely, the inherent "fairness" of CAP transfers and, by extension, the integrity of the entire system of federal-provincial transfers. The most recent manifestation of this is growing popular sentiment among western Canadians that they are transferring too many funds out of their region to the rest of the country. Thus, in addition to the potential sustainability issue, the underlying "taste" for the existing degree of interregional distribution on the part of many Canadians may be diminishing. My personal twist on this latter issue is that the long-standing concern for the welfare of one's fellow Canadians is alive and well, but what is being discredited is the particular set of programs that embody this redistribution.

Regional Adjustment Impediments: The Gold Standard Analogy

The final piece of background relating to the existence and persistence of regional/provincial disparities comes at the issue from a quite different perspective: an analytical exercise that views interregional transfers from the conceptual framework of the operations of the gold standard adjustment mechanism.

Assume for present purposes that Canada is the "world." In this stylized world, there are ten "countries" (provinces), linked together by a single currency — the Canadian dollar. By definition, exchange rates between these countries are fixed, irrevocably, at parity — that is, one Nova Scotia "dollar" trades for one British Columbia "dollar." This is, in effect, the gold standard (or Canadian-dollar-standard) analogy transferred to the Canadian economy.

Now assume that the Atlantic region runs a balance-of-trade deficit on current account. (Actually, this trade deficit for the Atlantic region *vis-à-vis* the rest of Canada was $6.4 billion in 1984 [Proulx 1991, 128] and roughly $7 billion if one adds in the rest of the world, so that this assumption is entirely realistic.) Under the gold standard equilibrating mechanism, gold (dollars) have to flow out in order to pay for this deficit. The resulting decrease in the Atlantic region's money supply would trigger declines in wages and domestic prices. In reality, while wages are lower in the Atlantic region, they are not falling on an annual basis. Indeed, the opposite is true over the past decade — wages in Atlantic Canada are moving toward the national average. The question at issue then becomes the following: what mechanism is at work to allow the Atlantic provinces to run these substantial balance-of-payments deficits year in and year out?[4]

To a degree, this payment deficit could be financed by rest-of-Canada purchases of Atlantic Canadian assets, by a drawing down of savings of residents of Atlantic Canada, or by borrowing on the part of the governments and citizens in Atlantic Canada. No doubt all of these come into play from time to time. But these sources cannot come anywhere near to accounting for the magnitude of these annual external deficits.

Hence, one cannot escape the conclusion that the (dis-)equilibrating mechanism at work here is the federal tax, expenditure, and transfer system. Ottawa effectively rechannels these funds back into the Atlantic region via the comprehensive interregional and intergovernmental transfer system (equalization, unemployment insurance, the operations of the personal income tax system, and so on). In effect, this "sterilization" of the gold (dollar) outflows allows the Atlantic region to run deficits in perpetuity. It is as if the Atlantic region has latched on to the fabled "widow's cruse" or, equivalently, holds an "annuity" against the rest of Canada that permits it to escape the rigors of the gold standard adjustment mechanism.

It is true that this gold-standard analogy will come into play in modern welfare states whenever and wherever there are pockets of poverty or of low income — for example, elsewhere in Canada and even in unitary states. What makes the analogy so telling for Canada, however, is the fact that both levels of government have the ability to interfere (and *have* interfered), with the way in which the gold-standard analogy operates across regions. While the analysis of

---

4 Calculations from Statistics Canada, *The Daily, August 24, 1993*, reveal that the trade deficit on goods and services for the Atlantic region for 1989 was roughly $8 billion.

this interference and how it relates back to the provincial economies is critical to the thrust of this chapter, it is also quite technical in nature. Accordingly, it is relegated to an appendix to this chapter. However, the basic ideas emerging from the analysis are highlighted in the remainder of this section.

The starting point of the analysis is that the federal government is committed to the alleviation of regional disparities. In the normal course of events, a "have-not" region would experience some job creation and some outmigration. Underpinning this observation is that there is an outmigration function with the characteristic that there will be more outmigration from the "have-not" region if its wages are lower (relative to the Ontario or national average). Likewise, there is also a job creation function that has more jobs being created in the "have-not" region when wages are lower. However, if policy initiatives shift the outmigration function downward[5] — by Ottawa's providing preferential regional UI benefits or by the province's directing any training to within-region skills — and shift the job creation function downward — by the province's enacting high minimum wages — the appendix demonstrates that the result will be a substantially larger inflow of federal transfers to the region. In the process, the region develops an "equilibrium" that departs further and further from the traditional neoclassical equilibrium.

There are many more insights contained in the technical appendix, but these will suffice to introduce three concepts that ought to play a far more important role in both regional and social policy discussions in Canada — transfer dependency, policy-induced equilibria, and intergovernmental gaming.

A Triad of Dysfunctions

Transfer Dependency

The consequence of the operations of the constellation of forces described above has come to be known in policy circles as "transfer dependency." This need not imply that transfers are the cause of disparities. Rather, the essence of transfer dependency is that decades of interrupting the natural adjustment processes via both the magnitude of, and incentives within, the transfer system was bound to serve to entrench and, in many cases, exacerbate the pre-existing degree of disparity. Moreover, this is not merely a regional issue — it applies with equal force to the inappropriate incentives within, say, the welfare system that serve

---

5 A shift "downward" in the outmigration function means that fewer persons will migrate for a given wage differential. Likewise, a downward shift in the job creation function means that fewer jobs will be created in the "have-not" regions for a given wage differential.

as welfare or poverty traps. One must hasten to add that this is a "system dysfunction" and not in any way related to the character of individuals that may get caught in these transfer-dependency syndromes. By and large, individuals have acted *entirely rationally* in the face of a wholly inappropriate set of incentives. It is true that, over time, transfer dependency has proved to be pervasive enough to alter values and lifestyles, but again this is due to the persistence and, eventually, the acceptance as normal of these inappropriate incentives. It is essential that this perspective be carried throughout the ensuing analysis, particularly those sections dealing with adjustment, since it is inappropriate to force the burden of adjustment on individuals who were, in fact, acting rationally.

Policy-Induced Equilibria

Government after government comes to power with the intent of ameliorating Canada's regional disparities. Undoubtedly, the underlying notion here is that low incomes and/or high unemployment in certain provinces or regions represent a *disequilibrium* that must be "curable" by some or another federal policy initiative. In part, this explains the incredibly long period of experimentation with all manner of regional policies and initiatives.

But this is precisely the wrong perspective. The flip side of the concept of transfer dependency is that the consequent results in terms of income, employment or productivity relatives (as reflected in Tables 1 and 2) represent *equilibrium* situations, not disequilibrium ones. Moreover, they are *policy-induced equilibria*. We may not like the results, such as persistently higher unemployment rates, but they represent equilibrium positions nonetheless.

To see this, consider the province of Saskatchewan. Granted that its current prospects are hardly rosy, given the collapsed grain prices. But suppose that, in 1957, the self-employed farmers had been granted the same "privilege" as the self-employed fishers — namely, eligibility for UI in the off-season. Is there any doubt that, today, there would be far more farmers in Saskatchewan, that the farms would be much smaller, and that the entire socio-economic climate of the province would be different? This is the essence of a policy-induced equilibrium.

The recognition that unemployment disparities and the like may not represent a disequilibrium but, rather, a policy-induced equilibrium is obviously critical to policy formation. For one thing, one then has to recognize that existing government largesse in terms of the nature of the expenditure/transfer frameworks may be part of the problem rather than part of the solution. And from a different perspective, while Canadians may still want to pump funds into these provinces and regions, at least they should not then express surprise at the outcomes and should not view them as disequilibrium situations that call for yet more intervention.

As will be noted later, we have made some important strides in recognizing the errors of our ways. For example, we have now put in place a special program for Newfoundland fishers. Without commenting at this point on the nature of the program, this approach seems much preferable to the earlier tendency to tilt or alter national programs to serve the needs of certain regions and/or industries.

Intergovernmental Gaming

At the core of how a comprehensive transfer system falls into the transfer-dependency syndrome is what I have referred to as "intergovernmental gaming." This is the potential for a range of perverse interactions between and among levels of government that arise, again, from the incentives within the system. But intergovernmental gaming can go beyond this and reflect the quite different preference functions of the two levels of government, which in turn may reflect the allocation of constitutional responsibilities.

Examples are not only easy to come by but quite familiar to Canadian policy analysts. As an intergovernmental gaming process that leads to a vicious circle, Quebec policy in the 1960s and 1970s comes to mind. That province had the highest minimum wage not only in Canada but in North America. It could afford to do this because the bulk of the cost of such a policy was transferred to the rest of Canada via the federal transfer system. For example, to the extent that unemployment increased, the UI program would kick in; when UI benefits ran out, Ottawa would absorb 50 percent of any welfare payments. And if the effect was to decrease Quebec's revenues, equalization would come to the rescue. But the story does not end here. Because of its deteriorating employment situation, Quebec could and did lobby Ottawa (successfully) for tariffs and quotas to protect its labor-intensive industries (such as textiles and clothing). For a variety of reasons, Quebec has now backed off this minimum wage leadership, perhaps because the impact of the Canada-US and North American free trade agreements no longer allows it to close this circle with protectionist measures.

More familiar still to Canadians was the experiment with 50-50 cost sharing for health until 1977. Because the provinces could spend these 50 cent dollars only on doctors (not paramedics) and on accredited hospitals (not convalescent homes, and so on), we became locked into high-cost and institutional health care, the problems of which are now fully evident.

Still with us are the provincial ten or twelve week make-work programs designed to transfer persons from welfare to UI. What is new in terms of this intergovernmental gaming is that Ottawa has now begun to return the favor by curtailing UI in the context of a constrained system of federal-provincial transfers. The losers here are the persons directly affected and the economy generally. These initiatives persist, however, because they make economic sense to the governments in question in the context of the incentives in the intergovernmental transfer system.

Finally, but hardly exhaustively, for the four "have-not" provinces that are not part of the "five-province standard" for equalization purposes — that is, the Atlantic provinces — it matters not a whit in terms of their access to per capita revenues whether or not their policies serve to increase or decrease their economic base since the equalization program will tax away in a confiscatory way any and all revenue increase and will fully compensate any revenue loss. While the mechanics of why this is so will be deferred to Chapter 4, the relevant point here is that the time has undoubtedly come to ensure that the transfer system rewards initiatives that are in provinces' and individuals' long-term interests.

Admittedly, it is probably impossible to remove all the incentives for governmental or intergovernmental gaming from a transfer system that is as large and comprehensive as Canada's. But the way to attempt to tackle the problem is to introduce greater accountability into the system. One approach is to strive for "fiscal coincidence" — namely, that the level of government that is responsible for the spending decision should also be responsible for the associated revenue raising. And where it is not possible to achieve this, then the incentives in the transfers should at least attempt to ensure that agents (provinces, individuals, businesses) bear as much of the costs (and reap any benefits) of their own decisions.

An Australian Interlude

To this point in the analysis, there is a danger of throwing out the baby with the bathwater, as it were: transfer dependency relates to the *excesses* associated with the transfer system and interregional distribution, not to the concept of redistribution itself. After all, even the most "efficient" tax, expenditure, and transfer system will (and should) result in redistributing resources away from rich persons and regions to poorer persons and regions. And this would obviously apply to a unitary state as well. To anticipate the later analysis, an underlying theme is that sharply cutting or paring the social envelope is not an acceptable solution because economic success in a knowledge era depends critically on having an appropriate social envelope in place. Nonetheless, some cutting and paring of existing programs is inevitable (from a fiscal vantage point) and appropriate (from a social policy vantage point) because financing of the emerging social policy needs has to come in large measure from the existing envelope.

Thus, redistribution is not the real issue. Rather, it is the nature (incentives within) and magnitude of this redistribution.

An alternative way to address this redistribution issue as it relates to the theme of this chapter — namely, the viability of the provincial economies — is as follows: must a generous societal social conscience, including a generous system of interregional transfers, lead rather inevitably to the degree of provincial disparity that characterizes Canada? The answer appears to be no, as the evidence from Australia indicates.

Table 3 presents data for 1991 regional disparity relatives for the six Australian states. One is immediately struck by the fact that these data reveal much less disparity than is the case for the Canadian provinces. The high/low ratios for GDP per capita (column 1) are 1.80 and 1.30 for Canada and Australia, respectively, and for GDP/E they are 1.47 and 1.24. In Australia, the differences between GDP/P and GDP/E by state are not as large as they are for the Canadian provinces because there is little variation across the Australian states in terms of E/LF and LF/P — 1.03 and 1.07, respectively, for the high/low ratios, or roughly one-quarter of the Canadian differences.

I leave to the reader the task of completing the comparison between Tables 3 and 1, noting only that HDI (household disposable income) is the Australian equivalent to PDI (personal disposable income) and average weekly earnings (column (7)) is presumably a close proxy for average hourly earnings in column (9) of Table 1.

Why are Australian state disparities in income and employment rates so low or, equivalently, why are Canadian provincial disparities so high? The tables in this chapter cannot answer this question. And I do not claim to know the answer. But I offer the following observations. Australia, like Canada, has a generous equalization system. But there is no unemployment insurance system in Australia (and, therefore, no "regional" component to UI). Indeed, the Australian Constitution prohibits the federal government from engaging in preferential treatment of one state over another.[6]

Under this interpretation, Australia has avoided Canadian-style transfer dependency in part because it has not engaged in Canadian-style regional policy.[7] While I recognize fully that correlation is not causation, I nonetheless

---

6 Section 99 of the Australian Constitution reads: "The Commonwealth shall not, by any law or regulation of trade, commerce, or revenue, give preference to one State or any part thereof over another State or any part thereof."

7 An alternative interpretation is that Australia's regional disparities are narrower because Australian wages are rather uniform across regions. However, this would only guarantee relative equality in terms of GDP/E. The fact that the disparities in GDP/P across the Australian states are also much narrower implies that labor mobility is full and free and not the target of specific regional policy.

Table 3:   ***Regional Disparities in Australia, 1991***
              (relative to the national average)

	GDP/P (1)	*GDP/E* (2)	*E/LF* (3)	*LF/P* (4)	*HDI/GDP* (5)	*HDI/P* (6)	**Average Weekly Earnings** (7)
New South Wales	1.035	1.047	1.008	0.981	1.035	1.018	1.022
Victoria	1.053	1.051	0.991	1.010	0.984	1.043	1.008
Queensland	0.888	0.891	0.989	1.008	1.001	0.891	0.931
South Australia	0.883	0.889	0.990	0.974	1.048	0.926	0.952
Western Australia	1.037	1.020	0.981	1.036	0.858	0.889	1.005
Tasmania	0.810	0.850	0.982	0.970	1.061	0.859	0.968
Australia	1.00	1.00	1.00	1.00	1.00	1.00	1.00
High/Low Territory	1.30	1.24	1.03	1.07	1.24	1.21	1.10

Sources: Australia, Australian Bureau of Statistics, *The Labour Force, Australia* (July 1991), 6203.0; *Australian National Accounts*, 1990–91, *State Accounts*, 5220.0; *Estimated Resident Population by Sex and Age, States and Territories of Australia* (June 1990 and Preliminary June 1991), 3201.1; *Distribution and Composition of Employees, Earnings and Hours, Australia* (May 1991), 6306.0.

take heart from the Australian experience because it provides evidence that a generous transfer system (both interpersonal and interregional) need not lead to the sorts of disparities we witness in Canada. Thus, while we have overdone things on the regional/provincial front and created a made-in-Canada, policy-induced equilibrium, the problem lies in the way we have designed these transfers and not in the fact that Canadians have opted for a substantial degree of interpersonal and interregional/interprovincial distribution.

Further Perspectives on Canadian Regional Policy

The line of analysis articulated above and culminating with the focus on transfer dependency has a reasonably long policy history, including my own work in the late 1970s. However, expressing concern about the perverse incentives in the social envelope is, thankfully, no longer limited to economists. In his Eric Hanson Memorial Lecture, former top federal bureaucrat Arthur Kroeger focuses on the prospects for job growth in the millennium. Of interest here are his comments, *inter alia*, on the role of UI. Beyond noting that UI spending has increased 36-fold over the past 20 years, he remarks:

> The Unemployment Insurance program has for over fifty years been one of the most important components of the Canadian social safety net, providing

badly needed income support to several million individuals every year. One of its major weaknesses, however, is that it was originally designed to cover temporary interruptions in employment, and is ill-suited to deal with contemporary problems such as the growth of long-term unemployment. In addition, it includes a number of features that invite abuse and, others which — however desirable in themselves — have little to do with an insurance system. Finally, some elements of its design such as the variable entrance requirement have provided an incentive for individuals to remain in high-employment regions. (Kroeger 1994, 50.)

Even more intriguing and more important to the rethinking of regional policy are New Brunswick Premier Frank McKenna's comments on welfare and UI at the 1993 Couchiching Conference. The premier's purpose in this address was to describe the innovative measures taken by New Brunswick under the rubric of the new program "NB Works." (The features of this program will be detailed in chapter 9.) Part of the motivation for this new initiative, apart from the fact that "re-engineering" is inevitable because the fiscal crisis means that New Brunswick soon will not "have anybody around to bail us out," is that the old social policies are no longer delivering the goods, as it were:

Welfare was never meant to be a way of life, but it becomes so for thousands of Canadians. And we do them a disservice by allowing it to spread from one unsuspecting generation to the other. Canada is the only country that I know in the world that offers such generous programs that there is absolutely no incentive in return to divert yourself towards education or training. Passive assistance programs grind away at our ability to move our province forward and they are destroying those that they meant to help. Maintaining a culture of cradle-to-grave dependency is no longer viable. (McKenna 1993, 21.)

The premier expresses even more concern when it comes to UI:

I think that a lot of Atlantic Canadians would now tell you...the truth is that the generosity of Canada has in many ways been the principal impediment to our growth. In Atlantic Canada, we've been the victim of your generosity....Unemployment insurance was reformed so that not only were people out of work able to obtain unemployment to fill in the gaps, but that everybody who could get 10 weeks of work would be able to draw unemployment for the rest of the year....I inherited the province in 1987 where we had 128 fish plants, every one of them geared to work 10 weeks, because that's all they needed. (McKenna 1993, 20–21.)

What the 10/42 system implies is that working for $5,000 for ten weeks (at $500 per week) will generate roughly $12,000 in UI benefits over the remainder of the year. Thus, the societal cost of these ten-week jobs is at least twice as much again as the private cost. Recently, in what the *Toronto Star* ("Villages Make UI a Way of Life," September 6, 1993, A8.) referred to as "a kind of Canadian milestone," Statistics Canada reported that in two New Brunswick counties, 100 percent of two-earner households accessed UI at some time during 1992 and the ratio was well above 90 percent for many other counties in Atlantic Canada. While these examples are drawn from Atlantic Canada, it is important to recognize that these phenomena are country-wide in scope. "Fishing for stamps" also applies on the West coast, as a recent "W5" television program made evident, and much of the tourist industry in all provinces is now geared to the existence of UI. The result of all of this is transfer dependency. It has become so ingrained in our society that Canada's most profitable firm in 1992 (Bell Canada) had no qualms in requesting that UI cover Bell employees for day 5 in the context of moving to a four-day work week. Thankfully, the UI authorities turned down the request, but the general point is that as a society we have embarked on a series of programs on the social/regional policy fronts that embody poor economic policy, and poor social policy, and that are making all of us poor!

Debts/Deficits and Domestic/International Viability

To conclude this section on comparative provincial economic fortunes, it is appropriate to direct attention to fiscal-balance measures, both current (deficits) and cumulative (debts). These measures appear in Table 4, which was adopted from tables prepared by the Economic Research Department of the Toronto Dominion Bank. The table incorporates the actual fiscal year 1992/93 data, the revised estimate of the 1993/94 data and, finally, the projections for 1994/95 as reflected in the 1994 budgets of Ottawa and the provinces.

Focusing first on the upper panel of Table 4, the combined federal/provincial deficits for fiscal years 1992/93 and 1993/94 were unchanged at roughly $66 billion. However, the composition of this $66 billion over these two years reflected a $5 billion increase in the federal deficit (from $40.5 billion to $45.7 billion) combined with a roughly similar fall in the level of aggregate provincial deficits (from $25.3 billion to $20.3 billion). The budget projections for 1994/95 indicate a fall in the aggregate deficit of some $9 billion, with two-thirds of the improvement accounted for by the projected fall in Ottawa's deficit. In terms of the deficit per capita (the last column of the upper panel of Table 4), Ontario leads the way with a projected per capita deficit of $782 for 1994/95, followed closely by Nova Scotia. Over the three years shown in the table, Quebec's fiscal position exhibits the least progress — from a deficit of $690 per person in 1992/93 to a projected deficit per person of $609 in 1994/95. Several of the other provinces have made substantial strides in deficit control. This is especially the case for Saskatchewan and Prince Edward Island.

Turning now to the accumulated debt (the bottom panel of Table 4), the worrying aspect is that, even with these deficit reductions, the aggregate debt/GDP ratios are still rising. In fiscal year 1993/94, the combined debt/GDP ratio equaled 101.7 percent and it is projected to rise to 105.1 percent in 1994/95. As of May 1994, Moody's had downgraded Ontario's credit rating to double-A-3, which now stands four "notches" lower than its triple-A rating in 1991.

These deficit and debt figures raise the specter of running into the proverbial "wall" on the fiscal and/or international capital markets front. Some analysts would argue that we have already hit the wall. Regardless, the relevant point is that Canada's fiscal crisis, at both levels of government, is emerging as a potent force in the reworking of our social envelope. This fiscal crisis is also influencing the social envelope in quite another way. As the residents of some provinces perceive that they are being subjected to harsher provincial budgetary measures than citizens in other provinces, this has the potential for bringing an entirely new perspective to the system of federal-provincial transfers. There is no delicate way to express this issue, so one might as well be up front about it. Will the citizens of Alberta, who perceive themselves to be experiencing dramatic provincial budgetary cuts, make a case that in order to continue to receive the existing level of, say, equalization payments the "have-not" provinces must also engage in comparable deficit control measures? To the best of my knowledge, this notion of "equal burden sharing" has never played a significant role in the deliberations relating to the east-west transfer system[8] and it may not surface now. But the potential clearly exists.

Finally, Figures 5 and 6 provide an international perspective on some of these issues. Figure 5 reveals that Canada's net international indebtedness is far and away the outlier among the Group of Seven (G-7) industrial countries. The graphics are so stark that this literally is the case where a picture is worth a thousand words. To be sure, net indebtedness can be viewed an "asset" if the proceeds have been invested fully in capital and infrastructure that will generate income adequate to pay off these debts. As the earlier tables in this chapter indicate, along with evidence relating to investment (which is not included in the above analysis), this is not the case: we are borrowing largely to provide for current consumption.

---

8 Other notions of unequal burden have, of course, arisen, the most obvious of which was the National Energy Program and its impact on energy royalties of the Western provinces.

Table 4: *Fiscal Positions of Ottawa and the Provinces, fiscal years 1992/93 to 1994/95*

	Deficits								
	Deficit ($ millions)			Deficit/GDP (percent)			Deficit per Capita		
	Actual 1992/93	Revised 1993/94	Budget 1994/95	Actual 1992/93	Revised 1993/94	Budget 1994/95	Actual 1992/93	Revised 1993/94	Budget 1994/95
Total federal and provincial	65,789	65,962	56,692	9.6%	9.3%	7.6%	$2,314	$2,294	$1,945
Federal	40,500	45,700	39,700	5.9	6.4	5.3	1,424	1,589	1,362
Provincial	25,289	20,262	16,992	3.7	2.9	2.3	889	705	583
Newfoundland	266	223	197	2.9	2.4	2.1	457	383	339
Prince Edward Island	82	69	19	3.8	3.0	0.8	632	527	144
Nova Scotia	772	700	600	4.3	3.8	3.2	838	758	646
New Brunswick	481	438	270	3.5	3.1	1.8	642	583	359
Quebec	4,932	4,895	4,425	3.1	3.1	2.7	690	679	608
Ontario	12,428	9,430	8,548	4.5	3.3	2.9	1,171	878	782
Manitoba	566	461	296	2.4	1.9	1.2	508	413	263
Saskatchewan	592	294	189	2.9	1.4	0.9	590	293	187
Alberta	3,409	2,468	1,550	4.7	3.2	1.9	1,295	927	571
British Columbia	1,761	1,284	898	2.0	1.4	0.9	510	363	250

Table 4: Fiscal Positions of Ottawa and the Provinces, fiscal years 1992/93 to 1994/95 - cont'd.

	Net Public Debt			Debt/GDP			Debt per Capita		
	Actual 1992/93	Revised 1993/94	Budget 1994/95	Actual 1992/93	Revised 1993/94	Budget 1994/95	Actual 1992/93	Revised 1993/94	Budget 1994/95
	($ millions)			(percent)					
Total federal and provincial	651,750	722,680	780,209	94.7%	101.7%	105.1%	$22,920	$25,134	$26,767
Federal	465,300	511,000	550,700	67.6	71.9	74.2	16,363	17,772	18,893
Provincial	186,450	211,680	229,509	27.1	29.8	30.9	6,557	7,352	7,874
Newfoundland	4,718	4,938	5,135	51.1	52.6	53.6	8,119	8,498	8,838
Prince Edward Island	351	421	440	16.3	18.5	18.6	2,696	3,197	3,327
Nova Scotia	6,742	7,530	8,082	37.5	41.2	42.8	7,322	8,158	8,701
New Brunswick	3,900	4,190	4,311	28.1	29.2	28.9	5,206	5,580	5,725
Quebec	58,899	65,706	69,100	37.5	41.0	41.4	8,237	9,115	9,497
Ontario	68,607	80,166	90,360	24.7	28.1	30.4	6,466	7,460	8,264
Manitoba	6,179	6,831	7,014	25.8	28.0	27.6	5,552	6,121	6,232
Saskatchewan	8,185	8,460	8,817	40.4	39.4	40.0	8,148	8,434	8,724
Alberta	15,719	18,525	20,075	21.5	24.0	24.9	5,971	6,958	7,394
British Columbia	13,149	14,913	16,176	15.2	16.2	16.7	3,810	4,219	4,496

Notes: These data are current as of May 24, 1994. Some net public debt data are estimates only. Net public debt includes government debt net of the debt of self-financing Crown corporations. Population forecast as at May 1994; GDP forecast as at May 1994.

Sources: Federal and provincial budgets; Investment Dealers Association (for some historical data); Statistics Canada; and the Toronto-Dominion Bank.

Figure 5: *International Indebtedness of the G-7 Countries, 1991*
           (as a percentage of gross domestic product)

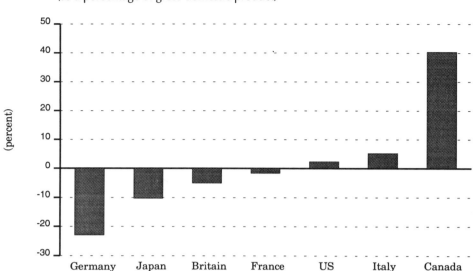

Note: The data for Canada and the United States are from 1991; for Germany, Italy, Britain, and Japan, from
       1990; and for France, from 1989.

Source: IRPP 1993.

Figure 6 is equally ominous. It suggests that we have precious little room
to solve our problems on the revenue side. I am not fully abreast of what is
transpiring in Europe, but the post-1991 revenue grab in Ontario and elsewhere
will clearly push our revenue/GDP ratios higher still, and we may well find
ourselves competing for the title as the top G-7 revenue-raiser. But with close
to 80 percent of our trade with the United States and with the NAFTA providing
an umbrella for integrating many of our trading practices, the ten-percentage-
point gap with the United States is very troubling. Every bit as troublesome are
the recent data on total taxes (realty, business, and other taxes) per square foot
of commercial prime space: Toronto ($19.60), Vancouver ($15.25), New York
($14.40), Atlanta ($2.40), Seattle ($1.44).[9] These are startling statistics in their
own right in a world where capital and plant locations are mobile. But they are
also very significant in another sense: at what point do "have" provinces such
as Ontario and British Columbia begin to fear for their own economic futures

_____

9 Joanne Chianello, "Tops in Taxes," *The Financial Post* (Toronto), August 4, 1993, p. 1.

Figure 6: *Tax Revenues of the G-7 Countries, 1991*
(as a percentage of gross domestic product)

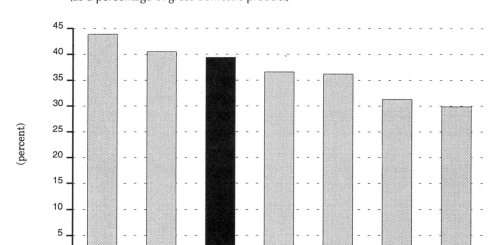

Note: The data for Japan and the United States are for 1990.

Source: IRPP 1993.

and begin to recognize that their own economic vulnerability may be due to the excesses of the transfer system. In Ontario's case, the $9.5 billion provincial deficit (for fiscal year 1993/94) matches fairly closely the net outward transfers (including UI) from Ontarians to the rest of Canada.

Thus, these more macro data not only confirm the message arising from the earlier sections of the chapter — that there is a sustainability issue in terms of the status quo; they also suggest that there is precious little room to maneuver on the revenue side. In turn, this focuses attention once again on the expenditure side and, inevitably, on social policy restructuring and reorientation.

Conclusion

The purpose of this monograph is to describe and evaluate Canada's social policy envelope with an eye toward developing the mandate for and the principles associated with social policy reform, and a blueprint for carrying it out. While most of the ensuing analysis will focus on policies, programs, and interactions within the social envelope itself, the emphasis in this chapter has been on the economic realities that underlie Social Canada. The theme is hardly new: the prospects for an effective social policy are rather bleak in the context of a faltering economy. What is more novel, perhaps, is to view Canada's economic prospects largely from the vantage point of the viability of the provincial economies. This is appropriate, however, because the provinces design and deliver much of Canada's social envelope and because provincial efforts in this area are supported by a system of federal-provincial transfers. Indeed, much of what has passed for social policy reform over the years in Canada has related to the reform of these federal-provincial transfers. While not denying that these issues of fiscal federalism are, and will remain, a key element of Social Canada, the thrust of the later analysis will argue that they ought to be derivative rather than determining — that is, social policy reform ought to begin with designing programs appropriate to individual Canadians and only later should the focus be directed toward who should deliver these programs and how they should be financed. But this is getting way ahead of the story.

What emerges from the brief analytical/statistical overview of the provincial and national economies in this chapter is not particularly good news:

- Provincial economic disparities in terms of GDP per capita are severe.
- These disparities have persisted for a long time. While one can point to some convergence (Helliwell 1994), much of this appears attributable to the increasing role of government in the economy.
- One can also make a case that these disparities are, in fact, worsening in that, compared to a decade ago, there are more provinces (for example, Saskatchewan) whose long-term economic viability is suspect.
- All of the above points relate to GDP per capita. The situation in terms of personal income or personal disposable income is much better: Canada's generous and comprehensive set of transfers to persons and provinces comes to the rescue of the "have-not" provinces and to lower-income Canadians in general.
- However, the role of these transfers in an increasing number of provinces is reaching significant, if not alarming, proportions. In two of the Atlantic provinces, personal income exceeds GDP.
- None of this ought to be surprising. Whether the focus is on the perverse nature of the incentives within the transfer system (elaborated in later chapters) or on the gold-standard analogy, decades of impeding the natural adjustment process was bound to lead to an entrenchment of disparities.
- In more familiar terms, Canada is suffering from "transfer dependency."
- The economic result is a "policy-induced equilibrium." We may not like the characteristics of this equilibrium, but it is an equilibrium nonetheless.

- None of this should be construed as an argument against a generous social conscience or against a generous transfer system. As casual empiricism from Australia indicates, a generous transfer system and a generous social conscience need not lead to transfer dependency.

- However, we must be prepared to contemplate that government largesse, at least as embodied in the current nature of our transfer envelope, is part of the problem rather than part of the solution.

- Arguably, this interprovincial and interpersonal social envelope was sustainable in the context of "old Canada" — that is, a cushion of resource rents, tariff walls, and east-west trade flows. With globalization, all of this is now gone. More to the point in terms of the immediate term, the industrial heartland is now bleeding, so that the issue of sustainability comes to the fore. To be sure, the severity of the recession triggered the collapse of the center. But the forecasts are for a low-employment recovery.

- I think that a case can be made that a good deal of the ongoing economic/fiscal transfer woes is attributable to the overall macro policy mix over the past decade. But even if this is correct, it does not alter the severity of the current situation.

- At the aggregate level, we have very little room to maneuver. Our overall (federal and provincial) ratio of debt to GDP is now over 100 percent and rising. Our international indebtedness as a percent of GDP literally towers above that of our G-7 partners.

- One way out of this dilemma is to Increase taxes, and Ontario and Quebec hiked taxes sharply in their 1993 budgets. But we do not have much room to maneuver here either, given that Canada is already one of the most highly taxed of the G-7 countries, and we certainly fare "poorly" on this score when the comparison is with our largest trading partner.

- This high tax/high debt/high transfer environment is leading, rather predictably, to fiscal paring and, I think, to an erosion among Canadians of their traditional taste for the existing degree of redistribution.

All in all, a rather alarming backdrop within which to be negotiating the future of Canadian fiscal federalism and the social envelope.

But as the focus on globalization and the information/knowledge revolution in Chapter 8 will reveal, these interprovincial tensions, significant as they may be in their own right, will inevitably be magnified. Globalization means, *inter alia*, that the appropriate definition of an economic region in Canada will shift to a north-south axis and away from an east-west conception. This pits east-west interregional equity against north-south international competitiveness and, I think, ultimately implies much greater scrutiny of east-west transfers. Moreover, the information revolution inevitably means an increased emphasis on individual Canadians and their opportunities for acquiring human capital. In terms of the provincial economies, this has to imply a shift toward "people prosperity" and away from "place prosperity," at least for federal policy. This presents yet another set of challenges in terms of the economic viability of the individual provinces.

If the result of all of this is that we simply begin to cut back sharply on the social envelope, then another series of problems will develop. As Judith Maxwell (1993) noted recently:

> If we simply let the programs wither, or limit ourselves to tinkering, our society will polarize into rich and poor, or educated and uneducated. Programs will remain generous to the elderly, but will permit new pools of poverty to build up around young families. This in turn will foster crime and other social pathologies. Governments may spend less on social programs but they will spend a lot more on fighting crime, protecting property and combatting racism. In short, Canada begins to look more like the United States.

The message that I take from the analysis thus far, and that will be developed further in the ensuing analysis, is that Canada's social policy envelope is in need of profound reform and restructuring. This is not the time for "tinkering" or "incrementalism" or "steady at the helm" (or whatever term one prefers). Such an approach will only grind down Social Canada and saddle us with US social policies at Scandinavian (or should we now say "Canadian") tax rates. More correctly, perhaps, this approach will lead to our social and fiscal environment being redesigned by the gnomes of Zurich (the international capital markets). The challenge, addressed in the following chapters, is to restructure Social Canada so that the social envelope is, and is perceived to be, indispensable to our economic future in a knowledge era. This is markedly different from the status quo, where social policy is increasingly perceived more in terms of a dead-weight cost that is hampering our competitiveness and, therefore, must be minimized.

Technical Appendix:
A Geometry of Transfer Dependency

This technical appendix develops a model in which an interregional or inter-provincial transfer system can lead to what the text refers to as "transfer dependency" and a "policy-induced equilibrium." What gives rise to transfer dependency in the model is the set of incentives that allow both levels of government to alter the processes of natural economic adjustment, or what in the text has been referred to as "intergovernmental gaming."

The Nature of the Model

The starting point of the analysis is the assumption that the federal govern-ment's goal is to minimize the variation in unemployment rates across regions. This is not quite Ottawa's goal, but it is close enough to reality that the analysis will lead to useful implications. For convenience, Canada is viewed as being composed of two regions — the Maritimes and Ontario, where Ontario can be viewed as the rest of Canada. The diagrammatic representation of the analysis is presented in the appendix figure. The vertical axis represents "numbers of people." Equal distances along this axis, whether above or below the origin (or, for that matter, straddling the origin) represent correspondingly equal numbers of people. The horizontal axis depicts relative wage rates. To the right of the origin wages are higher in the Maritimes than they are in Ontario — that is, $W^m - W^o$ is positive and increasingly so the further right one goes. To the left of the origin, the opposite prevails: $W^o - W^m$ is positive — that is, wage rates are higher in Ontario. Obviously, at the origin, $W^o = W^m$.

Curve JJ represents new jobs created for the Maritimes. For convenience, it is drawn as a straight line. The positive slope of JJ is intuitively plausible — the lower wages are in the Maritimes (relative to Ontario), the greater will be the number of new jobs created there. For example, where $W^o - W^m$ equals OF, the number of new jobs in the Maritimes will be OD. At a relatively lower Maritime wage (OE), job creation will rise to level OB. Curve JJ is drawn so that even when relative wages are equal (at the origin), there is still some positive Maritime job creation.

Curve OM is designed to represent the probability of outmigration from the Maritimes. An increase in Ontario wages relative to Maritime wages will lead to a greater outflow of persons to Ontario — for differential OF, the outmigration flow is OC, and for wage differential OE, it is OA. The OM function is drawn so that even where wage rates are identical, there is some outmigra-tion, but this is of no special significance to the analysis.

Appendix Figure: *A Geometry of Transfer Dependency*

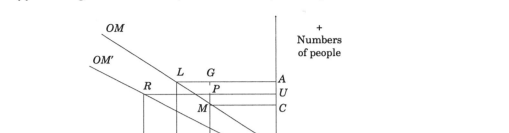

JJ = job creation function
OM – OM = outmigration function
Wages M = wages in Maritime region
Wages O = wages in Ontario

The starting assumption is that the two economies are currently in equilibrium, and the task at hand is to allocate the new entrants into the Maritime labor force between new jobs and outmigration. Let the number of new entrants in the Maritime job market be equal to the vertical distance AB in the diagram. (Note that this is an *exogenously determined* number of people. While it is represented thus far by the vertical distance, AB, it can also be represented by any other equivalent vertical distance in the diagram — for example, UV.)

The Separate Currency Area Solution

If the Maritimes had a separate currency, the system would, in the absence of government intervention, settle down at an "effective" wage differential equal to OE in the appendix figure. This effective wage differential is obtained by taking the vertical distance representing the numbers of new entrants into the labor force and sliding it between the curves OM and JJ until it "fits" exactly — that is, until distance KL equals distance AB. At this effective wage differential, OA new entrants would migrate and OB new entrants would find jobs in the Maritimes. Since OA plus OB equals AB, this "looks after" all the new entrants, so to speak. If the actual wage differential were only equal to OF, then

OC persons would migrate, *OD* would get new jobs, and the remainder (*AC* plus *DB*) would be unemployed, which would put downward pressure on the effective wage rate and move the differential back toward *OE*.

The analysis has been conducted in terms of what I have referred to as the effective wage rate. What would presumably generate this effective wage differential is a movement in the exchange rate between the Maritimes and Ontario (we are assuming for the moment that the regions have their own currencies). If the actual wage differential is, say, *OF*, the Maritimes' currency would depreciate until the effective wage differential equals *OE*.

Even though regions and provinces do not have their own currencies, there is some value in using this as the starting point for the present analysis since it provides a useful benchmark for comparing other solutions to the regional problem. In particular, the next section will demonstrate that this "flexible exchange rate" solution to the appendix figure can be "reproduced" by means of a set of subsidies. This suggests that, even though the two levels of government in a federation are normally constrained in certain actions by, say, the provisions of the constitution, other policy instruments frequently can accomplish much the same result. For example, provinces are not allowed to mount tariffs against goods from other provinces. However, provincial purchasing preferences have the same impact as a tariff for the goods in question. Indeed, these purchasing preferences can be viewed as altering the province's exchange rate for the protected goods.

The Optimal Subsidy Scheme

Let us breathe a bit of reality into the appendix figure and assume that the Maritimes does not have its own currency. Moreover, let us further assume that, while wage rates are lower in the Maritimes, the differential is only *OF*, which is less than the "separate currency" effective wage differential *OE*. As noted above, associated with wage differential *OF* is outmigration of *OC* and job creation *OD*, leaving *DB* plus *AC* Maritimers unemployed. One obvious solution would be for Maritime wage rates to fall relative to those in Ontario so that wage differential *OE* is reached. But suppose that there are sufficient rigidities in the system (minimum wage laws, nationwide wage bargaining, uniform scale of federal wages across the country, union strength, and the like) such that the wage differential remains at *OF*. Under these circumstances, what is the optimal (or probably more correctly, the least-cost) policy? One answer is that which duplicates the separate currency area solution.

To see this, assume that the government has full information with respect to the outmigration and job creation functions and, further, that it can act as a perfect discriminator — that is, it will pay only what is needed to require the additional migrant to move and to have the additional worker employed. Under these assumptions, it will offer subsidies to both outmigration and job creation such that, at the margin, the effective wage differential again becomes *OE*. Thus, the cost of having the marginal person migrate (*GL*) is equal to the marginal cost of employing an additional worker (*HK*), where these costs are measured horizontally (and, ideally, should be expressed in present value terms). The total cost of the subsidy program is the sum of the two triangles *NHK* and *LGM*.

The assumptions underlying this result are very restrictive. If firms and people are able to conceal their preferences, it is possible that *all* new jobs and *all* outmigrants will receive a subsidy. In this case, the marginal subsidy cost of employing the last person will be *BK*, not *HK*. (This assumes that the job-creation function goes through the origin.) David Springate found, using interview techniques, that many recipients of regional development grants would have invested in the Maritimes without the grant (Springate 1973). Hence, subsidies will often find their way even to those who would not need them to motivate their action. For the present, however, we shall maintain the assumption that governments have full information with respect to these reaction functions.

Therefore, under the assumption that the federal government is committed to a policy of full employment and that it takes the existing relative regional wage rates as given, an optimal subsidy scheme would involve both outmigration (bringing people to jobs) and job creation (bringing jobs to people) subsidies. What should be clear, however, is that the cost of achieving this goal will be increased substantially if the provinces mount development policies of their own.

Provincial Strategies

Suppose that the Maritime provinces know that the federal government is committed to absorbing any and all new labor force entrants. This sets the stage for the provinces to take advantage of Ottawa's commitment, or to hold the federal government to ransom, as it were. One obvious strategy for these provinces would be to attempt to shift the outmigration function downward, for example, from *OM* to *OM* in the appendix figure. One way this might be accomplished is to allow the provinces the right to select the training or retraining programs for their residents. If these programs were designed to train people for within-region skills rather than skills that would equip them better for employment in other regions, the result would be to tilt the outmigration curve downward. Similarly, these provinces could lobby the federal government to incorporate regionally differentiated benefits within unemployment insurance (as is now the case, since beneficiaries can collect UI for longer periods of time if they reside in high-unemployment regions), which would also move the *OM* curve in the direction of *OM*.

What happens if the outmigration curve shifts from *OM* to *OM*? The new equilibrium is at *X* — that is, the effective equilibrium wage differential now becomes *OX*. Outmigration equals *OU* and job creation equals *OV*, where by construction *UV* (that is, *OU* + *OV*) is equal to *AB* or, what is the same thing, *RS* = *LK*. The marginal cost of employing or moving the last labor force participant is now equal to *QS* (which equals *PR*) compared with the previous marginal cost of *HK*. The net result is that the federal government is enticed to devote more resources to the regional problem and in the process to shift its policy mix in the direction of bringing jobs to the Maritimes rather than sending people to jobs in other regions.

Obviously, the policies of the other provinces can also influence the cost to the federal government of achieving this regional goal. Were the richer provinces to mount barriers to internal migration (via provincial licensing of skill accreditations, for example), this policy would be equivalent to the previous example — that is, a downward shift in the outmigration function in the appendix figure. Were the richer provinces to counter the federal initiative by offering competing job creation subsidies, this policy would shift the job creation function upward (toward the horizontal axis) in the figure. Not only would this result in larger overall costs (as in the previous case), but now more of the adjustment arising from the imposition of an optimal set of subsidies would be thrown on outmigration from the Maritimes and less on job creation in the region.

With a little bit of creativity it is not difficult to envision scenarios where the effective wage rate in the Maritimes would fall relative to Ontario (that is, the equilibrium exchange rate *vis-à-vis* Ontario would fall) but where the *actual* wage rate relative to Ontario would rise. In terms of the figure, this implies that the separate currency area solution moves leftward from *E* but the actual wage differential moves rightward from *F*. This is, of course, the classic case of transfer dependency, where regional wages are progressively patterned after national wages and where the population is enticed to stay in the region via a comprehensive set of distortive transfers. Moreover, the new situation is appropriately described as an equilibrium and, specifically, a policy-induced equilibrium. Thus, what presumably began as an attempt by governments to minimize the adjustment burden has actually entrenched and exacerbated both the initial problem as well as the ultimate adjustment — that is, the role of the transfers is no longer to facilitate adjustment but rather to accommodate the nature of the new, policy-induced, equilibrium.

One final note: this geometry was developed by Geoffrey Young sometime in the mid-1970s when he served as a summer research assistant in the

Department of Finance. To the best of my knowledge, the paper no longer exists. The essential point, though, is that the analysis is hardly novel. The intriguing issue of why it has taken so long for this and similar analyses to have an impact on regional and social policy is the subject matter of Chapter 6.

Part III

The Federal Government and Social Canada

Chapter 3

Ottawa's Social Policy Presence:
Direct Programs

The analysis now turns to the description and evaluation of the multitude of programs that comprise Canada's social envelope. This chapter and Chapter 4 will focus on the federal role in Social Canada, while Chapter 5 will direct attention to the provincial role in the design and delivery of social programs.

Ottawa plays a multitude of roles in Social Canada. One of them, detailed in this chapter, is to deliver social programs to Canadians. A second role is to provide a system of federal-provincial transfers to enable the provinces to mount their own set of social programs. Focusing on these transfers (equalization, Established Programs Financing, Canada Assistance Plan) is the purpose of Chapter 4. A third key federal role is that of preserving and promoting the socio-economic union. Aspects of this role will be addressed in the relevant contexts of most of the remaining chapters, with special emphasis as part of the Social Canada blueprint developed in Chapter 11.

This chapter begins with an overview of the $75 billion of direct federal transfers to persons and business for 1991. The remainder of the chapter focuses in more detail on a selected set of these transfers — the unemployment insurance (UI) system, the retirement income subsystem and the day care/child care area. It may have been appropriate to deal with training in this chapter as well, but because of its close interaction with postsecondary education it will be highlighted, instead, in Chapter 5.

This focus on individual programs is not intended to be exhaustive. In the first place, and as already noted, not all programs will be highlighted. In the second, the analysis of any particular program will not be exhaustive. Thus, the discussion of the retirement income subsystem will not allow the reader to come away with a full grasp of the interaction among private pension systems, registered retirement savings plans (RRSPs), the old age security (OAS) and Guaranteed Income Supplement (GIS) programs, and the various provincial "add-ons." This required degree of comprehensiveness and detail is well beyond the scope of the monograph. Rather, the intent is to present sufficient documentation and information to serve as a backdrop for assessing the strengths and weaknesses of the existing social policy order as well as for evaluating alternative approaches to Social Canada.

An Overview of Federal Transfers to Persons and Businesses

Part A of Table 5 details, by category, federal government transfers to the residents of the various provinces. Basically, Ottawa's transfers to persons are concentrated in three areas. By far the largest of these is transfers to the "golden agers" — military pensions, veterans' allowances, federal public service pensions, OAS/GIS payments, and Canada Pension Plan/Quebec Pension Plan (CPP/QPP) benefits — which total in the neighborhood of $34 billion. However, this aggregate includes $14.8 billion of CPP/QPP benefits, which some analysts may prefer to include in provincial rather than federal transfers. In particular, it is difficult, conceptually, to include the QPP as part of Ottawa's transfers to Quebec residents. On the other hand, the contribution levels are identical across the provinces and the system is following a "pay-as-one-goes" strategy, so that the provinces probably will not be called on to run down their accumulated CPP/QPP "assets" (which are largely illusory in any event, except perhaps for those in Quebec). Whatever the responsibilities may be, *de jure*, if pay-as-one-goes becomes the rule, the program is, *de facto*, a "national" one. However, even this would not make it a *federal* transfer, *per se*, since the benefits would be financed by contributions and not out of Ottawa's consolidated revenues. But the CPP clearly is federal in that it is driven by federal legislation. For all of these reasons, Table 5 sandwiches the CPP/QPP entry between the subtotal and total rows of part A. Readers are free to choose either row for total federal transfers to persons. But even if one excludes the CPP/QPP, transfers to the elderly are still the largest category of federal transfers.

Unemployment insurance transfers are the second-largest federal transfer category for 1991 — the $17.3 billion of UI benefits is only slightly less than the OAS total of $17.95 billion. Were the table to refer to 1992, UI would have exceeded OAS. Note that both of these are "gross" transfers in the sense that the income tax system will tax (or claw) back some of these benefits.[1] Again, one can question whether UI is a *federal* transfer. Here the issue is not one of

---

1 In terms of the OAS clawback for the 1992 taxation year, if one's "net income before adjustments" on the tax form exceeds $53,215, then the OAS is clawed back at 15¢ for each additional dollar of net income. The provisions for UI are such that if one's "net income before adjustments" exceeds $55,380, the clawback is 30¢ on each additional dollar of net income, up to a maximum of 30 percent of UI benefits. The value of this clawback is then deducted from net income, but the remaining UI benefits (that is, 70 percent for high-income persons) are still taxable.

Table 5: Ottawa's Social Policy Role in the Provincial Economies: Transfers to Persons and Businesses, 1991

	Nfld.	PEI	NS	NB	Que.	Ont.	Man.	Sask.	Alta.	BC	Canada[a]
					($ millions)						
A. Transfers to persons											
Family and youth allowances	67	15	93	78	685	1,016	121	117	293	327	2,824
Pensions (war)	12	13	65	42	103	305	52	35	63	154	844
Veterans' allowance	28	6	29	21	96	174	13	11	20	41	439
Unemployment insurance	966	185	747	785	5,247	5,251	483	360	1,177	2,060	17,323
Pensions (federal public service)	42	23	225	108	511	1,407	125	80	195	462	3,186
Old age security payments	406	112	713	573	4,750	6,210	844	818	1,277	2,231	17,954
Scholarships	11	1	29	11	151	269	17	22	59	106	691
Miscellaneous	149	36	232	211	1,246	1,874	549	507	606	866	6,331
Subtotal	1,681	391	2,133	1,829	12,789	16,506	2,204	1,950	3,690	6,247	49,592
Canada Pension Plan/ Quebec Pension Plan	231	62	552	378	3,509	5,921	619	553	1,058	1,865	14,807
Total	*1,912*	*453*	*2,685*	*2,207*	*16,298*	*22,427*	*2,823*	*2,503*	*4,748*	*8,112*	*64,399*
% of personal income	*19.4%*	*20.3%*	*15.9%*	*16.9%*	*11.2%*	*9.1%*	*13.3%*	*13.7%*	*8.26%*	*10.8%*	*10.6%*
B. Transfers to businesses											
Subsidies	119	58	155	164	1,317	2,061	571	1,377	1,055	495	7,443
Capital assets	67	26	78	76	466	411	78	52	130	133	1,523
Total	*186*	*84*	*233*	*240*	*1,783*	*2,472*	*649*	*1,429*	*1,185*	*628*	*8,966*
C. Total direct transfers	2,098	537	2,918	2,447	18,081	24,899	3,472	3,932	5,933	8,740	73,365
% of personal income	*21.3%*	*24.1%*	*17.3%*	*18.8%*	*12.5%*	*10.1%*	*16.3%*	*21.6%*	*10.3%*	*11.6%*	*12.0%*
% of GDP	*22.8%*	*25.9%*	*16.5%*	*17.8%*	*11.6%*	*9.0%*	*14.9%*	*19.6%*	*8.3%*	*10.5%*	*10.9%*
$ per capita	*3,658*	*4,108*	*3,242*	*3,370*	*2,641*	*2,511*	*3,177*	*3,956*	*2,352*	*2,716*	*2,717*

[a] The Canada totals include expenditures by the Yukon and the Northwest Territories.

Source: Statistics Canada, *System of National Accounts*.

allocating UI to Ottawa or the provinces. Rather, given that Ottawa has, in principle at least, recently bailed out of any financing of the program, UI is really an interpersonal transfer system financed by premiums. Nonetheless, Ottawa controls the basic parameters of the program and covers temporary deficits from the consolidated revenue fund, so I have followed the National Accounts approach and included it as a federal program. (Note that these concerns do not only apply at the federal level. For example, while workers' compensation is viewed as a provincial program, it too could be viewed as a contributory, within-province, interpersonal transfer program.)

Apart from transfers to the elderly and the unemployed, the bulk of the remaining itemized federal transfers to persons in Table 5 go to children (family and youth allowances). As the table indicates, this category weighs in as a very distant third ($2.824 billion). In the February 25, 1992 budget, however, the federal government proposed a sweeping revision of child benefits, to take place in 1993. Family allowances, the refundable child tax credit, and the nonrefundable children's tax credit will all disappear and be replaced by a new, integrated (refundable with "clawback") monthly credit worth $1,233 for each child age 6 and under and $1,020 a year for each child age 7 to 17. Maximum credits are paid to families with net family incomes under $25,921, and this level will be indexed by the inflation rate in excess of 3 percent. Beyond this income threshold, the credit is taxed back at 2.5 cents for every additional dollar of net income for one child and 5.0 cents for 2 or more children. Thus, for one or two children over the age of 6, the credit falls to zero when net family income is in excess of the threshold by $40,800 (or $64,921 of net family income). For three children over 6 years of age, the zero-credit net family income level exceeds the threshold by $61,200 (that is, $3,060 ÷ 0.05), and so on. The cost of this program is close to $5 billion.

This prompts two observations. The first is that social policy is evolving at such a rapid pace that it is virtually impossible to keep abreast of the most recent developments. In order to ensure full comparability across all programs, I decided to use data for fiscal year 1991/92. But as the discussion of the new child tax credit illustrates, the first row of Table 5 is already outdated and the relevant entry is probably double that in the table. Distressing as this may be to the reader and author alike, this is an unavoidable occupational hazard in researching a fast-breaking area.

The second observation is to alert the reader to the presence of the Appendix to this monograph, which provides a bullet-form history of the evolution of federal social programs and taxes over the 1985–93 period. This Appendix is from a recent publication by Ken Battle and Sherri Torjman (1993a), and I am very grateful to them for their permission to reproduce it. This extremely valuable source document is the sort needed for each of the provinces as well.

That these three programs should feature prominently in federal direct transfers to persons is hardly surprising since they correspond to Ottawa's constitutional competencies. Unemployment insurance became a federal head of power (section 91(2a)) by virtue of a 1940 constitutional amendment, and its ability to legislate in the areas of old age pensions and supplementary benefits, including survivors and disability benefits regardless of age (section 94a), was the result of a 1951 constitutional amendment. Actually, section 94a is more in the nature of a concurrent power with provincial paramountcy, but the provinces have generally given Ottawa a free hand with respect to the OAS and GIS, opting instead for a bit of topping up here and there, in terms of both income and in-kind benefits such as free drugs. Where concurrence is really an issue is in the operations of the CPP/QPP. In effect, both the federal and provincial governments have to agree on such things as changes in contribution rates.

In terms of the third area — benefits to children — Ottawa has now moved away from the (former) family allowance approach and toward delivery of refundable child tax credits through the personal income tax system (where powers are concurrent, but with federal paramountcy).

In short, the federal government has used its constitutional flexibility in providing transfers to individual Canadians. This gives Ottawa both "visibility" and "accountability" in terms of these programs, unlike its contributions to major social programs such as health, welfare, and postsecondary education, which take the form of transfers to the provinces. One of the themes that will be pursued later is the alternative of converting these transfers to the provinces into more visible and more accountable transfers to persons (for example, vouchers for postsecondary education or converting Canada Assistance Plan transfers into a much-expanded refundable child tax credit). The issue then becomes one of whether this enhanced visibility and accountability is consistent with either or both fiscal federalism and the challenges on the social policy front. I broach these issues in due course.

Part B of Table 5 documents federal transfers to businesses. The clear outlier here is Saskatchewan, with transfers to businesses and capital assistance that amount to more than one-half of federal transfers to persons in that province. Presumably this reflects transfers (subsidies) to Saskatchewan farmers relating to the depressed grains economy, triggered in large measure by European protectionist policies toward agriculture, and the US decision to follow suit. Were the data in Table 5 to relate to more recent years, federal transfers would also record the substantial payments to Newfoundlanders under the Northern Cod Adjustment and Recovery Program.

Part C of Table 5 presents the provincial totals for transfers to persons and businesses. The $73.4 billion Canadian aggregate represents 12 percent of personal income, 10.9 percent of gross domestic product (GDP), and $2,717 per person. Note that a focus on transfers across provinces as a percentage of income can lead to quite different results than a comparison based on per capita transfers. For example, total transfers as a percent of GDP (the second-to-last row) are three times higher in Prince Edward Island than in Alberta (25.9 percent versus 8.3 percent). However, much of this has to do with the behavior of the denominator (GDP) across provinces — per capita GDP is considerably higher in Alberta than in Prince Edward Island. Per capita transfers (the last row) are only 1¾ times higher in Prince Edward Island than in Alberta ($4,108 versus $2,352). Thus, using provincial GDP as a denominator or a "scaler" can impart a significant bias to provincial comparisons.

This aside, one can distinguish three classes of provinces in terms of these per capita transfers — the high-transfer-recipient provinces (Saskatchewan, Newfoundland, and Prince Edward Island), the middle-transfer-recipient provinces (Manitoba, New Brunswick, and Nova Scotia) and the low-transfer-recipient provinces (Quebec and the three "have" provinces). While the presence of Saskatchewan in the high-transfer-recipient group of provinces is consistent with some evidence in the previous chapter, the pattern of transfers for this province is quite unlike that for Prince Edward Island and Newfoundland. For example, Newfoundland has less than 60 percent of Saskatchewan's population, but receives more than 2½ times the amount of UI transfers. And Saskatchewan receives the lowest per capita CAP transfer from Ottawa (see Chapter 5). As already noted, the reason for its high-transfer numbers in Table 5 has largely to do with grain subsidies.

With Table 5 as an overview of Ottawa's role in the provision of programs and services to Canadians, attention is now directed to profiling several specific programs, beginning with unemployment insurance.

Unemployment Insurance

Because the range of policies, programs, and issues covered in this study is very extensive, it is impossible to focus in full detail on any single one. This observation applies with even more force at the provincial level, where there are ten policies for health, for postsecondary education, and for welfare, and where documentation of these programs must, of necessity, be very partial. Therefore, my approach will be to highlight selective aspects of certain programs. For example, in terms of UI, this section will provide some information on aggregate benefits and contributions by province as well as some data on the time profile of benefits. Other features of UI are assumed to be well known and therefore I mention them only in passing. One of these relates to the perverse incentives in the program: recipients can earn up to 25 percent of their benefits without penalty, but beyond this benefits fall dollar for dollar with earnings. These confiscatory tax rates are, in effect, an open invitation to participate in the underground economy. Surely it is preferable to have less-than-confiscatory taxes in the transition from UI to work. Not surprisingly, this will be an integral part of the UI proposal offered later in the monograph.

As noted in the Appendix, the qualifying period for UI was increased in 1990 from 10–14 weeks to 10–20 weeks depending on the regional unemployment rate, with the result that the maximum duration of UI benefits is reduced from 46–50 weeks to 35–50 weeks. (As an important aside, the 1994 federal budget introduced further changes to UI. Rather than rewriting most of the chapters to incorporate all these late-breaking initiatives, Chapter 9 is designed to collect them in a single place and to make "back references" when appropriate. For present purposes, it should be noted that these new UI measures relate more to tinkering than to fundamental reform). Table 6 presents the details pertaining to this 1990 change in UI regulations. What is intriguing is that this so-called tightening of the regulations means that a claimant with 10 weeks of work in an area where the unemployment rate is over 16 percent will qualify for 39 weeks of benefits, but a claimant with 52 weeks of work (or 152 weeks for that matter) in an area where the unemployment rate is 6 percent or less will qualify for only 35 weeks of benefits. Alternatively, a worker with 19 weeks of contributions is ineligible for any benefits at all if he/she files in an area where the unemployment rate is less than 6 percent. However, a person losing a job after 19 weeks in a region with less than 6 percent unemployment has the option of filing (and being available for work) in an area with more than 16 percent unemployment, so that benefit weeks can be 48 instead of zero! Much has been written over the years in terms of the perverse incentives here, let alone the fact that two otherwise identically situated Canadians will be treated very differently according to place of "filing" (*not* place of work). If anything, these recent regulations have exacerbated these problems and surely have made a mockery of the notion that UI has anything to do with social "insurance."

The results of this set of incentives are fully predictable and are part and parcel of what was earlier referred to as "transfer dependency." This is evident from Table 7, which presents data for 1988.[2] From column (3), the benefit/contribution rate for Newfoundland is 416 percent — over 8 times the Ontario ratio. Indeed, there is a rather dramatic interregional transfer of funds from Ontario and the Prairies to the five easternmost provinces, with British Columbia roughly "breaking even" in terms of benefits and contributions. For example,

---

2 Although the data in Table 7 relate to 1988, the regulations in Table 6, with focuses on the more recent arrangements, basically represent a tinkering of sorts with respect to the pre-existing set of regional features of UI, so that the general results from Table 7 are still relevant.

Table 6: *Canada's Unemployment Insurance Program in 1990*

A. *Proposed Amendment to UI Benefit Schedule: Number of Weeks Claimant Can Receive Benefits*

(unemployment rate in claimant's region)

Weeks of Work	(1) 6% and under	(2) over 6% to 7%	(3) over 7% to 8%	(4) over 8% to 9%	(5) over 9% to 10%	(6) over 10% to 11%	(7) over 11% to 12%	(8) over 12% to 13%	(9) over 13% to 14%	(10) over 14% to 15%	(11) over 15% to 16%	(12) over 16%
10											37	39
11										36	38	40
12									35	37	39	41
13								34	36	38	40	42
14							33	35	37	39	41	43
15						30	34	36	38	40	42	44
16					27	31	35	37	39	41	43	45
17				24	28	32	36	38	40	42	44	46
18			21	25	29	33	37	39	41	43	45	47
19		19	22	26	30	34	38	40	42	44	46	48
20	17	20	23	27	31	35	39	41	43	45	47	49
21	18	21	24	28	32	36	40	42	44	46	48	50
22	19	22	25	29	33	37	41	43	45	47	49	
23	20	23	26	30	34	38	42	44	46	48	50	
24	21	24	27	31	35	39	43	45	47	49		
25	22	25	28	32	36	40	44	46	48	50		
26	22	25	28	32	36	40	44	46	48			
27	23	26	29	33	37	41	45	47	49			
28	23	26	29	33	37	41	45	47	49			
29	24	27	30	34	38	42	46	48	50			
30	24	27	30	34	38	42	46	48				
31	25	28	31	35	39	43	47	49				
32	25	28	31	35	39	43	47	49				
33	26	29	32	36	40	44	48	50				
34	26	29	32	36	40	44	48					
35	27	30	33	37	41	45	49					
36	27	30	33	37	41	45	49					
37	28	31	34	38	42	46	50					
38	28	31	34	38	42	46						
39	29	32	35	39	43	47						
40	29	32	35	39	43	47						
41	30	33	36	40	44	48						
42	30	33	36	40	44	48						
43	31	34	37	41	45	49						
44	31	34	37	41	45	49						
45	32	35	38	42	46	50						
46	32	35	38	42	46							
47	33	36	39	43	47							
48	33	36	39	43	47							
49	34	37	40	44	48							
50	34	37	40	44	48							
51	35	38	41	45	49							
52	35	38	41	45	49	50	50	50	50	50	50	50

50 weeks maximum

Table 6: *Canada's Unemployment Insurance Program in 1990* - cont'd.

B. *Variable Entrance Requirements*

Regional Unemployment Rate	Weeks of Insurable Employment Needed in Qualifying Period
6% and under	20
over 6% to 7%	19
over 7% to 8%	18
over 8% to 9%	17
over 9% to 10%	16
over 10% to 11%	15
over 11% to 12%	14
over 12% to 13%	13
over 13% to 14%	12
over 14% to 15%	11
over 15%	10

Source: Canada Employment and Immigration Commission, Human Resources Development Communications (Insurance).

in 1988 Ontario "transferred" nearly $2.5 billion of UI contributions to citizens outside of Ontario. It is, of course, true that any national unemployment program will involve the transfer of monies from rich to poor areas — but of this magnitude?

With the recent recession, Ontario has fallen on hard times so that the snapshot for 1991 will be different from that for 1988. Table 8 presents summary data for 1991. As expected, Ontario's contribution/benefit ratio is now 0.85, up from 0.50 in 1988. (However, these ratios are misleading because in Table 7 overall contributions exceed benefits by nearly $1 billion (last row), whereas the system is in deficit by $2¼ million according to the data in Table 8. This means that overall benefit/contribution ratios will, perforce, be higher in 1991.) Otherwise, the pattern across provinces remains roughly similar. The major difference is that the benefits have literally skyrocketed, from $10.9 to $17.3 billion, reflecting the severity of the recession.

Table 9 sheds some light on the transfer dependency aspects of UI. From column (2) of Table 9, the *nominal* value of UI benefits tends to increase substantially during recessions, *but not to drop back* when better times emerge. However, the appropriate comparison is in terms of *real* benefits, column (3), not nominal benefits. This pattern still seems to hold. The unemployment rate in both 1981 and 1989 was 7.5 percent (column 8), yet benefits in real terms were $7.6 billion in 1989 and $4.8 billion in 1981. Some of these real increases

Table 7: *Unemployment Insurance Operations, 1988*

	Contributions by Province[a,b] (1)	Benefits by Province (2)	Ratio of Benefits to Contributions[c] (3)	Number of Contributors (4)	Monthly Average Number of Beneficiaries (5)	Ratio of Beneficiaries to Contributors (6)	Unemployment Rate	Average Weekly Payment
	($ millions)	($ millions)		(thousands)	(thousands)	(percent)	(percent)	($)
Newfoundland	180.5	751.7	4.16	247.7	71.0	28.7	16.4	197
Prince Edward Island	41.0	151.0	3.68	59.9	12.7	22.4	13.0	199
Nova Scotia	338.5	567.0	1.67	406.1	50.0	12.3	10.2	193
New Brunswick	258.0	628.0	2.43	326.0	57.0	17.5	12.0	197
Quebec	2,838.5	3,727.0	1.31	3,162.0	322.0	10.1	9.4	199
Ontario	4,932.7	2,469.0	0.50	5,142.0	216.0	4.2	5.0	211
Manitoba	436.0	380.0	0.87	490.0	35.0	7.1	7.8	195
Saskatchewan	378.5	315.0	0.83	384.0	29.0	7.5	7.5	197
Alberta	1,086.7	898.0	0.83	1,200.0	78.0	6.5	8.0	209
British Columbia	1,326.0	1,521.0	1.15	1,404.0	135.0	9.6	10.3	206
Canada	11,815.0[b]	10,852.0[b]					7.8	202

[a] These data are employee contributions grossed up by the employers' share.

[b] Contributions exceed benefits by roughly the cost of administration of the plan. In 1988 the federal government contributed a substantial amount — $2.764 billion — but this was almost exactly the "surplus" of the fund's operation for the year so that this contribution is ignored.

[c] Column 2 divided by column 1.

Source: Statistics Canada, *Unemployment Insurance Statistics, Annual Supplement 1990*, cat. 73-202S (Ottawa, 1990), Tables 9, 18, 21, 26.

Table 8: *Unemployment Insurance Operations, 1991*

	Contributions	Benefits	Net	Ratio of Benefits to Contributions
	($ millions)	*($ millions)*	*($ millions)*	
Newfoundland	221	966	+744	4.35
Prince Edward Island	53	185	+132	3.49
Nova Scotia	425	747	+322	1.76
New Brunswick	337	785	+448	1.84
Quebec	3,515	5,247	+1,737	1.49
Ontario	6,153	5,521	− 902	0.85
Manitoba	529	483	− 46	0.91
Saskatchewan	408	360	− 48	0.88
Alberta	1,497	1,177	− 320	0.79
British Columbia	1,834	2,060	+226	1.12
Canada	15,064	17,323	+2,259	1.15

Source: Statistics Canada, *Provincial Economic Accounts, Annual Estimates, 1981–91*, cat. 13-213.

come from an increase in real average weekly benefits, but not as much as column (6) indicates. In effect, UI benefits in constant dollars were almost 70 percent greater in 1989 than in 1981, whereas average weekly benefit levels were only 10 percent higher. Much more of the rise in real benefits comes from the increase in the number of beneficiaries (column 1) and still more from the number of weeks paid (column 4). Thus, real benefits ratchet upward during recessions and then tend to remain at these higher levels. In other words, what begins as a *stabilization* initiative, triggered by recession, tends to become converted into part of the permanent *redistribution* system. If this pattern holds for the current recession (and the recent dramatic upturn in benefits), this will be frightening news indeed. All of this is, at first blush, consistent with the concepts of transfer dependency and policy-induced equilibria.

Reform Options

The mandate for reforming UI is clear, since it is almost universally recognized as a disaster area. It has long ceased to have much to do with insurance and, in effect, has become an important income support system for individuals and even communities. Indeed, many Canadians find themselves pawns in the ongoing jurisdictional shuffle. Make-work programs still persist whose primary goal appears to be to employ welfare recipients for periods long enough to qualify for

Table 9: Cyclical Aspects of Unemployment Insurance, 1979–91

	Number of Beneficiaries (1)	Benefits Paid (2)	Real Benefits Paid (3)	Number of Weeks Paid (4)	Average Weekly Benefit (5)	Average Weekly Benefit (6)	Real GDP Growth (7)	Unemployment Rate (8)
	(thousands)	*($ millions)*	*(1981 $ millions)*	*($ thousands)*	*($)*	*(1981 $ millions)*	*(percent)*	*(percent)*
1979	2,332	4,008	4,966	36,896	108.63	134.4	3.9	7.4
1980	2,274	4,393	4,941	36,333	120.92	135.8	1.5	7.5
1981	2,432	4,828	4,828	37,011	130.45	130.5	3.7	7.5
1982	3,123	8,575	7,739	60,441	141.88	127.9	3.2	11.0
1983	3,396	10,169	8,676	66,585	152.72	130.3	3.2	11.8
1984	3,221	9,985	8,164	61,862	161.42	131.9	6.3	11.2
1985	3,181	10,226	8,039	59,788	171.05	134.8	4.8	10.5
1986	3,136	10,513	7,940	58,063	181.07	136.7	3.3	9.5
1987	3,079	10,440	7,554	54,875	190.26	137.6	4.0	8.8
1988	3,016	10,852	7,546	53,526	202.75	141.0	4.4	7.8
1989	3,025	11,528	7,634	53,399	215.88	143.8	3.0	7.5
1990	3,260	13,189	8,336	57,052	231.18	146.1	0.9	8.1
1989 January	1,233	1,179		5,447	216.58			7.6
1990 January	1,256	1,286		5,543	232.07			7.8
1991 January	1,492	1,788		7,319	244.29			10.2*

* February 1991.

Sources: Statistics Canada, *Unemployment Insurance Statistics*, cat. 73-001, various issues; idem, *National Income and Expenditure Accounts, Annual Estimates*, cat. 13-201, various issues.

UI. With the recent tightening of some aspects of UI, Ottawa is returning the favor by forcing erstwhile UI recipients onto welfare. The status quo is unsustainable, both economically and socially, yet we are incapable of meaningful reform. This is cold comfort to many Canadians who are shifted commodity-like from federal to provincial and then back to federal support programs without either jurisdiction appearing to have a whit of concern about their longer-term well-being.

Thus, social policy advocates should be focusing on the characteristics of an equitable transition and a new future for UI, since the existing program is clearly no longer economically viable and is consistent with neither individual and interprovincial equity on the one hand nor international competitiveness on the other. Even the recent Cashin Report (Canada 1993) on the Newfoundland fishery argues that the UI system as it applies to the fishery is in need of substantial overhaul. And the provinces are now in the restructuring game. (The December 1993 proposal by Newfoundland to restructure UI in the context of a negative income tax for Newfoundlanders is described and evaluated in Chapter 9.)

What all of this means is that Canada is still awaiting meaningful UI reform. Allow me to suggest (but not elaborate on) several reform options. The most obvious is to convert UI into a true unemployment insurance scheme — for example, a single qualifying period (say, 30 weeks) and a benefit structure that is identical everywhere in Canada (say, 3 weeks of work for each week of benefits with a maximum benefit of 52 weeks). Implicit in this proposal is that meaningful UI reform must favor long-term labor force attachment. Under the 30 weeks' entry feature and 3 weeks of work for each week of benefits, a person would need to log three years of work to qualify for a maximum benefit. In any reform package, it is critical that UI no longer be open to manipulation as part of short-term "fixes" to longer-term structural problems. While a proposal along these lines is hardly novel at the analytical level, it would have some dramatic impacts on the role that social assistance would have to play in the system. Ottawa could not simply rework UI in this fashion and then walk away from the impact on social assistance. In part, this is the same issue that stymied the Forget Commission (Canada 1986). Its recommendation for "annualizing" UI (see Chapter 10) presumed the existence of some version of an income-tested guaranteed annual income. With the latter not in place, the recommendation fell on deaf ears. Thus, major UI reform also requires a rethinking of social assistance.

An even more radical proposal would follow from addressing the following question: why do we need two income support systems? Why not simply abolish UI and convert welfare into some version of an income-tested support system reconcilable, say, every six months? The existing UI payroll tax could be abolished, maintained to finance the new income-support programs, or converted into a training fund. Elaboration of any such proposals must await further discussion relating to jurisdictional issues, the discussion of provincial welfare schemes, and the imperatives arising from globalization and the knowledge revolution.

Presumably, there will always be a role for government support for devastated regions or economies (for example, payments to the grains economy and the Cod Moratorium). The major concern here is that these programs should facilitate adjustment rather than entrenchment, particularly if the underlying problem is longer term in nature. It was an enormous mistake to address issues relating to fishing within the context of a national unemployment insurance program: industry-specific issues or challenges should not be allowed to distort otherwise national programs. As already alluded to, it is heartening to note that the Cashin Report envisages a complete rethink of the UI program as it applies to the fishery. Likewise, the Liberal minister of agriculture has signaled Ottawa's intention of revisiting the $4 billion plus grains subsidy. All such programs should embody "sunset clauses" (for reconsideration and/or renewal) and any resulting transfers to provincial residents from such programs should be taken into account when assessing the overall level of federal-provincial transfers. With some of these special cases out of the way, the prospects for UI reform become much brighter. A rather far-ranging set of UI options will be addressed in Chapter 10.

Profiling the Retirement Income Subsystem

Public Pensions

Another federal transfer program, or set of programs, that merits highlight is what might be referred to as the "retirement income subsystem." Table 10 provides a convenient conceptual overview of the subsystem. As the table indicates, the first line of defense is the transfer system — the federal OAS and GIS, spouses allowances, and provincial supplements. Level two is the public contributory pension system (CPP/QPP) while the third level is the private pension system — occupational pensions and RRSPs. The fourth level — private non-pension-related savings for retirement — will not feature in the following analysis. I turn now to a brief discussion of all three levels.

As of January 1992, OAS was worth $4,488 per pensioner (Table 11) while the GIS guarantees another $5,334 for a single pensioner and $6,732 for a two-pensioner couple ($3,366 each). Thus, the minimum annual income is $9,822 per year for a single pensioner and $15,708 for a pensioner couple (see the first three rows of Table 11). The GIS was introduced in 1967 as a bridge

Table 10: *A Schema for the Retirement Income Subsystem*

Level One	• Old age security • Guaranteed Income Supplement • Spouse's allowance • Provincial/Territorial Supplements
Level Two	• Canada Pension Plan • Quebec Pension Plan
Level Three	• Occupational Pension Plans • Registered Retirement Savings Plans
Level Four	• Private wealth accumulation

Source: Adapted from National Council of Welfare 1989, Appendix A.

between the introduction of the CPP and the time when persons would be eligible for a full CPP. Over time, however, it has played an increasingly important role. Although GIS payments are not themselves taxable, the value of the GIS payment is reduced by 50 cents for every dollar of outside income.[3] OAS is treated as taxable income and, as noted in the Appendix, if a pensioner's net income exceeds $53,215 (for the 1992 tax year), the benefits are subject to full clawback at 15 cents for each additional dollar of net income. In the mid-1980s, the Progressive Conservative government attempted to partially de-index OAS and GIS (from full CPI indexation to CPI minus 3 percent indexation), but abandoned the proposal in the face of widespread criticism. As a result, both OAS and GIS remain fully indexed to the consumer price index.

Prior to focusing on the remainder of Table 11, it is convenient to direct attention to the various provincial supplements for the elderly. These appear in Table 12.[4] For example, for seniors receiving the full OAS/GIS amount, Alberta tops this up by $1,140 for a single pensioner and $2,280 for a two-pensioner couple. These top-ups are income-tested. Ontario duplicates the GIS treatment — for each dollar of outside income, Ontario's supplement (GAINS-A) falls by 50 cents. This means that, for a two-pensioner couple, there is a confiscatory (100 percent) tax on the first $3,984 of outside income — GIS falls by $1,992 as

---

3 Income that is not taxable under the *Income Tax Act* is not considered in calculating offsets for the GIS. As well, the *Old Age Act* specifically exempts the following sources of income for GIS purposes: Old age security payments, family allowances, death benefits under the CPP/QPP, provincial and territorial welfare payments, and home insulation grants. This footnote is from National Council of Welfare (1989, fn. 3).

4 While the data relate to 1988, for the two provinces where I requested updates (including Ontario), the rates still applied in 1992. More interest attaches to the manner in which these top-ups interact with OAS/GIS than in the precise dollar amounts.

Table 11: *The Retirement Income Subsystem:*
OAS, GIS, CPP/QPP Payments

	Single Pensioner		Married Couple[a]	
	Monthly	Annually	Monthly	Annually
OAS (January 1992)	$ 374	$ 4,488	$ 748	$ 8,976
GIS (January 1992)	445	5,334	561[b]	6,732[b]
Total OAS/GIS	819	9,822	1,309	15,708
Full CPP/QPP	636	7,633	636	7,633[f]
GIS offset[d]	−318	−3,817	−318	−3,817
Net GIS for full CPP/QPP	127	1,518	243	2,915
Total — OAS/GIS/full CPP/QPP[c]	1,137	13,638	1,627	19,525
One-half CPP/QPP	318	3,816	318	3,816[f]
GIS offset[d]	−159	−1,908	−159	−1,908
Net GIS for one-half CPP/QPP	286	3,426	402	4,824
Total — OAS/GIS/one-half CPP/QPP	978	11,730	1,468	17,616
LICO (1990)[e]		13,271		17,509

[a] Both persons are assumed to be over 65.

[b] This is $280.50 per month for each pensioner and $3,366 annually.

[c] Sum of CPP/QPP plus OAS plus net GIS. Also equals total OAS/GIS plus one-half of value of CPP.

[d] This is not quite correct, since there is a threshold below which there is no GIS offset for outside income (including CPP/QPP).

[e] Statistics Canada's "low-income cut offs" for cities of 100,000–500,000 persons.

[f] The full CPP or one-half CPP is assumed to apply only to one person of the married couple.

Sources: Author's calculations.

does Ontario's GAINS-A payment. Alberta's scheme reduces the supplement by 25 cents for each dollar of outside income, for a combined Alberta/GIS tax-back rate of 75 percent. From a work-incentive point of view, one might argue that confiscatory or near-confiscatory taxes may not be as deleterious for groups that are anticipated not to enter the labor force. However, with life-expectancy rates rising, many recent retirees will be deterred from earning extra income (or perhaps deterred from "reporting" extra income) with tax rates in this range. Moreover, if they have access to nonemployment income or savings, there is every incentive to receive this in a manner that minimizes the tax take — a simple approach would be to attempt to take this income every second year rather than every year. Other problematic aspects of these near-confiscatory tax-back rates will be highlighted later in connection with the CPP/QPP.

Beyond these income supplements, many provinces have a variety of tax credits for seniors (for example, rental assistance, property tax relief) as well as

Table 12: *Provincial and Territorial*
Income Supplements for the Elderly, 1988

	Maximum Annual Benefit	
	Single Person	**Two-Pensioner Couple**
Nova Scotia Special Social Assistance	$ 219	$ 438
Ontario GAINS-A	996	1,992
Manitoba 55 Plus	421	906
Saskatchewan Income Plan	960	1,620
Alberta Assured Income Plan	1,140	2,280
British Columbia GAIN	592	1,446
Yukon Seniors' Income Supplement	1,200	2,400
Northwest Territories Senior Citizens' Benefits	1,200	2,400

Source: National Council of Welfare 1989, Table 3.

other programs relating to home repair and renovation, drug plans, and so on. And, of course, under the personal income tax system, pensioners were allowed a nonrefundable age credit of $592 for the 1992 taxation year and a pension income credit of up to $170.[5] Both of these credits relate only to the federal share of the personal income tax (PIT). For a province with, say, a 60 percent PIT rate, the provincial value of these credits would be 60 percent of the federal value.

With this information on provincial supplements, I return to the analysis of Table 11 and, in particular, to the impact of the CPP/QPP system on incomes of the elderly. The assumption here is that a full CPP/QPP or a half CPP/QPP is the only outside income received by the pensioner. A full CPP/QPP pension generates (after the GIS offset) an annual income of $13,638 for a single pensioner and $19,525 for a two-pensioner family (but where only one of the spouses receives the CPP/QPP). Of some considerable interest is the situation where the CPP/QPP is not a full pension. The table provides an illustration with a half-pension. For the two-pensioner family, the couple maintains, after the GIS offset, $1,908 of the $3,816 CPP/QPP pension. However, if this couple lives in Ontario and is eligible for GAINS-A, its income would be supplemented by $1,992 (from Table 12). Thus, the $15,708 annual total would be $17,700. Now the addition of a half-CPP/QPP *will not add one cent to this couple* — GIS takes back $1,908 of the $3,816 pension and the GAINS-A supplement also falls by $1,908. In a sense, this is precisely what GIS (and presumably the provincial

---

5 CPP/QPP pensions are not eligible for the pension credit. As Chapter 9 documents, as a result of the 1994 federal budget, the age exemption is now subject to a clawback.

supplements) were originally intended to do — fill the income gap for those not in receipt of CPP/QPP. However, there may be some quite unintended consequences arising from this confiscatory taxation.

To see this, it is necessary to devote a word or two about the operations of the CPP/QPP. The CPP/QPP was designed to replace roughly 25 percent of earnings up to the average industrial wage. Thus, in CPP/QPP terminology, the Year's Maximum Pensionable Earnings (YMPE) is set roughly in line with the average industrial wage — $33,400 for 1993. There is a lower threshold, the *Year's Basic Exemption* (or YBE), which is set at roughly 10 percent of YMPE — $3,300 for 1993 — below which no contributions are required. Currently, the contribution rate is 5 percent (2.5 percent for employers and 2.5 percent for employees) of earnings between YBE and YMPE.[6] The CPP/QPP was, by design, not fully funded. Thus, contribution rates have risen by 0.2 percent in each of the past six years and, as noted, they now stand at 5 percent, shared equally by employers and employees. The steady state rate is estimated by CPP/QPP actuaries to be 13.7 percent by 2035 in order to fund the *existing real level of benefits* in the future. (As noted later in this chapter, other analysts suggest that the equilibrium "pay-as-you-go" rate could be as high as 16 percent.) Whichever is the more likely equilibrium rate, the point is that this will represent a major tax hike that is *unrelated* to (and will not lead to a reduction of) the current deficit/debt crisis, since unfunded CPP/QPP liabilities do not enter into budget calculations.

How does all of this relate to the two-pensioner, half-CPP/QPP example from Table 11? It seems to me that we may be placing far too much emphasis on the generation of future income (pensions) and not enough on the ability to earn current income. As already noted, persons working at the $20,000 level in 1993 (who will earn roughly a half CPP/QPP pension) will not benefit at all, at least in Ontario, because of their half-CPP/QPP. But they are clearly penalized by a 5 percent "payroll tax," soon to rise to something like 13–16 percent. Combined with other payroll taxes, such as UI and workers' compensation contributions (which are also rising) and health payroll taxes in Ontario, these wage costs are surely curtailing the employability of Canadians. Part of integrating the social and economic sphere means coming to grips with issues such

---

6 The contribution rate *as a percent of earnings* follows an intriguing pattern. Given that the YMPE for 1993 is, as noted, $33,400, that YBE is $3,300, and that the contribution rate is 5 percent, a person earning $3,300 will have an effective contribution (as a percentage of earnings) rate of zero. This effective rate rises linearly to its maximum, which is at earnings of $33,400. However, the maximum is not 5 percent but 4.5 percent of earnings, because the 5 percent rate is applied to (YMPE minus YBE) and YBE is one-tenth of YMPE. For earnings beyond YMPE, the rate begins falling again. When earnings equal twice YMPE, the effective rate falls in half, to 2.25 percent, and so on.

as these. New conceptions are needed. In terms of this particular issue, is there not a way to integrate OAS/GIS and the public contributory pension system into a single integrated income support program for the elderly?

Private Pensions: RPPs and RRSPs

To conclude this brief overview of the retirement income subsystem, Table 13 contains 1990 income tax statistics for private pension contributions by income class.[7] Turning, initially, to CPP/QPP contributions, several points stand out. First, the percentage of Canadians contributing to the public pension system literally overwhelms the percent contributing to private plans, especially for the lower-income classes. Since the CPP/QPP is compulsory, this is hardly a novel observation. What it does drive home, however, is that less than one in three Canadians in the $25,000–30,000 income range, for example, has access to occupational pensions or choose to contribute to RRSPs whereas 83.6 percent are covered by CPP/QPP. Second, with regard to the earlier discussion of the half-CPP/QPP not generating any additional income for the two-pensioner couple, Table 13 reveals that, for 1990 at least, a very substantial number of Canadians acquire something like a half-CPP/QPP — roughly the $15,000–20,000 category and lower.

In terms of Registered Pension Plans (RPPs, or occupational pensions), access is clearly related to earnings. Canadians in the $40,000–50,000 income class are twice as likely to have occupational plans as those in the $20,000–25,000 income class (that is, 46.9 percent versus 23.4 percent). As an important aside, the average dollar value of contributions for the CPP/QPP is fully matched by employers. This is also typically the case for RPPs, but not for RRSPs, which are, in effect, tax-assisted individual pension vehicles.

In virtually every income class, the number of persons taking advantage of RRSPs exceeds those contributing to RPPs. This is probably to be expected since RRSPs are the only pension vehicle available to the self-employed. Nonetheless, it is intriguing that total RRSP contributions are nearly double the value of individual contributions to RPPs. The fact that, without exception, both the proportion of taxpayers contributing to RRSPs and the average amount contributed rises with higher incomes is also easily explainable. First, the amount one is allowed to contribute to an RRSP increases with increasing income (up to the contribution limit, which, itself, is now rising). Second, the "tax savings" for a given level of RRSP contributions rises across the three tax

---

7 Income class relates to taxable income so that anomalies can appear, particularly in terms of the zero-income class (labeled loss or nil in Table 13).

Table 13: *Pension Contributions by Income Class, 1990*

Income Class	Loss or Nil	$1–5,000	$5,000–$10,000	$10,000–$15,000	$15,000–$20,000	$20,000–$25,000	$25,000–$30,000	$30,000–$40,000	$40,000–$50,000	$50,000–$100,000	$100,000 plus	All Returns
Number of filers (thousands)	815	2,305	2,609	2,266	1,968	1,785	1,552	2,326	1,395	1,496	240	18,759
RRSP contribution												
Percent contributing	*	1.0	3.6	9.6	16.2	24.6	30.9	40.2	49.2	52.9	64.2	22.1
Amount ($ thousands)	607	7,287	76,644	264,602	479,972	782,092	961,809	2,224,782	1,788,142	2,937,639	1,102,663	10,626,239
Average amount	5,519	387	803	1,214	1,503	1,781	2,005	2,376	2,607	3,708	7,162	2,567
RPP contribution												
Percent contributing	*	1.4	2.4	6.1	11.2	23.4	31.1	40.7	46.9	45.4	18.0	19.7
Amount ($ thousands)	4,071	4,795	15,910	52,512	125,275	331,591	509,508	1,399,308	1,343,131	1,976,857	177,473	5,940,431
Average amount ($)	1,642	148	251	379	539	792	1,053	1,415	1,958	2,908	4,116	1,608
CPP/QPP contribution												
Percent contributing	1.4	19.4	53.8	66.9	73.9	80.2	83.6	87.6	90.9	89.4	80.4	66.0
Amount ($ thousands)	3,008	12,879	130,495	277,868	415,658	566,001	651,483	1,115,034	726,892	788,422	131,598	4,859,280
Average amount ($)	270	29	93	183	286	382	502	567	578	589	685	392

* = less than 1 percent, rounded.

Source: Canada, Department of National Revenue, *Taxation Statistics for 1990* (Ottawa, 1992), Table 2.

brackets. This is because RRSP contributions (and RPP contributions as well) are treated as *deductions* from income and not as *tax credits* valued at the lowest federal tax rate, 17 percent, as is the case for CPP/QPP contributions. Moreover, RRSP contributions are probably about to mushroom. Ottawa is raising the overall maximum and is permitting the carrying forward of unused contribution opportunities. At today's high tax rates, the access rate will rise substantially. Yet, when these tax-assisted[8] RRSP contributions are eventually drawn into income, they benefit from yet another set of tax gifts — the elderly and the pension tax credits. Surely we can improve on this. At the very least we can clawback these "gifts" from upper-income elderly. Alternative approaches will be detailed later.

Postscript

As a postscript to this section, after the above analysis was completed I came across a publication by Newman Lam, Michael Prince, and James Cutt (1993), which basically updates many of the earlier analyses of the CPP/QPP, such as those associated with the Ontario Economic Council study *Pensions Today and Tomorrow* (1983a). Readers may wish to consult this informative study directly. I shall highlight a few of its findings. As already noted, the CPP/QPP was not designed to be fully funded at its inception. What is surprising is the degree of underfunding that already exists. Lam, Prince, and Cutt (1993) indicate that the CPP could afford a starting pension of $1,464 for people retired in 1990 if the average life span is assumed to be 80 years. However, the 1990 pension for a person with an average income was $6,675. This difference creates an annual shortfall of $5,211 per person, which, under a "pay-as-you-go" system, has to be absorbed by the current generation of contributors. Their calculation of equilibrium contribution rates in order to finance the current level of benefits are of the order of 16 percent (well above the 13.7 percent of the CPP actuaries). However, were the CPP assets invested at the average rates of return obtained by private sector funds (rather than turned over to the provinces at federal government bond rates), the equilibrium contribution rates would be cut in half — that is, 8 percent. Indeed, Lam, Prince, and Cutt (1993, 70) go much further:

> A comparative analysis of the present "pay-as-you-go" CPP and a fully funded alternative [with the same contribution rates but with profit-maximizing investment policies] shows that the fully funded system provides a higher

---

8 They are "tax assisted," not only in terms of deductions at the time of contribution, but as well because the interest accumulates tax free until redemption. This "tax deferral" benefit is already very substantial and is rising as marginal tax rates rise. Moreover, there is flexibility to make "spousal" RRSP contributions, which can reduce taxes further at the benefit stage.

level of pensions than the CPP. Indeed, in most of the cases simulated, the *fully funded pension was greater than the CPP and OAS combined* [italics added].

In much the same light, another option is to follow the United States and, more recently, Sweden in raising the qualifying age for full access to the public pension system. About a decade ago, the Ontario Economic Council (1983, 195) estimated that the savings arising from raising the qualifying age from 65 to 66 years would be approximately $1 billion in 1983 dollars, with a similar annual savings from raising the qualifying age from 66 to 67. These savings would be much higher now.

More generally, while our programs for the elderly represent one of the postwar success stories on the social policy front, there is a growing perception that the programs may well be too generous both in absolute terms and even more obviously relative to those available for, say, children and the working poor. The combination of OAS/GIS and a full CPP generate incomes for pensioners that exceed Statistics Canada's low income cut-offs (LICOs). Indeed, the combination of OAS/GIS and provincial top-ups comes close to the LICOs even without a CPP. Note that these LICOs are really "inequality indices" and are well above any measure of "necessities" (see Chapter 5 for more detail). To be sure, there are still some areas where improvements are essential but, by and large, this area of the social envelope will increasingly be viewed as unsustainable and will be targeted for reform and restructuring. Some initiatives have already been implemented — for example, the clawback of OAS for the elderly rich and, in the 1994 federal budget, the clawback of the age exemption. But this is probably only the beginning. As Battle and Torjman (1993b, 23) note:

> In the area of elderly benefits, in particular, changes have to be made to the current set of programs. It will not be possible to sustain an adequate system of payments for the elderly, given the projected future demand. One possible solution is to replace Old Age Security, the Guaranteed Income Supplement, the Spouses Allowance as well as certain refundable tax credits, such as the age credit — with a single, adequate income-tested program. The new scheme would pay its maximum benefit to low and modest-income persons ages 60 and older, with partial and diminishing benefits to middle-income seniors.

Difficult as this may be to sell politically, it is really a straightforward option. Not so straightforward would be to bring reform of the CPP/QPP into the package. But why not? Why do we need two near-comprehensive public programs for the elderly? Prior to addressing these issues, it is necessary to detour a bit and to focus on some aspects of the philosophy underpinning the income tax system. While this analysis relates to a broad set of issues in the social policy arena, it is also critical to sorting out several of the concerns relating to the retirement income subsystem.

Income Taxation,
Horizontal Equity, and Tax Credits

Until the mid-1980s' reform of the personal income tax, personal and other exemptions were addressed via a series of *deductions*. Since tax reform, most of these deductions have been converted to *tax credits*. Under the deduction system, horizontal equity issues were never far from the surface. Horizontal equity implied equal treatment of equals. This is best seen in the context of child benefits.

Consider two families that have identical incomes but one of the families has three children and the other has no children. To facilitate the comparison, assume that all of the family income is earned by a single breadwinner in each of the families. It was accepted wisdom and philosophy for most of the postwar period that these two families should not be treated identically by the income tax system. Horizontal equity considerations dictated that the taxation on the family with children should be lower. And it was. Early on, for example, family allowances were not taxable. This guaranteed a smaller tax take from the family with children regardless of the income level. When family allowances were converted to, or combined with, deductions, the same principle obtained.

The switch to a credit system altered all of this, not so much because of the credit system itself but because the system moved to refundable credits, replete with clawbacks. Thus, if our two families have a sufficiently high income level, they will now be treated equally since the child tax credits will be fully clawed back. Horizontal equity no longer obtains, at least in the way that we were used to defining it.

What triggered this shift to credits was the increasing emphasis that we began to place on *vertical equity* and, in particular, on the notion that these benefits ought to be targeted to those most in need. Readers will recall that this issue was crystallized in the query as to whether wealthy bankers ought to receive family allowance.

Conceptually, however, these former deductions (now credits) were being diverted to social policy or income distribution concerns rather than horizontal equity concerns.

Compounding this shift is another set of issues relating to the philosophy underlying the nature of income taxation. The Carter Commission's approach to personal income taxation was that a "dollar is a dollar," so that all income should be treated in an identical manner for tax purposes. The alternative approach is based on a consumption or expenditure approach — namely, that the system should tax only expenditures and that all savings should be exempt from taxation. This provided the rationale for full deductions for RRSPs and RPPs. Thus, our system was somewhat of a hybrid — it resembled an expenditure approach in terms of RRSPs and RPPs but not for other types of savings. Many analysts express a preference for an expenditure approach to taxation, and in international taxation circles the Canadian tax system often received high marks for embodying aspects of an expenditure tax. As an interesting aside, the goods and services tax can be viewed as a move in this direction, since one is not taxed on what is not spent.

However, this income versus expenditure debate also became more complicated with the shift toward tax credits. One obvious aspect relates to the fact that CPP/QPP premiums are now treated as a credit at the lowest federal rate, whereas RPPs and RRSPs remain a full deduction. Given that these credits are viewed more in social policy or income distribution terms, it becomes much harder to defend the existence of a full deduction for RPPs and RRSPs, especially since the amounts that one can contribute, at least for RRSPs, also increase with the level of income. The expenditure tax rationale for full deduction still exists, but it is harder to make a persuasive case in the context where all of the former deductions have come to be viewed as "tax expenditures." And just as the international community approved those components of our system that moved it toward expenditure taxation, Canada was also congratulated for its shift to a credit system and, more recently, for embracing substantial aspects of a negative income tax approach to taxation.

Thus, there are alternative and competing theoretical or analytical approaches to the philosophy that ought to underpin the structure of the personal income tax system. Moreover, the issues at stake go well beyond those that were aired in the above paragraphs. For example, should capital gains be taxed at all and, if so, should the inflation component of any gain be exempt? Sorting out these fundamental issues is well beyond the scope of this book, especially since these issues transcend the Canadian tax system. Nonetheless, overall I welcomed the move from deductions to credits, even refundable credits. The CPP/QPP versus RRSP/RPP issue is more complicated and I will comment on it in the following section on reform options for the retirement income subsystem.

Reform Options for the Retirement Income Subsystem

Treatment of the elderly is clearly one of the successes of Canadian social policy. However, we are probably now at the stage where, for the first time in our history, the current generation of the elderly is better off than the current generation of children. (The same is true of the United States.) And the soon-to-be elderly will be far richer still, given that they are probably the last generation to reap the full benefits of a resource-based economy — including good middle-class jobs replete with occupational pension plans. Quite appropriately, we have begun to target these transfers (for example, the clawbacks of OAS for the elderly rich).

But more is needed here since the unfunded liabilities of the retirement income subsystem are truly staggering. What is the rationale for the age exemption when most (but not all) of the elderly are above the LICO inequality lines, let alone more appropriate definitions of poverty? (Ottawa, in its 1994 budget, has agreed — see Chapter 9.) What is the continuing rationale for the pension exemption, particularly since the tax treatment of pensions is already very generous? Surely these monies can be put to better use elsewhere in the social envelope or in the economy.

At a more basic level, I reiterate my earlier query: do we really need (or can we afford) two near-comprehensive public programs for the elderly — the OAS/GIS on the one hand and the CPP/QPP on the other? This area is really a ticking societal time bomb. It borders on the immoral, let alone inequitable, to saddle future generations of Canadians with an eventual (combined) 16 percent CPP/QPP contribution rate given that

- it is principally an intergenerational transfer to that group of Canadians that is also saddling the young with a horrendous debt overhang;
- the impact of a 16 percent "payroll tax" will have a deleterious impact on the next generation's employment prospects, especially when one realizes that workers' compensation contribution rates will have to rise and UI contribution rates have also risen recently; and
- the eventual benefits of a less-than-full CPP/QPP (which will likely characterize large segments of the elderly of the future) are fairly minimal given the existing set of programs for the elderly (as documented in Table 11).

Radical alternatives are inevitable. Indeed, the writing was clearly on the wall as far back as 1984 when Hamilton and Whalley proposed a series of restructuring options. The first was to merge OAS and GIS into a single program administered on a GIS income-tested basis. This is a variant of the Battle/Torjman proposal quoted above. With the full clawback of the OAS, we have now moved somewhat in this direction. The difference is that, with the OAS rolled in, the GIS, the clawback would begin at a much lower income level.

The second approach would also fold CPP into the negative income tax to be funded out of general revenue. As Lam, Prince, and Cutt (1993, 26) note, New Zealand and Australia have adopted this approach — that is, they have abolished social security taxes and used the personal income tax for funding income support to the elderly.

The third approach proffered by Hamilton and Whalley (1984) is to blend OAS/GIS/ CPP into a single, pay-go, contribution-based scheme. This is close to the US system. Note that the benefits under this approach could also take the form of a universal GIS or negative-income-tax scheme.

All of these approaches merit further research, especially those that take some pressure off the payroll tax as the principal funding source. There is a limit to how much of the current financial burden we can pass on to the next generation of workers. At what point will they simply renege on the intergenerational contract?

Another option is to follow the Americans and Swedes in raising the qualifying age for full access to the public pension system. As noted, about a decade ago, the Ontario Economic Council (1983a, 195) estimated that the savings arising from raising the qualifying age from 65 to 66 years would be approximately $1 billion in 1983 dollars, with an even larger annual savings from moving from 66 to 67 years.

In terms of RRPs and RRSPs, the pressures on the status quo are severe. Canadians from many quarters do not buy into the expenditure-tax conception, elaborated earlier, but prefer to view these as lucrative tax expenditures. As already highlighted, the complicating problem is that CPP/QPP contributions are treated as a tax credit at the lowest federal tax rate. The expenditure tax solution might be to treat the CPP/QPP the same as the RRSP system. Or even more radical, why not allow Canadians to opt out of CPP/QPP provided that they switch these contributions to the equivalent of an RRSP scheme (or an RPP scheme if the employer contributions are also transferable)? The message here is fairly clear, however. Those wishing to maintain the full deduction approach to RRSPs and RPPs will probably have to turn their attention to finding acceptable solutions to the intergenerational burden levied on lower-income Canadians.

As a final comment on the public pension system, anecdotal evidence suggests that Canadians are well ahead of their politicians with respect to the need for change. Many of the baby boomers are already reconciled to the fact that there will likely be no CPP/QPP to collect when they retire. To the extent that the CPP/QPP is one of our "sacred cows" on the social policy front, it is clearly more sacred to the politicians than to the citizenry. More to the point, the full force of the fiscal crisis in this subsystem has not yet hit us. We can avoid much of this if we act now.

Family Benefits and Day Care

The Appendix details the 1985–93 evolution of policy initiatives with respect to family benefits and child care. Most of the description and evaluation of family benefits will be undertaken in the context of the discussion of welfare in

Chapter 5 and to some extent in tandem with Ontario's social policy blueprint, *Turning Point*, in Chapter 9. In what follows, emphasis is directed toward the societal debate on child care/day care. An excellent overview of these issues, from which I shall draw heavily, is that by Powell (1992).

In terms of the evolution of social policy, child care/day care is one of those issues that did not feature significantly in the 1960s' conception of social policy. This is not to say that it was not an important issue for many Canadians, only that it was not high on the policy agenda. One of the underlying themes of this monograph is that, because of the changing nature of society (economic, demographic, and social changes, including the simultaneous dramatic changes in the role of women in society and in the nature of family arrangements), the current and emerging needs on the social policy front do not square well with the goals of the existing social envelope. Chapter 6 will address the issue of why Canada's social envelope has not been able to evolve to accommodate these changing needs. More generally, given the constraints on the fiscal side, it is probably the case that some or most of the funds needed to accommodate these emerging social policy needs (day care, enhanced training, and so on) will have to come from elsewhere in the social envelope. In an important sense, therefore, what is holding back progress on the social policy front in terms of day care and/or training is our collective unwillingness to reform programs such as UI.

Beyond these considerations, however, there is the fact that child care/day care is one of the more complex policy issues in the social arena. As Powell (1992) notes, the first issue to be sorted out has to do with the distinction between day care and child care. I shall, following Powell, define the former as involving the care of children while parents are in the paid labor force. Thus, day care has to do with enhancing or easing labor force participation of parents, and particularly spouses and heads of single-parent families. In other words, day care can probably be cast in terms of efficiency, at least in part. Child care, on the other hand, is "concerned with the care of children regardless of the labor force participation decision of parents" (Powell 1992, 157). This is more along the lines of a societal goal than a labor market issue. In the limit, it also involves concern about the proportion of children living in poverty.

This distinction is important because the appropriate policy instruments for day care and child care may be quite different. The latter can be addressed in part via the recently inaugurated child tax benefit or, as proposed by Ontario's *Turning Point*, some version of a negative income tax for children. One approach to addressing day care, particularly for lower-income families, would be to convert the existing child tax expense deduction (which, from the Appendix, now stands at $5,000 for each child under 6 and $3,000 for each child 7 to 14) into a "refundable" tax deduction or credit. To trigger this "voucher," it would be necessary to provide evidence of labor force attachment.

Intriguingly, the Mulroney government initially framed the issue in terms of day care — that is, it centered the discussion around labor market issues. But by the time the proposed *Child Care Act* of 1988 died on the order paper, the legislation had shifted toward a child care conception, on grounds that subsidies should not only be provided to families or women who choose to work but should also support those who choose to stay at home and rear their children (Powell 1993, 157).

The day care debate became even more complicated by further series of controversial issues:

- Should subsidies be limited to "licensed day care" centers or should parents be allowed to access the informal (for example, relatives) or unregulated market?
- Should licensed day care centers be restricted to the nonprofit sector?
- Should day care be universal (for example, like the public school system) or be targeted, say, to lower-income groups?
- Relatedly, should subsidies go to "institutions" (creating subsidized day care spaces) or to "persons" (for example, vouchers)?

There is no "solution" to these issues in the sense that they are either ideological (for example, profit versus not-for-profit) or embedded in deeper societal values (for example, universal versus targeted). But among the perspectives that the analysis in this monograph can bring to the issue are the following. First, and as noted by Powell, the dramatic rise in female participation rates was not propelled by an equivalent subsidization of day care, or at least not by a proliferation of subsidized day care "spaces." To be sure, the child expense deduction under the income tax system probably played an important role. Thus, a move to universal day care, as in the Scandinavian countries, will not trigger a major increase in labor force participation of females: they are already in the labor force. It could enhance the quality of day care and, therefore, play a part in human capital formation of children. But much of the impact would probably be to alter existing day care arrangements.

Nonetheless, there probably would be some increase in labor force participation as a result of greater availability of day care. Frequently, however, day care is not the sole reason for lack of labor force participation. As elaborated later (Chapter 5), one of the principal reasons for "welfare traps" is the presence of children in welfare families — working at wages, even when they are considerably above the minimum wage, cannot dominate what a single mother with three children, say, would receive from welfare. Subsidized day care, even free day care, would not solve this problem. Rather, something like an income-tested guaranteed annual income for children is more likely to entice labor force participation. With such a scheme in place, then a system of day care vouchers may become an important factor in this transition. Thus, the second point is that day care systems or programs should be conceived in the context of the overall tax transfer/training system.

Third, given the growing concern that our monopolized school system is not delivering value for money (Chapter 5), it seems wholly inappropriate to extend the monopoly to include universal day care. Even if there were no financial or cost issues at stake, it would be preferable to proceed with vouchers so that parents could opt for the day care of their choice (Montessori, public school system, workplace, and so on). Others, of course, may and will disagree with this. Indeed, when Ontario reduced the age for admission to kindergarten in 1989, this could be viewed as a move in the direction of both day care (for those that worked from 9 to 5) and child care (Powell 1992, 169). However, beyond this initiative, it seems to me that the last thing we need to do is to saddle day care with the expense and rigidities of teachers' union rules and salaries. The more general point here is that we have gone way too far in subsidizing "institutional spaces" (whether in day care or in housing, which receives no attention in this monograph). This creates inequitable "lotteries" — one either gets access to subsidized or free spaces or one does not. Much better to let the market do its thing and to attach subsidies (income tested) to individuals or families.

Finally, but not exhaustively, Ottawa has much greater leeway in addressing child care than day care. As already noted, the new refundable child tax credit can be viewed as an instrument related to child care. However, the licensing and provision of day care services surely falls into the provincial domain. What Ottawa can do and has done is to provide funding, either via the tax system (the child care tax deduction, which, as an aside, should be called the day care tax deduction in terms of the terminology adopted here) or via the Canada Assistance Plan (which cost shares certain provincial day care subsidies). In this context, an interesting question arises: could Ottawa provide day care funding with the proviso that the monies be used for subsidizing licensed, nonprofit, day care centers? This is, of course, what much of the early cost sharing in health was all about — the provinces got federal funding provided that health delivery was by physicians (not paramedics) and that the hospitals were accredited (half-way houses were not eligible for funding). The courts would probably have to sort this out. But my view is that this would not be an appropriate way to proceed. To be affective, day care should be integrated into the overall welfare/tax-transfer system within each province, and it is unlikely that some central vision emanating from the center would be appropriate, let alone cost effective.

In summary, I believe that day care is a policy whose time has finally arrived. It is much easier to rationalize day care in the emerging knowledge-based society than in the former resource-based society, since one can make human capital formation arguments for parents and children alike. However, it is a big ticket item and the only way that we can probably afford even a limited system is in the context of a wholesale restructuring of the existing social envelope. Moreover, since there are many policy instruments that can be brought to bear on the range of issues associated with day care and labor force participation, it is important that Ottawa not straightjacket the system to evolve in some predetermined way.

Conclusion

Ottawa's current role in the social policy area is largely twofold: to deliver selected programs directly to Canadians and to provide financial support to the provinces to enable them to deliver key programs such as health, education, and welfare. This chapter dealt with the former. Since most of the reform proposals have been attached to the relevant sections of the above analysis, I shall use the conclusion to make a few summary comments.

Ottawa basically engages in direct program delivery in those areas where it has the constitutional right to do so — the elderly, the unemployed, and, via the tax system, children. However, perhaps because Ottawa has felt itself to be constrained constitutionally on the social policy front, it has diverted its contributory social insurance programs (UI and CPP) in ways that have incorporated other social policy goals. It is these other features that are in the forefront of creating problems with these programs.

This summary section is a convenient place to highlight two anomalies associated with the philosophy underlying our social programs. The first is that we have managed to get things backward when it comes to the income support of the young (welfare) and the old (the retirement income subsystem). We apply needs testing for the former (see Chapter 5) but apply income testing to the latter. While I am not suggesting that needs testing is appropriate for the elderly, I am suggesting that income testing makes eminent sense for the welfare and working poor. The very conception of means testing leads rather naturally to the confiscatory tax rates that characterize the welfare system.

The second and related anomaly arises from this last comment about confiscatory taxation. It is rather incredible that the UI system still involves confiscatory taxation. A person receiving benefits can earn up to one-quarter of these benefits without any loss of benefits. But earnings beyond this threshold are "taxed" dollar for dollar in terms of benefits. We would never think of saddling higher-income Canadians with confiscatory tax rates. Why does society view these as appropriate for UI and welfare recipients? Surely, we have no grounds for surprise when these individuals channel their activities toward "rational" directions (for example, the underground economy) because of these perverse incentives.

Beyond these issues, what is disconcerting in all of this is that the challenges with respect to UI and the retirement income subsystem are long-standing. As already noted, the Hamilton/Whalley analysis relating to the reform of the retirement income subsystem was penned in 1984. And on the UI front, the Report of the Newfoundland Royal Commission on Employment and Unemployment was published in 1986 and most of the problems that are now besetting UI were highlighted much earlier than this. Because the reform of UI is so critical to the overall restructuring of Social Canada, I shall conclude this chapter by listing some of the concerns with respect to UI that were highlighted by the Commission (Newfoundland 1986, 406–410):

- The UI system undermines the intrinsic value of work.
- The system undermines good working habits and discipline.
- The system undermines the importance of education.
- UI is a disincentive to work.
- UI undermines personal and community initiatives.
- UI discourages self-employment and small-scale enterprise.
- The UI make-work system encourages political patronage.
- UI make-work distorts the efforts of local development groups.
- The system is vulnerable to manipulation (for example, job rotation; employers' submitting records for higher salaries than they are paying; employers' having employees on the payroll for 10–20 week periods but not actually paying them; provincial social services agencies' providing short-term employment for recipients of their benefits so that the financial burden of caring for these people is shifted from the provincial to the federal government, and so on).

Fundamental reform is surely the order of the day.

Chapter 4

Ottawa's Social Policy Presence:
Fiscal Federalism

Much of the current public discussion and debate relating to social policy centers around the future of federal transfers to the provinces — equalization, Established Programs Financing (EPF), and the Canada Assistance Plan (CAP). The purpose of this chapter is to describe and to some extent evaluate each of these major transfers. The more controversial issue — assessing and evaluating the impact on the provinces of the various caps, ceilings and freezes to these transfer programs — will be the subject of Chapter 7, although a description, as distinct from an evaluation, of these changes will be part and parcel of the present discussion.

The chapter begins with a statistical overview of federal-provincial transfers. This is followed by a detailed focus on each of the three major transfer programs. The penultimate section presents some aggregate data relating to the overall federal presence in the social policy area — that is, combining the transfers to persons and business from the previous chapter with the transfers to provinces. The concluding section touches on selected aspects of the mandate for the reform of fiscal federalism although, as already noted, a more complete assessment of reform possibilities will come later in the monograph.

One final introductory note is in order. The term "fiscal federalism" as employed here refers to the three major federal transfers. This is, however, a rather narrow interpretation of the term. As used in the Canadian public finance literature, it also encompasses areas such as the tax collection agreements, the use of the spending power to promote the internal economic union, and more generally all aspects of the financial and, in some cases, the economic, interface between Ottawa and the provinces. While most of these nontransfer aspects of fiscal federalism will not be dealt with in this chapter, they will feature prominently later in the monograph.

An Overview of Major Federal Transfers

Table 14 presents a statistical overview for fiscal year 1991/92 of the major transfers to the provinces — equalization, EPF, and CAP transfers. EPF transfers to the provinces total $20.8 billion, of which $9.6 billion is in the form of cash and the remainder in the form of various sorts of tax transfers. CAP transfers total $6.7 billion and equalization totals $7.6 billion, for an overall total of roughly $34 billion (or just over $23 billion in terms of cash transfers).

The per capita value of these transfers varies widely across provinces, from a high of $2,355 for Newfoundland to a low of $994 for Alberta. Most, though not all, of this variation arises from the equalization program. Note that the staggering value of per capita transfers to the territories (Yukon gets $9,248 per capita and the Northwest Territories $15,885) are attributable to their extremely generous "formula financing" arrangements. Although the Yukon and the Northwest Territories are included in Table 14, the focus for the remainder of the chapter will be almost exclusively on the provinces. Readers interested in some detail relating to the formula financing arrangements for the Yukon can consult Courchene and Powell (1992).

The role of these transfers is to ameliorate both vertical and horizontal fiscal imbalances in the federation. The former relates to the fact that the federal government has a share of revenues in excess of its share of expenditure responsibilities, while the transfers relating to horizontal imbalance (largely, but as we shall see not wholly, equalization) are designed to enhance revenue access for the "have-not" provinces. As a first cut at sorting out vertical and horizontal transfers, one might argue that the vertical component is $994 per capita (that is, Alberta's total) with the excess for any province representing the contribution toward generating horizontal balance.

With this brief overview, attention is now directed to an analysis of each of the major transfers, beginning with equalization.

Profiling Equalization

Introduction

Equalization payments are the cornerstone of Canada's federal-provincial redistribution. Programs such as EPF are much larger in dollar value, but they do not embody anywhere near the degree of ameliorating horizontal fiscal inequities across the provinces that equalization does. In effect, equalization is what gives life to Social Canada because, paraphrasing section 36(2) of the *Constitution Act, 1982*, equalization provides funds to the poorer provinces to allow them to deliver reasonably comparable public services at reasonably comparable tax rates. From part C of Table 14, offsetting these horizontal fiscal inequities across provinces means that, at the high end, Newfoundland receives

Table 14: The Federal Presence in the Provincial Economies:
Major Transfers to Provinces, fiscal year 1991/92 - cont'd.

	Manitoba	Saskatchewan	Alberta	British Columbia	Northwest Territories	Yukon	Canada
				($ millions)			
A. EPF transfers							
1. Cash transfers (total)	448.6	407.2	1,003.2	1,319.2	21.51	11.9	9,657.5
of which: postsecondary education	(116.7)	(105.9)	(258.1)	(340.3)	(5.4)	(3.1)	(2,407.7)
health	(331.9)	(301.3)	(745.1)	(978.9)	(16.1)	(8.8)	(7,249.8)
2. Tax transfers (total)[a]	373.6	339.2	921.2	1,184.3	23.8	9.5	11,178.0
of which: postsecondary education	(120.0)	(109.0)	(259.9)	(380.5)	(7.7)	(3.1)	(3,590.8)
health	(253.6)	(230.2)	(625.3)	(803.9)	(16.2)	(6.5)	(7,587.2)
including: Quebec abatement[b]	(95.7)	(105.5)					(1,098.4)
associated equalization							(829.6)
3. Total (cash and tax)	822.2	746.4	1,924.4	2,503.6	45.4	21.4	20,835.5
of which: postsecondary education	(236.7)	(214.9)	(544.0)	(720.8)	(13.1)	(6.2)	(5,988.5)
health	(585.5)	(531.5)	(1,370.4)	(1,782.8)	(32.3)	(15.2)	(14,837.0)
B. CAP transfers (total)	251.1	166.4	582.5	761.9	23.3	8.3	6,746.7
of which: Quebec tax[c]							(644.2)
C. Equalization (including associated equalization)	840.4	473.8	0.0	0.0	805.0*	220.0*	7,606.8[e]
$ per capita	768.0	476.0	0.0	0.0	14,690.0	8,178.0	
D. Total major transfers[d]	1,817.9	1,281.1	2,506.9	3,265.5	837.7	249.7	34,359.3[e]
of which: cash	(1,540.0)	(1,047.4)	(1,587.5)	(2,081.1)	(849.8)*	(240.2)*	(23,381.8)
$ per capita (total major transfers)	1,663.0	1,288.0	994.0	1,015.0	15,885.0	9,248.0	1,278.0

[a] This reflects 13.5 points of personal income tax and one point of corporate income tax.

[b] This reflects 8.5 additional personal income tax points for Quebec for postsecondary education.

[c] This reflects 5 points of personal income tax for Quebec under CAP.

[d] This total only counts "associated equalization" once; that is, it is the sum of rows A.3, B, and C less the associated equalization under A.2.

[e] These totals exclude the formal financing for the Northwest Territories and the Yukon, which appear in the Equalization row.

Source: Canada, Department of Finance.

Table 14: *The Federal Presence in the Provincial Economies:
Major Transfers to Provinces, fiscal year 1991/92*

	Newfoundland	PEI	Nova Scotia	New Brunswick	Quebec	Ontario
			($ millions)			
A. *EPF transfers*						
1. Cash transfers (total)	231.8	52.9	391.2	302.1	1,761.4	3,726.0
of which: postsecondary education	(60.1)	(13.8)	(96.6)	(78.6)	(391.0)	(939.1)
health	(171.6)	(39.2)	(274.6)	(223.5)	(1,360.3)	(2,788.5)
2. Tax transfers (total)[a]	195.7	44.1	309.2	251.6	3,480.0	4,043.0
of which: postsecondary education	(63.4)	(14.2)	(99.3)	(80.8)	(1,118.1)	(1,298.9)
health	(134.0)	(29.9)	(209.9)	(170.8)	(2,362.4)	(2,744.5)
including: Quebec Abatement[b]					1,098.4	
Associated Equalization	(87.1)	(17.4)	(78.3)	(87.7)		
3. Total (cash and tax)	429.3	97.1	680.4	553.6	5,241.0	7,769.9
of which: postsecondary education	(123.6)	(27.9)	(195.9)	(159.4)	(1,509.1)	(2,236.9)
health	(305.7)	(89.1)	(484.5)	(394.3)	(3,732.8)	(5,533.0)
B. *CAP transfers* (total)	133.6	31.9	219.5	203.1	2,218.0[d]	2,147.2
of which: Quebec tax[c]					(644.2)	
C. *Equalization* (including Associated Equalization)	874.0	186.6	860.0	951.1	3,420.8	0.0
$ per capita	1,524.0	1,428.0	955.0	1,310.0	500.0	0.0
D. *Total major transfers*[d]	1,349.7	298.2	1,681.6	1,620.2	10,522.8	9,917.1
of which: cash	(1,239.4)	(271.5)	(1,450.7)	(1,450.7)	(6,755.9)	(5,873.8)
$ per capita (total major transfers)	2,355.0	2,276.0	1,866.0	2,232.0	1,537.0	1,000.0

$1,524 per capita while Saskatchewan receives $476 per capita and, of course, the three "have" provinces — Ontario, British Columbia, and Alberta — receive no equalization. These payments come out of Ottawa's consolidated revenue fund and *not* directly from the coffers of the "have" provinces. Equalization transfers are unconditional — they can be spent on anything the recipient provinces choose.

Intuitively, equalization allows the provinces with low tax bases to have access to revenues equal to what they would get from applying national average tax rates to the "average tax base" in five designated provinces, rather than what they would get from applying national average tax rates to their own tax bases.

At one level, perhaps, this is all one needs to know about equalization, particularly given the inherent complexity of the equalization formula. Phrased differently, acquiring additional insights relating to the operations of equalization can only come with immersing oneself in some rather technical, and even antiseptic detail that, heretofore, has largely been the preserve of the relevant bureaucrats at both levels of government and a few academics and policy analysts.

Notwithstanding, I have decided to offer the reader an opportunity to become familiar with this financial cornerstone of our federal system. There are several reasons for this. First of all, as a result of the ongoing social policy review, there is a possibility that equalization will not only increase in importance but, in terms of some proposals for reform, be the only surviving federal-provincial transfer. Second, much of what Canadians perceive themselves to be as a federal nation is embodied or embedded in the equalization formula. Third, and relatedly, it is far from evident that the philosophy underpinning the existing equalization arrangements is appropriate to the Canada of the millennium where, among other things, trade will increasingly be north-south rather than east-west. Fourth, and practically, there are problems with the current equalization system (even within its existing philosophy) that should be sorted out in the process of reworking Social Canada.

Accordingly, the second section will focus on the basic mechanics relating to equalization. The third section will then focus on what I refer to as some of the "bells and whistles" associated with the programs — for example, floors and ceilings. Those readers who want to put some limits on just how much they care to know about the operations of equalization may wish to skip that section. The analysis then turns to a section entitled "equalization in action," which traces the history of the program over the past decade or so. The final section focuses on the key issues that are up for grabs in any program redesign. Several "Thematic Tableaux," designed to address selected features of equalization are also included in the analysis.

The Basic Equalization Formula

Canada's formal equalization program began in 1957. Initially, only the three "shared taxes" (personal income taxes, corporate income taxes, and succession duties) were subject to equalization. The first comprehensive formula came into being in 1967. With the *Constitution Act, 1992*, the twenty-fifth anniversary of the initial formula, equalization was formally enshrined in the Constitution. Section 36(2) reads: "Parliament and the Government of Canada are committed to the principle of making equalization payments to ensure that provincial governments have sufficient revenues to provide reasonably comparable levels of public services at reasonably comparable levels of taxation."

The first order of business is to document the manner in which Canada implements this principle of equalization. Later sections will focus on evaluating the conceptual underpinnings of the program. Thematic Tableau 1, "How Equalization Works," reproduced from the Department of Finance publication *Federal Transfers to the Provinces* (Canada 1992b) provides a pictorial and verbal overview of the program. In somewhat more detail, one can envisage the following four steps in the determination of equalization:

- determining the revenues which are eligible for equalization;
- calculating the "fiscal capacity" associated with these revenues for each province;
- defining the equalization "standard" to which the fiscal capacity measures in the second bullet are to be compared; and
- calculating equalization entitlements and payments.

Revenues to be Equalized

As noted in Thematic Tableau 1, over 30 different provincial revenue sources now enter the equalization formula. And many of these revenue sources have more than one category, so that there are more like 40 separate revenue categories. The underlying operational principle here appears to be that, as provinces enter new taxation fields, these become integrated into the formula. For example, lottery revenues now enter the formula. If, as seems likely, many provinces establish casinos, the logic of the formula suggests that we would eventually establish a separate revenue category for "casino royalties or profits."

Calculating Fiscal Capacities

The concept of fiscal capacity is at the core of the equalization formula. The two key ingredients in calculating fiscal capacity are i) the concept of *standardized tax bases* and ii) the calculation of *standardized tax rates*. In terms of the former,

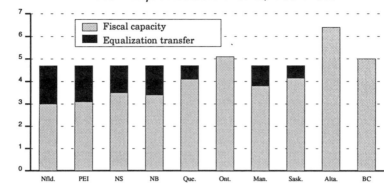

Thematic Tableau 1
How Equalization Works, 1991–92

Legend:
- Fiscal capacity
- Equalization transfer

Vertical axis: ($ thousands per capita), 0 to 7

Horizontal axis: Nfld., PEI, NS, NB, Que., Ont., Man., Sask., Alta., BC

The chart above illustrates how Equalization is calculated, as expressed in per capita terms. Equalization payments are calculated on the basis of a formula set out in federal legislation that compares the overall capacity of each province — together with its local governments — to raise revenues from all of the various taxes and fees levied by these governments. This includes personal income taxes, corporate income taxes, general sales taxes, taxes on gasoline, tobacco, and alcohol, natural resource levies, property taxes and numerous smaller taxes.

The comparison of revenue raising capacity is made each year by estimating the revenues that would be raised in each province if they were all levying the same taxes with commonly defined tax bases and the same tax rates. This involves developing a standardized tax system known as the Representative Tax System. This Representative Tax System classifies provincial-local government revenues into 32 separate sources, each having a base defined for it that is typical of the bases actually taxed by provinces. The size of these bases is then estimated for each province and, using an average provincial rate of tax for each source, the revenues each province would receive are estimated and totalled for all sources.

The Equalization due to a province is then determined by comparing the total revenues per capita that each province would receive from the Representative Tax System to a prescribed per capita revenue standard. Any province whose per capital total is below the prescribed per capita standard receives Equalization. The amount received is equal to its shortfall from the standard multiplied by its population.

The prescribed Equalization standard is the total per capita revenues that would result from applying the Representative Tax System in five provinces: Ontario, British Columbia, Saskatchewan, Quebec, and Manitoba. For [fiscal year 1991/92], the standard is $4,704 per capita. It is, however, lowered to $4,641 per capita as a result of a ceiling provision which limits the rate of growth of total Equalization to the rate of growth of the economy (GNP). Equalization also has floor provisions which protect each receiving province against a sharp annual decline in its Equalization.

Source: Canada 1992b, Figure 5.

each revenue category is assigned a tax base. In many cases, the tax base is obvious. For tobacco revenues, it is the quantities of cigarettes, cigars, and so on that are sold; for gasoline taxes, it is the quantity of gas sold. For some other revenues, like lottery revenues, the tax base is not as obvious, so that some measure of income is typically designated as the tax base. The key point here is that there will be a common or uniform base for each revenue source and it will be calculated in the *same* manner across all provinces — that is, the base will be "standardized." While Alberta has no retail sales tax, it *does* have a retail sales tax *base* and this base is used to calculate fiscal capacities.

The second ingredient in terms of calculating fiscal capacity is the "standardized tax rate." In principle, this standardized tax rate for each revenue source is calculated by dividing the *actual* aggregate revenues of the ten provinces from this revenue source by the (ten-province) aggregate tax base for this source. This standardized tax rate is, in reality, a "national (ten-province) average tax rate."

Calculating the fiscal capacity for each province is now straightforward: it is the product of standardized tax bases and standardized tax rates for all the revenue sources that enter the formula. In Thematic Tableau 1, these (standardized) fiscal capacities, by province, are depicted as the lightly shaded area of the figure, expressed in per capita terms.

Defining the "Standard"

The next step is to define a "standard" against which to compare the provincial fiscal capacities. In the 1957 version of the equalization formula, the standard was the two richest provinces (Alberta and Ontario). In the comprehensive 1967 revision, the "national average" became the standard. For reasons associated with the role of resource revenues (see Courchene 1984), from 1982 onward Canada has adopted a five province standard comprising Ontario, Quebec, Manitoba, Saskatchewan, and British Columbia. As noted in Thematic Tableau 1, the five-province standard is the average per capita fiscal capacity in the five provinces. This value of the five-province standard (henceforth, FPS) for fiscal year 1991/92 is $4,704 per capita.

Equalization Entitlements
and Equalization Payments

Equalization entitlements for each province equal the difference between the fiscal capacity of that province and the five-province fiscal capacity. In principle, one could set entitlements at 50 percent or 75 percent or 90 percent of the difference. But our equalization system provides 100 percent of the difference.

Thus, if a given province has a standardized per capita fiscal capacity of $4,204, its equalization entitlement will be $500 per capita to bring its revenues up to the $4,704 per capita of the FPS.

Equalization *entitlements* are not always the same as equalization *payments* because of the various "bells and whistles" associated with the program (for example, floors, ceilings, and transitional payments). Thus, as Thematic Tableau 1 indicates, there was a ceiling in effect for fiscal year 1991/92, which reduces the equalization standard from $4,704 per capita to $4,641 per capita (more later on the impact of the ceiling provisions). Ontario, British Columbia, and Alberta receive no equalization because their fiscal capacities are above the FPS. As already alluded to, these provinces do not contribute, as provinces, to the financing of equalization. Rather, the financing comes from Ottawa's consolidated revenue fund (see Chapter 2, note 3, for the shares across provinces). Note that while Alberta's (standardized) fiscal capacity is well above $6,000 per capita, its *actual* revenues are not this high because it does not levy a tax on retail sales. But for equalization purposes it is assumed to be levying a sales tax.

Table 15 provides a tabular history of equalization over the past decade. The entries for the provinces relate to fiscal capacities — namely, national average tax rates applied to the provinces' standardized bases. The third-to-last column is the FPS standard, and the last column is the national average standard. Sandwiched between these two is the "average" fiscal capacity for the "have-not" provinces. Per capita equalization entitlements for each year equal the shortfall between the FPS and the "receiving provinces" column. (I trust that, by now, readers will not be surprised that the figures in Table 15 for fiscal year 1991/92, in terms of the FPS standard for example, do not square with the figures that appear in Thematic Tableau 1. Living with constantly changing numbers and forecasts simply goes with the territory, as it were.) Among other things, Table 15 reveals that the differences between the national average and FPS standards is much less now than it was when the FPS was inaugurated in 1982.

To this point, the assumption has been that the equalization program has driven actual equalization payments. This has not been the case throughout most of the 1980s. Rather, actual equalization payments have been driven by a series of "bells and whistles" and, in particular, by the existence of the equalization ceiling. Detailing these is the purpose of the next section.

Bells and Whistles

Columns (3) and (1) of Table 16 present data on equalization entitlements and actual payments, respectively. The difference between the two, whether in terms of floors, ceilings, or transitions, appears in column (2). The purpose of this

Table 15: Per Capita Yield of the Representative Tax System, by Province, fiscal years 1982/83 to 1993/94

	Nfld.	PEI	NS	NB	Quebec	Ontario	Manitoba	Sask.	Alberta	BC	Standard Provinces	Receiving Provinces	All Provinces
	(dollars)												
1982/83	1,559.48	1,512.28	1,801.09	1,731.70	1,997.59	2,490.98	2,108.03	2,763.05	5,490.01	2,801.91	2,368.03	1,941.46	2,601.98
1983/84	1,673.75	1,707.82	2,024.10	1,893.19	2,206.62	2,766.73	2,293.02	3,079.97	5,811.79	3,005.03	2,610.30	2,139.72	2,845.98
1984/85	1,777.06	1,826.43	2,185.75	2,019.23	2,385.72	2,952.94	2,414.01	3,317.33	6,281.13	3,056.46	2,775.57	2,301.92	3,034.50
1985/86	1,885.86	1,964.95	2,344.02	2,178.30	2,610.04	3,271.22	2,627.16	3,367.88	6,305.76	3,248.24	3,028.79	2,507.05	3,256.31
1986/87	2,114.81	2,218.59	2,597.80	2,402.74	2,857.49	3,662.97	2,867.49	3,025.44	4,857.12	3,464.99	3,307.26	2,777.45	3,370.70
1987/88	2,255.56	2,412.11	2,852.00	2,658.73	3,223.74	4,086.05	3,035.10	3,431.33	5,459.57	3,927.29	3,705.34	3,098.48	3,771.43
1987/88[a]	2,279.20	2,417.42	2,864.45	2,684.10	3,221.89	4,081.98	3,025.74	3,405.47	5,489.45	3,917.77	3,699.87	3,097.95	3,771.43
1988/89	2,508.11	2,704.68	3,135.81	3,003.05	3,571.75	4,574.07	3,349.34	3,631.26	5,687.00	4,389.38	4,125.37	3,423.91	4,164.48
1989/90	2,807.54	2,896.85	3,378.16	3,143.11	3,874.02	5,029.30	3,493.22	3,740.20	5,936.92	4,837.76	4,502.51	3,671.33	4,515.07
1990/91	2,979.49	3,100.94	3,538.83	3,396.24	4,065.66	5,169.83	3,757.27	4,064.05	6,470.21	5,093.16	4,695.16	3,883.97	4,742.77
1991/92	2,990.64	3,019.20	3,506.06	3,170.80	3,957.81	4,760.93	3,684.83	3,970.90	5,936.67	4,840.84	4,439.91	3,787.00	4,477.58
1992/93	3,072.90	3,217.59	3,602.09	3,337.76	4,073.59	4,942.74	3,765.43	4,046.47	6,080.39	4,957.97	4,584.56	3,897.40	4,621.38
1993/94	3,144.05	3,315.24	3,688.80	3,432.39	4,214.37	5,095.34	3,880.82	4,177.87	6,297.82	5,096.76	4,730.98	4,024.06	4,770.84

[a] Represents the per capita yield of the representative tax system used to determine actual equalization entitlements.

Source: Canada, Department of Finance, Federal-Provincial Relations Division.

section is to focus on those ancillary aspects of the equalization system that account for these differences.

Transitional Payments

The three initial transitional payments in column (2) for fiscal years 1982/83 through 1984/85 relate to the switch in 1982 from a national average standard to a five-province standard. As already alluded to, the rationale for this shift was that Ottawa could no longer afford to fully equalize energy royalties. Excluding Alberta from the new standard accomplished this. By also excluding the four Atlantic provinces from the new standard (which have roughly the same population as Alberta), this insured that the value of the five-province standard would not fall too much below the previous national average standard. In principle, of course, the value of the FPS could exceed the national average standard. But in the time frame of the alteration, the new standard was lower — roughly $250 per capita lower in 1982/83. To compensate for this, Ottawa provided some "transitional guarantees,"[1] which meant that actual equalization rose above the equalization entitlements for these years.

Now that energy prices have fallen substantially from their early 1980s' levels, the difference between the five-province and national average standard is really quite minimal — about $40 per capita from this initial estimate of fiscal capacity for fiscal year 1993/94. But $40 per capita nonetheless represents a substantial sum — 8 percent of Quebec's equalization payments, for example (see Table 14).

The Equalization Ceiling

While the equalization-receiving provinces, not surprisingly, have argued in favor of a return to the national average standard (as long as the value of the national average standard is in excess of the five-province standard!), their much bigger concern and complaint is the imposition of the ceiling on equalization. The ceiling has been in place for the last three five-year fiscal periods — 1982/83 to 1986/7, 1987/88 to 1991/92 and for the 1992/93 to 1993/94 period.

---

1 The details of these transitional guarantees were as follows. For each province, take the dollar level of equalization in 1981/82 (the last year of the old system) and add to it the average annual dollar increase in equalization over the five-year period 1977/78 to 1981/82. This is the minimum level of equalization for 1982/83. For 1983/84, the minimum equals the 1981/82 level plus five-thirds of the value of the annual change over 1977/78 to 1981/82. For the last year of the transitional guarantee, the minimum was 1981/82 plus twice this annual average charge. Beyond this, equalization payments were driven by the new formula.

Table 16: Equalization in Action, fiscal years 1982/83 to 1993/94

	Actual Formula Entitlements (1)	Portion of Actual Formula Entitlements (+/-) Relating to Transitional, Ceiling, or Floor Provisions (2)	Total Entitlements without Transitional, Ceiling, or Floor Provisions (1 − 2) (3)	Total Revenues Subject to Equalization (4)	Provincial Disparity Factor (3 + 4) (5)	Calendar Year GNP (6)	Revenue Subject to Equalization as Share of GNP (4 + 6) (7)	Total Entitlements as Share of GNP Actual (1 + 6) (8a)	Without Transitional Ceiling, Floor (3 + 6) (8b)
	($ billions)	($ billions)	($ billions)	($ billions)	(%)	($ billions)	($ billions)	(%)	(%)
1982/83	4.87	+0.70 (T)	4.16	63.91	6.51	361.77	17.66	1.34	1.15
1983/84	5.23	+0.60 (T)	4.62	70.62	6.55	394.11	17.92	1.33	1.17
1984/85	5.42	+0.74 (T)	4.69	76.02	6.16	431.25	17.63	1.26	1.09
1985/86	5.14		5.14	81.70	6.29	463.66	17.62	1.11	1.11
1986/87	5.78		5.78	85.21	6.78	489.26	17.42	1.18	1.18
1987/88	6.60	− 0.05 (T)	6.66	96.33	6.91	535.15	18.00	1.23	1.24
1988/89	7.27	− 0.47 (C)	7.74	107.58	7.19	587.19	18.32	1.24	1.32
1989/90	7.81	− 1.42 (C)	9.22	118.12	7.81	629.25	18.77	1.24	1.47
1990/91	8.00	− 1.05 (C)	9.06	126.21	7.17	647.03	19.51	1.24	1.40
1991/92	7.61	+0.03 (F)	7.57	125.88	6.02	654.00	19.25	1.16	1.16
1992/93	8.02		8.02	131.49	6.10	664.34	19.79	1.21	1.21
1993/94	8.31		8.31	137.48	6.04	690.15	19.92	1.20	1.20

Notes:

Figures in the first three columns have been rounded.

Amounts for years from 1990/91 are preliminary. Amounts in columns (1) and (2) exclude supplementary equalization paid under separate legislation, totaling $220 million for 1985/86 and $65 million for 1986/87. The transitional amount for 1987/88 relates to a phase-in of tax base changes over two years — 1987/88 and 1988/89.

Figures for column (2) are denoted as transitional (T), ceiling (C), or floor (F).

Source: Canada, Department of Finance.

(Equalization was only renewed for two years in 1992/93). Since the ceiling is "rebased" in the first year of each of these five-year periods — that is, it is set equal to formula entitlements for that fiscal year — it cannot be binding in these three initial years, although actual payments can differ from entitlements because of other factors (as was the case in 1987/88, when there was a small negative transitional payment). For the remaining fiscal years in these five-year periods, equalization in aggregate cannot exceed the cumulative rate of growth of nominal gross national product (GNP) from the base year. Thus, the ceiling constrains equalization for 1993/94 so that total entitlements for all provinces may not grow more rapidly from the 1992/93 base year than the rate of growth of GNP from the 1992 calendar year to the 1993 calendar year. Similarly, if the current two-year arrangements are extended through to 1996/97, the 1994/95 payments cannot grow from the 1992/93 base year by more than 1994 GNP exceeds 1992 GNP.

If the ceiling applies in 1993/94, or in any other year, the entitlements of each eligible province will be reduced by an equal per capita amount to the point where the overall growth rate of total entitlements between the 1992/93 fiscal year and 1993/94 will not exceed the growth rate of GNP between 1993 and 1992. Because the program standard (five-province standard) for any given year is equal per capita for all provinces, the reduction of equalization entitlements when the ceiling applies *is equivalent to a lowering of the "effective" standard, so that the effective standard falls below the five-province standard*. This is not the only way in which one could apply a ceiling.[2]

As column (2) of Table 16 indicates, the ceiling became binding for three years in the 1987/88 to 1991/92 fiscal arrangements period — indeed, to the tune of $1.4 billion in fiscal year 1989/90. The figures in column (8) of Table 16 help explain the operations of the ceiling. The base-year (1987/88) ratio of entitlements to GNP was 1.24 percent (row 8(b)), because the row 8(a) figure reflects the transitional reduction itemized in column (2) as detailed in the notes

---

2   To see this, some elaboration is warranted. For illustrative purposes only, suppose that Quebec's per capita equalization entitlement was $100 and that for Newfoundland was $2,000. Suppose further than the ceiling is binding and that equalization payments have to be rolled back by 10 percent. The equalization program does this by lowering the standard by 10 percent. If this amounts to, say, $50 per capita, then Quebec's equalization will be $50 and Newfoundland's will be $1,950 per capita — that is, a 50 percent rollback for Quebec and a 2½ percent rollback for Newfoundland. An alternative approach would be to roll back all entitlements by 10 percent. Under this scenario, Newfoundland would receive $1,800 per capita and Quebec $90 per capita. Both these approaches would bring equalization down to the ceiling level, *but the distribution of rollbacks is markedly different*. One could even imagine a province with an initial entitlement of $45 per capita that would be brought down to zero if the overall standard were to be reduced by $50 per capita. I remain surprised that there is not more public debate in terms of how Ottawa has decided to implement the equalization ceiling.

to the table). This 1.24 ratio applies in column 8(a) for the next three fiscal years, whereas an unconstrained (column 8(b)) formula would have generated entitlements of 1.47 percent of GNP for fiscal year 1989/90. In other words, equalization is limited to the growth of GNP, which is what a constant 1.24 ratio implies. With the recession and the collapse of the Ontario economy in 1991/92, the ceiling ceased to be binding — as column (3) indicates, the "unconstrained" entitlements fell from $9.2 billion in 1989/90 to $7.6 billion in 1991/92.

The impact of the ceiling was very significant, especially the $1.4 billion reduction in 1989/90, which converts into $125 per capita for the seven recipient provinces. I shall have more to say about the ceiling later in this chapter and, not surprisingly, it will feature prominently in Chapter 7, on deficit shifting.

Equalization Floors

Perhaps as an offset to the ceiling, the equalization program also contains "floor" provisions. Each recipient province is guaranteed against a year-over-year reduction of its total equalization entitlement of more than 5, 10, or 15 percent, with the applicable percentage for each province depending on its fiscal capacity. At the present time, the following floor levels to *actual* equalization payments apply:

- Newfoundland and Prince Edward Island are protected against more than a 5 percent decline in actual equalization from one year to the next (because their per capita fiscal capacities are below 70 percent of the national average).
- New Brunswick is protected against more than 10 percent decline (because its per capita fiscal capacity is between 70 and 75 percent of the national average).
- Quebec, Manitoba, Saskatchewan, and Nova Scotia are protected against more than a 15 percent decline (because their fiscal capacities are above 75 percent of the national average).

As column (2) of Table 16 indicates, these floor provisions increased equalization in 1991/92 by $31.9 million. All of this went to Newfoundland and reflects the above-noted, recession-induced decrease in *actual* equalization payments over this period — compare the Newfoundland column in Table 15 with the "standard provinces" column for fiscal years 1990/91 and 1991/92.

At this juncture, a slight detour is warranted. In Thematic Tableau 1, the equalization system for 1991/92 incorporated a ceiling. Yet in Table 16, the floor provisions, rather than a ceiling, apply for this year. Both sets of data come from the Department of Finance. The difference is that the Table 16 figures are more recent. The initial estimates for equalization are frequently well off the mark. This should hardly come as a surprise given the fall 1993 announcement by Finance Minister Paul Martin of the massive forecasting errors in the deficits for fiscal years 1992/93 and 1993/94.[3] Hence, the reader should put little faith in the Table 16 figures for these fiscal years. Indeed, the revenue side of the system has collapsed to such a degree that yet another equalization-related feature has come into play for the 1993/94 fiscal year — namely, "stabilization payments."

Fiscal Stabilization Programs

Operating alongside the equalization program is the "fiscal stabilization program." Essentially, this program puts a floor of sorts not under equalization, but under total provincial revenue. If a province suffers an overall decline in total revenues from one year to the next, *at unchanged tax rates*, then it is eligible for compensation. The current arrangements provide for compensation up to $60 per capita, with ministerial discretion to extend an interest-free loan to cover any shortfall beyond the $60 per capita.

My recollection is that the rationale for this fiscal stabilization program had more to do with helping the provinces out with the bond-rating agencies. At its inception at least, it was deemed unlikely that it would ever come into play. British Columbia was the first province to draw on the program when its revenues collapsed in the early 1980s. Alberta followed suit in the mid-1980s when the bottom fell out of energy prices. And already in the 1990s, Ontario has qualified at least twice for stabilization payments.

The more recent surprise is that several of the equalization-recipient provinces have now filed for stabilization payments. Indeed, part of what has led to the finance minister's upward revision of the estimates of Ottawa's deficit represents a decision to pay these stabilization payments immediately. Normally, these claims are subject to considerable delay, even negotiation, because it is not easy to rework the figures from one year to the next under the assumption that tax rates remain unchanged.

What all of this means is that, in terms of the data in Table 16, there will likely be only two years (1985/86 and 1986/87) when the equalization formula *itself* determined the level of equalization payments. The rest of the time, the system was driven by the various bells and whistles. This is troubling in the sense that it raises issues about the value of having a formula when the payments are determined by a series of nonformula constraints.

---

3 Much of the forecasting error was associated with the shortfall of revenues from the personal income tax. Since the provinces' share of the personal income tax is roughly 40 percent, it is evident that this will have an impact on provincial revenues and, therefore, on equalization.

Equalization in Action

Analytical Reflections

Because the equalization formula is amenable to mathematical manipulation much of the intricate evaluation and assessment in the literature has been quite technical in nature. For those who are inclined, the note below contains the full mathematical description of the FPS formula.[4] Readers wishing the full analytic evaluation of the FPS formula can consult Boadway and Hobson (1993) or a more comprehensive but less recent analysis by Courchene and Wildasin (in Courchene 1984, Appendix).

Thematic Tableau 2 attempts a nontechnical approach to selected key features of the FPS formula, under the assumption that the bells and whistles are not in force. While Thematic Tableau 2 does not delve deeply into some of the more arcane features of the formula, it does try to shed some light on the philosophy underpinning the current formula. A few comments on the tableau are in order.

To get at the fundamentals underlying equalization, it is convenient to focus on a particular province, say, Nova Scotia, and to make an important

---

4 The FPS equalization formula can be expressed as follows:

$$\frac{E_{ij}}{P_i} = t_{cj}\left(\frac{B_{Rj}}{P_R} - \frac{B_{ij}}{P_i}\right), \tag{N.1}$$

where

$\quad E_{ij} =$ equalization to province i from revenue source j.

$\quad P_i =$ population of province i,

$\quad E_{ij}/P_i =$ per capita equalization to province i from revenue source j.

$\quad t_{cj} =$ the national average (all-province) tax rate, defined as total revenues from revenue source j (that is, TR_j) divided by the total base for source (that is, B_{cj}), where subscript c refers to Canada or, more correctly, the all-province total;

$\quad B_{Rj}/P_R =$ the per capita base for source j in the FPS provinces; and

$\quad B_{ij}/P_i =$ province i's per capita base for revenue source j.

It is equation (N.1) that is cast in terms of words in the context of Thematic Tableau 2.

In the literature, equation (N.1) has been referred to as the "base-per-capita" formulation of FPS equalization. With appropriate manipulation, FPS equalization can also be cast in terms of a "population-share" formulation:

$$E_{ij} = \frac{B_{Rj}}{B_{cj}} TR_j\left(\frac{P_i}{P_R} - \frac{B_{ij}}{B_{Rj}}\right), \tag{N.2}$$

where B_{Rj}/B_{cj} is the share of the total base located in the provinces that comprise the FPS, TR_j is the total revenues to be equalized and P_i/P_R is the province's proportion of the FPS population.

Thematic Tableau 2

Equalization:
Workings of the Five-Province Standard

Formula:

$$
\begin{array}{ccc}
\text{Equalization} & \text{national} & \left(\text{the five provinces'} \quad \text{province's own}\right) \\
\text{per} & = \text{average} & \left(\quad \text{per capita} \quad - \quad \text{per capita} \quad\right) \\
\text{capita} & \text{tax rates} & \left(\qquad \text{base} \qquad\qquad \text{base} \qquad\right)
\end{array}
$$

where these bases are all standardized and this expression is summed over all tax bases. If the overall sum is positive, this equals the province's equalization. If negative, equalization is set equal to zero. This assumes that there are no ceilings in place. The five-province standard excludes Alberta and the Atlantic provinces.

Changes in Tax Bases

If an Atlantic province (that is, a province *not* in the five-province standard) registers an increase, all other things unchanged, in one of its tax bases (say, retail sales go up by 10 percent in Nova Scotia), then it will see its equalization reduced by the full amount because the first term in the bracket will be unchanged and the second will incorporate the province's base increase. In other words, *there is 100 percent offset* and this also applies for a fall in a province's base. Actually, there is a second order effect: the 100 percent offset holds only if the province's tax rate on the base equals the national average tax rate. If its tax rate is lower, the offset will be more than 100 percent and vice versa. But this will be a negligible amount.

For a poor province that is part of the standard, the offset will be less than 100 percent, since an increase in the province's base will also increase the five-provinces' base. For example, given that, on average, Saskatchewan has a 6 percent weight in the five-standard base, a $100 increase in an average Saskatchewan base would cost the province $94 in equalization.

Ontario gets no equalization, but its weight in the five-standard base is over 50 percent. Thus, a $100 per capita increase in an Ontario base, other things unchanged, will increase equalization for each of the "have" provinces by at least $50 per capita. (Again, there could be minor second-round impacts because of changes in the national average tax rate.) Small wonder that some have claimed that the "have-not" provinces should be as concerned about Ontario's fortunes and budgets as their own!

Thematic Tableau 2 – cont'd.

Changes in Rates

Equalization-receiving provinces benefit from any increase in a tax rate relating to a base for which they are poor — that is, if the bracketed terms above are negative for a province, then an increase in tax rates by any province will increase this province's revenue. And vice versa if the tax increase relates to a base where the bracketed terms for the province are negative. Thus, if Prince Edward Island is a poor province for sales taxes, an increase in the sales tax rate in Prince Edward Island will increase its own revenues and also increase its equalization to the extent that its tax rate increases the national average tax rate.

Population Shifts

Population shifts are more complex to analyze. The most straightforward example is a loss of population for a "have-not" province that leaves all the values in the above equation unchanged — that is, the outmigration does not affect the province's per capita base and it does not affect the five-province average base either (because they migrate from, say, Nova Scotia to New Brunswick, both of which are out of the standard). In this case, per capita equalization will not change, but the dollar value will fall because there are fewer "per capitas." Beyond this, matters get very complicated (see Courchene 1984, Appendix; or Boadway and Hobson 1993).

Base Transfers

If a headquarters of a major company moves from Toronto (in the standard) to Alberta (not in the standard), the first term in the bracket would fall for the relevant tax base so that equalization for all provinces would fall, and vice versa for a shift from Calgary to Toronto.

If Nova Scotia loses a headquarters to New Brunswick, Nova Scotia's per capita equalization would rise because its own per capita base (the second term in the bracket) would fall. Its equalization would rise more, however, if the headquarters shifted to Quebec, since now the first term in the bracket would rise.

Under a national average standard, as distinct from the five-province standard, transfers of bases across provinces (for example, headquarters shifts) would still affect equalization, but where they shifted from or to would be neutral in terms of the formula.

simplifying assumption — namely, that Nova Scotia's tax rates are equal to the national average tax rates. Then, the total per capita revenues of Nova Scotia will, for any tax base, equal the sum of its own revenues and the revenue it gets from equalization. Given the assumption of tax rates identical to national average rates, Nova Scotia's *own revenues* will equal:

$$
\begin{matrix} \text{Nova Scotia's} \\ \text{own revenue} \\ \text{per capita} \end{matrix} = \begin{pmatrix} \text{national average} \\ \text{tax rates} \end{pmatrix} \times \begin{pmatrix} \text{Nova Scotia's} \\ \text{per capita} \\ \text{tax base} \end{pmatrix}. \tag{1}
$$

Thus, Nova Scotia's *total* per capita revenues will be the *sum* of its own revenues (equation (1)) plus its equalization revenues, as reflected in the formula in Tableau 1. Simple arithmetic manipulation leads to the following expression for Nova Scotia's total per capital revenues:

$$
\begin{matrix} \text{Nova Scotia's} \\ \text{total per capita} \\ \text{revenues} \end{matrix} = \begin{pmatrix} \text{national average} \\ \text{tax rates} \end{pmatrix} \times \begin{pmatrix} \text{the five–provinces'} \\ \text{per capita} \\ \text{tax base} \end{pmatrix}. \tag{2}
$$

Hence, the FPS system effectively guarantees that the per capita revenues of any "have-not" province will be brought up to a level equal to that which it would obtain if it were to apply national average tax rates to the average per capita tax base of the FPS.

The remainder of Thematic Tableau 2 focuses on some of the intricacies of the FPS approach to equalization. By far the most significant is the fact that equalization is a *fully confiscatory* "tax" on any changes in the tax bases of any of the "have-not" provinces that are not part of the five-province standard, and a near-confiscatory tax for any small provinces that are part of the FPS. Thus, there will be *zero* return, in terms of increasing provincial revenues, from any or all of Nova Scotia's policies designed to increase its various tax bases. Likewise, there is *zero* provincial revenue cost for Nova Scotia to engage in policies that may decrease its own-revenue base since the equalization program will fully compensate for this errant policy. (As an aside, a switch to a national average standard, instead of an FPS, would alter this result only in trivial ways.) To be sure, there are other "returns" to provincial governments to doing the right things, as it were. But the fundamental issue becomes: does it make economic sense, either to Nova Scotia or to Canada, to have in place an equalization program with such perverse incentives? This is particularly the case since one and all condemn the confiscatory tax rates in the transition from welfare or unemployment insurance to work. Why are confiscatory tax rates appropriate for provinces? Is this not part and parcel of the transfer-dependency syndrome?

Needless to say, these issues will loom large in terms of my preferred design for equalization to be elaborated in Chapter 11.

The only other comment on Thematic Tableau 2 relates primarily to the final paragraph under "changes in Tax Bases." Ontario's weight in the FPS exceeds 50 percent. Thus, Parti Québécois leader Jacques Parizeau's comments surely ring true — what happens to the revenues of most "have-not" provinces depends much more on what Ontario's budget (and to a lesser but nonetheless important extent on the Quebec budget, since it too has a large weight in the FPS) contains than what their own budgets contain. Does this make any economic or socio-economic sense? Did Nova Scotia's need for equalization in order to provide "reasonably comparable public services" rise dramatically during the Ontario 1983–89 boom and then suddenly collapse as the 1990s' recession ravaged Ontario? Surely not. Yet these are the characteristics inherent in the equalization formula. It is, admittedly, personally gratifying that many analysts in this area frequently quote my observation that equalization is an essential part of the glue that binds us together as a nation. While I still subscribe to this, my view has always been that we can overdo, and indeed have overdone, aspects of equalization. In response to these quotes, I would only add that I, too, have a favorite quote from my late University of Saskatchewan professor, Robert Kautz: Does mortar (or glue) hold bricks together or apart?

The task of analyzing the remainder of Thematic Tableau 2 is left to the reader. The rest of this section is devoted to focusing on equalization developments over the last decade from a related, but nonetheless different, perspective.

Practical Reflections

We now return to Table 16 in order to provide a perspective of what occurred on the equalization front in the 1980s. Notationally, we can also cast the operations of the equalization formula in terms of the following equation — namely, that equalization entitlements (column (3)) are the product of columns (4) and (5):

$$EE = TR \bullet \frac{EE}{TR} , \qquad (3)$$

where

$EE =$ equalization entitlements (column (3)),

$TR =$ total revenues to be equalized (column (4)), and

$EE/TR =$ equalization per dollar of revenue that enters the formula (column (5)).

From column (4), revenues subject to equalization (which include almost all provincial revenues) have doubled from fiscal year 1982/83 to 1993/94 and, except for 1991/92, have increased every year. Column (5) is designated as the "provincial disparity factor" in Table 16. This indicates the number of cents of equalization generated by each dollar of revenue (on average, across all bases) that enters the formula. Intuitively, an increase in the figures in column (5) is equivalent to an increase in provincial disparity. Were fiscal capacities identical across the provinces, there would be no equalization. Similarly, the greater the "average disparity" across provinces, the larger will equalization be for each revenue dollar that enters the formula. The peak value for the provincial disparity factor is 7.81 in 1989/90 — that is, each dollar of total provincial revenues in this year generated 7.81 cents in equalization. More recently, this ratio has fallen rather dramatically — each dollar of revenues to be equalized generated only 6.04 cents in equalization in 1993/94. This is only 77 percent of the value in 1989/90. As already noted, with Ontario having more than a 50 percent weight in the five-province standard, this provincial disparities factor closely tracks the boom and bust of the Ontario economy.

Note, however, that equalization payments, from either columns (1) or (3), bottom out in 1991/92 and then increase significantly to 1993/94, despite the fact that the provincial disparity factor for 1993/94 (6.04) is almost identical to that for 1991/92 (6.02). The resolution to this puzzle is that, despite the recession, revenues to be equalized have not fallen. This is true in terms of the absolute value of revenues to be equalized — except for a dip in column (4) for 1991/92, revenues to be equalized have risen monotonically. It is also true in relative terms — revenues to be equalized have increased in relation to GNP (column (7)). Indeed, in 1993/94, revenues to be equalized are close to 20 percent of GNP — and probably higher still since these data did not anticipate the significant tax hikes (retroactive to January 1, 1993) introduced by the Ontario and Quebec budgets.

This leads to a quite different reason the equalization ceiling became binding. The fact is that it was largely triggered by the Ontario boom in the latter half of the 1980s, not by a plunge in the economic fortunes of the equalization-recipient provinces. When the bubble finally burst with the 1990s' recession, equalization entitlements did fall but then rebounded quickly in spite of the *decrease* in provincial disparities (column (5)). The reason for this related to the fact that *tax rates* were increased sufficiently (largely, but not entirely, in Ontario) to increase "revenues to be equalized" more than enough to offset the fall in the column (5) disparity factor. This casts a somewhat different light on the operations of the equalization ceiling than what has emerged from the spokespersons of the "have-not" provinces (see Chapter 7).

Beyond this, however, the operations of the equalization program and the manner in which it is intricately intertwined with other aspects of fiscal federalism came sharply to the fore during this period and, particularly, during the past few years. The issue that captures this interrelationship most dramatically relates to the interplay of equalization with the cap on CAP. To this I now turn.

Interaction between Equalization and CAP

While the discussion of the Canada Assistance Plan is the subject of a later section in this chapter, it is nonetheless instructive at this point to recognize the potential for interaction between equalization and the cap on CAP. As will be noted, the cost of this cap to Ontario in the current time frame is about $1.7 billion annually. Assuming that Ontario's recent tax hikes reflect this shortfall, the $1.7 billion dollar increase in Ontario's revenues would enter "revenues to be equalized" in the equalization formula for 1994, and would generate roughly $150 million in equalization.[5] To say the least, this is a peculiar way to run a federation — punish the "have" provinces via CAP regulations, which, in turn, forces them to raise taxes, which then adds to the coffers of the "have-not" provinces (via equalization), and the ultimate bill for which largely comes out of the taxpayers of the "have" provinces (two-thirds of Ottawa's revenues to pay for equalization come from the three "have" provinces — see note 3 to Chapter 2). This is part and parcel of the ongoing concern that recent federal initiatives have undermined the very integrity of the federal-provincial transfer system.

Equalization and Social Policy Reform

There are several issues that the equalization-recipient provinces will want to place on the reform agenda. One of these relates to the equalization ceiling and, specifically, to the removal of the ceiling. Presumably, this would also mean the elimination of the floors, in which case the issue would not be so straightforward given that the floors are now in play. A second, and perennial, issue has to do with abandoning the FPS and returning to the national average standard. This issue, too, may have fallen in terms of priority now that the values of the FPS and national average standard have converged substantially over the past decade. However, there are some intrinsic values that, other things equal, would

---

5 Row 5 of Table 15 indicates that, on average, each dollar of new revenues to be equalized for 1993/94 generates 6.04 cents of increased equalization payments. For personal income taxes, however, the "provincial disparity factor" is of the order of 9 cents of equalization for each dollar of revenue.

favor the national average standard. For example, the headquarters-shifting peculiarities aired in Thematic Tableau 2 would not exist under a national average standard.

My general comment on these issues are that they are worthy of consideration, but only in the context of a more thorough reassessment of equalization as discussed later in this section. A more significant issue, and one raised by many of the "have-not" provinces, is to introduce "fiscal need" into the formula.

Fiscal Need

Canada's approach to ensuring that all provinces can supply reasonably comparable public services at reasonably comparable tax rates is to focus solely on *equalizing revenues*. Implicitly, if not explicitly, this assumes that the costs of delivering services are identical in per capita terms across provinces. Analytically, a more comprehensive approach would be to incorporate "fiscal need" into equalization. In turn, this would involve giving considerations to both "costs" and "needs" in determining equalization levels. For example, even if needs in all provinces were identical, it may nonetheless cost more in some provinces to deliver a given bundle of goods. Average wages, including civil service wages are higher in Toronto than in Vancouver. Rents are much higher in Toronto and Vancouver than in Saskatoon or Winnipeg. As the following chapter will show, health expenditures and medical fee schedules tend to be higher in the "have" provinces than in the "have-not" provinces. In other words, these largely market-driven factors become capitalized in wages, rents, property values, and the like. Equalization ignores all of this.

On the other hand, it is no doubt the case that "needs" can also vary by province — for example, provinces with high unemployment rates may have greater needs in terms of social assistance expenditures. While no one would disagree with this in principle, putting it into practice can be difficult, particularly since equalization payments are unconditional: one might determine that province X had a greater need in area Y, but there is no guarantee that any additional equalization would be spent in this area. Nonetheless, as already noted, many of the "have-not" provinces are pressing for a move in this direction of expenditure equalization or need equalization, particularly in terms of social assistance spending. This could be accomplished within the equalization program itself or within the operations of CAP; for example, allow 60 percent federal sharing under CAP for provinces that have unemployment rates or case loads above certain threshold levels. I have two general problems with such a proposal. The first is that one cannot alter a single program independently of what is happening elsewhere in the system. This will be elaborated in the context of the focus on the Canada Assistance Plan later in this chapter. The second concern arises from the analysis in Chapter 2: why would one follow this route when much of the higher unemployment in certain regions *already reflects* a policy-induced equilibrium?

This leads to the final and by far the most controversial issue: what is the appropriate level for equalization? There is no scientific answer to this, but there are conflicting philosophical positions that need to be aired.

Dynamic Efficiency versus Redistribution

An influential group of international fiscal federalism scholars, led by Queen's University's Robin Boadway, argues that we "underequalize" and this would still be the case if we adopted the national-average standard and removed the equalization ceiling. The arguments are cast in terms of equalizing "net fiscal benefits" (NFBs). Full equalization of NFBs would not result from equalizing to the national average level because this would still leave the "have" provinces with larger per-capital revenues. One solution to this would be to opt for a "net scheme." And one version of this net scheme (elaborated in more detail in Chapter 10) is to equalize to the national average level and to reduce the cash transfers (from other programs) to the three "have" provinces until their per capita revenues are also brought down to the national average level.

This view runs counter to the entire thrust of the present monograph. In effect, it argues, implicitly if not explicitly, that the entire rationale for fiscal federalism is redistributive. Relatedly, it embodies a concept of horizontal equity (equal treatment of equals) that, in my view, is inconsistent with the underpinnings of a federal state. (Principles other than horizontal equity can be drawn upon to support the principle of equalization.)[6] Effectively, a federal system is viewed as dysfunctional on the redistribution front and the only way to counter this is to convert it, via fiscal federalism, into a virtual unitary state.

My view is the opposite — namely, that we equalize too much in Canada, not too little. I shall attempt two general defenses of this proposition. The first relates directly to the NFB issue. The assumption that equalizing NFBs implies

---

6 In my work on equalization (Courchene 1984, chap. 3), I outlined two rationales for equalization. The first of these I referred to as a "federal rationale," which views equalization as the
cornerstone of a meaningful federal system. If the constitution assigns certain powers to the
provinces, they must have the financial capacity to fulfill these responsibilities. The second is
a "citizenship or nationhood rationale." This has to do with the notion that Canadians, wherever
they live, ought to have access to certain basic economic and social rights — rights that ought
to attend citizenship, as it were. Equalization is the vehicle that can ensure that these rights
are available to all, in the event that they fall under provincial responsibility. Both these
rationales are related to equity, but neither embodies the individualistic approach of the
horizontal equity calculus.

full equalization of revenues only holds if one ignores the capitalization issue raised earlier. For example, the United States has no formal revenue equalization program. There are no doubt many reasons for this, but one of them is that any regional disparities across the states are fully capitalized in wages, rents, property values, and the like, so that, in the final analysis, there is *nothing* to *equalize*. This has led one of the leading federal scholars in the United States (Oates 1972) to proclaim that equalization programs in federal states are a matter of "taste" rather than "principle."

The second defense of the overequalization scenario is that equalization (and fiscal federalism generally) has to encompass more than just a redistribution goal. In particular, it must balance redistribution against "dynamic efficiency" or adjustment concerns. The MacDougall Report (1977), which was the blueprint for European evolution, recommended that per capita revenues of member states be equalized to 65 percent of the all-member-state average. And a recent update (Commission of the European Communities 1993) does not even contemplate Canadian-style equalization. I recognize that this is comparing apples and oranges, since the European Union is confederal, not federal, in design and issues of social cohesion do not loom as large as they do in federal Canada. Nonetheless, it is noteworthy that much of the reason these European blueprints shy away from equalization as Canadians practice it is the fear of what the Europeans call "wage demonstration" effects. These effects are similar to what I have referred to as transfer dependency effects.

Balancing dynamic efficiency concerns with redistributive goals would surely mean altering equalization in ways to ensure that the system does not fully tax away all revenues arising from an increase in the tax bases of a "have-not" province. For example, provided there are appropriate offsets in the overall reform package, one approach could be (a) remove the ceiling; (b) move to a national average standard but (c) only equalize to a portion of the standard, for example, 90 percent. Other, more radical, approaches will be broached later in the monograph.

Despite these concerns, the equalization program has been very successful in redressing fiscal capacity differences across the provinces. Just how successful is best addressed after attention has been directed to the two major federal-provincial transfers — EPF and CAP — especially since they also embody some equalizing features.

Established Programs Financing

EPF was introduced in 1977 as a block fund to replace the cost-sharing system for hospital insurance, for medicare and for postsecondary education (PSE). At one level, it is at the same time the largest and simplest of the federal-provincial transfers — nearly $21 billion (from Table 14) distributed on an equal per capita basis. At another level, it is the most complicated of the transfers, involving as it does tax point transfers, associated equalization, tax abatements and cash transfers. Understanding the analytical underpinnings of EPF requires some history of the program, which is provided in the first section. Attention is then directed to the rather complicated composition of EPF payments, and, finally, to the range of issues that are playing center-stage in the social policy review. Readers wishing to avoid some of the detail can proceed directly to the section entitled "The Anatomy of EPF."

A Brief History of EPF

Thematic Tableau 3 presents a chronology of EPF. The role of this section is to elaborate on selected entries of the tableau.

The first point to make is that, while Ottawa paid 50 percent of the total costs of hospital, medical, and PSE (operational) expenditures in the pre-EPF era, this percentage varied considerably across the provinces. For medicare, the provincial shares varied from 41 to 75 percent; for hospital insurance, from 47 to 60 percent; and for PSE, from 43 to 76 percent (Canada 1992b, 19). In terms of provincial breakdown, data for fiscal year 1975/76 reveal the following percentage of federal contributions in terms of overall operating expenditure for hospital insurance, medicare, and PSE: Newfoundland (58 percent); Prince Edward Island (64 percent); Nova Scotia (52 percent); New Brunswick (60 percent); Quebec (50 percent); Ontario (49 percent); Manitoba (51 percent); Saskatchewan (53 percent); Alberta (50 percent) and British Columbia (48 percent) (Courchene 1979). Thus, there was already considerable *implicit equalization* in the pre-1977 shared-cost programs and, as we shall see, EPF introduced even more.

Indeed, among the objectives of the 1977 arrangements was to bring about equality among the provinces with regard to the amount of federal funds they received under the programs. Of equal importance was to break the shared-cost link — that is, to make the provision of funding independent of the growth of health and PSE. This was an important federal goal since the federal officials were not comfortable with the situation where Ottawa's spending was driven by decisions in the ten provincial capitals. For their part, the provinces would henceforth not be spending 50 cent dollars in some areas and "full" or 100 cent dollars in others.

In terms of the financial basis for EPF, the base year was Ottawa's per capita contribution to these programs in fiscal year 1975/76, escalated to 1977/78 (the first year of EPF) by the three-year growth in per capita GNP over the interim. Half of this was to be paid in cash and the other half in tax transfers. Since the provinces were already in receipt of 4.357 personal income tax (PIT)

Thematic Tableau 3

A Chronology of EPF Events

1958   *Hospital Insurance and Diagnostic Services Act* becomes effective. Provinces to get 25 percent of their per capita costs, and 25 percent of the national per capita costs, times their population.

1964   *Established Programs (Interim Arrangements) Act*: allows "opting out" with compensation. Only Quebec chooses to exercise this option.

1967   Postsecondary Education (PSE) Cost-sharing Agreement: Quebec receives 8.5 personal income tax (PIT) points abatement. Cost-sharing was 50 percent of operating cost or a specific per capita amount of a province preferred.

1968   *Medical Care Act*, 1966–67 becomes effective. By 1972, all provinces and territories had signed on. Ottawa pays 50 percent of national-average costs for medicare distributed to provinces on an equal per capita basis.

1972   Federal government caps its PSE contribution at 15 percent.

1975   Federal Anti-inflation program. Federal restraints put on medical payments.

1976   Federal Anti-inflation program. More federal restraint on medical payments.

1977   Established Programs Agreement (EPF). Effectively put hospital, medicare, and PSE under one funding formula. Provinces receive 13.5 percent PIT and 1 percent corporate tax points, plus cash payments, to a roughly equalized per capita amount, indexed to three-year average nominal GNP and provincial population growth.

1982   EPF renewed. Original revenue guarantee removed, and funding formula slightly amended so that the national per capita combined transfers are equal everywhere. Within provincial totals, health gets 67.9 percent, PSE 32.1 percent.

1983   Federal government adopts "Six and Five" restraint program. PSE component limited to 6 percent growth.

1984   PSE component limited to 5 percent growth.

1984   Ottawa enacts the *Canada Health Act*, which penalizes provinces allowing user fees or extra billing by reducing the EPF cash payment dollar for dollar.

1986   Ottawa introduces Bill C-96, reducing the GNP escalator by 2 percent.

1989   Ottawa reduces the GNP escalator by another 1 percent, effective fiscal year 1990/91.

1990   Ottawa announces a two-year freeze on per capita EPF transfers.

1991   Ottawa extends the per capita freeze another three years, to the end of fiscal year 1994/95, when it will revert to the GNP minus 3% formula.

Source: Adapted from Jenness and McCracken 1993b, A-5.

points and one corporate income tax (CIT) point, the overall tax transfer came out to 12½ PIT points and one CIT point. Further negotiation relating to the termination of the former "revenue guarantee"[7] led to an increase in transfers equivalent to two further PIT points. One of these points was to be in the form of a tax point transfer and the other in terms of a cash transfer.

The overall transfer was split equally between cash and tax points, with the tax transfer component being 13.5 PIT points and one CIT point. The value of the tax point transfer was set so that the average yield in the base year, 1975/76, for British Columbia and Ontario (the two highest-yield provinces in terms of the personal income tax) represented one-half of the overall transfer. Even though these tax points were equalized, equalization brought the revenue up only to the national average level, not the level of British Columbia and Ontario. To ensure equal payments per capita, Ottawa agreed that there would be "transitional adjustment payments," so that no province's total transfer would be less than double its cash transfer. This is "super equalization," which I shall return to later. In the meantime, it is appropriate to note that, in addition to the "implicit equalization" embedded in the pre-1977 arrangements (documented above), the new arrangements generated the following additional per capita benefits (additional in the sense that they were beyond the level of Ontario's incremental benefits); Newfoundland ($23); Prince Edward Island ($52); Nova Scotia ($12); New Brunswick ($20); Quebec ($1); Manitoba ($13); Saskatchewan ($29); and British Columbia ($26) (Courchene 1979, Table 5). Given that the average per capita transfers under the pre-1977 arrangements were about $250, this additional "implicit equalization" is quite large — 20 percent for Prince Edward Island, for example. Thus, although the EPF block funding arrangements were cast (largely) in terms of equal per capita payments, this involved very substantial increases in funding for the "have-not" provinces.

It is important to note that the two components (cash transfers and tax point transfers) were to be *independent* of each other. In particular, the cash component was to be escalated by the three-year average growth in per capita GNP. Phrased differently, there was, at this point, *no ceiling* on overall EPF transfers.

---

7 The revenue guarantee dates back to 1972. Ottawa was intent on introducing significant tax reforms, especially in respect of the personal income tax system. To ensure that the provinces went along with these reforms, Ottawa promised that their equalized income tax receipts under the reformed tax regime would be no less than they would have received under the old regime. Originally designed for two years, this revenue guarantee was extended through to fiscal year 1976/77. The value of the guarantee increased over the years and, as noted in the text, the compensation for its termination as part of the 1977 Fiscal Arrangements took the form of the equivalent of two PIT points. Ottawa, but not the provinces, always viewed the revenue guarantee as temporary and, as the text later notes, Ottawa took back these two PIT points in the 1982 arrangements. For more detail, see Courchene (1979, chap. 9).

We now come to the 1982 arrangements, which are critical to understanding the recent evolution of EPF. Two key changes took place that year. The first was the removal of the dollar value of the two tax points associated with the revenue guarantee. This is really the first of several "hits" on EPF. And it was one of the most expensive for the provinces, since it effectively reduced EPF by 7 percent on an ongoing basis. As important was that the reduction of the dollar value of the two tax points *took the form of a decrease in the cash transfer*. This speaks to a later issue: whether the tax points ought to be considered a federal transfer or provincial own-source revenues. What the 1982 arrangements suggest is that these two points are indeed provincial revenues and cannot be taken back by Ottawa, since the reduction in EPF payments took place entirely in terms of a reduction of EPF cash transfers.

The second change was probably more important, since it led to the imposition of a ceiling on EPF. Specifically, the value of the tax point transfer for Alberta was rising substantially (triggered by energy prices), so rapidly in fact that it was outstripping the value of the cash transfer. This meant that Alberta's overall EPF revenues were now in excess of double the cash transfer. Ottawa decided to strip away this "fiscal dividend," by taking the original 1975/76 benchmark (see earlier), escalating it forward to 1982/83 by the three-year average per capita GNP growth rate, and then *treating this funding level as the EPF ceiling*. Because the value of the tax points for Alberta pushed that province's total EPF payments above the ceiling, Ottawa reduced Alberta's cash payments by a corresponding amount. Henceforth, therefore, *the cash transfers became a residual*. For a given level of the ceiling, an increase in the value of the tax point transfer would *decrease* the cash transfer. It is this change that has allowed the various recent de-indexing initiatives to occur. And it is the presence of a de-indexed or frozen ceiling that implies that, at some point, the cash component of the EPF transfer will fall to zero. I doubt whether this implication was fully appreciated back in 1982. But it became clear as the EPF ceiling was progressively constrained and then frozen. About the time of the EPF freeze, the decline of cash to zero was forecast to occur near the turn of the century and much earlier for Quebec (because of its special abatement), but the recession has prolonged this day of reckoning.

The remainder of Thematic Tableau 3 should be straightforward.

A Technical Detour on the EPF Tax Transfer

A tax transfer involves the transfer of tax room from one order of government to another (so far in Canada, from the federal to provincial governments) as an alternative to cash transfers. As noted, EPF initially incorporated 13.5 PIT points and one CIT point. However, the one CIT point already existed and so did 4.357 PIT points. Thus, the net personal income tax point transfer was 9.143 points. To vacate the tax room, Ottawa reduced its tax base from 100 points (or percent) to 100 minus 9.143, or 90.857. In terms of this new base, the 13.5 points represent 14.86 percent (that is, 13.5 ÷ 90.857 = 14.86). Even though everybody still refers to EPF as transferring 13.5 PIT points, the reality is that, as a percentage of Ottawa's current base, the effective transfer is 14.86 percent or 14.86 tax points. Therefore, in determining the value of the tax point transfer in 1992/93 for Ontario, for example, Ottawa calculates the value of federal PIT revenues arising from Ontario residents and then assigns 14.86 percent of this as Ontario's tax point transfer. *No money changes hands here.* It is a notional transfer used for calculating the rest of EPF. The provinces are assumed to have taken up this vacated federal tax room (see the following paragraph). This notional transfer is assumed to be equalized via the regular equalization formula, since the transfer is defined as 13.5 (or 14.86) *equalized* tax points. This is referred to as "associated equalization" in Table 14 (category 2 under part A). This associated equalization is also a *notional*, not real, transfer, since it is already incorporated in the equalization formula. Over time, the value of this transfer changes if and when federal income tax revenues from the respective province changes. Obviously, this will be affected by the growth of income. But it will also be affected by changes in *federal* tax rates and/or changes in other tax parameters.

How did the tax transfer affect the provinces? Let us take Ontario as an example. In 1976, Ontario's rate of tax (assessed against basic federal tax) was 30.5 percent. To this one must add the new tax room, 9.143 points, for a total of 39.643. (Recall that incorporated in the existing Ontario rate were the 4.357 tax points transferred earlier.) As a percentage of the *new* (and lower) federal base, this 39.643 tax points converts to an Ontario tax rate of 43.6 percent (that is, 39.643 ÷ 90.857 = 43.6, where 90.857 is the post-tax-transfer federal tax base). Ontario's new tax rate was set at 44.0 percent — that is, it took advantage of this tax change to increase its tax rate a bit. So did Newfoundland, Saskatchewan, and British Columbia. The other provinces set their new rates in accordance with the tax room made available (Courchene 1979, Table 4). Overall, therefore, the tax take of the provincial income tax did not change much, but the proportion allocated to the provinces increased significantly as a result of the EPF changes.

Over the years, Ontario has raised this tax rate to well into the 50 percent range. So have virtually all the other provinces. But this does *not* affect the value of the tax points for EPF — these are determined by the procedures outlined in the first paragraph of this section.

Since the tax transfer is incorporated in the provincial taxes, they become provincial own-source revenues. Thus, it is not obvious that much, other than confusion, is achieved by referring to the tax-point transfer under EPF as *federal transfers*. What these tax point transfers are really used for in the context of EPF is essentially to determine how much in the way of cash transfers to the various provinces is needed to bring each province up to the EPF ceiling.

The Quebec Tax Abatement

One last issue relating to tax point transfers: in the 1960s, all provinces were offered the opportunity to take some federal program funding in the form of tax point transfers instead of cash. Only Quebec chose this option and these additional tax point transfers for Quebec are referred to as "tax abatements." Thus, Quebec receives 16.5 additional PIT points in terms of a tax abatement. Of this total, eight and a half points are associated with EPF, five points are related to the CAP, and three points for other programs.[8] These tax abatements are not equalized. Quebec's cash transfers are reduced to offset these abatements. What this means is that Quebecers pay less federal tax than other Canadians and pay more provincial tax. While comparisons are difficult to make, it is probably the case that an Ontarian would pay about 60–65 percent of his/her PIT to Ottawa whereas the Quebec proportion would be more like 50 percent.

Anatomy of EPF

With this backdrop, understanding Figure 7 should be straightforward. The equal per capita ceiling for 1992/93 is $752. The solid black portion of the bars for each province records the value of the notional tax transfer (notional, because these are really provincial revenues). Ontario's value of this transfer is more than double that for Newfoundland. These tax point transfers are equalized via

---

8 These three tax points were associated with the former Youth Allowance program and were obtained by Quebec in 1967. Now that this program is gone, Quebec essentially "rents" these tax points from Ottawa. That is, they are incorporated in the Quebec income tax (and taken out of the federal income tax for Quebecers) but Quebec transfers the equivalent amount of cash to Ottawa. Another way to visualize these would be that Quebec's equalization payments are reduced by the amount of these three tax points. Note also that, while one may wish to associate the eight and a half EPF points with either PSE or health, the fact of the matter is that in the context of the 1977 block funding for EPF these tax points became associated with EPF in general and not any particular program. Historically, however, these tax points were associated with hospital insurance, dating back as early as 1967. I wish to thank Stefan Dupré for the information in this footnote.

Figure 7: *How Established Programs Financing Works, fiscal year 1992/93*

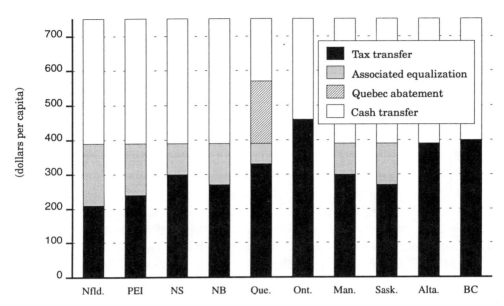

Source: Canada 1992b, Figure 9.

the formal (five-province standard) equalization program. This brings all provinces up to a level just under $400 per capita. Quebec's eight and a half point PIT abatement is represented by the hatched area in the Quebec bar. *To this point, there is no real or financial transfer from Ottawa to the provinces. All of this is notional.* Therefore, all that is truly transferred under EPF is the cash component — the white part on the top of each province's bar, up to the $752 maximum.

EPF as Super-Equalization

Later in this chapter and monograph, it will become useful to refer to EPF as embodying "super-equalization." Given that the overall EPF grant is equal per capita, one way of viewing this is that all provinces' per capita revenues are brought up to the level of Ontario (the top province for income tax fiscal capacity) rather than to the five-province standard. We can use Figure 7 to illustrate this. All we have to do is draw a horizontal line across the chart that touches the top of the tax transfer for Ontario. "Eyeballing" the figure would suggest that this hypothetical line would be in the $460 per capita range. Super-equalization is the amount *above* regular equalization (the light-shaded component) needed to bring each province to this $460 level. Beyond this, EPF payments are equal per capita, except for the province of Quebec, because of its EPF tax abatements.

Issues Relating to EPF

The first point is that EPF is not a $20.8 billion transfer, as might be assumed from Table 14. Rather, it is a $9.6 billion transfer (the cash component), with potentially an extra billion or so for the Quebec abatement. This still makes it the largest federal transfer, but this will soon change if the ceiling remains in place.

Second, EPF is *not* directly related to the financing of health care or PSE. These monies are, in effect, unconditional, and can be spent anyway that the provinces wish. What is true, however, is that *any* monies that the provinces spend on health must satisfy the five provisions of the *Canada Health Act* — universality, comprehensiveness, accessibility (which includes the prohibition of user fees and extra billing), portability, and public administration.

The third point is that, if the ceiling rate continues to the fully or partially de-indexed, then the cash component will tend toward zero. Quebec will get to zero well before the rest of the provinces because of its tax abatement. What happens then is anything but clear. Ottawa has passed legislation to the effect that, when Quebec's cash component becomes negative (because the combination of the tax point transfer, associated equalization, and the eight and a half point abatement will exceed the ceiling), these funds can be recouped from other transfers to Quebec. In my view, this is a retroactive "confiscation" of the Quebec abatement, and Ottawa will not get away with it. Relatedly, the utter unpredictability of unilateral federal alterations of EPF will lead all provinces to ask for the same abatement as Quebec. How can Ottawa refuse? These issues will feature prominently in the later chapter on deficit shifting.

The final set of issues relates to alternatives for reforming EPF. In the do-nothing scenario, EPF will revert to GNP minus 3 percent escalation beginning in fiscal year 1995/96. However, reform proposals abound, including the conversion of the PSE cash component into a portable PSE voucher for students and the conversion of the cash component for health into a further equalized tax point transfer. This combination would remove EPF, as we know it, from the system. While these and other approaches will be described and evaluated in more detail later, the option of converting the cash component of EPF into a further tax point transfer merits attention in the present context. One attraction to the provinces is that this new EPF would be beyond tinkering by Ottawa, since it would now be in the form of *provincial own-source revenues*. But this, in turn, raises an important issue. If all, or most, of EPF is replaced by an increase in provincial tax points, how would these tax points be equalized? One obvious answer is that they would be run through the formal equalization program, which would bring the equalized value of the points up to the five-province standard level. At present, however, EPF transfers are effectively equalized not only to the level of the top province, given the equal per capita nature of the ceiling, but also in terms of the top province in respect of personal income taxation — namely, Ontario (even though Ontario is not the top province overall in terms of the equalization program). Thus, we effectively have *two equalization programs* that are operative — one for general revenues and one for the tax points associated with EPF. These two equalization programs will not co-exist for long — pressures from the "have-not" provinces would surely develop to convert *all* equalization into the more lucrative EPF variant.

This would be wholly inappropriate. EPF already embodies over-equalization. As I shall argue in the following chapter, Ontario's per capita spending on health and postsecondary education exceeds that of most, if not all, "have-not" provinces, so that there is no equity rationale for the existing EPF scheme to be in the form of equal per capita grants. But since these EPF monies are effectively unconditional, it is probably inappropriate to refer to the cost of health in particular provinces as an argument against equal per capita payments. The more appropriate point to make is that unconditional tax point transfers not related to the EPF system are equalized to the five-province standard while unconditional tax point transfers within EPF are equalized to the level of the top province. As argued in the previous section on equalization, my view is that we already over-equalize within the formal equalization program. By way of elaboration, it seems to me that, if Ottawa delivers programs *directly* to people, they must be identical across all citizens. But if Ottawa supports programs *indirectly* via transfers to the provinces, it is appropriate that these transfers allow the provinces to deliver comparable services. Differences in capitalization (for example, provincial average wages) would surely not imply identical treatment across provinces as reflected in EPF super-equalization.

Complicating all of this that the remaining major transfer program, the Canada Assistance Plan, now embodies 28 percent sharing for Ontario and 50 percent sharing for the "have-not" province. To this I now turn.

The Canada Assistance Plan

From its inception in 1966 until 1990, the Canada Assistance Plan was a 50–50 shared-cost program for financing social assistance benefits and social services for Canadians. The 1990 federal budget contained a "cap" on CAP: for fiscal year 1990/91 through fiscal year 1994/95, the growth in CAP transfers to the three "have" provinces (Ontario, British Columbia, and Alberta) would be limited to 5 percent annually. All other provinces would continue with the 50–50 sharing.

The provinces challenged this in the courts, but the Supreme Court rejected the challenge, arguing, in effect, that CAP is a "federal" transfer program and can be altered at will by the Parliament of Canada.

The impact of this arbitrary federal initiative has been much more severe on Ontario than on the other two rich provinces — 85 percent of the CAP "losses" due to the cap have occurred in Ontario (Jenness and McCracken 1993a, 7). In fiscal year 1992/93, Ontario's losses were $1.7 billion, roughly equal to the "savings" generated by the province's "social contract" legislation. As already alluded to, the result has been that Ontario now receives 28 cents for every dollar spent on welfare whereas the "have-not" provinces receive 50 cents. This issue clearly dominates CAP reform and reform of the transfer system generally.

Prior to addressing further aspects of this cap on the CAP, I will focus on some more general aspects of the program. In fiscal year 1991/92, aggregate CAP expenditures total $6¾ billion (Table 14). Figure 8 presents data on per capita CAP transfers by province. What is anomalous is the position of Newfoundland in this ranking. With the highest unemployment rate in Canada, Newfoundland's $233 per capita of CAP transfers do appear to be below what one otherwise might have anticipated. Some of this is no doubt due to lower benefit levels for those on welfare in Newfoundland compared with those in, say, Ontario. But by far the dominant explanation must surely be that Newfoundland has been very "successful" in transferring its citizens from social assistance to unemployment insurance (UI). As was documented in the previous chapter, Newfoundland's *net* inflow of UI funds for 1991 was $750 million, or $1,300 per capita. Numerically, this swamps the CAP transfer.

Another way of viewing this is to focus on the rate of growth of CAP payments over the 1969/70 to 1991/92 period, where the former year predates the introduction of the major revision of the UI reform. For Newfoundland, this increase is roughly 650 percent, or 6.5-fold. All other provinces have significantly higher multiples: Prince Edward Island (10.6); Nova Scotia (14.3); New Brunswick (17.5); Quebec (14.2); Ontario (16.3); Manitoba (15.4); Saskatchewan (10.4); Alberta (20.1); British Columbia (17.4). While it is obviously the case that many factors are at play over a span of 20-plus years (for example, Saskatchewan's multiple is lower than it would be if it had experienced the national average population growth and Ontario's number is lower than it would be if the cap on CAP were not instituted). Nonetheless, the difference between Newfoundland and the rest of the provinces is such that one must assume that UI has played some role in keeping the growth in check.

The essential point here is, however, somewhat different. In the context of reworking the fiscal arrangements, many of the "have-not" provinces (including Newfoundland) are, as noted in the previous section, pressing for an equalization component to CAP. Specifically, the proposals tend to run along the lines

Figure 8:   *Canada Assistance Plan Transfers,*
                fiscal year 1992/93

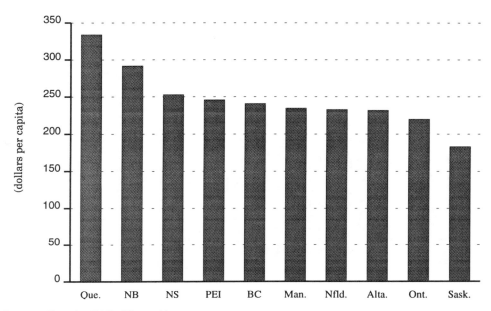

Source: Canada 1992b, Figure 11.

that those provinces with high unemployment rates should receive, say, 60 percent of social assistance expenditures while those with low unemployment rates
should receive less (say, 40 percent). The thrust of the above comments is that
it is inappropriate, analytically and empirically, to focus on reform of CAP *in
isolation* from the operations of other transfer programs, particularly UI.

A second dominant feature of Figure 8 is the high per capita transfer for
Quebec. Yet it was this province, in its budgets leading up to the introduction
cap on CAP, that argued that reform was needed because, over the 1980s, the
growth of overall transfers was higher for the "have" than for the "have not"
provinces. I am not sure whether this argument played a role in the introduction
of the cap on CAP, but given the size of Quebec's per capita transfer as shown
in Figure 8, it is difficult to understand how or why Quebec felt that it was being
short-changed. This is particularly true now, in the presence of the cap on CAP,
given that the value of the federal CAP transfer *per social assistance beneficiary*
for 1992/93 is $3,707 for Quebec and only $1,912 for Ontario (Jenness and
McCracken 1993a, 9).

Now that the cap on CAP issue has resurfaced, it is instructive to focus on
Figure 9 which depicts the evolution of Ontario's caseload and, on the funding
side, the fall in the cost-sharing percentage to 28 percent. While this general

Figure 9: *Social Assistance in Ontario,*
fiscal years 1988/89 to 1992/93

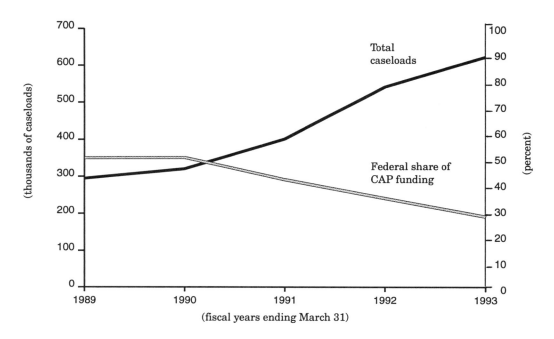

Source: Adapted from Jenness and McCracken 1993, 8.

issue will come up on several occasions later in this volume, it merits some elaboration here. From Jenness and McCracken (1993a, 1):

> A generation ago Ontario had the lowest proportion of social assistance beneficiaries per capita of any province, averaging about 4 percent of the population. Today, with 1.2 million persons dependent on social assistance, Ontario has the highest social dependency rate of any province, close to 12 percent. Within the three year span 1988/89 to 1992/93, Ontario's social assistance more than doubled [see Figure 9] and the share of Ontario's budget spent on social assistance rose from 5 percent to 11 percent.

As I have argued elsewhere, Ontario views the cap on CAP in much the same way as Alberta and Albertans viewed the National Energy Policy. (No doubt Alberta is once again infuriated since the cap on CAP is also starting to bite in this province, too.) Moreover, whereas one can conceive of equalization and EPF continuing to apply in the future, this is much less obvious for CAP. The existing legislation restores 50–50 sharing for 1995/96, but it is highly unlikely that Ottawa would contemplate a full "snapback" of the program, given the amounts of money involved. This has led some to propose alternatives to CAP, such as converting it to a guaranteed annual income for children (Chapter 5).

In any event, not only has the cap on CAP called into question the integrity of the entire transfer system, but the fact that it is not likely to be reconstituted in its former guise means that substantial rethinking of the entire transfer system and social envelope is inevitable.

Indexes of Fiscal Equality

Now that attention has been directed in turn to equalization, EPF, and CAP, it is appropriate to focus on their collective impact on provincial government finances. Toward this end, Table 17 presents indices of revenue equality for fiscal year 1991/92. Columns (1) and (2) present data on what has earlier been referred to as "fiscal capacity" — namely, the per capita revenues by province resulting from the application of national average tax rates to the provinces' own, standardized, tax bases. Newfoundland and Prince Edward Island, both with roughly $3,000 per capita in own revenues, weigh in at two-thirds of the national average and at one-half of Alberta's per capita total.

Equalization ensures that all provinces' per capita revenues are brought up to the five-province standard of $4,400. This is column (3) of Table 17, and the associated fiscal indices are in column (4). (As a technical aside, although the EPF and CAP data used in Table 17 are drawn from Table 14, the data for equalization are not. They are more up-to-date estimates for fiscal year 1991/92 and embody less equalization than the Table 14 figures. This alteration was necessary in order to obtain consistent data for the four concepts embodied in columns (1) through (4): fiscal capacity, the national average standard, the five-province standard, and equalization.

Since the five-province standard is 99.3 percent of the national average or all-province figure — that is, $4,440 is 99.3 percent of $4,478, the last entry in column (1) — one measure of the impact of equalization on provincial per capita revenues is that they are brought up to 99.3 percent of the national average fiscal capacity.

In the process of paying out all this equalization, however, the all-province average of provincial revenues (own revenues plus equalization) *rises* to $4,751 — see the last entry in column (3). Column (4) presents fiscal indices in relation to this $4,751 per capita average. The seven "have-not" provinces now record 93 percent of the all-province total. Ontario falls from 106 percent of the national average (from column (1)) to 100 percent. Alberta still tops the list with 125 percent, but the high/low ratio drops from the 1.99 for own revenues to 1.34 for own revenues plus equalization.

Table 17: *Indexes of Revenue Equality, fiscal year 1991/92*

	Own Revenues[a] (Standardized)		Own Revenues plus Equalization[b]		Own Revenues plus Equalization, CAP, and EPF				Net Transfers			
	$ per capita	(% of national average)	$ per capita	(% of national average)	$ per capita	(% of national average)	($ millions)[c]	Financing share ($ millions)	Net[d] ($ millions)	Net ($ per capita)	Net (as a % of own revenues)[e]
	(1)	(2)	(3)	(4)	(5)	(6)	(7)	(8)	(9)	(10)	(11)
Newfoundland	2,991	67	4,440	93	5,077	94	1,196	315	881	1,536	0.51
Prince Edward Island	3,019	67	4,440	93	5,089	94	271	82	189	1,446	0.48
Nova Scotia	3,506	78	4,440	93	5,118	95	1,452	754	698	775	0.22
New Brunswick	3,171	71	4,440	93	5,136	95	1,426	519	907	1,249	0.39
Quebec	3,958	88	4,440	93	5,186	96	8,377	5,393	2,984	436	0.11
Ontario	4,761	106	4,761	100	5,352	99	5,863	10,878	-5,015	-506	-0.11
Manitoba	3,684	82	4,440	93	5,080	94	1,526	764	762	697	0.19
Saskatchewan	3,970	89	4,440	93	5,017	93	1,041	653	388	390	0.10
Alberta	5,937	133	5,937	125	6,565	122	1,586	2,395	-809	-321	-0.07
British Columbia	4,840	108	4,840	102	5,487	102	2,081	3,067	-986	-306	-0.07
All provinces	4,478	100	4,751	100	5,397	100	24,819	24,819	-1	n/a	n/a
High/low		1.99		1.34		1.31					

[a] Revenues from representative tax bases at national average tax rates — that is, fiscal capacity.

[b] $4,400 is the five-province standard.

[c] Equalization plus CAP plus the cash components of EPF (plus the tax abatements for Quebec).

[d] The shares of federal taxes by province appear in note 3 of Chapter 2.

[e] The previous column divided by column (1).

Source: Author's calculations.

Columns (5) and (6) now add EPF and CAP to the analysis. There is an equalization component to EPF because all provinces' per capita transfers are brought up to the Ontario level. (Note that, while Ontario is well below Alberta in terms of overall fiscal capacity, column [1], it is the top province for personal income tax, which is the relevant fiscal capacity parameter for EPF.) CAP also embodies equalization in the sense that the transfers to the rich provinces are limited to 5 percent growth. Thus, the indices in column (6) reflect a further equalizing tendency. Ontario now has 99 percent of the (new) all-province average and Quebec is brought up from 93 percent to 96 percent. Saskatchewan remains at 93 percent, because its above-average cash transfer under EPF is offset by the fact that it receives the lowest per capita CAP transfer (see Figure 8). The high/low ratio falls from 1.34 to 1.31. Actually, if one were to compare *actual* per capita revenues across provinces, this high/low ratio would be much narrower. This is because the benchmark is revenue *potential*, or fiscal capacity, so that Alberta is assumed in Table 17 to be applying the national average tax rate to its retail sales base, whereas in reality it does not tax retail sales.

The remaining five columns of Table 17 derive measures of net transfers across provinces. Column (7) lists the values for the total transfer — that is, equalization, CAP (including the Quebec abatement), and the cash and Quebec abatement components of EPF. (Excluded from this are the equalized tax point transfers related to EPF because the tax component is already part of the provinces' own revenues in column [1] and the associated equalization is already included in equalization.) Column (8) then allocates the federal financing by province of these net transfers, using the shares of federal tax that appear in note 3 in chapter 2. The next two columns contain the net (after-tax) transfers in dollar and dollar per capita terms. The final column records the rates of net transfers as a percent of provincial own revenues.

Newfoundland's net transfer is $1,536 in per capita terms. As the last column indicates, this is 51 percent of Newfoundland's own revenues. Thus, without these net transfers, Newfoundland would have to raise its tax rates by 51 percent *across the board* to generate the equivalent revenue. Prince Edward Island is essentially in the same boat as Newfoundland. Net transfer to New Brunswick is at the 40 percent level, as a proportion of own revenues; Nova Scotia and Manitoba are at around 20 percent, with Saskatchewan and Quebec at roughly 10 percent. On the other side of the ledger, if there were no inter-provincial transfers, Ontario taxpayers could receive the same level of provincial services with an 11 percent *reduction* in taxes across the board. The corresponding reductions for Alberta and British Columbia would be 7 percent.

By way of summary, Figures 10 and 11 provide a graphical overview of the role of these three major transfers in provincial finances. Whereas the final column of Table 17 focused on *net* provincial transfers as a percent of own

Figure 10: *Major Federal Transfers as a Share of Provincial Revenues,*
fiscal year 1992/93

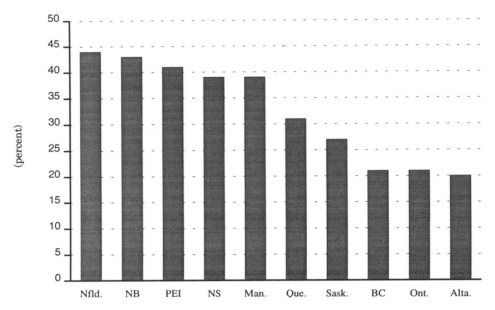

Source: Canada 1992b, Figure 4.

Figure 11: *Major Federal Transfers by Program,*
fiscal year 1992/93

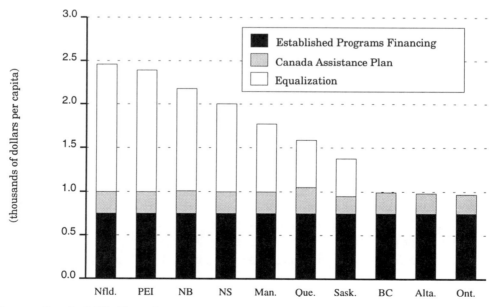

Source: Canada 1992b, Figure 3.

revenues, Figure 10 focuses on gross transfers as a percent of total provincial revenues (including transfers). Note also that, in Figure 11, the tax point transfer and associated equalization appears in EPF rather than equalization. Given the recent substantial upward forecast in the federal deficit for 1992/93, and given that much of this forecast error occurred on the tax side, it is likely that the data in these two figures will be subject to revision. One final point: these transfers now play a lesser role in provincial finances than in earlier years. In large measure, this is due to the fact that the provinces have increased their share (via tax hikes) of the overall personal income tax. This implies that the vertical fiscal imbalance in the federation has been ameliorated, which is appropriate in terms of accountability, as will be elaborated later.

The Federal Presence in the Provincial Economies

Table 18 attempts to provide an overview of the aggregate federal presence in the provincial economies by combining the data from the present and previous chapters. As usual, there are a few problems with these summary figures. Transfers to persons and federal expenditures on goods and services are National Accounts figures for calendar year 1991, whereas the major transfers to the provinces are on an Entitlement basis for fiscal year 1991/92 (except for row three — "other transfers to provinces" — which are also for calendar year 1991). The notes to the table are designed to alert the reader to these issues.

From row 4(a), total federal transfers represent at least 50 percent of wages and salaries for Newfoundland, Prince Edward Island, New Brunswick, and Saskatchewan. Manitoba and Nova Scotia are in the mid-40s while, in the "have" provinces, the shares are in the 20s.

Row 5 adds in federal expenditures on goods and services in the provinces. Presumably, the large Ontario figure ($11,206 million) reflects the fact that the capital is located in Ontario. Row 6 then totals up the federal transfer-plus-expenditure presence and divides this by what might be termed "own-source" net domestic income at factor cost — that is, *NDI* at factor cost *less* federal spending on goods and services in the province. The range of ratios is rather dramatic — Ottawa's presence is equivalent to two-thirds or more (80 percent for Prince Edward Island) for the three easternmost provinces and falls to 19 percent for Alberta. Quebec is at the national average level of 27 percent.

These figures add credence to the notion that Ottawa's principal role in the federation appears to be redistributive.

Table 18: The Federal Presence in the Provincial Economies: Summary Totals, fiscal year 1991/92

	Nfld.	PEI	NS	NB	Quebec	Ontario	Manitoba	Sask.	Alberta	BC	Canada
	($ millions)										
1. Transfers to personal and business[a]	2,098	537	2,918	2,447	18,081	24,889	3,472	3,932	5,933	8,740	73,365
2. (a) Transfers to provinces (cash and tax)[b]	1,350	298	1,682	1,620	10,523	9,913	1,818	1,281	2,507	3,266	35,382
(b) Transfers to provinces (cash only)[b]	1,239	272	1,451	1,456	6,756	5,874	1,540	1,047	1,586	2,081	24,399
3. Other transfers to provinces[c]	87	27	54	60	305	431	232	675	384	81	2,359
4. (a) Total transfers (1 + 2a + 3)	3,535	862	4,654	4,127	28,909	35,243	5,522	5,888	8,824	12,087	111,106
as a percentage of wages and salaries	0.68	0.73	0.46	0.54	0.33	0.22	0.44	0.61	0.24	0.26	0.29
(b) Total transfers (1 + 2b + 3)	3,424	836	4,423	3,963	25,142	31,204	5,244	5,654	7,903	10,902	100,101
as a percentage of wages and salaries[e]	0.65	0.71	0.44	0.52	0.28	0.19	0.42	0.59	0.21	0.23	0.26
5. Federal goods and services expenditures[d]	647	253	2,392	1,091	5,736	11,206	1,383	855	2,072	2,662	30,562
6. (a) Total federal government presence (4a + 5)	4,182	1,115	7,046	5,218	34,645	46,449	6,905	6,773	10,896	14,749	141,668
as a percentage of net domestic income at factor cost[f]	0.69	0.80	0.66	0.58	0.31	0.24	0.41	0.46	0.20	0.24	0.29
(b) Total federal government presence (4b + 5)	4,071	1,089	6,815	5,054	30,878	42,410	6,627	6,539	9,975	13,564	130,663
as a percentage of net domestic income at factor cost[f]	0.67	0.78	0.64	0.56	0.22	0.22	0.39	0.44	0.19	0.22	0.27

[a] From Table 5, National Accounts basis.

[b] From Table 14, Entitlement basis.

[c] From Statistics Canada, *Provincial Economic Accounts (1981–91)*, cat. 13-213, Table 17, selected items, calendar year 1991.

[d] From ibid., Table 6, calendar year 1991.

[e] From ibid., Table 1, calendar year 1991 wages and salaries.

[f] Net domestic income at factor cost for our purposes is defined as NDI at factor cost (ibid.) *less* federal government expenditures of goods and services.

Conclusions and Implications

The role of federal transfers to the provinces and the impact on social Canada will feature prominently in Chapter 7 on federal offloading. The focus in the present chapter has been to describe and evaluate aspects of these transfers, particularly as they relate to the amelioration of horizontal and vertical fiscal imbalance in the Canadian federation.

Given that the reform options with respect to CAP, EPF, and equalization will be detailed in later chapters, I shall use this conclusion to stand back a bit, as it were, and look at fiscal federalism in a much broader context. While these transfer programs are, as noted, geared to redressing horizontal and vertical imbalance, the broader framework within which they accomplish this also underpins much of Canada's social and economic union. The tax collection agreements, under which Ottawa collects the provinces share of the income tax, preclude the imposition of discriminatory tax credits at the provincial level and, more generally, have led to the development of what several international public finance experts refer to as a "model" form of income taxation for a federal state — decentralized yet harmonized. Moreover, aspects of the internal economic and social union (portability, no residency requirements, and so on) are a direct result of the moral suasion associated with these transfers. Indeed, whatever currently ails these transfers, the fact remains that they are the instruments by which Canada has developed a set of "national" programs, even if in some cases there are no national "standards" as such.

Continuing with this broader focus, there has been a significant trend in Canadian fiscal federalism away from conditionality in federal-provincial transfers. Equalization has always been unconditional. Since 1977, EPF has been unconditional in the sense that these transfers are no longer tied to PSE or health spending. And now that Ontario, British Columbia, and Alberta are, at the margin, spending 100 cent dollars on welfare, the CAP transfers for these provinces can be viewed as unconditional transfers that grow at 5 percent per year.

When one moves back to the level of the individual programs, however, it is apparent that all is not well. The provinces resent not only the series of caps, freezes, and ceilings placed on the various programs, but also the arbitrary and unexpected manner in which Ottawa has introduced these measures. More fundamentally, unless Ottawa is willing to return to 50–50 sharing under CAP (and willing to add the $2 billion in additional transfers that this would entail), the existing fiscal arrangements cannot be "reconstituted." In turn, this implies that system reform is inevitable and, not surprisingly perhaps, reform proposals are being generated from many quarters. Recently, the provinces (particularly New Brunswick and Newfoundland, as elaborated in Chapter 9) have got into the reform game in a serious way. While Ottawa has not as yet shown its hand, it too has major concerns, largely related to CAP.

Moreover, from Ottawa's vantage point, there is almost no federal visibility or accountability associated with these transfers, unlike the alternatives where, for example, CAP could be replaced by an additional income-tested guaranteed annual income for children and the PSE component of EPF could be converted into a system of portable postsecondary vouchers. This would restore parliamentary accountability for this spending and, of course, they would be highly visible to Canadians.

My final comment on the set of federal-provincial transfers anticipates the manner in which the ensuing analysis will evolve. In a federal system such as ours that has significant vertical and horizontal fiscal imbalances, it is inevitable that a process of social policy review will focus substantial attention on intergovernmental finances. However, an underlying theme of this monograph is that reforming the social envelope should *not* begin with a reform of fiscal federalism. Rather it should begin with determining what set of social programs will best suit the needs of individual Canadians as we approach the millennium. If we can put some broad parameters on what is needed at this fundamental level, then the nature of the associated reform on the federal-provincial transfer front in order to deliver these social programs will become more evident. Focusing reform attention at the outset on intergovernmental transfers may, and likely will, *predetermine* what is possible in terms of reworking the social envelope as it relates to individual Canadians. Surely, this is going about the reform process the wrong way — we need to work from the bottom up, as it were, and not from the top down. Much of the rest of the monograph is devoted to this theme.

I now turn to the role of the provinces in the design and delivery of Social Canada.

Part IV

The Provinces
and Social Canada

Chapter 5

The Provinces and Social Policy:
Health, Education, and Welfare Spending

The social policy focus now shifts to the provinces. Table 19 presents some aggregate numbers relating to the three major provincial social spending areas — health, education and welfare. Total health, education, and welfare (HEW) spending for fiscal year 1990/91 was $100 billion. When combined with federal transfers to persons, the value of the social envelope is in the range of $175 billion, or one-quarter of Canada's gross domestic product (GDP). The lower half of Table 19 expresses this HEW spending as percentages of overall provincial government expenditures. These HEW expenditure shares are really quite uniform. Except for Saskatchewan (with a 48 percent share), all provinces' percentages are within five points of the overall average — 57 percent. Ontario leads the way with HEW expenditures accounting for 62 percent provincial expenditures, but for each of the components at least one province matches the Ontario share.

The purpose of this chapter is to focus in greater detail on the design and delivery of each of the HEW components. In addition, attention will also be directed toward two other areas — workers' compensation and the general area of training. Workers' compensation is clearly in the provincial arena; it is less obvious that training is a provincial matter, but because it is closely related to welfare and education as well as unemployment insurance (UI), it was deemed appropriate to delay the analysis of training until all three of these related policy areas had been subjected to description and evaluation.

It should be immediately evident that what follows cannot possibly pass for a comprehensive evaluation of these policy areas. For example, a comprehensive analysis of the welfare area would require a focus on each of the ten provincial regimes. The same is true for education and health. For our purposes, however, this is not a major concern since we are not interested in assessing the adequacy of a particular program in a particular province. Rather, our interest is on the general structure of these programs and their interface with related programs.

The analysis begins with a focus on education — elementary and secondary, then postsecondary. As will also be the case with the other social program areas,

Table 19: *Provincial-Local Spending on Health, Education, and Welfare, fiscal year 1990/91*

	Canada	Nfld.	PEI	NS	NB	Que.	Ont.	Man.	Sask.	Alta.	BC
	($ millions)										
Health	40,127	748	151	1,306	980	9,109	15,934	1,647	1,527	4,052	4,995
Social Services	24,100	411	88	642	548	6,990	9,641	984	562	2,043	2,683
Education	35,863	804	156	1,209	876	8,818	14,041	1,268	1,152	3,609	3,795
Total HEW	100,090	1,963	395	3,157	2,404	24,917	39,616	3,899	3,241	9,704	11,471
Total provincial expenditures	177,378	3,582	752	5,311	4,252	46,340	63,527	7,496	6,765	18,480	19,390
	(percentage of total expenditures)										
Health	0.23	0.21	0.20	0.25	0.23	0.20	0.25	0.22	0.23	0.22	0.25
Social Services	0.14	0.11	0.12	0.12	0.13	0.15	0.15	0.13	0.08	0.11	0.14
Education	0.20	0.22	0.21	0.23	0.21	0.19	0.22	0.17	0.17	0.20	0.20
Total HEW	0.57	0.55	0.53	0.59	0.57	0.54	0.62	0.52	0.48	0.53	0.59

Source: Statistics Canada, *Public Finance Historical Data 1965/66–1991/92*, cat. 68-512. Data are based on consolidated provincial-local expenditures (Table H8) except on those (too many!) occasions where these consolidated provincial-local expenditures are smaller than the provincial expenditures for the category in question. In these cases, this table uses the provincial data. Statistics Canada is somewhat negligent here, either in terms of its calculations/methodology or in terms of explaining to the public why, for several provinces, the provincial-local totals are less than the provincial totals themselves.

the relative equality in terms of spending (as revealed in Table 19) masks a quite significant variation across provinces in terms of many important features of design and delivery. In effect, what makes Canada's social programs "national" is not their uniformity but their adherence to similar principles and the fact that their portability, universality, and lack of residency requirements means that Canadians have access to them no matter where they choose to live. Of interest in what follows, however, is not so much the inherent characteristics of the status quo as an assessment of how well these programs are serving Canadians.

Education

Elementary and Secondary Education

Table 20 presents data on fiscal year 1990/91 by province on institutions, full-time teachers, full-time enrollment, and expenditures for the education sector. I leave to the reader the task of sorting out the detail in this table and I turn, instead, to Table 21, which incorporates some summary statistics, largely drawn from Table 20.

In terms, first, of education "need," row 7 indicates that Newfoundland and Saskatchewan have a school-age (5–17) population in excess of 20 percent, with British Columbia and Ontario at the low end (17.2 percent). From row 4, however, overall spending per student (including postsecondary education [PSE] spending) has a quite different distribution. Newfoundland with $7,200 per student is near the bottom while British Columbia with $8,200 is near the top. Converting these per student spending totals as a percentage of per capita GDP (row 8) yields rather predictable and not very interesting results, because the ratios tend to be driven by differences in the denominator — that is, Ontario, Alberta, and British Columbia typically will have low ratios as a result of their high per capita GDPs. Of more interest are the data in row 9 — spending per student in relation to total provincial-local revenue per capita. The all-province average is 1.22 — that is, spending per student (from row 4) is 22 percent higher than per capita revenues. While there are some substantial differences (British Columbia and New Brunswick have ratios of 1.32 and Alberta has 1.06), all provinces are within 10 percent of the all-province average. One way of interpreting these ratios is that the provinces are all spending reasonably comparable amounts of their overall budgets on education.

In terms of performance data, however, the variations are substantial. Row 10 presents one measure of high school dropout rates. The five easternmost provinces have higher, sometimes much higher, dropout rates than the five western provinces. Indeed, the dropout rate for Prince Edward Island is 178 percent that of Alberta. As Figure 12 indicates, the performance results in terms

Table 20: *Education Data: Institutions, Full-Time Teachers, Full-Time Enrollment, and Expenditures, Canada and the Provinces, fiscal year 1990/91*

	Canada	Nfld.	PEI	NS	NB	Que.	Ont.	Man.	Sask.	Alta.	BC
Institutions (number)											
1. Elementary-secondary	15,638	535	73	537	460	2,925	5,516	846	990	1,715	1,901
2. Community college	203	12	2	10	8	89	32	10	1	18	19
3. University	69	1	1	12	5	8	22	6	3	5	6
4. Subtotal	272	13	13	22	13	97	54	16	4	23	25
5. *Total*	*15,910*	*548*	*76*	*559*	*473*	*3,022*	*5,600*	*862*	*994*	*1,738*	*1,926*
Teachers (number)											
6. Elementary-secondary	297,106	8,028	1,373	10,649	8,210	65,007	121,405	13,142	10,389	26,765	30,664
7. Community college[a]	24,950	310	80	290	310	11,700	7,200	380	380	2,200	2,020
8. University	37,435	1,051	177	2,160	1,268	8,400	14,448	1,734	1,578	3,376	3,243
9. Subtotal	62,385	1,361	257	2,450	1,578	20,100	21,648	2,114	1,958	5,576	5,263
10. *Total*[b]	*359,491*	*9,389*	*1,630*	*13,099*	*9,788*	*85,107*	*143,053*	*15,256*	*12,347*	*32,341*	*35,927*
Enrollment (number of students)											
11. Elementary-secondary	5,151,003	127,400	24,523	169,170	134,761	1,148,770	2,009,090	219,859	212,278	507,460	564,627
12. Community college	324,346	3,666	999	2,692	2,664	154,418	99,465	3,972	3,433	25,168	27,427
13. University	532,132	12,534	2,534	27,011	16,895	124,669	216,441	19,698	21,640	48,614	42,096
14. Subtotal	856,478	16,200	3,533	29,703	19,559	279,087	315,906	23,670	25,073	73,782	69,523
15. *Total*	*5,997,481*	*143,600*	*28,056*	*198,873*	*154,320*	*1,427,857*	*2,324,996*	*243,529*	*237,351*	*581,242*	*634,150*
Expenditures ($ thousands)											
16. Elementary-secondary	30,718,022	601,635	113,205	868,928	730,716	6,941,910	12,650,252	1,345,461	1,099,793	2,763,801	3,353,811
17. Community college	3,588,372	X	X	X	39,355	1,520,418	1,071,392	60,184	49,098	368,266	346,983
18. University	10,062,551	X	X	X	255,137	2,617,388	3,528,686	401,706	462,147	957,743	973,862
19. Subtotal	13,650,923	258,135	58,060	461,661	294,492	4,137,806	4,600,078	461,890	511,245	1,326,009	1,320,845
20. Trade	3,814,743	169,225	24,588	143,350	173,690	789,617	896,925	150,431	177,817	472,589	525,406
21. *Total*[c]	*48,183,688*	*1,028,995*	*195,823*	*1,473,939*	*1,198,898*	*11,869,333*	*18,147,255*	*1,957,782*	*1,788,855*	*4,562,408*	*5,200,062*

Note: "X" means that Statistics Canada does not break down the data in this category.

[a] Estimate.

[b] Excludes trade level teachers.

[c] Includes Canada's spending on education in foreign countries and undistributed expenditures.

Source: Statistics Canada, *Education in Canada, A Statistical Review, 1990–91*, cat. 81-229, Table 1.

Table 21: *Education: Summary Statistics*

	Canada	Nfld.	PEI	NS	NB	Que.	Ont.	Man.	Sask.	Alta.	BC
1. Student/faculty ratio for PSE[a]	13.7	11.9	13.7	12.1	12.4	13.9	14.6	11.2	12.8	13.2	13.2
2. Spending per student[b] ($ thousands)	15.9	15.9	16.6	15.5	19.5	14.8	14.6	19.5	20.4	18.0	19.0
3. Spending per capita[c] ($)	1,811	1,799	1,498	1,647	1,660	1,754	1,861	1,798	1,794	1,845	1,660
4. Spending per student[d] (all levels, $ thousands)	8.1	7.2	7.0	7.4	7.8	8.3	7.8	8.0	7.5	7.9	8.2
5. Community college/university ratio[e]	0.61	0.29	0.39	0.09	0.16	1.24	0.46	0.20	0.16	0.52	0.65
6. Community college/university spending ratio[f]	0.36	0.20	0.24	0.10	0.15	0.58	0.30	0.15	0.11	0.38	0.36
7. Education need: school-age population (5–17) as a percentage of total population[g]	17.8	21.6	19.9	17.9	19.0	17.5	17.2	18.6	20.3	19.4	17.2
8. Spending per student as a share of GDP per capita[h]	0.32	0.47	0.46	0.39	0.43	0.36	0.28	0.37	0.37	0.27	0.31
9. Spending per student in relation to provincial-local revenue per capita	1.22	1.29	1.22	1.25	1.32	1.21	1.20	1.16	1.11	1.06	1.32
10. High school dropout rate[i]	18	24	25	22	20	22	17	19	16	14	16
11. Postsecondary education enrollment[j]											
Community college as a % of population aged 18–21	20.8	8.5	12.1	4.8	5.7	41.7	17.4	6.0	5.9	16.5	15.6
University as a % of population aged 18–21	30.1	27.3	30.3	43.9	34.1	28.5	33.5	26.4	34.7	28.3	19.9
Graduate school as a % of population aged 22–24	5.3	2.5	0.5	5.4	2.5	6.3	5.4	4.5	3.3	4.7	5.4
Total PSE as a % of population aged 18–24	30.9	21.9	24.9	29.9	24.0	41.3	30.8	20.5	25.0	27.5	22.7

[a] Row 14 ÷ row 9 (Table 20).
[b] Row 19 ÷ row 14 (Table 20).
[c] Row 19 (Table 20) ÷ population.
[d] Row 21 ÷ row 15 (Table 20).
[e] Row 12 ÷ row 13 (Table 20).
[f] Row 17 ÷ row 18 (Table 20) except for Newfoundland, Prince Edward Island, and Nova Scotia, where the data refer to 1989/90.
[g] From Canadian Teachers' Federation 1993.
[h] Row 4 of this table divided by GDP per capita for 1990 (from Statistics Canada, *Provincial Economic Accounts* , cat. 13-213, Table 19).
[i] School leavers survey (1991), Canadian Teachers' Federation 1993, Table 18.
[j] Statistics Canada, *Education in Canada, A Statistical Review 1990–91*, cat. 81-229, Table 21.

Figure 12: *Science Achievement at the End of
Secondary School, by Province, mid-1980s*

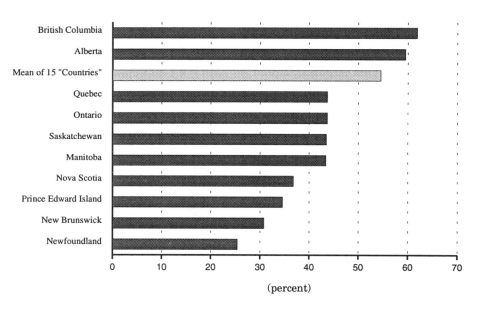

(percent)

Note: The population measured here consists of students in the final year of secondary school with a strong
scientific component in their academic program. The results are adjusted for years of schooling and
retention rates. Taking part in the study were 15 "countries," including two Canadian provinces and
two grade levels in Hong Kong. The test was administered over the 1983–86 period.

Source: Economic Council of Canada 1992, 8.

of science achievement for those remaining in secondary school also reveal
significant regional and provincial variance: British Columbia and Alberta top
the list, with the four Atlantic provinces well below the average.

In tandem with the dropout data, these are disturbing results. As earlier
evidence reveals, they cannot be attributed to variances in amounts of education
expenditures either per student or as a percentage of provincial revenues. One
possible answer, at least for Newfoundland, which fares poorly in terms of both
dropout rates and science achievement, is that it is part of the "transfer-
dependency" syndrome. Among the many broadsides leveled against UI by the
Newfoundland Royal Commission on Employment and Unemployment (Newfoundland 1986) is that the system "undermines the importance of education"
(p. 406). In more detail:

> Little or no qualifications are required to become an inshore fisherman, a
> fish-plant worker or a construction worker, or to be employed on a short-term
> make-work project. It is as easy to get the 10 weeks' work to qualify for UI

with a Grade 8 education as it is with a university degree — at least that is the local perception. Hence, there is little incentive to get a better education for the work world. In addition, the UI system actually penalizes people for aspiring to further their education by cutting off benefits if they become full-time students. (Ibid., 406.)

This issue will be revisited later in the study in the context of the necessity of making the transition from a resource-based economy to a human-capital based economy as well as in the context of whether provincial education systems are providing full opportunities for their residents to acquire and develop their human capital potential.

Prior to taking leave of the elementary and secondary education area, it is instructive to note that there are significant differences across the provinces in terms of how and where this education is financed. As Figure 13 indicates, the five easternmost provinces have a much more centralized (provincial) control over education. British Columbia is roughly at the national average while the Prairies and particularly Ontario maintain a relatively decentralized system of financing elementary and secondary expenditure. While I do not pretend to know the full ramifications of centralized versus decentralized financing of provincial education, these differences across provinces provide a convenient launch pad for several subjective comments and conjectures.

The first is that provincial education represents one of the last major monopolies in the system. My hunch is that, based on performance data (some of which are presented below) and on the decentralist tendencies being ushered in by globalization and the information revolution (see Chapter 8), this monopoly will come under increasing attack as we approach the millennium. A move toward standardized, even national, testing would introduce competition between provincial systems. But more significant will be the introduction of greater competition and choice *within* each provincial system. One might guess that this within-province competition is likely to emerge in a system such as that in Alberta, where the financing (and presumably the control) is already more decentralized. On the other hand, Quebec probably has more experience, in terms of both costs and performance, with "private" schools so that it might initiate the first significant move. In any event, I would be very surprised if this monopoly remained intact through to the millennium, even if only in the sense that greater powers will be transferred from bureaucrats and unions to parents and communities.

An equally speculative comment is that it is entirely rational for the five easternmost provinces to have moved in the direction of centralizing ("provincializing") elementary and secondary education. The motivation for this comment is that it was not until New Brunswick, for example, centralized education

Figure 13: *Total Expenditures on Elementary and Secondary Education,*
by Province and Source of Funds, fiscal year 1991/92 (estimated)

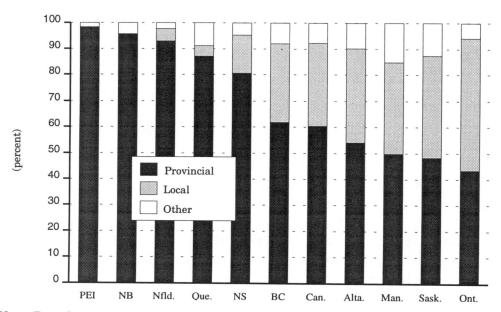

Note: Expenditures are for public, federal, and private schools as well as special education. "Other" includes
direct contributions by the federal government, fees, and other sources.

Source: Canadian Teachers' Federation 1993.

expenditures (and took over this aspect of the property tax) that the education component of the property tax entered the equalization formula, to the obvious benefit of the overall revenue position of that province and the other "have-not" provinces. Is this another example of moral hazard at work in the social policy envelope?

Finally, while elementary and secondary education is attracting increasing attention in the policy arena, it is something of an orphan in terms of the analysis in this monograph. This is because not only is it entirely under provincial jurisdiction, but it is little influenced by the operations of the major federal-provincial transfers. The component of education that is so influenced is postsecondary, to which the analysis now turns.

Postsecondary Education

The rest of Table 21 focuses on postsecondary education. The first three rows of the table present various summary statistics relating to the PSE sector (community colleges and universities). Manitoba has the lowest student/faculty ratio (11.2, as row 1 indicates) and one of the highest rates of spending per student

($19,500, row 2). The opposite is true for Ontario. Yet Ontario tops the list of PSE spending per capita ($1,861, row 3) because of the number of students enrolled per capita.

In terms of the split between university students and community college students (row 5), Quebec is a clear outlier because of its CEGEP system — it has 24 percent more community college students than university students. Quebec aside, it is the three "have" provinces (Ontario, Alberta, and British Columbia) that place substantial emphasis on community colleges — their ratios of community college to university students are between 46 and 65 percent. Prince Edward Island and Newfoundland hold the middle ground with 39 percent and 29 percent, respectively, while the remaining provinces, particularly Nova Scotia, assign preference to university training. In Nova Scotia's case, it has probably gone way overboard here, given that it has roughly twice as many universities as the rest of Atlantic Canada (Table 20, row 3). Row 6 of Table 21 (which shows the community college/university spending ratio) indicates that community colleges are, in general, cheaper to run than universities. For example, in Ontario, community college enrollment is 46 percent of university enrollment but these colleges receive only 30 percent of the monies spent on universities. The Quebec figures are more dramatic: there are more students in community colleges (CEGEPs) than in universities, but these colleges receive only 58 percent of the funds that go to universities.

The last four columns of Table 21 present age-related enrolment rates in PSE. Nova Scotia scores high in terms of university enrolment among the 18–21 age group (43.9 percent), but is slightly below Ontario in terms of overall PSE enrolment among the 18–24 age group (29.9 versus 30.8), because of its low community college enrollment (4.8 percent of the 18–21 population in Nova Scotia compared with 17.4 percent for Ontario). None of these data take account of out-of-province registrations, which tend to be relatively high in some provinces (for example, Nova Scotia). Again, the role of the CEGEPs makes Quebec an outlier here with overall PSE enrollment equal to 41.3 percent of the 18–24 age group.

Education, Employability and Income

Figure 14 provides a snapshot of the relationship between education, income levels, and employability by province for 1991. For Canadians with low education levels (less than grade 9), earnings do not differ much by province (somewhere in the $12–$15,000 range), but rates of unemployment certainly do. To be sure, there is probably a close correlation between the overall rate of unemployment in the province and the unemployment rates for low-educated persons in Figure 14. What is significant, however, is that this provincial

Figure 14: *Education, Earnings, and Unemployment, by Province, 1991*

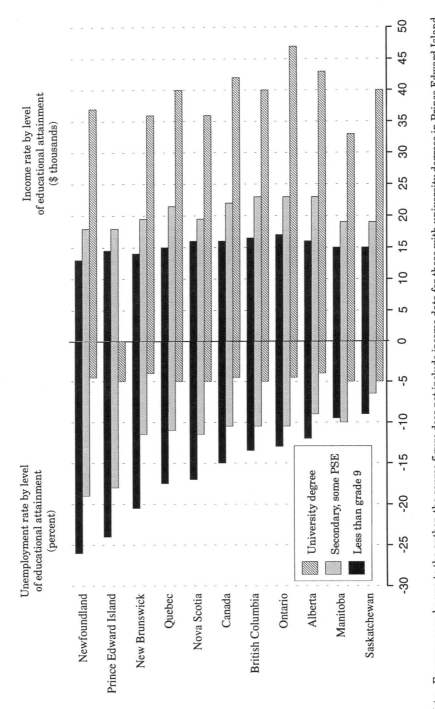

Note: For reasons unknown to the author, the source figure does not include income data for those with university degrees in Prince Edward Island.

Source: Canadian Teachers' Federation 1993.

disparity in unemployment rates vanishes entirely for Canadians with a university degree. I will return to this point later.

International Comparisons

Table 22 presents international comparisons of selected indicators relating to education. In terms of education spending as a percent of GDP, Canada is tied for fourth with the Netherlands. The Scandinavian countries top the list and, perhaps surprisingly, West Germany is at the bottom. Japan is second-to-last in terms of public spending on education, but rises to eighth place once private sources of education financing are included. The last column of Table 22 presents a subjective ranking of education status. As the notes beneath the table indicate, these are Economic Council of Canada rankings based on *The World Competitiveness Report* and data from the Organisation for Economic Co-operation and Development. West Germany (the lowest spender) tops the list. Canada ranks eleventh (or tenth, given that Finland, ranked second, is deleted from the comparison). What is clear from the table is that the correlation between amounts spent on education and the assessment of the effectiveness of this spending is not very high. Indeed, it is not obvious that the correlation is even positive. This has been an important issue in the public discussion on education: are Canadians getting their money's worth for their relatively generous spending on education? The anecdotal evidence, including test scores on various international comparisons, suggests that the answer is generally "no." This is yet another disturbing aspect of the education subsystem, particularly so as we are ushering in the era where human capital is at the cutting edge of competitiveness.

In terms of other sets of indicators, the Economic Council of Canada (1992a, 28–29) reports on a recent study that indicates that the average salaries of Canadian teachers in the first half of the 1980s were substantially higher than those of their US counterparts and higher still than those of teachers in Japan, South Korea, Britain, and Sweden. Salaries in Denmark and West Germany were also above the US scale, but well beneath Canadian salaries. All these comparisons are in terms of US dollar equivalents. The Economic Council concludes: "Canadian teachers are among the highest-paid in the world and occupy comparatively high positions on the economic ladder" (p. 28). If something ails our education system, one has to look elsewhere than teachers' salaries.

The PSE Reform

The Maxwell Critique

But something does ail the education system. In a recent paper critiquing PSE, Judith Maxwell (1994) zeroes in on four themes: bureaucratic deadlock, vested

Table 22: *International Education Indicators, 1989*

	Ratio of Education Spending to Gross Domestic Product				Education Indicator[d]
	Public Sector	Private Sources	Total	Ranking	Ranking
Norway	7.2	0.2	7.4	1	9
Sweden	7.1	—	7.1	3	3[e]
Denmark	7.0	0.3	7.3	2	5
Netherlands	6.5[a]	0.3	6.8	4.5	12
Canada	6.2	0.6	6.8	4.5	11
New Zealand	5.6[a]	—	5.6	10	16
Austria	5.5	—	5.5	11	6
France	5.3	1.0	6.3	7	13
Australia	5.3[b]	0.4[b]	5.7	9	14
United Kingdom	5.0[c]	—	5.0	13	15
Switzerland	5.0	—	5.0	13	7
Italy	5.0[b]	—	5.0	13	17
Belgium	4.9[a]	—	4.9	15	10
United States	4.8[b]	1.7[b]	6.5	6	8
Japan	4.7[a]	1.4[a]	6.1	8	4
West Germany	4.1[a]	0.2[a]	4.3	16	1

[a] 1988.

[b] 1986.

[c] 1987.

[d] The education ranking represents estimates by the Economic Council of Canada based on data from the Organisation for Economic Co-operation and Development and the *World Competitiveness Report*, 1990 and 1991. The indicator is a composite of, among other items, educational attainment and opportunities, universality and access, drop-out levels, interest in scientific fields, strength of vocational training, and so on.

[e] Finland is ranked second, but it is not included in the first four rows.

Source: Economic Council of Canada 1992, Tables 8 and 14.

interests, jurisdictional games, and a desperate need for innovation. To set the stage for the analysis, she reflects on the nature of the fundamental societal changes that have occurred:

> Globalization and technology have eliminated any prospect for low-skills jobs with high pay in Canada. We had more than our share of these jobs in the postwar period because of high levels of tariff protection and the robust resource sector. In every province, there were large sections of the male population who could leave school at age 16 and expect to live a full and

prosperous life working in the mines, the forests, the fishery, some parts of agriculture, and in standardized manufacturing jobs like breweries and metal bashing.

Those days are gone. A young man who leaves school at 16 today faces the prospect of a life pumping gas, flipping hamburgers, or brief seasonal work as a fishing or hunting guide. Even in the public sector, the jobs for young men who started work in the mail room and ended up as a $40,000 a year clerk with a fully indexed pension are disappearing. (Maxwell 1994, 218.)

This theme, which will be elaborated in Chapter 8, leads Maxwell to outline four objectives in terms of the evolution of the PSE sector:

1. A system that pays attention to the interface between theory and action. The key words are policy, empirical, and practical. (It is my impression that these three words are considered to be bad words in the lexicon of many university departments.) This can be achieved through cooperative education, the use of practitioners as instructors or as special guests in the classroom, university-industry cooperation, practical work assignments, and so on.

2. A system that works on the basis of teams. The key word is interdisciplinary. Society — the workplace, families and so on — works in teams. Skills are blended. Few university programs actively practice this. There is little or no cooperation across departments and faculties....Many departments do not work as a team in designing complementary courses, assignments, etc.

3. A system that offers coherent transitions from one institution to another and from one stage of study to another over a lifetime. The key words are lifelong learning, responsiveness, and articulation (recognition of credits). The typical adult will return to school several times over a life time. She or he should be able to get credit for previous study and for work experience. Most institutions still treat these mature students, especially the part-time ones, as second-class citizens.

4. A system that is performance driven. The key words are excellent, efficient, and accountable. Institutions have to be able to demonstrate that there is excellence in teaching and/or in research, and that time, assets, and money are being used efficiently. (Ibid., 224–225.)

The remainder of Maxwell's analysis with respect to PSE focuses on ways to ensure that these objectives can be met. Many of these are hardly novel (for example, increasing tuition fees). The one that is novel relates to restoring the former powers and autonomy of the boards of universities. These boards are now moving in the direction of involving administrators, faculty, students, as well as community outsiders as members of the board. Maxwell would like, first, to reverse this membership composition and to make it more like corporate governance in private sector corporations and, second, to mandate the board to engage in hands-on management of universities. While I am sympathetic to the notion that some "outside" pressures for reform are appropriate to be brought to bear on universities, I would have focused elsewhere than on restructuring corporate governance.

Prior to focusing on how these alternative external pressures might work, it seems appropriate to refer at some length to a recent essay in *The Economist* ("Towers of Babble," December 25, 1993, 72–74) on the future of universities. The essay begins by contrasting the past and the present: "Thirty years ago, universities were arguably the most pampered institutions on earth," whereas now "nothing less than a populist backlash appears to be under way" (p. 72). Part of this relates to equity:

> Investing public money in higher education makes less sense in terms of equity or efficiency than investing it in primary and secondary education. It yields a much lower return...The higher the stage of education, the more the benefits accrue to the individual rather than to society at large — not least because one of the main functions of universities is to screen people for elite positions. Public investment in higher education is regressive; students are usually middle class by origin, and nearly always middle class by destination. And much of it may well be superfluous; many students would still go to university even if they had to finance themselves.

This is not a criticism of universities, but rather a comment on how they are financed.

Far more intriguing, however, is that universities are finding that they are becoming eclipsed in the very time frame when they ought to be becoming increasingly indispensable. *The Economist*'s answer to this puzzle merits quoting at length:

> What about the argument that universities are crucial in this information age? How else can society train the people needed to staff knowledge-intensive industries or spur the innovations needed to fuel economic growth? True, universities continue to play a crucial role in producing graduates — thanks to their legal monopoly — and in conducting basic research. In other respects, when it comes to producing and disseminating knowledge, they are moving to the margins.
>
> Today, knowledge is too important to be left to academics. To make money, more and more companies need to know immediately what is going on and why. Investment banks employ economists to plot the movement of everything from broad money to lead concentrates. Consultancies hire sociologists

to analyze the effect of changing social structures on consumer preferences. Pharmaceutical firms produce multi-volume studies of global health-care.

Private entrepreneurs have been much better than their public-sector counterparts at harnessing the information revolution. They are flexible and ruthless enough to ride a rapidly changing market. Most universities are still mired in the public sector, in spirit if not in fact. The combination of academic tenure and cumbersome decision-making means that they are much better at conserving old subjects than they are at extending, let alone inventing, new ones.

Technical innovation means that universities have ever-less control over the dissemination of knowledge. When the older universities were founded in the high Middle Ages, anyone interested in scholarship had no choice but to visit them, either to consult their inhabitants or to read in their libraries. Since then a stream of technological innovations, starting with the printing press and extending to the computer disk and the videotape, have succeeded in divorcing knowledge from institutions.

Soon you will be able to enjoy many of the advantages of a first-class education without ever setting foot on a campus. If you want to learn economics, you will be able to watch a lecture delivered by a Nobel laureate; if you want to learn geometry, you will be able to interact with your computer screen; if you want to do some original research, you will be able to summon library-loads of information. Universities, far from responding to these developments, still expect their students to turn up to lectures — a ritual rendered superfluous by Caxton.

The result of all this is that governments everywhere are bent on university reform. (Ibid., 73–74.)

In terms of how to implement reform, three strategies are proving popular. Again, from *The Economist* at length:

The first and broadest is to subject universities to quasi-market disciplines. British universities remain in the public sector, free at the point of use. But the government tries to play the part of a discriminating purchaser. By linking funding to performance, and by separating money for research from money for teaching, the government has provided universities with two distinct ways of boosting their incomes, increasing the number of pupils or improving the quality of their research. The result is that different universities are pursuing different strategies for survival, with the prestigious universities trying to increase their research income while their less distinguished rivals try to sharpen their teaching....

A second approach to reform is to cut costs simply by shifting funds to cheaper institutions, such as the polytechnics in Germany or the community colleges in the United States, or else by encouraging new sorts of higher education. Part-time courses, which allow students to combine work with study, are especially cost-effective. So are distance learning (which enables people to work for degrees without setting foot on a campus) and academic credits (which allow students to advance at their own pace, cram several courses into a single year, combine study with part-time work, or move from one institution to another).

The third strategy is for universities to diversify their funding — by marketing their research, by improving their relations with local industry and above all by charging fees.

The internal and external pressures on universities are beginning to force a change. In Britain, academics have started to rethink some of their hallowed practices, such as the three-term year, the three-year course, the primacy of lectures and the equality of all academics. In the United States, industry-sponsored research has more than quadrupled in the past decade, reaching $1.2-billion (US) in 1991. Everywhere, universities are introducing tighter management, treating dons like employees rather than gentleman-scholars, paying star performers star salaries and, even more controversially, contracting out more of their teaching and research to nontenured staff. (Ibid., 74.)

Some Modest Proposals

Even were one to accept much or even all of the above critique, there is still the further challenge of converting all of this into meaningful reform proposals. I shall focus on a few such proposals, discussing them in the context of what has become the current buzzword in PSE financing: income-contingent-repayment (ICR) schemes.

Basically, ICR schemes incorporate access to borrowed funds, full-cost (or fuller-cost) tuition, and pay-back systems based on postgraduation earnings. The initial funding could come from up-front borrowing or, indirectly, from commitments to income-tax-based pay-back schemes. ICR has the backing of the Ontario Council of Universities and Colleges, and the Association of Universities and Colleges of Canada supports revamping the Canada Student Loan program along ICR lines. The most recent advocate of ICR is the *Globe and Mail* in its January 3, 1994, editorial. This editorial followed by a week or so the reproduction on the *Globe and Mail's* op-ed page of the essay from *The Economist* referred to in the previous section. Whereas *The Economist* recommends, as already noted, that universities be subject to "quasi-market discipline," the *Globe and Mail* views ICR as an approach that embodies "full market discipline."

This is a much more complex proposal than it might appear at first blush. In particular, it has the potential for incorporating several intriguing reform initiatives, depending on the details of the particular ICR scheme. Indeed, in evaluating aspects of ICR, I shall use it as a springboard for discussing a wider range of reform proposals.

One of the attractions of ICR is that it represents a way to finance PSE that throws more of the costs of education back to students, but it does so in a way that is likely to be "progressive," in the income distribution sense of this term. Specifically, if students remain unemployed after graduation or earn an income that is below some threshold (for example, $20,000), then they will not be required to pay back the loan (or will not be assessed an income tax surcharge, if the tax system is utilized as the reconciliation avenue). In this sense, the cost of PSE is related to "ability to pay" based on postgraduation income (which may differ substantially from ability to pay based on the students' pre-PSE income class). Moreover, evidence from Australia, where a variant of ICR is in place, suggests that many students (or their families) prefer to pay for their university *up front* without "enrolling" in the ICR scheme. This is also "progressive" financing in that choosing this option is presumably highly correlated with pre-PSE family income.

Implicit in an ideal ICR system would be deregulation of tuition fees. One important result of this is that competition among institutions for students would lead to a more appropriate structure, across disciplines, of tuition fees. The current structure is incredibly perverse. A few examples will make this clear. Students in general arts programs pay (via tuition) a much larger portion of the total costs of their education than, say, engineers, doctors, or dentists. This is inappropriate, in the sense that it is the professional degrees that embody more of a "private" than a "social" return. Because the returns for professional degrees are internalized or privatized, tuition should be higher — and higher proportionally, not just absolutely — for these professional programs. Intriguingly, Queen's University is contemplating the mounting of a full-cost MBA program, with tuition in the $20,000 area. It is hoped that this will be a precedent-setting initiative. In the interim, it would be highly instructive for someone to calculate the *implicit subsidy* by program to PSE students. Given that tuition is generally in the range of $2,000 and that this covers about 20 percent of the cost of operating the universities, the average subsidy is about $8,000 per student per year. However, as already alluded to, this subsidy increases substantially for precisely the wrong programs, such as dentistry and medicine.

Isolating the value of the subsidy to PSE education will be salutary in a couple of other areas. The first of these relates to the nature of treatment accorded PSE and non-PSE students. What is the rationale for favoring PSE students with an "average" subsidy of $32,000 for a four-year B.A. — that is, four times the average $8,000 subsidy — while society tolerates countless thousands of young Canadians dropping out of high school with no equivalent subsidy to allow them to apprentice or train further. Moreover, the social return to spending money on these high school leavers is probably much higher than on adding a few more doctors in Toronto, especially since the former group will likely end up on one or another of our income support systems. This issue will be addressed in more detail when the discussion turns to training. The relevant point in the present context is that making the implicit subsidies more *explicit* allows society to assess the inherent equity embodied in the subsidy schemes.

There is a related issue, one that will also be highlighted under the training section but one that also merits airing in this context. Provincial governments provide enormous incentives to entice students to enroll in subsidized community colleges rather than in private sector training institutions. To be fair, some governments provide both loans and grants to these latter students. But if the focus were put where it ought to be — on the benefits accruing to the students themselves — there is absolutely *no rationale* for subsidizing government owned and operated community colleges and not these private institutions. An ICR scheme would allow the system to finesse this problem, since students could "shop around" for their PSE education.

There are also several important competitive virtues that would follow in the wake of ICR or some alternative variant of full-cost or fuller-cost tuition. The first of these is that, in one fell swoop, universities and PSE institutions generally would become more responsive to students' needs and aspirations. This is exactly the sort of "external" market discipline that is currently lacking in the PSE environment. Universities would be forced to compete and, in the process, would become far more "service" oriented, including the likelihood that students would play a much more important role in university governance. This would be a welcome move, in my view.

Second, and in a sense much more exciting, were we to launch a full-blown ICR scheme with, say, $10,000 to $15,000 as the typical tuition fee, the way would be open for the establishment of new institutions. Our system is far too uniform and, if the truth be told, far too expensive, burdened as it is by both bureaucratic and tenure-related sclerosis. It seems to me that, at $15,000 per student, the stage would be set for some "academic entrepreneur" to mount a new institution that would provide, say, the first two years of a university curriculum at *much less* than the cost of the existing system. The only drawback is that provincial governments would probably be loathe to give this upstart institution a charter. But somewhere, someone would. The point at issue here is that we have nowhere near the optimal diversity or variety in PSE institutions. And we are not likely to achieve this desired degree of diversity (and cost-effectiveness) unless the system comes under "outside" pressure such as that which would arise from ICR.

To this point, the implicit assumption has been that an ICR scheme would involve the complete privatization of the cost of PSE education. This need not follow. For example, the provincial governments could convert part of their existing grants to PSE institutions into portable vouchers for students. Indeed, the EPF federal cash transfers related to PSE could also be converted into a portable student voucher. And the special wrinkle that I would prefer in any ICR scheme is that it begin only in the second year of PSE. I think that it is important that as many Canadians as possible have an opportunity to avail themselves of a postsecondary education. To encourage this, I would keep first-year tuition reasonably low. If students wish to continue beyond first year, then let the full-blown ICR scheme take hold. At this point, the students will know exactly what they are "buying" into.

What all of this means is that, even within an ICR scheme, one can integrate the desired degree of societal subsidy to higher education. This is an important point — freeing tuition fees need not imply the full privatization of PSE education because some of these fees could be covered by vouchers. An ICR scheme can combine both enhanced external pressure to encourage system adjustment as well as society's desired degree of subsidization to higher education. In any event, I would be surprised if the next few years do not usher in substantial tuition fee deregulation and the initiation of some variant of ICR. I shall return to some of these issues when the discussion focuses on the training imperative. Prior to this, attention needs to be directed to the way we approach welfare and, more generally, social assistance.

Social Assistance and Workers' Compensation

The social services data in Table 19 cover a multitude of provincial programs — for example, assistance for the elderly, drug plans, subsidized housing, workers' compensation, social assistance (welfare), and social services. Moreover, even if some principles carry over across provinces, each province has its own set of programs in these areas. For purposes of this study, I shall limit the discussion to two areas — social assistance (welfare) and workers' compensation.

Social Assistance

Principles

Welfare is paid under the terms of the Canada Assistance Plan (CAP), an arrangement that allows the costs to be shared by Ottawa and the provinces. Although Canadians view welfare as part of the "sacred trust," the program is "national" largely in the sense that there are no residency requirements for eligibility. In reality, there are ten quite distinct welfare systems (12 if one includes the territories). Indeed, as the National Council of Welfare (1992, 1) notes, there are literally hundreds of welfare systems because of the leeway allowed to municipalities, which run welfare programs in Nova Scotia, Ontario, and Manitoba. While the central CAP eligibility criterion is "need," regardless of cause, provincial welfare systems vary markedly in terms of how they implement this criterion and in terms of the amounts of income support that they provide.

However, there are also some general rules that apply across most provinces. For example, assistance is granted in most jurisdictions to unemployed employable applicants only when the administrative authorities are satisfied that the existing unemployment is due to circumstances beyond the person's control, the person is willing to accept employment, and the person is making reasonable efforts to secure employment. Other generally applicable eligibility criteria include the following:

- full-time students of PSE institutions may qualify in some jurisdictions if they meet specified conditions;
- single parents must try to secure any court-ordered maintenance support from their former spouses to which they are entitled;
- strikers are not eligible in most jurisdictions;
- immigrants must try to obtain financial assistance from their sponsor.

Once eligible, claimants must submit to a "needs test." In order to be eligible for federal cost-sharing, an applicant's fixed and liquid assets cannot exceed the maximums set by Ottawa (for example, liquid assets of $2,500 for a single person will disqualify him or her from welfare). Assuming that these asset requirements are not binding, the next step is to calculate the needs of the household for food, clothing, shelter, and other essentials. Some sources of income, such as family allowances, the federal refundable tax credit, and the federal goods and services tax (GST) credit, are normally considered exempt and, therefore, not an offset to the determination of income support. However, income from other sources, such as employment, pensions, and UI is considered as income available to the household and is subtracted (in whole or in part) from the total needs of the household. *No two provinces use the same method for calculating these benefit levels.* Indeed, since welfare is "needs tested," the whole process is almost by definition intrusive (in the sense that applicants must reveal a significant amount of financial and personal information) and quite discretionary in contrast, for example, to other income support programs such as the refundable child tax credit or the Guaranteed Income Supplement, which are determined by an income test. Social assistance benefits that are sharable under CAP are not considered taxable income under the *Income Tax Act*.

With this brief overview of aspects of the eligibility criteria for welfare, the focus is now directed to some summary data relating to CAP and welfare.

Social Assistance Data

Row 1 of Table 23 presents CAP transfers per capita by province for fiscal year 1990/91. This is the last fiscal year that all provinces received 50 percent funding for CAP-related welfare and social assistance. (Doubling these numbers may not provide a precise estimate of provincial social assistance spending, because not all provincial social spending qualifies for CAP sharing.) With $250 per capita in CAP transfers, Ontario is the second-highest recipient — only Quebec, with $278 per capita, is higher. (Note that more recent data for 1992/93, which reflect the operations of the cap on CAP, put Ontario in second-to-last place — see Figure 8.) As pointed out in the previous chapter, Ontario now has the highest percentage of social assistance recipients: 11.9 percent, row 2. Saskatchewan has both the lowest percentage of beneficiaries (6.1 percent) and the lowest levels of per capita CAP transfers ($159).[1]

Ontario is the runaway winner in terms of the growth of CAP spending during the 1980s: 464 percent. Indeed, this is twice the growth rate of CAP in five provinces — Newfoundland, Prince Edward Island, New Brunswick, Quebec, and Saskatchewan.

The remainder of Table 23 focuses in various ways on the benefit levels across provinces for a family consisting of a single parent and one child. These benefit levels (row 4) include basic social assistance, family allowances, the child tax credit, other child related benefits, sales tax/GST credits, provincial tax credits, and various other benefits in some provinces. The benefit levels range from $16,098 in Ontario to $9,841 in New Brunswick. Quebec has the second-lowest benefit level ($10,975), well below the benefit level in Newfoundland and Prince Edward Island, for example.

As row 5 reveals, Ontario's increased welfare bill is not only the result of an increase in the number of beneficiaries; the province has also enriched quite dramatically the level of benefits. The growth in real terms of benefits for a single-parent/one-child family in Ontario rose by 23.6 percent over the 1986–91 period. Apart from British Columbia and Nova Scotia (which enriched their benefit levels by 8.9 percent and 1.0 percent, respectively), all other provinces

---

1 The Saskatchewan data may reflect the fact that this province has the highest proportion (as a percentage of provincial population) of First Nations citizens, whose welfare payments (if living on a reserve) would come from the Department of Indian Affairs and Northern Development and thus do not come under CAP. However, the per capita dollar values in Table 23 relate to the total provincial population.

recorded *negative* growth: welfare benefits *fell* in real terms over this period. Had Table 23 focused on the benefit levels for a couple with two children, rather than the single-parent/one-child combination, the growth in real benefits (1991 constant dollars) in Ontario would have been even higher(29.6 percent). Thus, apart from the severity of the recession, the reason the cap on CAP has hit Ontario so hard (from 50 percent federal funding prior to the cap to an estimated 28 percent federal funding in fiscal year 1992/93) is that it caught the province in the process of substantially enriching its benefit levels. In dollar terms, Ontario's overall welfare expenditures in 1992 are in the $9.5 billion area, compared with $2.1 billion a decade earlier.

Row 6 of Table 23 expresses the benefit levels in row 4 as a percentage of Statistics Canada's low income cut-off (LICO) rates for a single parent with a single child. These LICO rates are levels of gross income (adjusted for family composition) that ensure that no more than 58.5 percent of this gross (before tax) income would be spent on food, clothing, and shelter. Welfare benefits for a single parent with one child fall well short of these LICOs — Ontario's benefit level is only 79 percent of the relevant LICO. Given that the ratios in row 8 (row 4 as a percentage of average incomes of working single females) are not much below those in row 6, this means that *average* incomes of working female single parents are barely above the LICO rates. In this sense, the LICO rates are more in the way of "inequality" indexes rather than poverty lines, although they are frequently viewed as the latter. Recently, Christopher Sarlo (1992) has constructed a "necessities" index. Row 7 presents the values of the row 4 benefits as a percent of these necessities indexes. All the ratios are above 100 percent, often well above. While I have no desire to become involved in a discussion relating to the appropriate poverty line, it is important to recognize that there is a significant difference between "inequality" indexes and "necessities" indexes.

I now address the issues of the incentives within the welfare system and the transition from welfare to work.

The Transition from Welfare to Work

As the Economic Council of Canada (1992b) points out, the Canadian welfare system was developed in an environment where full employment — or at least low unemployment — was anticipated to be the norm. Welfare recipients were, by and large, expected to be unemployable and UI was introduced to look after people who lost their jobs because of business cycle swings. Neither program worried much about the transition from welfare (or UI) to work and, in the case of welfare, the authorities did not anticipate that the burgeoning case load increasingly would involve beneficiaries who were able to work.

Table 23: Social Assistance:
Summary Statistics, fiscal year 1991/92

	Nfld.	PEI	NS	NB	Que.	Ont.	Man.	Sask.	Alta.	BC	Canada
1. CAP transfers[a] per capita (90/91) ($)	207	219	210	239	278	250	207	159	219	232	245
2. Assistance recipients per capita[b] (%)	10.5	9.0	10.3	10.8	10.2	11.9	7.4	6.1	7.5	8.7	10.1
3. CAP growth 1980/81 to 1990/91 (%)	226	231	312	221	223	464	328	220	357	239	244
4. Welfare benefits, 1991 Single parent, one child[c] ($)	12,347	12,343	11,961	9,841	10,975	16,098	11,167	12,028	11,630	12,478	
5. Growth rate of row 4 (real terms), 1986–91[d] (%)	−1.2	−3.3	1.0	−6.0	−7.8	23.6	−4.8	−6.9	−10.9	8.9	
6. Row 4 as a percentage of LICO[e]	69	71	67	55	54	79	55	68	57	62	
7. Row 4 as a % of Sarlo poverty line[f]	120	137	132	113	119	160	119	133	128	131	
8. Row 4 as a percentage of average income[g]	67	—	59	53	48	70	55	60	53	52	

[a] Canada, Department of National Health and Welfare, *Canada Assistance Plan Annual Report, 1991/92* (Ottawa, 1992), Table 7, divided by 1990 population.

[b] Number of persons assisted under the Canada Assistance Plan, as of March 1992. From ibid., Table 2, divided by 1991 population.

[c] National Council of Welfare, *Welfare Incomes 1991* (Ottawa, 1992), Table 1.

[d] This is a five-year growth rate, not an annual growth rate. From ibid., Table 4.

[e] LICO is Statistics Canada's "low income cut-off" rate for a single parent with one child (1991).

[f] Sarlo 1992. Sarlo's index for 1991 (from his Table 7-7) is really a "necessities" index.

[g] National Council of Welfare, *Welfare Incomes 1991*, Table 3. Average income is defined as the average incomes of female single parents in the workforce.

Thus, the initial thrust of welfare was oriented almost entirely to income support, not to training or the transition back to the labor market. While all provincial welfare programs now contain a number of measures designed to promote the entry or re-entry of able-bodied unemployed clients into the labor force and while most provinces have signed agreements with Ottawa to enhance the employability of social assistance recipients, it nonetheless remains the case that the prevailing mentality remains largely income support related.

One aspect of this is that average tax rates in the transition from welfare to work frequently tend to be confiscatory (that is, exceed 100 percent). This is especially true when one adds in the "noncash" components of welfare, such as free drugs, subsidized housing, and so on. Thankfully, some provinces are now experimenting with various types of tax rates that are less than 100 percent.

The above comments are intended to apply to those individuals or families who would be able to find employment at income levels that, given more appropriate tax rates in the transition, would make it worth their while to re-enter the work force. However, there is another group — families with children — that is, for all intents and purposes, effectively "trapped" by welfare. To see this, it is instructive to refer to an unpublished paper by Christopher Sarlo (1993). Using 1992 data for Ontario, Sarlo calculates the total value of welfare benefits to be as follows: employable single ($7,804); single parent, one child ($15,772); single parent, two children ($18,864); single parent, three children ($22,365). The *market-income equivalencies* of these welfare levels are $7,350, $18,425, $22,800, and $29,625, respectively. Were one to add subsidized housing for welfare recipients, earnings equivalencies would be higher still — $32,225 for a single parent with three children. Few single parents on welfare can step into the workforce and command a $32,000 income. In effect, therefore, the so-called welfare trap is really due to the presence of children and how they are treated under welfare. One of the obvious solutions here is to devise funding mechanisms for children of low-income families that relate to income levels, not to whether the parent is or is not on welfare.

Ottawa embarked on a variant of this with the new child tax benefit, which replaced family allowances, the nonrefundable child tax credit, and refundable child tax credit with a single refundable monthly credit. The new benefit is worth $1,233 annually for each child age 6 and under and $1,020 for each child between 7 and 17. Maximum benefits are paid to families with net family incomes under $25,921, above which the credit is reduced by 2.5 cents for every additional dollar of net family income for families with one child and five cents for every additional dollar for families with two or more children. In addition, "working-poor" families get up to $500 more per household per year from an "earned income supplement" payable to those with employment earnings of $3,750 or more: the supplement phases in at a rate of 8 percent, so the maximum

$500 begins once employment earnings reach $10,000 and continues until a net family income of $25,921, above which the earned income supplement is reduced by 10 cents for each additional dollar earned.

This clearly eases the transition from welfare to work for families with children because the child tax credit provides income support independent of whether the family is on welfare. Indeed, one of the proposals offered in this monograph is to eliminate CAP and to transform it into *another* refundable tax credit for children. Were this new tax credit to replicate the existing one, there is enough money in CAP to more than double the existing credit — say, to something like $2,500 per child. But this would be the wrong way to proceed. The existing tax credit is not primarily an anti-poverty credit: it also has to do with ensuring horizontal equity between families with and without children in the tax system, at least up to middle-income levels. Because CAP funding relates to social assistance, converting CAP to any new child tax credit should also have *an anti-poverty focus*. This means that the new tax credit should probably break even (that is, fall to zero) about the same income level as the existing tax credit begins to be clawed back (that is, about $25,000 or preferably less). With this degree of low-income targeting, the value of the tax credit could be considerably larger, and we would be pretty close to the situation where provincial welfare or social assistance would target only adults (with Ottawa looking after the children). This would facilitate the linking of welfare/UI/training to labor force participation.

Worker's Compensation

While workers' compensation is one of the oldest forms of government social insurance, not only in Canada but across most of the industrialized world, it is also the least researched and, indeed, until recently it was never really featured in the social policy debates. This is about to change. Provincial workers' compensation boards (WCBs) paid out benefits of nearly $5 billion in 1991. Moreover, the annual growth rate of workers' compensation benefits over the 1970–90 period exceeded that of almost every other social program. As Jérôme-Forget (1993) documents, the annual growth in workers' compensation benefits in Quebec over the period equalled 6.9 percent, exceeding that of UI (5.6 percent), welfare (5.3 percent), and health (4.5 percent). The same was true for Ontario — WCB (7.2 percent), UI (4.9 percent), welfare (5.3 percent), and health (4.5 percent). Premiums, now ranging upwards from $2\frac{1}{2}$ percent of maximum insurable earnings (for example, where maximum insurable earnings are 150 percent of composite industrial wages in New Brunswick and 250 percent in Newfoundland) are borne by employers, and most jurisdictions employ experience rating — higher premiums for industries with higher accident records.

Indeed, Nova Scotia hinted recently that the debt position of its WCB is such that the average payroll premium of 2.54 percent may have to be raised to 5 percent or higher within a year ("N.S. fund may boost premiums," *Globe and Mail* [Toronto], January 28, 1994, p. B3). Along with recent UI premium hikes and increases in Canada Pension Plan/Quebec Pension Plan (CPP/QPP) contribution rates, these workers' compensation contribution increases are pushing payroll taxes to levels that presumably are having a very deleterious impact on employment. As an aside, an abundance of anecdotal evidence indicates that payroll tax increases inhibit employment, but this area, too, is under-researched.

Compensation rates are based on the earnings of the injured worker at the time of the accident, up to the legislated maximum (Canada 1991, 148). Most jurisdictions base wage loss compensation at 90 percent of a worker's "net" pre-accident gross earnings, where "net" refers to wages after deductions for income taxes, UI, and CPP/QPP. Injured workers may receive one or a combination of the following types of benefits: cash compensation, medical aid, or rehabilitation services. Cash compensation may be payable to the injured worker in respect of a temporary or permanent disability, and to surviving dependents in the case of death. Although workers' compensation benefits are reduced by the amount of any CPP/QPP disability entitlement in some jurisdictions, no other assets or sources of income are considered. Moreover, in all jurisdictions payments are nontaxable. As Jérôme-Forget notes, this feature is partly responsible for workers' preferring to shift from UI to workers' compensation wherever circumstances permit. And there is growing anecdotal evidence that, in depressed areas (mine closures, and so on), there is mounting pressure on physicians to "back up" workers' compensation claims.

Tables 24 through 26, reproduced from Chaykowski and Thomason (1994), present data, by province, on the operations of workers' compensation. Table 24 focuses on the benefit characteristics across provinces. The benefit maximum and benefit minimum columns in this table refer to weekly benefits. Immediately apparent are the striking differences across provinces, although there does appear to be relative uniformity in terms of cost of living adjustments (last column).

Table 25 contains assessment rates, by selected industry and by province. These rates, which are presented as the rate per $100 of payroll, are experience rated — for example, by the industry's accident experience over the previous three-to-five year period. Again, the variations are enormous — both across provinces by industry group and across industry group by province.

Table 26 contains the costs of workers' compensation in 1991, classified by type of benefit. As already noted, the overall total is touching $5 billion. Ontario and Quebec top the list with expenditures of $210 and $190 per capita respectively. Three provinces — Saskatchewan, New Brunswick, and Prince Edward

Table 24: *Workers' Compensation Benefit Characteristics,*
by Province, 1993

	Formula	Benefit Maximum	Benefit Minimum	Maximum Earnings Covered	Cost of Living Adjustment
British Columbia	75% of gross	727.81	261.44	50,000	Automatic Semiannual
Alberta	90% of net	525.83	217.48	42,000	Ad hoc
Saskatchewan	90% of net	551.20	317.77	48,000	Automatic Annual
Manitoba	90% of net (80% after 24 months)	541.09	171.28	47,000	Automatic Annual
Ontario	90% of net	647.27	285.83	52,500	Automatic Annual
Quebec	90% of net	568.26	213.91	46,500	Automatic Annual
New Brunswick	80% of net (85% after 39 weeks)	459.39	None	41,000	Automatic Annual
Nova Scotia	75% of gross	519.23	147.11	36,000	Automatic Annual
Prince Edward Island	75% of gross	389.42	60.00	27,000	Ad hoc
Newfoundland	75% of net (80% after 39 weeks)	466.54	200.00	45,500	Automatic Annual
Northwest Territories	90% of net	640.31	301.44	47,500	Ad hoc
Yukon Territory	75% of gross	719.18	306.85	50,000	Automatic Annual

Source: Chaykowski and Thomason 1994, Table 1.

Island spend less than $100 per capita. Again, there is incredible variation, with a high/low ratio of 2.5 (Ontario and Saskatchewan).

One measure of the degree to which workers' compensation programs have been operating outside public scrutiny is the (admittedly anecdotal) evidence that physician fee schedules relating to expenditures for hospital and medical care (column 3 of Table 26) are typically above those prevailing for general health treatments in the respective provinces. Presumably, this will ensure prompt treatment and perhaps reduce the ultimate workers' compensation claim, but this raises important societal issues.

As important as these actual payments across provinces is the fact that these workers' compensation funds are only partially funded. Figure 15 reveals that Ontario's cumulative deficit is in the $9 billion range and rising rapidly.

Table 25: Workers' Compensation Assessment Rates, by Industry and Province, 1993

	BC	Alta.	Sask.	Man.	Ont.	Que.	NB	NS	PEI	Nfld.	Yukon	NWT
Dairy farms	3.00	6.89	1.50	3.68	4.88	9.18						
Fruit and vegetable farms							2.65	3.18	4.12	2.59	2.00	1.70
Underground coal mining	2.80	7.92	5.25	3.81	4.41							
Open pit coal mining							3.81	20.86		19.31	2.50	19.75
Poultry packing plants	2.04	9.63	4.65	6.19	4.13	6.84	5.48	3.34	3.94	10.10	1.25	4.00
Manmade fibers and yarns	1.79		1.40	2.06	2.53	2.64	1.75	1.79	0.82	0.90	1.25	
Sawmills	3.46	6.11	3.50	7.89	8.21		6.55	4.13	7.50	6.47	2.50	21.00
Printing	0.74	0.99	0.30	1.08	1.80	2.36	0.45	0.41	0.82	1.29	1.25	1.20
Steel fabrication	3.99	5.33	6.25	4.88	6.07	4.61	6.63	5.72	2.00	6.80	2.50	
Commercial construction	6.14	5.14	9.50	7.01	5.97	11.05	4.25	5.14	6.18	6.15	2.50	10.25
General trucking	4.03	6.76	4.00	6.44	5.91	8.23	4.37	3.32	2.76	6.73	2.50	6.25
Supermarkets	1.09	2.10	1.40	2.08	2.75	3.30	0.70	1.00	0.92	2.07	1.25	1.20
Credit unions	1.09	0.29	0.05	2.08	0.50	0.57	0.31	0.39	0.35	0.45	0.75	0.55

Source: Chaykowski and Thomason 1994, Table 2.

Table 26: *Workers' Compensation Benefit Costs, by Province and Type of Benefit, 1991*

	Pensions for Permanent Disability or Survivors	Payment for Temporary Disability	Expenditures for Hospital and Medical Care	Total	Total per Capita
	($ thousands)				
British Columbia	176,084	207,922	119,582	503,588	156
	34.97%	*41.29%*	*23.75%*	*100.00%*	
Alberta	127,634	164,229	122,316	414,179	164
	30.82%	*39.65%*	*29.53%*	*100.00%*	
Saskatchewan	28,035	36,967	17,685	82,687	83
	33.90%	*44.71%*	*21.39%*	*100.00%*	
Manitoba	27,175	68,874	22,065	118,114	108
	23.01%	*58.31%*	*18.68%*	*100.00%*	
Ontario	665,000	679,000	741,000	2,085,000	210
	31.89%	*32.57%*	*35.54%*	*100.00%*	
Quebec	338,060	755,209	232,995	1,326,264	194
	25.49%	*56.94%*	*17.57%*	*100.00%*	
New Brunswick	15,676	31,878	17,607	65,161	90
	24.06%	*48.92%*	*27.02%*	*100.00%*	
Nova Scotia	47,116	51,394	27,888	126,398	140
	37.28%	*40.66%*	*22.06%*	*100.00%*	
Prince Edward Island	4,237	3,363	3,328	10,928	84
	38.77%	*30.77%*	*30.45%*	*100.00%*	
Newfoundland	4,527	33,471	27,845	65,843	115
	6.88%	*50.83%*	*42.29%*	*100.00%*	
Northwest Territories	9,848	1,862	888	12,598	
	78.17%	*14.78%*	*7.05%*	*100.00%*	
Yukon Territory	1,077	1,825	721	3,623	
	29.73%	*50.37%*	*19.90%*	*100.00%*	
Canada	1,444,473	2,035,999	1,333,923	4,814,394	178
	30.00%	*42.29%*	*27.71%*	*100.00%*	

Source: Chaykowski and Thomason 1994, Table 3.

Figure 15: *Cumulative Workers' Compensation Deficit,
Ontario and Quebec, 1980–90*

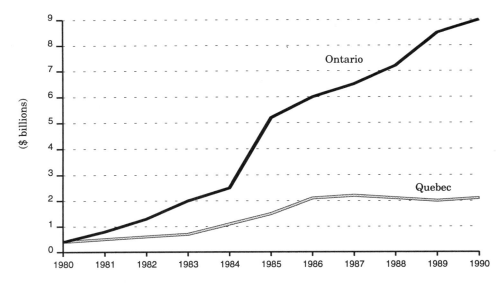

Source: Jérôme-Forget 1993.

(More recent data put Ontario's workers' compensation unfunded debt at
$11.5 billion.) As Jérôme-Forget (1993) points out, some of this is due to
generous indexation of benefits and some relates to the marked increase in the
duration of injuries. In terms of the latter, Jérôme-Forget (1993, 58–59) notes:

> In Quebec in 1988 the average time spent off the job due to injury was
> 43.6 days. By 1991, this had increased by 69 percent to 73.9 days. Such a
> dramatic jump cannot be accounted for by increased risks alone: through this
> period, progress has been made on improving occupational health and safety,
> and automation in the workplace has relieved workers of many of the riskier
> tasks in the manufacturing sector.

Intriguingly, the decision of the Ontario Workers' Compensation Board to press
ahead with its expensive new headquarters (in spite of its massive debt over-
hang) may finally direct some needed attention to the operations of the WCBs
across the provinces, not only in their own right but also in terms of how they
relate to overall social policy. As Jérôme-Forget (1993, 59) concludes:

> It is obvious that workers' compensation costs are becoming an important
> factor in the cost of production. For instance, the mean cost to the manufac-
> turing sector of WCB contributions is 2 percent of production outlays in
> British Columbia and 3.12 percent in Quebec.

According to a comprehensive survey of US employers, workers' compensation costs are out of control. Costs in the United States for workplace accidents were said to have reached $60 billion in 1990. Fully 60 percent of manufacturers surveyed in the US claim that the cost of workers' compensation would influence their decision on whether to settle in one state as opposed to another.

The good news is that cost containment strategies can and do work. The BC Board has been able to control costs and is in the enviable position of having a surplus in the bank to alleviate pressures in difficult times. BC pays only 75 percent of gross income [see Table 24 — TJC] and has put in place a rehabilitation program that seems far more effective than most.

One trusts that WCBs will no longer escape the attention of social and economic policy analysts. Of importance here is the forthcoming conference volume on workers' compensation from the Industrial Relations Centre of Queen's University edited by Thomason and Chaykowski (1994).

Summary Comments

Social welfare policies and programs vary markedly across provinces. No two provinces have identical approaches to eligibility, to determining need, or to calculating benefits. Moreover, all provinces are increasingly concerned that their welfare rolls are filling up with able-to-work persons. Some of this is obviously recession related. However, some also is incentive-related (in terms of the nature of welfare programs) and skills related (in terms of individuals). What is emerging is a series of experiments across the provinces in the dual directions of emphasizing skills development and providing more appropriate incentives to facilitate the welfare-to-work transition. In later chapters, the focus will be on whether these initiatives are enough or whether more dramatic changes are likely to be required.

Training and Skills Formation

Now that the analysis has focused, in varying degrees of thoroughness, on UI, on PSE, and on welfare, the stage is set for a discussion and analysis of the training and skills challenges facing Canadians in this increasingly global and information/knowledge era. Admittedly, focusing on training at this juncture of the monograph is "leap frogging" the analytical flow, in the sense that the detailed discussion of the impact of globalization and the knowledge/information revolution for a range of social policy issues, including the training or skills development imperative, occurs in Chapter 8. Many of the insights in Chapter 8 are, however, already in the public domain — the shift from a resource-based economy to a human-capital based economy, the "professional" orientation of Canadian society replete with a lack of respect for (and of training infrastructure for) para-professionals and technologists, the resulting "disappearing" middle class as the labor market becomes increasingly polarized, and so on.

While my personal biases are doubtless apparent in virtually every aspect of this monograph, nowhere are they stronger than with respect to the woeful and wasteful way in which Canadian society has attempted to address the skills competency of individual Canadians. When resources and raw materials ruled the roost, Canada had little difficulty in ensuring that it ranked in the very top echelon of global economies. In the new world order, we will be able to regain and maintain such status only to the extent that the skills and knowledge of our people can command high incomes. The status quo is serving Canadians poorly here. Maxwell (1994, 235) has captured my concerns in a direct and powerful way — Canada has latched onto the worst of both worlds, as it were: "a secondary school system that does not prepare young people for work and a training system that does not compensate for that failure."

What all of this means is that one cannot redress the training/skills/human capital inadequacies by focusing solely on redressing training or skills formation policies. The problem goes way deeper and is intimately intertwined with the manner in which we design and deliver education, welfare, and UI. The challenges here are formidable in that there is, arguably, no other area that is more caught up in the federal-provincial tug-of-war than is training. At the same time, it is also the case that nowhere in the social envelope is it more important to rethink programs and processes from the "bottom up" (from the vantage point of individual Canadians) and to realign such programs in the areas of primary and secondary education, PSE, welfare, and UI so that they are consistent with a skills-formation culture.

Prior to proceeding, at least three caveats are in order. First, we ought to celebrate the fact that Canada does an excellent job at the high (professional) end of the knowledge/skills continuum. This is not at issue in what follows.

Second, there is to my surprise rather strong resistance to a move toward a training culture. Much of this takes the form of a straightforward question: training for what? Underlying this question is the assumption that much of what ails Canada is a demand-side problem, not a supply-side (skills) problem. It is no doubt true that the best social policy is a fully employed economy. Moreover, when labor markets are tight, the returns to training and, more generally, to an "active" labor market policy are not only more apparent but more immediate. But if all that is needed is a demand-side focus, then we would not be in the situation where an aggregate deficit in the $60 billion range cannot drive unemployment rates below double-digit levels. My position is that we have no alternative but to remake Social Canada in a manner consistent with the emerging global economic order. Implicit in this is the assumption that, if we put in place an appropriate social and human capital infrastructure, then physical capital investment will be forthcoming. Moreover, the correct way to view the demand side is that the global demand for Canadian products is potentially infinite if we can but meet the test of competitiveness. Training and skills development is not a panacea, but it is surely a critical part not only in terms of specific programs but in the more general sense of making the inevitable transition from a resource-based mentality to a human-capital or knowledge-based mentality.

The third caveat may well be the most telling: I am far from an expert on most of these issues. In particular, I am not *au courant* when it comes to the myriad training programs and schemes that have been proposed and/or implemented over the last few decades. For this reason, I shall draw rather heavily on recent papers by Maxwell (1994) and Dupré (1994) as well as the Economic Council of Canada (1992a). However, I have come away from a casual look at the literature with the impression that, in general terms, these programs and our overall approach to skills enhancement have been sadly lacking — what else is one to assume when presented with evidence to the effect that there is a 44 percent illiteracy rate in Newfoundland (Makin 1994).

While there will be some reference to past approaches (for example, the "procurement federalism" section that follows), much of the discussion-*cum*-analysis will be forward looking and rather general in nature, with an emphasis not so much on what might constitute an ideal training program or set of programs but on what might constitute an environment sufficiently fertile to encourage the development of a training culture.

The Nature of the Challenge

It is not difficult to document what ails Canada on the training or learning front. Among the concerns that can be gleaned from the literature are the following:

- high secondary school dropout rates;
- Canadian students' performances are mediocre by international comparison (one example of which is apparent from Figure 12 above);
- an unacceptable level of illiteracy;
- private sector spending on training that is low compared with other industrialized countries (see Figure 16).
- an apprenticeship system that is narrowly focused, provides little guarantee of consistent standards, and has few established links to the education system (see Table 27 for a comparison between West Germany and Canada); and
- evidence that the quality of education has been declining over time.

Figure 16: *Private Sector Training Expenditures,*
Various Countries

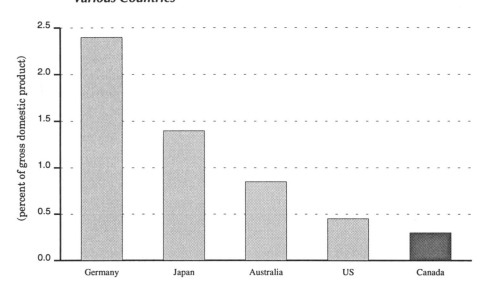

Not surprisingly, the results are fairly predictable (some of which have been noted earlier in other contexts):

- a growing segmentation of the labor market and the polarization of jobs and earnings (see Beach and Slotsve 1994; Vaillancourt 1994);
- an increase in long-term unemployment;
- a widening of potential regional disparities in the sense that certain regions are more at risk in this process than others;
- an increasingly reliance on income support programs that do not mesh well with the training imperative and that tend to be financed via payroll taxes which further diminishes the income (earnings) prospects of low-skilled Canadians.

Perhaps more seriously, there is another polarization developing. Under the pressures of the debt and deficit overhang and the competitive environment following in the wake of the free trade agreements with the United States and Mexico, and because of our inappropriate policies in these various areas, my perception is that corporate Canada is coming to view Social Canada more and more as a "cost" that ought to be minimized, rather than as an investment in the future of Canada and Canadians.

Table 27: *Apprenticeship Statistics,*
          Canada and West Germany, 1987

	Canada	West Germany
Population (millions)	25.6	61.2
Labor force (millions)	12.8	29.4
Apprentices		
Total number (thousands)	122	1,800
As a proportion of the labor force (percent)	0.95	6.1
Average age of apprentices (years)	26	17
Length of apprenticeship (years)	4–5	2–3
Cost of apprenticeship[a] ($ thousands)	170	51
Apprenticeship wages ($ thousands)	120	25

[a] The apprenticeship programs examined here lasted five years in Canada and three and a half years in West Germany. The cost of apprenticeship includes the wages of apprentices.

Source: Economic Council of Canada 1992a , 21.

In more general terms, there appear to be two sorts of generic failures in the system. The first falls under the heading of inefficient or ineffective school-to-work transitions. Table 28 presents alternative philosophies with respect to this school-to-work transition.

The second generic failure has to do with the inadequacy, if not the perversity, of the UI/welfare-to-work transition. Most of these issues have already been alluded to — the income support rather than active labor market mentality, the "entrapment" nature of the incentives in UI/welfare, the self-defeating manner of financing much of the income support system, and so on. While there have been some recent provincial proposals — by Newfoundland and New Brunswick, for example — that attempt to redress this UI/welfare-to-work subsystem, there has been little in the way of provincial innovations in what is probably the "core" problem — namely, the school-to-work transition.

Procurement Federalism

Turning now to training, *per se*, in a recent paper Dupré (1994) waxes eloquently on what he refers to as the "day before yesterday" approach or the "procurement federalism" approach to training that was inaugurated during the Pearson era:

Table 28: *Models of the School-to-Work Transition*

	Market Model	**Institutional Model**	
Premises	human-capital theory; individual competition on free markets ⇒ better worker/job matching	signal and information networks theories; institutional relations ⇒ importance of information and confidence in partners	
Representative countries	Canada, United States	Germany	Japan
Type of administrative control	decentralized	decentralized	centralized
Formal involvement of educational institutions in the transition process	none	growing, but still limited	strong at all school levels ⇒ preliminary employee screening by teachers
Formal involvement of employers in the transition process	none	strong, but government employment services important as intermediary	strong and direct⇒ relationships between companies and schools
Signals sent by employers to students	vague, no clear criteria or general values; not much consideration for high school grades	clear ⇒ direct link between academic results and "quality" of apprenticeship positions	precise and standardized ⇒ academic marks accorded high importance
Signals received by young people	confused, if any ⇒ no incentive/motivation for school work; weak relationship between marks and quality of jobs	clear ⇒ strong incentive to work hard; school streaming takes marks into account	clear, teachers used as relay
Main means of entry to first job	friends: 27.7% (in the US) family: 15.7%	(not available)	school: 49.2% family: 11.6%
Company recruitment policy	according to immediate need	according to need, but considering the social role of hiring young people	regular and annual
Layoff practice	fast, based on seniority; young people go first	constrained by legislation and collective agreements; major role for work councils	last resort only; then emphasis on pre-retirement
Unemployment rates: young people (15–24)/ total population (1990)	United States: 10.7%/5.4% Canada: 12.8%/8.1%	Germany: 8.1%/7.1% (1987)	Japan: 4.3%/2.1%

Source: Economic Council of Canada 1992a, 47.

What was the day before yesterday's approach to labor market training? It was Tom Kent's brainchild, the conceptually innovative program of adult occupational training launched by the newly created Department of Manpower and Immigration in 1966. Fiscal federalism was out; procurement federalism was in. The longstanding shared-cost programs that had linked the old Training Branch of the federal Department of Labour to the like-minded vocational education divisions of provincial Departments of Education were abruptly terminated. Henceforth, the federal government would purchase, at full cost, training courses for adults selected by its community-based employment counsellors on the basis of these counsellors' assessment of their clients' attitudes and future employment prospects. The desired training could be purchased either from public institutions under provincial control or from private sources. (Ibid., 251.)

But this program runs into our perennial challenge — federal-provincial relations:

In brief, what happened was that the provincial Departments of Education interposed themselves between the federal adult occupational training program and postsecondary institutions, and forced federal officials to deal with them as "exclusive brokers" of training courses. Provincial insistence on exclusive brokerage not only hobbled private sector trainers as potential competitors; it forced the formation of bilateral federal-provincial committees where the so-called purchase and sale of training became a negotiated, shared-cost planning process that made labor market needs subservient to provincial institutional and enrollment strategies. The federal economists, those would-be purchasers of training as a labor market adjustment tool, were trumped by the provincial educationists. (Ibid.)

Maxwell (1994, 245, fn 9.) is even more direct on this point: "it seems that they [the provinces] were prepared to protect teaching staff at the expense of providing relevant training." In the jargon of this monograph, this is a "top-down" social policy, catering to the "needs" of government rather than of people.

From Dupré's vantage point, the key to more effective procurement federalism is to recognize that institutions are such a formidable constituency on the supply side of labor market training that they must be balanced by an equally strong constituency on the demand side, an essential part of which is a wide-open procurement approach that does not discriminate between public and private suppliers. Dupré sees a further advantage to such an approach:

A tough-minded, wide-open procurement approach to labour market training is precisely what can rescue the university-college interface from the waste-land it has been, especially in Ontario. To the extent that the knowledge society generates unmet demand for para-professionals and super-technologists, this need can only be met by graduates of programs that will be joint university-college endeavours. The cold cash offered by a determined buyer will do more to promote such joint endeavours than all the exhortations in all the reports that could ever be written on the university-college interface. (Dupré 1994, 252–253.)

Some version of procurement federalism is a rather natural outgrowth of a situation where, as Maxwell (1994) notes, the provinces have jurisdiction over education, apprenticeship, industrial standards, and 90 percent of the labor force but where Ottawa accounts for the dominant share of government spending on labor markets and training (Table 29). More generally, training is the one area where Canadians will not be able to avoid revisiting the concepts of the constitutional and referendum debates — devolution, asymmetry, and the internal economic union. Most of the remaining discussions of training initiatives will take place under this rubric.

Training, Federalism, and the Economic Union

The Canadian Labour Force Development Board

The most innovative recent institutional development was the formation of the Canadian Labour Force Development Board (CLFDB) in 1991. As Maxwell (1994, 235–236) elaborates:

> The underlying principle was simple: transfer the responsibility for design and delivery of training to the private sector — to labor, business and the equity-seeking groups appointed to the Board. This national board was to be matched by provincial boards (which would mobilize and coordinate all provincial inputs to the training system) and by community level boards which would be responsible for determining which courses would be offered locally and who would qualify for them. The whole exercise was intended to be a vehicle for putting all the federal and provincial training resources into one pot. Eventually, it was hoped that there would be a "single window" for training, placement and counselling at the community level....
>
> Thus was launched one of the most important institution-building exercises of the 1990s — an effort to reform the training system *and* to build a bridge of cooperation between business and labor leaders. This was an ambitious task, and it is important to recognize that the pathway was strewn with institutional barriers — the ongoing federal-provincial turf war; the reluctance of federal and provincial officials to delegate their functions to a private board; and the total lack of experience of the labor market partners

Table 29:   *Sources of Funds for Vocational Training,*
                  fiscal year 1988/89

	($ billions)	(percent)
Federal[a]	$2.1	60%
Provincial	1.1	31
Fees	0.2	6
Other	0.1	2
Subtotal	3.4	
Employer-based training (1991)[b]	3.6[c]	

[a] Since the passage of Bill C-21 in 1990, over $1.5 billion in additional funds from the UI system are being applied to training, despite a general pattern of expenditure cuts.

[b] Government subsidies covered about 9 percent of employer expenditures on training other than apprenticeship; 20 percent of apprenticeship training was funded by governments and a further 19 percent was jointly funded by the employer and governments.

[c] The 1991 National Training Survey estimated structured training expenditures by the private sector at $3.6 billion based only on those organizations that provided actual or estimated structured training costs. The margin of error for the $3.6 billion estimate is in excess of 50 percent. Only half of the 8,000 organizations that provided detailed training information were able to provide usable information on training costs and only 13 percent of organizations providing training reported actual costs.

Source: Maxwell (1994.

in working together, let alone with the equity and educational groups also participating.

What is also intriguing about this development is that, while it represents a potential "devolution" of power, it is not a devolution to the provinces, *per se*, but rather to community or provincial level boards that would represent business, labor, the provincial government, the federal government, and other interests. On the optimistic front, New Brunswick has designed its own LFDB along the lines of the federal board so it is likely that it can be the principal channel (and single window) for federal training funds flowing into the province. Ontario was already in the process of rationalizing its training structure in the form of the Ontario Training and Development Board (OTAB) when the CLFDB was formed, so that their roles are different. In particular, OTAB has line responsibility for designing and delivering programs; it was not designed to channel federal funds into Ontario. Moreover, Dupré (1994) senses a serious design fault surrounding OTAB, since the minister to whom OTAB reports is also the minister responsible for Ontario's colleges and universities. This does not augur well for what is vital to effective procurement practices — an arm's-length relation between purchasers and suppliers. OTAB is probably not the answer, but these are still early days with respect to such initiatives, and the general directions are surely appropriate.

Standards

Integral to the functioning of an internal common market for skills is the existence of a set of mutually recognized training and occupational standards. In general, however, there are few training standards in Canada. Maxwell (1994) notes that fewer than 30 occupations are certified under the federal Red Seal program, which means that they are accepted by all provinces, and these 30 are largely occupations associated with construction and the "old economy." Maxwell then adds:

> [D]eveloping standards will be an immense task. We probably need standards for 400 occupations. In Germany, it takes about two years for the social partners to agree on the standard for one occupation. No province can afford either the time or the money required to do all 400. No country can run an effective training system without them. Why not cooperate? The actual programs being delivered will vary according to the needs of each community, but once a Canadian has completed the program in Nanaimo, her qualifications should be recognized in all parts of the country. (Ibid., 239–240.)
>
> It is important to note that the provinces have already had 35 years, since the need was first recognized, to develop these standards. And the federal government, which has no jurisdiction, has continued to fund training despite this pitiful performance. The [Canadian Labour Market and Productivity Centre] Task Force on Apprenticeship, composed of labor, business and educational representatives, issued a scathing report in 1990 in which it recommended that the federal government should give the provinces three more years to develop standards for all apprenticeship programs. After that, the Task Force said, funding should be cut off.

I agree. If the provinces wish greater powers in the training area, then they have to accept the responsibility that goes with these powers and one aspect of this responsibility is the development of processes that permit skill transferability across provinces.

Asymmetry

While standards are critical to a successful training and apprenticeship system — and so is portability — the fact remains that it is most unlikely Canada could end up with a "centralized" approach to training and all its forward and backward linkages. Training and apprenticeship have to have close and logical linkages with schooling (both secondary and PSE), with the incentives in and structure of the welfare system, and with the needs of the associated industrial economy. Even apart from the special situation posed by Quebec, the economic diversity of Canada's regions likely will call for different integration priorities. This is especially important because, *a priori*, there is no one best approach to this general area. We need to experiment and let the winning strategies be imported to the other regions/provinces.

The remaining critical element in this equation is the UI system. New Brunswick and Newfoundland now have formal proposals for integrating federal UI into what University of Western Ontario's Bob Young calls the WUTE subsystem (welfare, unemployment insurance, training, and education). The provinces are the logical level for this integration to take place because they control education and welfare. But some provinces are probably unable or unwilling to undertake this integration. Either Ottawa will have to provide the lead in these provinces or the provinces will have to forge alliances to make the integration cost effective.

But, as Maxwell (1994) notes, the role of the federal government here is to begin to use the leverage that comes from being a major funder — leverage in terms of standards, portability, accountability and access or opportunity for all Canadians. This latter aspect merits further attention.

Individuals and the Canadian Economic Union

It is intriguing that, in discussions relating to preserving and promoting the Canadian economic union, the *cause célèbre* has typically been Moosehead beer and the barriers that until recently have precluded non-Maritimers from buying it. To be sure, the free flow of goods across provincial boundaries is important to our economic future, but as the knowledge economy becomes more entrenched, the free flow of persons and labor across boundaries becomes increasingly important. As already noted, some of this has to do with mutually recognized standards for training and certification. However, we must be willing to address a more fundamental and sensitive issue: do all Canadians have roughly equivalent access to avenues and opportunities to develop and enhance their human capital? Or, and here is the sensitive part, are some Canadians becoming "human capital prisoners" of the policies of their respective provinces? As part of the earlier analysis of the PSE sector, there was a focus on the potential role of portable vouchers as a vehicle for encouraging competition and restructuring of the sector. The analysis went as far as to suggest that the cash component of EPF that relates to PSE could be converted to a transfer to students and incorporated in this voucher. This proposal also has merit in the present context: the federal component of the voucher would ensure portability from the system's standpoint and enhance access and opportunity from the individual's standpoint. The remedy also accords well with one of Maxwell's

(1994, 243) conclusions: "the central problem with the fiscal arrangements for education and training is that the federal government has been writing cheques for services without specifying or monitoring desired outcomes." I do not think that Ottawa ought to have much of a role in determining the design and delivery aspects of specific training programs, but it must be willing to live up to its responsibility associated with ensuring equality of access and opportunity for all Canadians.

Toward this end, it is absolutely essential that the Canadian economic union incorporate national accreditation of skills and their free flow across the country. This ought to be a right inherent in citizenship and not an area where balkanization is permitted. If the provinces do not act, then Ottawa must. Notwithstanding our experience with referendums, I predict that a constitutional referendum to this effect would pass with flying colors. But Ottawa need not go this far. A straightforward court challenge to a discriminatory provincial skills-licensing provision would surely succeed, given that the judges are now seeped in the rhetoric of free trade. Indeed, even the hint of such action should push the provinces into a European-type "mutual recognition" compact. The essential point is that, in an increasingly skills-intensive world, individual Canadians must have the opportunity to acquire training that is accredited and transferable across the country. This is integral to a bottom-up approach to social policy.

Other Issues in Training

Much of the above discussion of training has been conducted in the context of integrating UI, welfare, and PSE on the one hand, and with facilitating the transition to the paid labor force on the other. However, critical to the development of a training or skills culture is an enhanced degree of partnership between industry and the vocational aspect of training in the secondary school system. The Economic Council of Canada (1992a, 19) comments favorably on the interface between Quebec industry and the CEGEPs:

> In Quebec, some 15 CEGEPs provide courses designed to impact the latest skills and techniques pertinent to local industries. These range from fibre optics and laser technology in the association between Bombardier and the La Pocatière CEGEP, to mineral technology in the asbestos industry, and fashion design at Collège La Salle, a private institution. What is especially important, in these Quebec examples, is the role of private firms. Local businesses transfer recent technology to the colleges by providing machinery, equipment and staff; and the colleges train technicians to work in the local industries. The bulk of the costs of the public college system are usually covered by the province; typically, less than 10 percent is raised from fees.

But in Quebec's industry/ college partnerships, 50 percent of project costs, on average, is covered by participating enterprises.

While this quote refers to Quebec's CEGEPs, which are a transition institution from a (shortened) secondary school system to either occupational training or university, this degree of integration should begin to move down into the vocational component of secondary school education. This would serve to complete the interactive feedback loop among education, income support/insurance, training, and work. Moreover, this conception of the overall training subsystem would lend support to the earlier proposal — namely, that given the nature of the feedbacks, the responsibility for integrating training should fall to the provinces with Ottawa providing the necessary framework policies and environment.

My final comment on training may catch some readers by surprise. It is motivated by the belief that in this new era we need to lever off our societal assets, whatever and wherever they may be. In the area of training, there is clearly one institution that has done this very well — the military. On the occupational front, the evidence is that roughly 80 percent of civilian jobs have a military counterpart. Would it be possible or would it make economic sense for civilian Canada to access aspects of this significant training capacity of Canada's military? Courchene and Campbell (1994) have undertaken some exploratory research relating to this potential. Our tentative conclusion is that the possibility exists for much closer coordination and cooperation between the military and civilian training establishments, particularly given that the military is likely to have substantial excess training capacity in this period of downsizing.

But even if, in the final analysis, such interaction may prove inappropriate or noneconomic, the important issue is the one raised earlier: in this paradigm shift from the old conception of the social envelope to the new one, it is critical that we be open enough to draw on our inherent strengths wherever they may be. For example, it would appear foolish to close down the communications and electronics training center at CFB Kingston only to realize a few years down the line that we need to recreate a civilian equivalent somewhere.

Health Care

If there is a "sacred cow" in the social policy arena, it is clearly medicare (which I shall use as a generic term for health care). Tuohy (1994, 207) elaborates on this "symbolic" aspect of medicare as follows:

Polls have consistently demonstrated that medicare is by far the most popular public program in Canada. A 1988 cross-national poll showed that Canadians were more satisfied with their health care system than were either American or British respondents, and that they overwhelmingly preferred the Canadian system to the British or the American. A large majority of American respondents, on the other hand, preferred a Canadian-style system to their own....Subsequent polls have reinforced these results....This level of public support exists not only because of the tangible benefits that medicare yields, though that is clearly an important factor. It exists also because medicare is a central part of Canadian public mythology. It has become an important element by which Canadians distinguish themselves from other nations, and particularly from the United States. During the heated and wrenching public debate over the Free Trade Agreement with the United States in 1988, politicians opposing the agreement repeatedly invoked medicare as one of the things that distinguished Canada from the United States, and alleged that it was threatened by the agreement. Public opinion polls showed that this allegation was the most effective way of galvanizing opposition to the FTA.... Given the volatility of symbolic politics, it is difficult to judge how tightly the mythological status of Canadian medicare constrains fundamental constitutional change. But it is fair to say that proposing structural change in medicare, especially in the direction of the "American" model of managed competition now gaining increasing prominence on the policy landscape, carries great political risk.

The thrust of the Tuohy analysis is that the combination of this symbolic aspect of medicare in tandem with the distributional (vested interest) aspect implies that we will not likely see much in the way of fundamental change in the design and delivery of medicare. Simeon (1994) offers a similar view of the entire social envelope, which I shall elaborate in the following chapter. While not in any way underestimating these powerful symbolic and distributional factors, my view is that the fiscal crunch is such that fundamental change is not only inevitable but already well under way. Admittedly, some of this presumed difference in viewpoints may well be semantic, that is, turning around the definition of what constitutes fundamental change. In any event, the purpose of this section is to focus on some of the fault lines in medicare and to isolate the nature of some of the emerging forces.

Myth versus Reality

National Standards

Canadians may well value medicare highly, but in doing so they harbor a view of medicare that does not always square with reality.

The first myth is that medicare is driven by "national standards." What is true is that the 1984 *Canada Health Act* reinforced the five previously existing principles — public administrative, comprehensiveness, universality, portability, and accessibility. The act also allowed the federal minister of health to withhold cash transfers from provinces that contravened the act. At issue were the imposition of user fees and the practice of extra billing, both of which were prohibited under the act. However, as Boothe and Johnston (1993, 7) point out, these five principles do not constitute a meaningful national standard defined as a set of health care services common to citizens of all provinces. In more detail:

> [S]ince insured health services are defined by the Act simply as "all medically necessary services," each province has been free to determine which services are medically necessary. An examination of provincial health plans shows significant differences in what services are insured in each province; these differences exist both in hospital services and in medical services provided by doctors outside of hospitals. Together with the variation in spending levels [documented later — TJC], this variation in the mix of services provided shows that the provinces have been little constrained by the putative national standards of the *Canada Health Act* in managing health care restraint. (Ibid., 8.)

Among the recent initiatives in the various provinces (drawn largely but not entirely from Boothe and Johnston 1993) are the following:

- A trend toward closing hospital beds. Between 1990 and 1991, the number of hospital beds in Newfoundland was cut by 8.9 percent and Ontario cut beds by 2.9 percent. More recently, Saskatchewan has closed or restructured 52 hospitals, one of which had not yet opened.
- A movement in many provinces toward de-insuring some services. Insured services are, as already noted, not uniform across provinces: abortions are not available in Prince Edward Island. Ontario is the only province where *in vitro* fertilization is insured.
- Some provinces have instituted "global caps" on medicare budgets.
- Quebec is proposing to put physicians at university hospitals on salary rather than fee for service.
- Ontario has reduced out-of-country payments for long-duration stays, which effectively means that persons going south for the winter have to buy private insurance.
- Queen's University's medical school and its three associated hospitals are embarking on a pilot project under which funding that now flows to the Faculty of Medicine and its members from many sources will be replaced by a single envelope. In particular, this will eliminate fee-for-service fund-

ing and remove the incentive to maximize fee-for-service activities and associated costs as a major basis for funding academic medicine. Among the potential benefits is enhanced management of health care costs through optimization of physician encounters and procedures and, it is hoped, increased opportunities and incentives for other health care professionals to do work currently provided by physicians. In the words of the Dean's Letter (Queen's University 1992, 2) this alternative funding plan will "establish one-stop shopping for the Faculty and our affiliated hospitals with respect both to our financing and our accountability for productivity, and for the government with respect to the educational, research, and clinical services we and our members provide...in southeastern Ontario." This experiment is unique in North America and may well have significant implications for the evolution of physician care and physician payment.

As the fiscal purse strings tighten, these variations will surely intensify. Perhaps this is not fundamental change in the Tuohy (1994, 203) sense, since she notes that while there are cross-province variations in costs, supply, and utilization, "what is remarkable is that variation is not greater than it is, given the loose constraints of the federal legislation."

Beyond this, however, there have been significant structural/institutional changes in at least six provinces as a result of a series of provincial health commissions. Table 30 summarizes the new structure in these six provinces. Saskatchewan and British Columbia have transferred decisionmaking power to local boards. Manitoba has undergone greater centralization, strengthening the role of bureaucratic professionals and the research community. The remaining provinces have created or strengthened regional boards. Underlying these reorganizations are a host of other important changes that are as significant as the altered structures themselves (see Hurley, Lomas, and Bhatia 1993). Amid these differences, the authors point to one important commonality:

> All the provinces that create regional and/or local governance institutions adopt systems of closed funding envelopes. Within such systems of "restrained local government," the noncentral bodies have discretion in allocating their budgets, but the center restricts the size of the budgets. (Ibid., 11.)

They conclude by remarking (p. 23) that "more so than at any time in medicare's history the provinces have embarked down divergent paths within the framework established by the Medical Care Act and the Canada Health Act."

One might add that, in Saskatchewan's case at least, each of the 30 regional/local boards will have access to a massive information bank relating to general socio-economic data (demographics, family types, rural/urban breakdown) to medical and hospital data (number of patient days, types of medical and hospital services in fine detail, the specialist/general practitioner breakdown, and so on) and to drug use (number and type of prescriptions). This is only one aspect of how modern technology will alter management of health care in Canada. It allows managers to detect different physician practice in different parts of the province and provides data appropriate for future rationalization of the system.

Expenditure by Province

Somewhat related to the issue of national standards is that per capita spending on health varies quite substantially across provinces. The first two columns of Table 31 present total health expenditures per capita for 1991. These data incorporate private as well as provincial government spending on health care. Ontario, Saskatchewan, and British Columbia top the list, and all five westernmost provinces spend more than the five easternmost provinces. Focusing only on provincial spending and using a different data base, Boothe and Johnston (1993) find even greater disparities (see Figure 17). Nonetheless, the same general pattern exists.

These differing per capita expenditures by province need not imply differing levels of services, since the cost of a given service may also vary in the same proportion. The last two columns of Table 31 contain a comparison of physician fee schedules for all provinces but Quebec. Care must be taken with these comparisons because they represent a composite of service mixes (national or Ontario practice profiles). In general, there seems to be a positive correlation between these data and those in, say, Figure 17 in that the three provinces with the highest fee schedules are also the provinces with the highest level of per capita provincial health expenditures.

International Comparisons

As a percent of GDP, Canada spends much less on health than does the United States — 8.8 percent versus 11.2 percent (see Table 32). While Canada spends more than France, Germany, Japan, and Britain on health, the proportion of this spending from the public sector is lower for Canada. Of more interest, however, is the pattern of private and public expenditure on health within Canada. As Tuohy (1994, 192–193) notes:

> In most other nations public and private expenditures are divided on a "tiered" basis — with private alternatives to publicly funded services *within* each category of service. In Canada, however, public and private expenditures

Table 30: *Elements of Restructured Provincial Health Care Governance Systems*

	British Columbia	Saskatchewan	Manitoba
Provincial level	Ministry of Health	Ministry of Health	Ministry of Health
	Health Council	Health Council	
	Composition unspecified	*Composition* 12–15 individuals representing • consumers • urban/rural • labor/business • educators • interest groups	
Regional level	Regional Health Boards *Composition* • representatives of the region's Community Health Councils • appointees of Minister of Health		
Local level	Community Health Council Boards *Composition* • elected community representatives • appointees of Minister	Local Health District Boards *Composition* • 8 elected community representatives • 4 appointees of Minister from community nominees	

Table 30: *Elements of Restructured Provincial Health Care Governance Systems* - cont'd.

	Quebec	New Brunswick	Nova Scotia
Provincial level	Ministry of Health	Ministry of Health	Ministry of Health
			Health Council
			Composition 12 Ministry appointees representative of Nova Scotian society
Regional level	18 Regional Health and Social Service Boards	8 Regional Hospital Boards	6 Regional Health Agencies
	Composition • 20 elected from Regional Assembly • executive director • Regional Medical Commission representative • 1–2 co-opted from Assembly by board	*Composition* Voting: •3–4 appointees of Minister •members selected according to regional hospital bylaws •2–3 others selected by board	*Composition* 12–18 appointees of Minister • representative of users/ providers • nomination process present
	18 Regional Assemblies	Nonvoting: •CEO of Regional Hospital Corp. •Regional Director of Medical Staff	

	Composition
	• up to 150 in specified proportions representing:
	  • institutions
	  • community organizations
	  • socioeconomic groups
	  • municipalities		

Local level			

Source: Hurley, Lomas, and Bhatia 1993, 12.

Table 31:   *Comparative Provincial Health Costs*

| | Total Health Expenditures per capita, 1991 | | Physician Payment Schedule Comparison, 1990[a] | |
	Amount ($)	as % of Canadian Average	National Practice Profile	Ontario Practice Profile
Newfoundland	2,107	0.88	0.89	0.83
Prince Edward Island	2,140	0.90	0.87	0.87
Nova Scotia	2,248	0.94	1.05	1.07
New Brunswick	2,107	0.88	0.89	0.89
Quebec	2,282	0.96	—	—
Ontario	2,511	1.05	1.15	1.15
Manitoba	2,373	0.99	0.91	0.92
Saskatchewan	2,454	1.03	1.01	1.02
Alberta	2,288	0.96	1.14	1.13
British Columbia	2,412	1.01	1.30	1.30
Canada	2,388	1.00	1.00[b]	1.00[b]

[a] These are the indexes of fee-for-service benefit rates for general practice. The first column is based on the national practice profile (weights) and the second on an Ontario practice profile. These profiles determine the weighting systems in calculating the fee-for-service benefit rates. The ten-province median is set at 1.00.

[b] Ten-province median, as noted above.

Source: Canada 1990; 1994, Table 1.2.

are segmented. Certain segments — notably medical and hospital services — are almost entirely publicly funded; others, such as dental care, drugs, and eyeglasses and other prostheses, are in the private sector....Private insurers, then, are effectively confined to certain segments of the system.

If the fiscal crunch intensifies, it would be surprising if several provinces did not take a closer look at the way in which the Europeans bring private sector funding into the core areas of medical and hospital services.

Federal Funding

While the issue of federal offloading is the subject of Chapter 7, it is instructive to focus briefly on the role of federal funding in the provision of medicare (even though these funds are, in effect, unconditional). For this purpose, I shall follow Boothe and Johnston (1993) and focus only on the cash portion of the notional EPF component relating to health. What is surprising is just how small the federal share of funding is — less than 15 percent for fiscal year 1991/92, down

Figure 17: *Health Care Spending, by Province, fiscal year 1991/92*
(percentage deviation from national average)

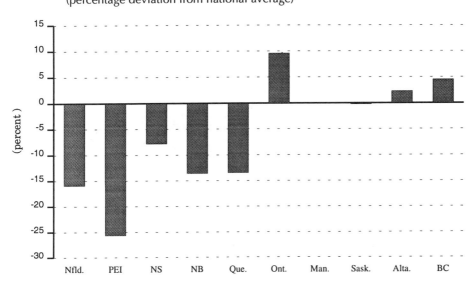

Source: Boothe and Johnston 1993, 7.

from 20 percent in 1988/89 (ibid., 5). Obviously, as the overall cash portion of EPF falls to zero (see Chapters 4 or 7), so will federal funding of health.

While many Canadians look to Ottawa as the ultimate defender of medicare, the federal government is losing its ability to dictate to the system as it pulls back on funding. Phrased differently, Ottawa's version of the "golden rule" is less and less sustainable: as it stops supplying the gold, it is also losing its moral authority to continue to make the rules. One can even find a silver lining here. Medicare does not exist now because of federal funding, although the federal role was crucial in the beginning. Rather, medicare exists because Canadians want it to exist and have made this clear to politicians of all stripes in all provinces.

Physician Practice

Canadians frequently compare Canadian and US medicine in terms of a private system and a public system, respectively. This is not correct. The US system is largely privately financed and delivered (except for areas like care for the elderly). While the Canadian system is publicly funded, it, too, is privately delivered since the doctors, with their fee-for-service payment systems, are effectively in the private sector. In other words, we have "contracted out" the delivery of medicare to self-regulated physicians. Intriguingly, one might make an argument to the effect that, in comparison with US physicians, Canadian

Table 32: *Spending on Health Care,*
Various Countries, 1989

	Total Health Care Spending	Government Health Care Spending	Government Share
	(as a percentage of gross domestic product)		
Germany	8.0	6.3	0.79
Canada	8.8	6.3	0.72
United States	11.2	4.6	0.41
France	8.5	6.4	0.75
Japan	6.8	5.0	0.73
United Kingdom	6.1	5.2	0.85
Average	8.2	5.6	0.69

Source: Canada 1992a, Table 6.15.

physicians have been willing to forgo income in order to maintain greater professional freedom — US physicians are increasingly constrained in their approach to practice by powerful third-party insurance companies. Thus, "socialized" medicine has turned out to be more consistent with professional freedom. One big difference is that the US approach to malpractice has not (yet) made significant inroads into Canada. If it ever does, watch out for cost escalation!

There are several other key differences as well. Setting aside what the future holds for the US health care system in terms of the Clinton initiative, the existing environment in the United States is characterized increasingly by health maintenance organizations (HMOs), one feature of which is "capitation," whereby a single per capita or per family fee covers all medical services. While there has been some experimentation with versions of HMOs in Canada, this approach is somewhat alien to the Canadian system because it limits physician choice on the part of citizens. Nonetheless, it does have other advantages, such as an emphasis on preventative measures and an incentive for efficient delivery within the HMO (since the up-front funding is fixed) including the use of less costly paramedics and other nonphysician personnel. In my view, it is only a matter of time before some "Canadian" version will begin to take hold.

Growth and Limits

Physician Willard Gaylin (1993) argues that, while the cost escalation in medicare can be partly attributed to technology, a more basic reason is that we have radically altered our concept of what it means to be healthy or sick. As he explains,

> the patients I deal with in my daily practice would not have been considered mentally ill in the nineteenth century. Mental illness was then rigidly defined...[Then] Freud invented a new category of mental diseases now called "neuroses," thereby vastly increasing the population of the mentally ill. Some thirty years later, Wilhelm Reich decided that one does not even have to display mental symptoms to be mentally ill, that one can suffer from "character disorders." The personalities of even completely asymptomatic individuals might so limit their productivity or pleasure in life that we are justified in diagnosing them as mentally ill. Then medicine "discovered" the psychosomatic disorders. These are people with no symptoms of mental illness who have *physical* conditions with psychic roots — peptic ulcers, ulcerative colitis, migraine headache, allergies and the like. These people, too, were now classified as mentally ill. By such sophisticated expansions of the category, we eventually managed to get some 60 percent to 70 percent (as one serious study found) of the residents of the Upper East Side of Manhattan into the population of the mentally ill.
>
> What has happened in mental health has happened across the board in medicine....Probably the best way to understand this is to consider how medicine goes about "discovering" new diseases.
>
> Most people assume that medical researchers first uncover an illness and then seek a cure for it. This, of course, does happen: the infectious diseases are the paradigm case. What is less familiar, but is becoming more common, is the opposite mechanism: we discover a cure and then find a disease to go with it....
>
> The vast expansion of the concept of health can be demonstrated in surgery, orthopaedics, gynaecology — indeed, in any field of medicine. Infertility, for example, was not considered a disease until this generation; before, it was simply a God-given condition. With the advances of modern medicine, including artificial insemination, in vitro fertilization and surrogate mothering — new cures were discovered for "illnesses" that now have to be invented. (Gaylin 1993, 60.)

Obviously, there has to be a limit to this somewhere and somehow. We simply cannot do everything for everybody. While Canadians tend, quite appropriately, to look down on some aspects of the US health system, there is one development south of the border that should be taken seriously — namely, the Oregon experience on how to make tragic choices among competing health needs. Gaylin's summary of the Oregon model is as brief, yet as comprehensive, as any:

Oregon sought to guarantee a basic health-care package to everyone; at the same time, it acknowledged that doing so would bankrupt the state unless some hard choices were made about what should constitute "basic health care." Not all health services could be included. In other words, Oregon faced up to the issue of allocation, and it did so out in the open: in a series of town meetings and a statewide "health parliament," issues of access and medical priorities were debated publicly, sometimes fiercely. The state's health commission then published a comprehensive list of medical conditions and treatments, each ranked according to its costs and benefits. More debate ensured; the list was revised. Finally, the legislature decided exactly where on the revised list the state could afford to draw the necessary cutoff line: it would pay for hip replacements and neonatal care, for example, but not liver transplants or in vitro fertilization. (Oregonians who still wanted such treatments were free to pay for them.) By conducting much of this process in public, the health commission was able to develop a consensus behind some otherwise unpopular decisions.

The Oregon plan is by no means perfect. But at least the state has addressed the uncomfortable truth that they cannot have equity in their health-care system without making anguished, even tragic choices. (Ibid., 64.)

It seems to me that Canada cannot expect to avoid the tradeoff between the ever-expanding nature of health and the consequential need, given limited resources, to place some limits on access or to make some societal rules about allocation. Different provinces may go in different directions in terms of grappling with this challenge, but a failure to address it has the potential for bringing the whole system down.

Sickness versus Health

To this point, the analysis has not really been about health care. Rather, it has been about "sickness care." One of the major recent developments has been a quite dramatic shift of attention (and some resources) away from sickness and toward health. The literature in this area is burgeoning and I shall not attempt to summarize it except to make one point. Among the findings is that socio-economic status has a major bearing on health status. At the more operational level, Quebec is, or at least was, way in the forefront here with its network of CLSCs (centres locaux de services communautaires), which, under one roof, combine medical, social, and sometimes legal services. These CLSCs are essentially engaged in primary care. Physicians can serve as the "gatekeepers," but patients will be directed to nutritionists, for example, if the problem relates to diet or to a social worker if that is the nature of the underlying problem. This system works effectively because the physicians in CLSCs are on salary, not on fee for service, so that there is no incentive not to channel the patients to the appropriate primary care professional. Much attention has been focused on this Quebec model, not only by other provinces but by other countries as well. (As a trivial aside, this focus on holistic health in Quebec may have been facilitated because Quebecers got their definitions straight — what we in Ontario refer to as health insurance, they call *assurance maladie* — that is, sickness insurance.)

This concept of holistic treatment is occurring in many provinces at the local level, but typically, as one moves up the bureaucratic ladder, this degree of integration vanishes. A few years ago, I suggested that an alternative way of organizing the bureaucracy was to place the "compensation" side of health and social services (for example, payments to hospitals, physicians, and welfare recipients) in a single "statistical" department and channel the social services side of welfare and the "well-being" side of health into a separate well-being department. This may or may not be a useful reform, but there is no question that conception of health or, rather, well-being both in and of itself and its relation to other spheres is here to stay, and this will have a significant impact on the evolution of health policy and social policy generally. In this emerging context, the *Canada Health Act* represents an unacceptable straightjacket to the evolution of our health systems.

Incentives and the Price System

Economists, more so than other policy analysts, tend to emphasize the need for altering incentives, (preferably via the price system) in health care design and delivery. I recognize that even the mention of user fees and medicare in the same breath is akin to "destroying" medicare in the minds of many, perhaps most, Canadians. Nonetheless, in as sweeping a treatment of social policy issues as is contained in this monograph, it would be inappropriate to delete any and all references to using the price system in medicare. In any event, we do use prices now in many areas.

Copayment and Ability to Pay: Drugs

In Ontario, both welfare recipients and the elderly are entitled to free drugs. While this may have once been standard fare across the provinces, it is no longer the case. In part, the march of technology is making alternative systems more feasible. As I noted a few years ago (Courchene 1989, 199):

> Saskatchewan now has a version of a "smart card" [magnetic card] in place for its drug plan. Already two interesting effects have been noted. The first is

that it has been a source of substantial savings since it is now impossible to run up a series of rapid-fire prescriptions from various doctors for the same drug. Secondly, the card is serving as a useful adjunct to the payment mechanism. Saskatchewan has an initial annual deductible — I think it is $125. Payment records are kept in the system, so that if the deductible has already been paid this fact is known and the drugs are free. This should prove to be an important convenience for the consumers (rather than waiting six weeks or so to be reimbursed) as well as for the administration of the plan.

More recently, presumably under fiscal pressure, Saskatchewan dramatically altered the nature of its drug benefit program. The new deductible is $850, beyond which citizens pay 35 percent of the cost of drugs. But there are all sorts of "catastrophic" limits to ensure that drugs remain affordable to Saskatchewan residents, based both on income and intensity of drug usage. In terms of welfare recipients, for example, there is a copayment of $2 per prescription, unless the recipient is in a nursing home in which case drugs are free, as they are for children of welfare families. In terms of the elderly, the deductible for recipients of the Guaranteed Income Supplement (GIS) is $200 (or $100 if they are in nursing homes). Note that all of this information (for example, whether on welfare or whether in receipt of GIS) is accessible to the druggist from the magnetic card.

The intriguing feature here is that high-income elderly are treated in the same manner as high-income non-elderly — that is, any special provisions (which reduce the deductible) are targeted to income, not to age. Apparently, the introduction of this scheme was not greeted with substantial protest from the elderly.

Ontario, and other provinces, ought to take note of this. In an era where large segments of the elderly will be among the middle- and upper-income echelons of Canadians, a blanket approach of free drugs to all elderly does not square with equity (or at least with ability to pay).

Copayment and Ability to Pay: Medical Services

Quebec's proposal to introduce a $5 charge for an emergency room visit during hours where alternative (and very much cheaper) clinics are available was initially labeled by federal politicians and others as the unwinding of medicare. But surely this is wrong. The fee is simply a rationing device for allocating patients to clinics (where there would be no user fee) and away from the more expensive hospital emergency rooms. Thus, while this Quebec initiative probably should not be classed as a user fee, there are, nonetheless, some user fees in the system. For example, nursing home accommodation and semi-private and private hospital rooms typically carry user fees.

With the spread of magnetic health cards, most provinces will soon be able to provide citizens with annual or semi-annual information relating to their use of medicare services. This would be valuable in its own right because it alerts citizens to the costs and benefits of health and ultimately would allow them a greater say in system evolution. As an important aside, it would also serve to enhance physician accountability. In any event, it would not be difficult to convert this usage data into some form of a taxable benefit for income tax purposes. The advantage of this approach is that the deferred fee (or tax) could be geared closely to income. For example, the taxable benefit obviously would not trigger payments from the poor. In other words, what Saskatchewan has done with its drug benefit plan could be replicated in the medicare area.

The goal would not be primarily one of economizing on health care. Rather, it would be to shift some of the financing toward users, but based on ability to pay, and away from other forms of taxation. For example, suppose that Ontario were to develop such a system that would generate sufficient revenues to allow the repeal of its health payroll tax on corporations. My view is that this would be a net benefit for Social Canada, since we would be gaining employment (reducing the payroll tax) by transferring some of the health care costs to individual Canadians based on ability to pay.

Readers are free to refer to this as a "tax on sickness" if they wish. But others are also free to view the present Ontario system as a "tax on employment." It seems to me that the issue is not so clear-cut when it is cast in the framework of what the alternatives are.

The Physician-Hospital Interface

Under the present system, there is little incentive for physicians to make "efficient" use of hospitals. Indeed, the incentives are such that physicians quite appropriately view hospitals as a free, complementary input to their own delivery of health care. There are several possible remedies for this situation. With the reduction in the number of hospital beds in the system, access is increasingly a scarce input. Why not impose a "user fee" on physicians? More generally, a case can be made for placing all physicians who work virtually full time at a hospital on salary. As Alan Hay noted nearly two decades ago (1976):

> Physicians whose work is virtually all hospital-based should not be reim-
> bursed on an open-ended, fee-for-service basis. We have suggested instead a
> negotiated salary, because it would eliminate the dilemma of the physician

whose personal income [rises] from increasing, rather than limiting, the volume of services the hospital provides.

Presumably, several of the provinces are now launched in this direction.

Physician Incentives

It has become fashionable, in some health conferences at least, to lower the boom on the medical profession in terms of diverting our resources to sick care and away from health care (for example, overprescribing drugs or engaging in costly procedures that may not be effective). While I have no intention of defending the medical profession, *per se*, this is an unfair rap, in the same way that blaming Newfoundlanders for "ripping off" UI is unfair. Both groups are reacting in exactly the way that the incentives in the system dictate. With obvious exemptions that apply to all groups, the problems here are "systemic," not professional. My best guess is that, if the system wants to emphasize health care rather than sick care, we will find that physicians will (after readjustment) eventually be in the forefront of health care, provided the incentives are appropriate. As Blomqvist (1989, 80) notes, under the present system "physicians do not derive any financial benefit from combining health inputs in an efficient manner." If one wants to place medicare in the balance, there is probably no better way than to pick a fight with physicians by devising a set of expectations for physician behavior that is completely at odds with the incentives they face in terms of the internal operations of the system.

Federalism and Medicare

In rethinking Social Canada, it might appear that medicare is a case apart — that is, off on its own with little scope for interaction with the rest of the social envelope. But this is clearly wrong. If we do not regain control of the medicare envelope, the casualties will likely be elsewhere in the social envelope. More to the point, on the delivery front, it is increasingly difficult to separate medical treatment from some of its underlying causes (drug abuse, family violence, low incomes, and so on). Focusing on this more holistic approach to medicare in terms of the overall social envelope is presumably on the priority list of all provinces.

Countries everywhere are wrestling with the challenges of health care. And so are all ten provinces. We have already focused on the recent major reorganizations in six of the provinces. But all of them are innovating, experimenting, and rationalizing in order to make design and delivery more efficient. In my view, this is cause for optimism. The fiscal pressure is such that innovations that prove successful in one province will spread across the system in the same way that Saskatchewan's innovations did more than a quarter-century ago.

Ottawa's role here is to develop some national principles within which this ongoing (and soon to mushroom) provincial experimentation will take place and then to let the system evolve. Indeed, to ensure that Ottawa is not tempted to interfere, why not convert the cash transfer associated with the health component of EPF into a further tax point transfer (*à la* Norrie 1993)? With this process in full swing, we can look forward rather confidently to the restructuring of a made-in-Canada medicare system for the millennium. This is one of the inherent strengths of a federal system.

Conclusion

While this chapter has covered a wide range of programs and issues, the analysis has barely scratched the surface in most of these areas. Moreover, some important areas were left out — social housing and social services. In terms of the latter, there was some oblique reference to it in the context of the discussion of well-being or holistic health. I would guess that social services will evolve in an integrated manner that will incorporate the full range of services — health, substance abuse, family violence, legal concerns, pre-natal nutrition, and so on. As such, it will become divorced from its current link to CAP and become a sort of one-stop depot related to well-being.

I have now focused on federal direct programs to Canadians (UI, the retirement income subsystem, the family benefits package), on provincial programs (health, education, welfare, workers compensation, and training) and on the programs that are part of the federal-provincial financial interface (EPF, CAP, and equalization). In a sense, the last three chapters have dissected these programs analytically and statistically. The task in the remaining chapters is to repackage the programs to create a social infrastructure appropriate to the needs of Canadians in the millennium. This process of restructuring Social Canada begins with a focus on the various elements relating to the political economy of social policy reform.

Part V

The Political Economy of Social Policy Reform

Chapter 6

The Political Economy of
Social Policy Reform I:
The Inertial Power of the Status Quo

This and the following two chapters focus on what I shall refer to as the political economy of social policy reform. This chapter addresses the following question: why have some critical aspects of our social infrastructure not evolved? Phrased differently, what are the series of forces that have, thus far at least, forestalled the sorts of reform that the previous chapters have alluded to? In the remaining two chapters of this trilogy, the emphasis shifts toward those factors, or sets of factors, that are facilitating or even compelling reform. Chapter 7 deals with the most obvious of these — namely, deficit shifting or federal "offloading" to the provinces. Chapter 8 presents, at long last, the analytics of the new world economic order — globalization and the knowledge/information revolution — and their implications for both Social and Economic Canada.

This chapter proceeds as follows. The first section focuses on the role of vested interests in preserving existing entitlements. As part of this analysis, focus is directed to the wage premiums favoring public sector employees. Attention then turns to the set of powerful political forces that traditionally have held the upper hand in any process of social policy reform.

At this point in the assessment of the inertial powers of the status quo, the analytical framework incorporates some of the insights from the recent macro growth literature, especially its emphasis on feedback mechanisms and path dependency. Creative destruction, *à la* Schumpeter, is an alternative way to view this perspective. Everywhere one looks in the private sector, there has been dramatic restructuring. Why has this evolution not carried over, or not carried over to a greater degree, to the social sphere? The response that the former is subject to the market and the latter to nonmarket (political/bureaucratic) forces is surely part of the answer. But it is not the full answer because nonmarket systems are also capable of evolution. In any event, the purpose is to explore the range of forces, both internal and external to the social sphere, that not only have impeded evolution but in several cases have probably served to entrench the status quo. Accordingly, attention is directed in turn to health care policy, to the role of the courts, to monopolies and sinecures, and, finally, to jurisdictional overlap. Throughout this analysis, and in the concluding section as well, there is an emphasis on some emerging countervailing forces that will challenge the status quo and tilt the social policy envelope in evolutionary directions.

Prior to proceeding, it is important to recognize a quite different set of arguments that would serve to entrench the status quo. This is that the so-called reform and restructuring of the social envelope is not really about reform or restructuring. Rather, it is about "Americanizing" Social Canada in order to level the Canadian playing field to be consistent with the North American Free Trade Agreement. No doubt, influential elements of our society might prefer an Americanization of our social envelope. And thus far, all that a dedicated social policy advocate may see is a series of caps, cuts, and freezes on the social policy front, and deficit reduction and the pursuit of zero inflation on the macro front. The "new" Social Canada is not yet in view and, from their perspective, may never materialize. While I respect this position, it is no longer tenable. The surest way to undermine and, indeed, unwind our postwar social policy accomplishments is to attempt to adhere to an outmoded social policy paradigm in the context of a dramatically altered global economic order. More to the point, I believe that the vast majority of Canadians who have major concerns about the status quo also believe very strongly in the creation of a new Social Canada. Admittedly, there are no guarantees here, but restructuring appears to be the only viable route toward a made-in-Canada social policy for the millennium.

At the same time, we should not delude ourselves. It is inevitable that the pervasiveness of government in the social policy sphere will decline somewhat and the responsibility for aspects of social policy will devolve to agents outside the public sector. I have already alluded to several examples in earlier chapters — the move by Saskatchewan and, more recently, Alberta to curtail the access of highly subsidized or free drugs to the elderly rich, the inevitable rise in tuition fees (particularly as they relate to professions where the returns to education are largely internalized in the students' future earning powers), and the need for incentives everywhere in the social envelope to shift away from dependency and toward self-reliance. These pressures are in evidence everywhere in the industrialized world and especially in traditional social democracies such as Sweden. The puzzle is why these emerging trends elsewhere have not made their mark on Social Canada.

One final introductory point: while the focus in this chapter is on why the status quo has remained so entrenched for so long, some parts of the system *have* undergone substantial evolution over the years. The shift from universal payments to tax credits and then to refundable tax credits (as in the case of family allowances) is clearly an example of creative evolution. The issue thus becomes: why has the overall system not experienced this sort of evolution?

I begin by turning to the standard economic explanation for system entrenchment — namely the "capture theory" of regulation.

The Role of Vested Interests

What has come to be known in the regulatory literature as Stigler's Law posits that regulation tends rather inevitably and invariably to be in the interests of those being regulated — that is, the regulated "capture" the regulators. Sometimes, this is cast in terms of generating "clientele" effects. In any event, deregulation becomes extremely difficult because the regulated frequently perceive themselves to have acquired quasi-proprietary rights to the status quo. (This was the theme of my 1980 Innis Lecture to the Canadian Economics Association.) This difficulty is typically magnified because the potential losers from deregulation are often a readily identifiable and concentrated group whereas the winners are not only more numerous but dispersed across the system. It obviously "pays" the former groups to invest in significant lobbying because their potential losses from deregulation are large. Not so for the potential gainers because the amount of gain on a per capita basis is typically too small to warrant an equivalent counter lobby. All of this is further complicated if the regulation in question is in the nonmarket sector because the lobbying is then focused largely in the political arena — that is, the perceived entitlements are then buttressed by political clout.

The principal proponent of this vested interest or capture theory as it relates to the social order is John Richards of Simon Fraser University (1994). Richards isolates three broad interest groups that have a substantial stake in defending the existing social order, particularly as it relates to the federal-provincial transfer system and the UI/welfare subsystem:

- public sector unions;
- groups representing the beneficiaries of major transfer programs; and
- regional alliances in "have-not" provinces.

In order to elaborate on these categories, it is instructive to note what would happen under regulation if substantial outmigration were to occur. Richards (ibid., 359) notes that such outmigration would levy losses across a broad swath of interest groups with fixed assets in "have-not" regions: "the threatened fixed assets range from the obvious (commercial real estate in communities of declining population) to the subtle (the 'style-of-life' values placed on farms by people wanting to live in stable rural communities or attractive civil service jobs, many of which could disappear with outmigration)." Richards (ibid., 360) then adds: "These alliances [across the three groups] have been a formidable obstacle to any would-be political 'entrepreneurs' advocating change. In the long run, however, 'have-not' regional alliances are unstable; countervailing alliances arise in 'have' regions." Among the countervailing alliances, one could probably point to the rise of the Reform Party or, offshore, to the support among Italians for the Northern League.

While this example relates to the "have-not" provinces, the analysis carries over to other areas of the social envelope (witness the reaction to Ontario's "social contract") and, of course, to the rest of the economy as well. At the individual or micro level, all of us presumably would prefer the status quo to a situation where we would perceive ourselves to be worse off. This may even be the case if being "worse off" applies only to the short term. But it is easier to stand up against the winds of change in some cases than in others. For example, it is difficult to counteract the march of technology. Global restructuring and the shift away from a resource-intensive economy have wrought havoc with many Canadians and even communities, but it is difficult for citizens to know where or at whom to vent their anger or frustration. However, restructuring of the social envelope is much more difficult to accomplish because citizens clearly know where to target their lobbying. While this may be rational behavior at the level of the individual or even the group, the fallacy of composition sets in once everyone gets into the act. What is true for the individual is no longer true for the aggregate — the whole may be better off if everyone backs off from their individual crusades. This is what ultimately leads to countervailing alliances.

Beyond this highlighting of the alliances against social policy restructuring, Richards' contribution is to argue that some of this is misplaced. Specifically, the public sector payroll is excessive and, therefore, represents an obvious area for both cost savings and restructuring. Basically, this is because the compensation advantage of public sector wages over comparable private sector wages (except at the very top) has become unjustifiable, even were there not the need for budgetary restraint. It is important to add that Richards is not out to unwind the welfare state. Far from it, as his concluding paragraph indicates (ibid., 363):

> A generous welfare state is one of the major achievements of industrial society in the twentieth century. It must co-exist, however, with a market economy and that implies serious analysis of the appropriate limits to be placed on each. In summary, I could state the thesis...as follows: do not confuse the case for a generous and efficient welfare state with the case for extrapolating the past quarter century's trends in public expenditure growth and, *a fortiori*, do not confuse the case with extrapolating trends in public sector collective bargaining.

While there is much of value in Richards' work that I have not attempted to summarize, the above extracts lead to several comments. First, these vested interests are indeed powerful. One need only think back to the 1985 budget where Finance Minister Michael Wilson had to backtrack on his attempt to partially de-index payments to the elderly. Second, it is probably difficult to generate change from within: some external force is probably essential. And one of the key external forces is the advent of globalization and the information revolution, as Chapter 8 will detail.

The third comment relates to the premium on public sector wages. Figure 18 presents comparisons by province for public sector (federal, provincial and municipal) and private sector wages. This figure and the following one as well are reproduced from a 1993 research report from the Canadian Federation of Independent Business (CFIB). Except for municipal wages in Prince Edward Island, these public sector premiums exist across all provinces — in Manitoba, for example, they exceed 20 percent for both federal and provincial employees. The CFIB study notes that, where the pay gaps are smaller (as in Alberta and British Columbia), this is generally a result of much higher rates of pay in the private sector compared to the national average. Government pay levels, on the other hand, were much closer to the national average (CFIB 1993, 11).

The data in Figure 18 relate only to wages. Figure 19 presents an aggregate comparison of the combination of wages, hours of work and benefits. The aggregate federal government compensation advantage exceeds 20 percent with the provincial advantage just under 20 percent. All of this is by way of lending support to Richards' claim that there ought to be concern about public sector wages and, by extension, the public sector payroll.

Detouring a bit, one might be able to mount a case that, in terms of what the Europeans refer to as "social cohesion" or what Canadians might call "horizontal equity," wage rates across the provinces ought to be fairly uniform. But the *quid pro quo* would then be that governments, particularly the federal government, would then leave the labor markets alone. Canada's problem is that we strive for national wage grids but then build a socio-economic transfer system designed in large measure to accommodate or even offset any resulting negative economic fallout associated with this wage policy. This is the "policy induced" equilibrium that featured prominently in Chapter 2 and the associated appendix.

Federalism as Regulation

Returning to the political economy of social policy reform, the University of Toronto's Richard Simeon (1984) has adopted some of these concepts from

Figure 18: *Public Sector Wage Advantages, by Province, 1991*
(percentage premium over private sector wages)

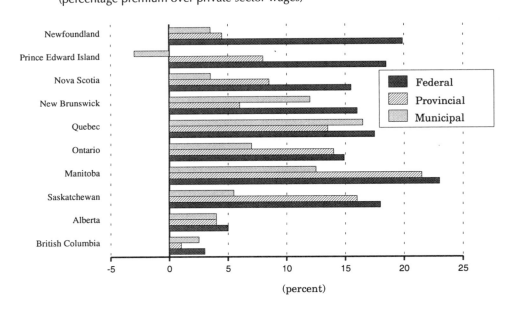

(percent)

Source: Canadian Federation of Independent Business 1993.

regulatory theory and applied them to the Canadian federal system itself. In a highly insightful paper on federalism and social policy reform, Simeon begins with the observation that issues of distribution — which, in other advanced countries might be played out in terms of class or economic sectors — are played out in Canada in terms of distribution across provinces and regions. In a sense, aspects of this observation have already been incorporated in some of the previous chapters. For example, our federation has developed a guaranteed annual income for provinces (equalization), but not for people. Another aspect of this is that any social policy problem tends quickly to become an issue of federal-provincial transfers.

However, Simeon uses this observation to articulate a series of "trumps" that characterize the Canadian federation. The first of these is that, in federal-provincial relations, the Constitution and related issues of national unity tend to trump or dominate debate on substantive, functional policy issues. The second is that regional politics trumps other dimensions of distribution; the third is that fiscal federalism trumps social policy.

These are powerful insights and even a casual glance back at our recent history will attest to their significance. In an important sense, this is the traditional "capture" theory in new raiment: federalism is a regulatory process,

Figure 19: *Total Public Sector Compensation Advantage*
over the Private Sector, 1991

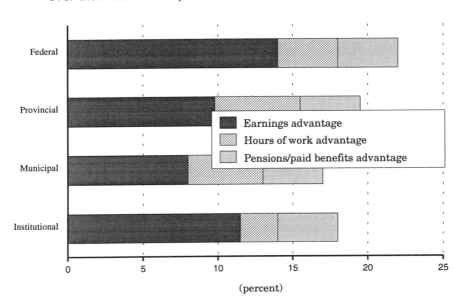

(percent)

Source: Canadian Federation of Independent Business 1993.

and the regulated — Ottawa and the provinces individually and in groups (for example, "have-not" provinces) — have captured the process at the expense of both individual Canadians and functional policy issues. In effect, it points toward a system of institutional or constitutional sclerosis that incorporates another level of vested interests or, alternatively, another "process" that has to be accommodated prior to undertaking substantive policy reform.

There is no question that this represents a significant challenge to social policy reform. In the language that will be used later, the "feedbacks" from this process tend to entrench the existing set of arrangements. More to the point perhaps, these forces will never be far from the forefront *during* any process of social policy restructuring.

Nonetheless, as I have argued elsewhere (Courchene 1994a), I do not think that these trumps will maintain their former influence. Chapters 7 and 8 are devoted to isolating a formidable set of challenges to the status quo, so much so that the underlying nature of the game has changed: fiscal stringency and the globalization/information revolution will effectively checkmate these trumps! Intriguingly, there is a second way in which this institutional sclerosis can be circumvented — namely, for major restructuring proposals to come from the have-not provinces. This is exactly what we are witnessing in the innovative (but not necessarily appropriate) social policy reform proposals coming from New Brunswick and Newfoundland. This dramatically alters the underlying regulatory dynamic because the challenge to the status quo is coming from some of the very provinces that were perceived or presumed to have "captured" the federal regulatory process. Why this has occurred, as well as an evaluation of these proposals, is the subject of Chapter 9.

In the final analysis, it may well be wishful thinking on my part that the politics of social policy reform is do-able. But then the alternative is to run into the fiscal and financial "wall" and to turn over the restructuring, in part at least, to agents outside Canada. If this is the bottom line, then I think that Canadians will realize that a made-in-Canada restructuring is preferable.

I now want to focus on some recent analytical literature relating to the process of economic and social change, and then to subject selective areas of the social envelope to this analytical framework. What will emerge is a different, perhaps even novel, perspective on the inertial power of the status quo as well as a set of countervailing forces that will tilt the system in an evolutionary direction.

Path Dependence and Positive Feedbacks

Recent developments in the literature on economic growth provide a quite different perspective from which to view the processes of change. This new growth literature speaks in terms of path dependency, positive (or negative) feedbacks, and increasing returns. From an equilibrium position, suppose that there is a new innovation in a process or product. If this innovation is deemed to be profitable, it will generate a set of feedbacks that will catapult it forward, typically at the expense of existing processes or products. This is akin to Schumpeter's creative destruction process and the dramatic restructuring of the 1980s bears witness to its powers and influence. However, because the process can involve increasing returns, initial conditions can matter. This is path dependence: the most appropriate innovation may not win out. The example, *par excellence*, is Beta versus VHS. Although Beta was (and is) arguably the preferred technology, the fact that Sony prevented the interplay of positive feedbacks (such as compatible software) caused the industry settle on VHS and effectively to leap-frog the Beta technology.

Admittedly, there are dangers in carrying over this approach to the social policy arena. Nonetheless, the remainder of the chapter will attempt to argue that these concepts can lend insights to the nonevolution of major aspects of the social envelope. I shall focus on several areas. One of these relates directly to the social envelope (the health care sector). Another deals with the impact of the courts as an institution for social change. Yet another focuses on the role that monopolies and sinecures play in maintaining the status quo. The final area relates to a series of issues arising in the context of the jurisdictional overlap that characterizes the social order.

Health Care

From my vantage point, the major stumbling block to the process of creative destruction in the health care area occurred in the 1970s.[1] Quebec (and perhaps other provinces as well) was anxious to substitute, where feasible, services of lower-cost paramedics for the services of physicians and to substitute convalescent homes or "half-way hospitals," as it were, for higher-cost institutional care. But Ottawa said "no" — the cost sharing under health programs was limited to physicians and to accredited hospitals. This was an incredibly important (that is, incredibly perverse) decision that has had lasting implications well beyond the health area.

First, it locked Canada into high-cost health care: the health sector would be in far better shape today if the provinces had been allowed the flexibility in the 1970s to experiment with appealing alternatives to a reliance on physicians and hospitals for the delivery of health care services. In this case, the federally enforced "positive feedbacks" served to *entrench the existing system* and to stifle evolution and innovation.

Second, and relatedly, we were rich enough in the 1960s to ignore the cost and societal advantages associated with paraprofessionals (paramedics, para-engineers, paralegals, paradentals, and so on). Had Canada allowed paramedics to qualify for shared-cost funding, this would have provided an invaluable counter to the prevailing wisdom that our ample resource base was such that we could afford to maintain a professional society, almost to the complete exclusion of paraprofessionals. Our disappearing middle class is, in part at least, traceable to this and similar decisions.

Third, this is a classic example of the problems that can and frequently do arise in a federal system: Ottawa used its spending power to enforce underlying parameters (*beyond* the five principles underlying the health care system) within which the provinces must design and deliver the services. What this meant was that any Schumpeterian process of "creative destruction" was effectively stymied.

---

1 This section and the following one on the courts often reproduce major portions of Courchene 1993 verbatim. Indeed, that article was designed to be incorporated into the present study.

One could, of course, argue that as long as Ottawa was providing 50 percent of the funding, it had some responsibility for program design, irrespective of what the Constitution might say. However, whatever rationale this may have had initially disappeared with the block-funding arrangements introduced in 1977. The problem was, however, that by this time the underlying nature of the health care system was pretty effectively locked in. More to the point, when the provinces attempted to flex their muscles a bit in the 1980s in terms of cost containment (partly because, after 1977, Ottawa's share of provincial health financing was falling rapidly), Ottawa responded with the 1984 *Canada Health Act*. I view this piece of legislation to be every bit as destructive of meaningful federalism as the National Energy Program or the recent targeted provincial caps on the operations of the Canada Assistance Plan. Politically, the issue was user fees, extra billing, and, arguably, the existence of premiums. Analytically, the issue was again one of federally imposed positive feedback — that is, locking in the existing system. What was afoot in those days were creative proposals to cofinance aspects of health care, typically via the income tax system. But these were stymied. The assumption underlying the federal legislation was that the various provinces would allow the spread of user fees and the like to "destroy" our medicare system. As I argued in the previous chapter, I do not believe that this would have been the case. To the extent that medicare is a "sacred trust," the electors would not long tolerate a provincial government that attempted to unwind the system.

Indeed, the reverse is really the case. The series of these federal initiatives, in tandem with the recent freezes in Established Programs Financing, are the real challenges to our medicare system. Had the provinces been given the flexibility and leeway to adjust and/or to adapt the system in light of the emerging reality, the future of Canada's health care system would be much brighter than it currently is. Nonetheless, I remain optimistic because, under the burden of the provincial fiscal crises, a wide-ranging and exciting degree of experimentation is emerging. Ottawa will probably not have the same ability to stifle innovation this time around, largely because Canadians realize not only the extent of the health care crisis but also that federal deficit shifting is partly responsible for the provinces' being backed into a fiscal corner. As noted earlier, winning strategies in any province will be quickly adopted by other provinces, in much the same way that Saskatchewan's medicare strategy carried the day in the 1960s. To facilitate the information flow, it would be useful to have some agency (private or public) dedicated to monitoring and evaluating the various experiments and models across provinces.

Whatever emerges, however, it is likely to be inferior to what could have been had Ottawa allowed the Schumpeterian process of creative destruction to flourish much earlier.

Readers will be able to apply these same concepts to other areas of the social envelope — the welfare/unemployment insurance (UI) subsystem, the retirement income subsystem, and the usurping by the provinces of procurement federalism on the training front to suit their own ends. As an important aside, some of these feedbacks in the UI area, for example, served not only to entrench the existing programs but also to alter the entire environment. This broadens the set of agents who might support the continuance of the status quo.

I shall now turn to a much more controversial area — the role of the courts in social policy evolution.

The Courts and Social Policy

Apart from some high-profile decisions such as striking down federal unemployment insurance legislation in the 1930s, the courts were largely on the sidelines in terms of social policy until the Charter of Rights and Freedoms was implemented in 1982. Since then, and particularly since the coming into force in 1985 of the equality provisions (section 15), the Charter has had a profound influence on social policy. The role of the courts has been to give effect to aspects of the Charter.

While the Charter and the courts are in effect agents for change in the social policy arena both in terms of individuals (for example, mandatory retirement) and groups (pay and employment equity), the Charter and the courts cannot really address the globalization and knowledge/information challenges in terms of social programs. Indeed, the opposite is the case: because the courts are typically constrained to operate within the *existing* legislative framework, their path-breaking decisions with respect, say, to equity or equality issues tend also to entrench the existing framework relating to the social order.

By way of elaboration, I want to focus initially on those areas where the Charter and the courts are interacting with the existing social programs. The first relates to the age limits associated with the various social programs. This is not limited only to the elderly or to the retirement end of the social policy spectrum. For example, under the income tax provisions, a single parent can claim a spousal exemption for a child under 18. Why not 19?

The second area relates to the definition of family status in order to qualify for benefits. The most glaring issue here is the existence of the spousal allowance for widows and widowers 60–64 years of age, regardless of when the spouse died. Why should divorced persons, 60 to 64, whose former spouses have died not qualify? Or those who have never married?

The third area relates to the definition of income that triggers a reduction in benefits. The various programs have different definitions of what constitutes "outside income" that would reduce the benefits under the particular program.

Given that Canada's social policy network has evolved largely by responding piecemeal to perceived needs of certain groups in society, it is hardly surprising that the overall system would fare very poorly when subjected to section 15(1) of the Charter: "Every individual is equal before and under the law and has the right to equal protection and equal benefit of the law without discrimination." The courts can exercise several options here. First, they can defer entirely to Parliament, essentially recognizing the existence of inconsistencies or inequities, but viewing these as falling within the limits that, in the words of the Preamble to the Charter, "can be demonstrably justified in a free and democratic society." Second, they can strike down the offending pieces of legislation or programs and, in effect, again defer to Parliament, this time to enact new legislation consistent with Charter principles. Third, the courts can take on a far more activist stance and impose a legislative scheme to replace that found constitutionally defective. The extreme variant of judicial activism is for the courts to extend benefits *judicially* — that is, effectively to appropriate public funds for a purpose not authorized by Parliament.

Presumably, the courts will invoke all three approaches, depending on the nature of the various challenges or cases. It is instructive, however, to focus on the recent decision in the Schachter case, where the plaintiff (Shalom Schachter) challenged the UI maternity provisions that restrict benefits to mothers (*Schachter v. The Queen* (1992) 93 D.L.R. (4th) 1 (S.C.C.)). Part of his Charter-related challenge was based on the fact that child care leave for adoptive parents can be taken by either parent. The lower court did not find in favor of Schachter in terms of his rights to maternity benefits under UI. But it then pointed out that child care benefits for adoptive parents are quite different from maternity benefits under UI for natural parents, so that there existed a basic inequality. The remedy recommended by the lower court was to rewrite the relevant provision of the UI maternity leave benefits to incorporate an additional 15 or so weeks for child care — which can be accessed by either parent. At the Federal Court of Appeal, one of the main issues centered on the role of the judiciary in circumstances where the granting of a Charter remedy results in a judicial amendment to the legislation, and where it also entails the appropriation of public monies from the Consolidated Revenue Fund for a purpose not authorized by Parliament. The court upheld the remedy in a split decision. Recently, the Supreme Court has overruled the lower courts, but in the meantime the UI legislation had been changed in a direction consistent with the lower courts' ruling.

The general point is that if the courts engage in judicial activism of the type reflected in the Schachter case — where the approach to remedy in cases of discrimination or inequality is to "level up" to the most generous existing provisions — then the revenue costs could be enormous. For example, leveling up the widow and widower allowances for those aged 60 to 64 to include divorced and never-married individuals would result in an estimated five or sixfold increase in costs. All told, we are probably talking about billions of dollars of additional social policy costs, which would easily swamp any potential savings from initiatives such as the old age security and family allowance clawbacks. Effectively, what would result is a new version of universality, this time based on Charter principles.

In general, my position is that the courts are largely constrained to seek redress *within the existing social order*. For example, were the courts' decisions to have the impact of expanding social envelope spending by, say, $3 billion annually, these funds inevitably would relate to enhancing spending with respect to some *existing* programs that fall short of the equality provisions of the Charter. This is not an attempt to downplay equity or Charter issues; rather, it is a straightforward observation that this extra $3 billion of spending may have little relationship to our emerging social policy needs. Effectively, the courts generally grant entitlements with respect to the existing social policy framework, not with respect to a conception of the overall social envelope that is more appropriate to globalization and an information society. In terms of the new growth theory, the feedbacks are all in the direction of entrenching the status quo, albeit with a nod toward equality here and there.

It is, of course, possible to conceive of cases where the courts *could* play a quite different role. To see this, consider the following hypothetical case (although I remain astonished that it has remained hypothetical and has not been brought before the courts). Suppose two identically situated people (in terms of sex, family status, age, and so on) lose their jobs after working 14 weeks with a national firm — say, a bank. Their situations differ only in that one person resides in an area where the unemployment rate is 10.5 percent and the other where the unemployment rate is over 16 percent. Under current UI provisions,[2] the former would have no claim to benefits whereas the latter would qualify for 43 weeks of UI. This is an incredible inequality in terms of individual rights. How would the courts respond to a Charter challenge by the person denied benefits? One option would be for the courts to argue (falling back on, say, section 36 of the *Constitution Act, 1982* relating to regional equity) that the discrimination based on the unemployment rate does not run counter to section 15. But I have made the case too easy: suppose both people worked in the low-unemployment area but that one of them went back to the high-unemployment area (his/her home) to file for benefits. This would make the deferring-to-Parliament option much more difficult. The other options are: a) instruct Parliament to rewrite

---

2 In this context, "current" means the provisions as they applied prior to the 1994 federal budget. These new provisions will change the numbers somewhat, but not the issues being addressed.

the legislation to remove this inequality; and b) in activist fashion, award the 43 weeks to the client. The costs of b) would likely be in the billions of dollars and it would be difficult politically for Parliament to then turn around and abolish all regional benefits (including differentiated qualifying periods). Option a) gives far more flexibility to Parliament but does not make the decision much easier.

The point of this hypothetical example is to recognize that the courts do have the *potential* for major reformulation of the social envelope. However, the more likely result is that they would not strike down the entire legislation but resort to remedies that would remove inequalities *within* the existing social legislation. Arguably, this makes substantive reform more difficult because the "reworked" existing legislation now carries the imprimatur of the judicial system.

It is important to recognize that not all court decisions in the social policy arena relate to the Charter — the ruling that Ottawa could, mid-agreement, renege on the Canada Assistance Plan provisions with respect to "have" provinces (Ontario, British Columbia, and Alberta) is still reverberating through the system.

Despite the analysis to this point, it is *conceivable* that the courts could, inadvertently, end up being an effective catalyst for a complete overhaul of our social policy infrastructure. To see this, suppose that the courts pursued an activist stance and, as part of this activism, insisted on a fully consistent definition of family status across all social programs, on identical treatment of "outside" income for benefit-offset purposes for all programs, and on eliminating all discrimination with respect to age and gender. It seems to me that the only way in which Parliament could handle these edicts, short of allowing social policy costs to mushroom, would be to jettison the existing patch-work system and to embark on some version of an individual-based guaranteed annual income or negative income tax. While I do not attach much likelihood to this scenario, it is nonetheless within the realm of possibility.

In any event, the courts are now a major social policy player, with some potential for creative destruction in the evolution of social policy, but with much greater potential for positive feedbacks that serve to entrench the existing social order (path dependence), *albeit* in a way that is consistent with Charter principles.

Monopolies and Sinecures

The problems that have recently affected such corporate giants as General Motors and IBM impress one with the realization that there are few sinecures left in the private sector. The public sector is another matter. This may not be surprising, but it surely is anachronistic. Governments have had a bird's-eye view of the brutal restructuring of the private sector over the past decade.

Hierarchical corporations became unlayered and flexible and, in the process, often furloughed several levels of middle management. Long-established and even "heritage firms" have closed their doors. But until very recently, none of this appears to have influenced the mentality of the public sector and public sector employees. Pay equity "obviously" means levering the salaries of women and minorities upward, never the salaries of others down. And employment equity is one of the more inequitable programs ever conceived. Consider my own sector, the universities. Tenured faculty (largely male) in all universities have either instigated or supported a policy of preferential hiring of women and minorities. The result is massive intergenerational discrimination against young white males by older tenured males. However, it is done in a very clever and politically correct way — how can young, white males mount a case against establishing gender balance in universities? Moreover, this also directs attention away from the real issue — tenure. In this Charter age, there is much less in the way of rhyme or reason for tenure. Ten-year (not tenure) contracts, even if renewable, would appear to be far more appropriate. Thus, while the private sector is restructuring to stay alive, the public sector is preserving sinecures and in the process ensuring that the current generation of university students is deprived of full access to innovative ideas.

In this environment, one that effectively eliminates the possibility of competition, the processes of creative destruction cannot really get off the ground. This would not be such a problem if productivity were continuously improving. But as Drucker (1993, 84) notes, no one would maintain that the teacher of 1990 is more productive than the teacher of 1930.

This situation cannot continue, nor will it. What is not immediately apparent, however, is just how these public sector privileges will be eroded and how the public sector will be submitted to more competition. One approach is simply to strip some of these privileges away. This is what Alberta and other governments are doing in selected areas (for example, MLAs' pensions in Alberta). It is also what the rollbacks under the rubric of Ontario's "social contract" are partly about (the social contract is much more than this, but elaboration is beyond the scope of this book). However, these measures relate more to "downsizing" than to "restructuring" the public sector.

Of more significance is the manner in which globalization and the knowledge/information revolution eventually will have an impact on the public sector. Let me illustrate this with a few examples that admittedly are a bit removed from the social policy area. But the process eventually will envelop that area, too.

A decade ago, a recession such as the one Canada has recently experienced probably would have seen an all-too-familiar struggle with the post office. But technology has largely tamed the post office and the postal workers. Specifically, the information revolution (faxes) and competition (couriers) have relegated the post office largely to the sidelines. Indeed, postal workers are becoming positively docile, probably because they want to ward off the next technological shift — replacing cheques in the mail with electronic transfers for the full range of federal and provincial spending and transfers. We are doing some of this, but we are behind many other countries. The potential savings appear to be substantial.

Telecommunications is another area where technology is dominating policy. The availability of "bypass" means that long-distance rates must become competitive. The system of cross-subsidization of local rates by long distance rates can no longer be maintained. Actually, this is just one aspect of a more pervasive phenomenon that is affecting the way we deliver social policy. With the advent of the North American Free Trade Agreement, as well as the avenues for bypass alluded to above, we can no longer use the allocative mechanism for distributional purposes. Henceforth, distributional goals will have to be delivered by distributional instruments (for example, the tax-transfer system). This is a welcome development because it means that distributional measures will now leave an identifiable statistical trail and, therefore, can be debated and/or defended on their own merits. Continuing with the telecommunications example, the fact that satellite dishes are now the size of a saucer and that prices of these are falling apace means nothing but headaches for the Canadian Radio-Television and Telecommunications Commission. Eventually, it will be rendered irrelevant.

A third example is Ontario Hydro. Whether the problem was the inflexibility of its hierarchical structure or straightforward strategic error, the fact remains that this "state within a state" is about to undergo radical transformation. This is the government equivalent of the restructuring of IBM and it carries with it a message that competition and the availability of bypass will infiltrate the operations of government well beyond the degree that Canadians and particularly governments might have expected.

Turning now to social policy, I think it is clear that government (monopolized) delivery systems, whether in education, training, or social services, will face challenges from two sources. The first is "outsourcing" or contracting out; the second is via direct competition. The former will be discussed in Chapter 8. Here, I shall devote a few remarks to the latter.

What I have in mind are innovations such as vouchers for postsecondary education and allowing greater competition in the area of secondary education. The most likely province to take initiatives here is Quebec, where private education has had a long tradition and where anecdotal evidence suggests that it is available at roughly two-thirds the cost of public education.

More likely, however, is that the cutting edge in terms of competition will come on the training front. If the devolution of training to the local level (via labor market training boards alluded to in the previous chapter) does indeed occur and if there is a will to integrate training fully into the local labor/industry structure, it would be surprising if private training facilities did not arise as viable alternatives to the community colleges, or their equivalent. It would be most unfortunate if this intriguing experiment in devolving training decisions to the local level became fully captured by the existing training establishments, (in the same manner as they captured the earlier experiment in procurement federalism). Not only am I optimistic that this will not happen, but if the results are positive then the feedbacks (or signals) will trigger an evolutionary dynamic of its own, which, in turn, will lead to further integration such as tailoring aspects of UI to be consistent with these local and regional training/educational networks.

By way of summary, two points are relevant. First, the presence of public sector monopolies effectively stymies much of the potential for Schumpeterian creative destruction. Second, these monopolies or sinecures will find it progressively much more difficult to maintain their former power and dominance.

I now turn to a final area that inhibits social evolution: jurisdictional entanglement.

Jurisdictional Overlap

Jurisdictional entanglement is endemic to federal systems. It cannot be eliminated in today's interdependent world because there is no such thing as "watertight compartments." There probably never was. The best that can be done is to minimize the impact of those jurisdictional overlaps that have the potential for wreaking havoc on the appropriate design and delivery of socioeconomic policy. There are several facets to this.

The Division of Powers

In many ways, the interaction between the division of powers and social policy has been highly successful. By clever use of the spending power and intergovernmental transfers, Canadians have mounted a set of social programs that are both decentralized and "national." This is a significant achievement.

The problem is that we designed the social envelope to interface with the economic and social realities of the 1960s and we have been singularly unsuccessful in ensuring that it has evolved in step with the changing economic and social realities. Part of this relates to the division of powers.

One aspect of this has to do with the fact that, on occasion, we used inappropriate instruments to deliver aspects of Social Canada. The best example here relates to the UI coverage for self-employed fishers and the set of regional UI benefits. Essentially, Ottawa wanted to enter the area of regional distribution and to help the fishing industry. However, it did not have access, constitutionally, to a set of redistributional instruments that could accomplish these goals. But it did have control over UI, thanks to an earlier constitutional amendment. Thus, it resorted to UI reform to deliver these distributional goals via an instrument that was inherently more allocative than redistributive in nature. We are now wrestling with the results of employing allocative instruments to deliver distributional objectives, let alone the results of using a national program to deliver regional benefits.

The second aspect is even more telling: constitutionally, there is no one level of government that can step in and rationalize the entire welfare/UI/training subsystem. Were Ottawa to undertake a meaningful restructuring of UI, the immediate result would be to transfer significant additional income support responsibilities to the provinces. Without a series of complementary initiatives, this is simply not politically feasible. Hence the current system remains intact. This is jurisdictional gridlock!

One approach would be for Ottawa to signal its attention to convert UI in, say, three years to insurance principles with the benefits accruing to substantial labor force attachment (for example, the proposal suggested earlier of a 30-week entry requirement and one week of benefits for each three weeks of contributions). Then it would invite proposals from the provinces in terms of how welfare might also be restructured and financed. Surely, *all* provinces would become engaged if they believed Ottawa would carry through with UI reform. Human Resources Minister Lloyd Axworthy has adopted a different approach. He has signaled Ottawa's intention of issuing a "white paper" on major aspects of Canada's social envelope. Of necessity, this will also have to involve a "constitution-like" consultation and participation process with the provinces.

In effect, what I think is happening is that this traditional jurisdictional gridlock is finally being overcome by the powerful set of forces addressed in the following two chapters — the fiscal crunch and the new global order.

Intergovernmental Gaming

Another issue relating to multiple jurisdictions has to do with accountability. At issue is the ability of provinces to pass off some of the costs of their decisions to the rest of the country or, worse, to deliberately engage in policies toward this same end. The real problem here relates to the incentives in the system, not to the fact that provinces take advantage of the incentives. They would be foolish to do otherwise. In this monograph I have referred to this as "intergovernmental gaming." Examples have already been presented in Chapter 2, so that they will not be reproduced here.

Once again, it is probably impossible to design an intergovernmental transfer system that will eliminate such moral hazard. Rather, the goal ought to be that the incentives in the set of intergovernmental transfers ensures, as far as possible, that the provinces (and Ottawa) bear the full costs of their own discretionary decisions. This leads rather naturally to a discussion of "fiscal coincidence."

Fiscal Coincidence

A maxim of public finance is that accountability is best served when the location of the expenditure decisionmaking responsibility coincides with the location of the revenue-raising responsibility. This has led a number of economists to argue for a transfer of additional taxing powers to the provinces to coincide with their larger expenditure responsibilities. While this obviously would not preclude the continued existence of equalization, it is undoubtedly the case that an enhanced degree of fiscal coincidence would contribute to enhanced accountability both within the social envelope and, more generally, across all policy areas. Many of the reform proposals advanced, both thus far and in future chapters, are influenced by ensuring that more accountability is brought to bear on the evolution of the social envelope.

Closely related to fiscal coincidence on the financial side is what might be referred to as "jurisdictional coincidence" on the political side. Federal systems will find themselves in accountability quagmires if unpopular decisions emanating from, say, the provincial level, lead citizens to "appeal" these decisions to the federal level. Again, some of this is inevitable in any federation. But if this proceeds to the point where, in the eyes of citizens, the location of the expenditure responsibility is not coincident with the location of the political responsibility, then accountability vanishes and, in all likelihood, so does cost control.

Conclusion

Restructuring is always difficult, and it is far more difficult in nonmarket sectors where the political system has control over the "prices" or "signals" that would trigger innovation in private markets. The purpose of this chapter has been to focus on selected features, processes, and institutions that contribute to the staying power of the status quo. Intriguingly, the casting of social policy in this evolutionary (or nonevolutionary) framework provides a quite different perspective on our social envelope. Basically, one can argue that aspects of the existing framework were appropriate to the economic and social needs of the time in which they were implemented (essentially the mid-1960s and early 1970s). But whereas the economic environment and the needs on the social front underwent a near-complete revolution, the social envelope failed to evolve.

There is an important lesson here. In our ever-changing world, no set of programs or policies is likely to be applicable for all time. For example, had I the power to put in place an "appropriate" social policy for 1994, it too almost certainly would be outmoded by 2004 or at least by 2014. What this means is that any new conception of Social Canada should be designed with an eye to its ability to evolve from within, as it were, with changing circumstances. Designing features that facilitate evolution is not an easy task. But let me suggest one principle — namely, that *all* benefits be subject to similar tax treatment. Currently, workers' compensation payments, for example, are tax exempt. This means that there are preferred benefits and, not surprisingly, many persons who have lost their blue collar jobs and are on UI are attempting to find ways to move from UI to workers' compensation. However, were all transfer payments treated in a similar manner, it would be much easier to adjust, readjust, or integrate the system in rational ways without affecting the well-being of recipients.

The division of powers poses a further complication in the restructuring of Social Canada. One of the key restructuring principles that pervades all the analysis is that rethinking Social Canada must begin from the "bottom up" — designing programs that make socio-economic sense to Canadians both as stand-alone programs and as an overall system. But even the discussion of such a design process will generate jurisdictional or "turf" concerns across governments. There are, I think, ways to accommodate both incentive-compatible design and jurisdictional flexibility (for example, concurrency with provincial paramountcy, as I will detail later), but there is no question that it will take some powerful forces, probably external to the social envelope, to shift the focus away from the traditional top-down or jurisdictionally driven approach and toward a bottom-up or individual-centered focus to policy formulation in the social policy arena.

This is the role of the following two chapters — to detail the nature of these powerful "external" forces that *will* overwhelm the inertial properties of the status quo. Unfortunately, the staying power of the status quo over all these years means that the degree of required restructuring will be much more dramatic than would otherwise have been necessary.

Chapter 7

The Political Economy of
Social Policy Reform II:
The Fiscal Crisis and Federal Offloading

Aspects of the fiscal straits of the provinces, including their debt and deficit burdens and credit ratings, were highlighted in Chapter 2. In Chapter 4, the focus was on federal-provincial transfers, including the nature of the various caps, freezes, and/or ceilings that have been attached to these transfers. One purpose of this chapter is to bring these two together, as it were, and to present an overview of the impact on the provinces of what has come to be referred to as "deficit shifting" or "federal offloading." Needless to say, attempting to put dollar values on this process is highly controversial. But even more controversial is how to interpret this federal offloading, whatever set of numbers one selects. Both of these exercises are part of the analysis that follows. One could argue that, since much of this offloading was probably inevitable and since much of it has already taken place, it might be preferable to simply focus on the impact of fiscal constraint as it relates to social policy evolution. However, the issue has played such a major role in both federal-provincial relations and in the run-up to the social policy review that it merits attention.

A second thrust of the chapter is to detail the manner in which the fiscal crisis in all its aspects is overwhelming some of the inertia that heretofore has inhibited social policy evolution. Not only is this, too, inevitable but the interaction between social policy and the deficit crisis is a two-way street. The debt and deficit overhangs are indeed forcing both a reworking and a downsizing of Social Canada. But it is also the case that an inappropriate, even blind, adherence to last generation's concept of social policy was a major contributing factor to the mushrooming of debts and deficits.

Readers are apt to be confused at times in the ensuing analysis. This is because I shall attempt to present both a provincial perspective and a federal perspective on some of the issues, such as the degree and desirability of offloading. Yet, almost by definition there can be no middle ground here because this tends to be, at best, a zero-sum financial game. To anticipate my approach to all of this, the following are some of the implications that I draw from the analysis:

- Within the strict confines of the three major federal-provincial transfers, there has been considerable federal deficit shifting.
- In the larger context of the rate of growth of federal goods and services expenditures and of the growth in the relative shares of taxation, it is much more difficult to make the case for federal offloading.
- While there are concerns relating to the manner in which federal transfers to the provinces have been curtailed, this constraint was inevitable in the face of mounting debt and deficits, and it should have been anticipated by the provinces.
- The salutary feature of all of this is that the provinces are now in a restraint and restructuring mode, particularly since the fiscal-transfer environment will remain constrained for the near future and, perhaps, indefinitely.

One further implication that derives from the analysis is that the financial interface between Ottawa and the provinces appears to be increasingly dysfunctional. The issue here relates in part to the resulting erosion of the perceived integrity of the system of federal-provincial transfers. It also relates to increased uncertainty and lack of accountability associated with these transfers. The likely result will be a rethinking and restructuring of fiscal federalism.

The chapter begins with a focus on the range of issues associated with deficit shifting.

Deficit Shifting

Table 33 presents one estimate of cumulative federal offloading from the base year, fiscal 1986/87, through to the projections for 1994/95. It is adapted from a handout prepared by the Canadian Teachers' Federation (1993) for one of its conferences. This particular version of offloading was selected from alternative choices partly because of its cumulative nature — even though the forecasts for gross national product (GNP) for 1993 and 1994 as elaborated in the notes to the table may well be way off the mark — and partly because it represents an extreme version of deficit shifting, one that would probably accord well with a "provincial" interpretation of these events.

Presumably, 1986/87 was selected as the base year because it was in this year (1986) that the federal government limited the indexation of Established Programs Financing (EPF) transfers to the increase in GNP less two percentage points (previously it was linked to GNP growth). In 1989, the indexation was lowered further to GNP less three percentage points. The federal government went further in 1991 and froze total EPF transfers (cash plus tax points) in per capita terms. This freeze was later extended through to the end of 1994/95, after which the GNP-less-three-percentage-points formula will kick in again. On the Canada Assistance Plan (CAP) front, Ottawa placed a limit of five percent growth on annual increases in transfers to Ontario, British Columbia and Alberta (the non-equalization-receiving provinces), effective in fiscal year 1990/91. As currently legislated, CAP will "snap back" (to use the relevant jargon) to a full 50 percent cost-sharing scheme in 1995/56. Most analysts do not expect that this legislation will remain intact since, from the CAP component in Table 33 for 1994/95, the cost to the federal treasury of a full snapback could be in the neighborhood of $2½ billion annually. (Readers wishing more information relating to these caps, freezes, and so on, can refer back to Chapter 4 where they discussed in greater detail.)

In terms of the data in Table 33, the fiscal impact of these federal measures for 1992/93, for example, is a shortfall in EPF transfers of about $5 billion (allocated roughly equally across the provinces in per capita terms) and about $2.1 billion for CAP ($1.7 billion of which is borne by Ontario). In cumulative terms, the 1986/87 to 1994/95 shortfall or offloading is (or will be) in the order of $26.7 billion for EPF and $8.5 billion for CAP, for an overall total of just over $35 billion.

To this total, the "have-not" provinces would surely add the implications of the imposition of the equalization ceiling, the cumulative impact of which over the 1987/88 to 1990/91 period is on the order of $3 billion. Thus, the overall deficit shifting from Ottawa to the provinces over the period covered by Table 33 is close to $38 billion.

What Do These Numbers Mean?

EPF Offloading

How should one interpret the numbers in Table 33? At the most basic level, they mean exactly what they claim to mean — namely, the annual and cumulative transfer shortfalls to the provinces resulting from all of the federal unilateral and negotiated changes to the transfer system since the mid-1980s. In other words, had Ottawa left the 1984/85 transfer system intact, EPF transfers in 1994/95 would be $5.6 billion more than they would otherwise be and CAP transfers would be $2.4 billion higher, with the cumulative impact being $26.8 billion and $8.5 billion, respectively. (Note that, for purposes of this chapter, it really does not matter if someone produces an updated/corrected set of estimates that indicates that these totals are off by, say, $5 billion in either

Table 33: *Offloading Federal Deficits: Estimated Losses in Federal Transfers to the Provinces and Territories, fiscal years 1986/87 to 1994/95*

($ millions)

	Nfld.	PEI	NS	NB	Que.	Ont.	Man.	Sask.	Alta.	BC	Yukon	NWT	Canada
1986/87													
EPF	7.1	1.6	10.9	8.9	81.5	113.6	13.3	12.6	29.6	36.0	0.3	0.7	315.9
CAP	—	—	—	—	—	—	—	—	—	—	—	—	—
1987/88													
EPF	15.0	3.4	23.2	18.9	174.5	245.3	28.6	26.9	62.9	77.4	0.6	1.4	678.2
CAP	—	—	—	—	—	—	—	—	—	—	—	—	—
1988/89													
EPF	23.9	5.4	37.0	30.0	279.0	396.2	45.5	42.6	100.3	125.2	1.1	2.2	1,088.4
CAP	—	—	—	—	—	—	—	—	—	—	—	—	—
1989/90													
EPF	33.9	7.7	52.8	42.7	398.1	570.0	64.6	59.8	144.2	181.2	1.5	3.1	1,559.6
CAP	—	—	—	—	—	—	—	—	—	—	—	—	—
1990/91													
EPF	67.8	15.5	106.9	86.2	811.4	1,172.3	129.8	118.6	297.5	379.2	3.2	6.7	3,195.0
CAP	—	—	—	—	—	389.5	—	—	0.0	36.2	—	—	425.7
1991/92													
EPF	90.0	20.4	142.6	116.1	1,099.0	1,629.0	172.4	156.5	403.4	524.9	4.5	9.5	4,368.1
CAP	—	—	—	—	—	1,166.4	—	—	41.5	142.4	—	—	1,350.3
1992/93													
EPF	100.4	22.5	159.7	129.5	1,232.5	1,835.7	192.2	173.9	455.5	597.9	5.2	10.8	4,915.7
CAP	—	—	—	—	—	1,714.8	—	—	63.6	306.3	—	—	2,084.7
1993/94													
EPF	103.0	23.1	164.0	132.9	1,269.6	1,904.3	196.9	177.4	473.4	622.1	5.4	11.2	5,083.4
CAP	—	—	—	—	—	1,700.0	—	—	66.7	506.8	—	—	2,273.5
1994/95													
EPF	111.3	25.1	178.4	144.1	1,384.9	2,094.2	214.7	193.2	521.8	684.3	6.0	12.2	5,570.1
CAP	—	—	—	—	—	1,785.3	—	—	70.0	532.2	—	—	2,387.5
Total 1986/87 to 1994/95													
EPF	552.5	124.7	875.6	709.1	6,730.5	9,960.3	1,058.0	961.4	2,488.7	3,228.2	27.8	57.7	26,774.5
CAP	—	—	—	—	—	6,756.1	—	—	241.8	1,523.9	—	—	8,521.8

Notes:

EPF: Established Programs Financing. The figure includes both health and postsecondary education and is the sum of both cash and tax points. Losses in EPF are calculated using 1985/86 as the base year. Cumulative losses due to restraints prior to 1986/87 are not included.

CAP: Canada Assistance Plan. This was capped at 5 percent for Ontario, Alberta, and British Columbia for 1990/91 to 1994/95, inclusively.

Totals may not add up due to rounding.

Nominal growth in gross national product was assumed to be as follows: 1993, 5.7%; 1994, 6.0%.

The federal share of total CAP shareable expenses was assumed to be constant from 1992/93 to 1994/95 for Alberta and from 1993/94 and 1994/95 for Ontario and British Columbia.

Data for fiscal year 1994/95 are projected.

Source: Canadian Teachers' Federation 1993, Table 10.

direction. In the immortal, but inflation-adjusted, words of the namesake of this Institute, what difference does a billion make, here or there?)

But this still raises the question: what do these numbers really mean? The first point I want to make is that an equivalent table based, say, in fiscal year 1955/56 — that is, prior to the transfer to the provinces of the bulk of their tax points and prior to the inauguration of the equalization program — would reveal *enormous deficit "onloading,"* and the cumulative positive totals would swamp the impact of the various caps and freezes over the most recent decade. Thus, these data are highly dependent on the benchmark year. Indeed, if one wanted to generate maximum offloading, the ideal benchmark year should probably be 1982, when the system was altered dramatically — that is, when the cash component of EPF became a residual rather than being escalated by the three-year average of GNP growth (see Chapter 4).

Second, in terms of EPF, there is a simple way to comprehend what is afoot here. Recall that, in 1977, the value of the overall transfer was effectively double the tax point transfer, the latter equaling 14.5 personal income tax (PIT) points and 1 corporate income tax (CIT) point — or 13.5 PIT points and 1 CIT point if one excludes the temporary "federal sweeteners" for the termination of the revenue guarantee. Let us assume that the latter is appropriate for the purpose at hand. The presence of the overall ceiling implies that somewhere down the road the cash component will fall to zero. When this occurs, what began as a transfer equivalent to 27 PIT points and 2 CIT points will have been reduced to 13.5 PIT points and 1 CIT point — that is, *the effective transfer will have been cut to half what it otherwise would have been.* This is the most effective and dramatic way of capturing the dynamics of the evolution of EPF. But this was triggered by what transpired in 1982. The recent set of caps and freezes obviously will hasten the day of zero cash transfer but not its inevitability. Indeed, while the shift from GNP minus 3 percent to a freeze on EPF transfers may be a major symbolic move, it has not had all that much impact because, over the past few years, the growth of income has been such that the GNP minus 3 percent regime would also have led to a freeze in EPF transfers.

A Federal Perspective

My third comment on Table 33 takes a federal perspective, under the assumption that the previous two approaches are closer to the provincial views of the degree of offloading. Ottawa would presumably counter with a few assertions of its own. The first would likely be that one should cumulate losses only *within* any given five-year negotiation period; they should not carry over to a new five-year period since this new agreement is a negotiated arrangement and the system begins afresh, as it were. In their evaluation of offloading, Boothe and Johnston (1993) essentially adopt this approach. One could counter that Ottawa effectively holds the hammer in these negotiations, but that is another matter.

A second assumption that Ottawa would surely insist on is that, if the provinces had their eyes open, they should have realized that their transfer growth would have been cut back (or de-indexed) in much the same way that Ottawa cut back or de-indexed its other programs in the social arena. For example:

- Indexation of family allowances was reduced to inflation minus 3 percent. In 1993, family allowances were folded into the new child tax benefit, which will also be partially indexed to the amount of inflation over 3 percent (which is really more restrictive than GNP minus 3 percent).
- Early in its first mandate, the Mulroney government attempted partial de-indexation of old age security (OAS) and the Guaranteed Income Supplement (GIS), but abandoned the effort in the face of widespread criticism. However, in 1989 it introduced a full clawback of the OAS for the elderly rich.
- The maximum number of weeks of unemployment insurance (UI) benefits was reduced in 1990 from 46–50 to 35–50, and the qualifying period was increased from 10–14 weeks to 10–20 weeks. In 1993, UI maximum benefits were reduced from 60 percent to 57 percent of insurable earnings. By itself, this latter measure is a 5 percent reduction (on a continuing basis) in what UI benefits would otherwise have been. And UI benefits have been reduced again (see Chapter 9 for the impact on UI of the 1994 federal budget).

Thus, if the comparison is what Ottawa is doing with the rest of its transfer envelope, it is not obvious that the EPF limits (especially the GNP minus 3 percent limit) depart much from the norm. This approach would allow Ottawa to argue that precious little EPF offloading has occurred. Indeed, over the 1985–92 period, federal transfers to the provinces (excluding tax transfers) increased by 36 percent whereas federal expenditures on goods and services increased by 30 percent: no deficit shifting here. But federal transfers to persons increased over this period by 67 percent. One could make the case that Ottawa cut back on federal-provincial transfers in order to enhance its transfers to persons. However, a significant portion of the increase in the latter relates to the explosion of UI in the early 1990s. While gross UI benefits are included in federal spending, the UI program is essentially on a pay-as-you-go basis, with Ottawa's role limited to picking up the temporary deficits. If one takes this into account, these aggregate data also suggest that the provinces have not been singled out for special offloading.

At this juncture, it is appropriate to refer again to the Boothe and Johnston (1993) analysis. As already noted, they are willing to accept that offloading calculations be limited to each five-year negotiated period. Moreover, in an attempt to find some middle ground between the federal and provincial positions on offloading, Boothe (1992) and Boothe and Johnston (1993) are also willing to accept that Ottawa should have the right to limit transfer growth to the growth rate of other federal expenditures. However, the transfer growth rate he focuses on is *cash* transfers, not the combined total of cash plus tax transfers. (As noted in Chapter 4, the cash transfer is the only actual transfer under EPF — that is, this is all that would disappear if EPF were abolished tomorrow, except perhaps for the Quebec tax abatement.) Thus, a "neutral" policy for Boothe would be for EPF cash transfers to grow at the rate of other federal expenditures or transfers. Of course, EPF *cash* transfers did not grow at this rate. Indeed, they *declined*, because of the growth of the tax transfer component and the existence of the overall EPF ceiling. The resulting deficit shifting is less than that in Table 33, but it is substantial nonetheless. One might speculate that updating the Boothe analysis to incorporate more recent data might actually produce an *increase* in cash transfers, because of the collapse of personal income tax revenues.

The final point I wish to make in terms of potential offloading is that it cannot be viewed in isolation from what has happened elsewhere on the taxation front. At the inception of EPF block funding (1977), Ontario's tax rate on basic federal tax under the personal income tax was 44 percent. It is now in the high 50s. The other provinces have also increased their tax rates under the shared PIT. Thus, offsetting any federal downloading with respect to EPF has been a rather dramatic increase in the provincial share of overall PIT revenues. Would the provinces have preferred that Ottawa increase its share of PIT revenues but keep up the level of EPF cash payments? Perhaps, but I doubt it. Setting aside the issue of whether overall income tax rates are too high, this shift away from cash transfers and toward an increase in provincial own revenues is the optimal approach from the vantage point of this monograph, because it reduces the degree of vertical fiscal imbalance and increases both "fiscal coincidence" (as defined in the previous chapter) and overall accountability.

CAP Offloading

Whatever the difficulty in identifying, let alone assessing, EPF offloading, there ought to be less confusion with respect to CAP offloading. As noted earlier, not since the National Energy Program in the early 1980's has there been a federal initiative so destructive to the integrity of federal-provincial fiscal relations as the cap on CAP. For whatever reasons (and I shall suggest some below), Ottawa has engaged in deficit shifting at the expense of the "have" provinces — in particular, Ontario. The amounts of this offloading to Ontario are staggering — $1.7 billion for fiscal year 1992/93 (Table 33) and larger still according to Ontario's estimates. To put this in perspective, this $1.7 billion figure is not far off the value of the anticipated savings to be achieved from the controversial "social contract." One might argue that, without the cap on CAP, there would have been no need for a social contract; this would be one way to view the implications on Ontario of the cap on CAP. More generally, Ontario taxpayers are in aggregate by far the largest contributors to the federal-provincial and interprovincial transfer systems. And Ontario has always been supportive of measures related to regional equity, even to the point of forgoing the $1.5 billion in equalization entitlements for which it qualified over the 1977–82 fiscal arrangements period. Moreover, Ontario is the destination of most of Canada's immigrants and refugees, and some of the services these people require fall under the CAP umbrella. Yet, when Ontario's economic fortunes turned sharply downward in the recent recession, the province (along with Alberta and British Columbia) was greeted with an arbitrary, selective, and huge reduction in its expected CAP transfers.

Again, there is probably a federal perspective to this. Much of the 1983–89 boom was really an Ontario boom. Rather than "saving" some of the resulting fiscal dividend, Ontario significantly increased its public expenditures. In turn, this created complications for both monetary policy and federal fiscal policy. In terms of the former, Ontario's spending fueled the fires of what already was a "made in Ontario" inflation problem — the result was that the Bank of Canada had to ratchet up interest rates (in pursuit of inflation control) to much higher levels than if Ontario had used its fiscal policy to temper its economic boom.

More relevant to CAP, Ottawa presumably realized that, in addition to compromising the overall approach to inflation control, the enrichment of Ontario's welfare/social assistance program had the potential to blow the lid off federal expenditure control since, under the provisions of CAP, Ottawa would be saddled with 50 percent of any and all increases in Ontario's welfare payments. Thus, one rationale for the cap on CAP was to shelter Ottawa's expenditures from the Peterson government's decision to enrich and extend Ontario's welfare system. At this point (fiscal year 1989/90), the recession had not yet arrived. In order to put the cap on CAP on a more acceptable footing, Ottawa extended it to all the "have" provinces, even though the target was undoubtedly Ontario. Obviously, these comments reflect my own views of the cap on CAP and not any official federal view.

The cap on CAP does not augur well for the existing framework of the fiscal arrangements. It is not at all evident how Ottawa can undo this selective offloading and return the three "have" provinces to equality with the other provinces. And if Ottawa fails to do so, Ontario is already on record that this could "dissipate" the support for equalization and the interregional transfer system generally (Ontario 1992). Unless Ottawa is willing to restore 50 percent cost sharing for the "have" provinces (which I deem unlikely), this means, in effect, that the existing CAP program is history and that some alternative arrangements will have to be introduced. It was partly for this reason that I recommended in an earlier chapter that Ottawa consider replacing CAP with some version of a negative income tax for children. Apart from the merits of this proposal (elaborated earlier), it would also restore equality across the provinces, albeit in a different manner.

Equalization Offloading

By contrast, I have little sympathy for any claim that the application of the equalization ceiling represents deficit offloading. First, unlike the offloading in Table 33, any equalization shortfall was *not* the result of an arbitrary federal initiative — the ceiling was initiated in the 1982 fiscal arrangements and was carried over unchanged to the 1987 and 1992 agreements. Second, the ceiling was "balanced" by provisions for stabilization payments and equalization floors (see Chapter 4), and these downside provisions are now kicking in for some of the "have-not" provinces.

This is not to say that the equalization ceiling did not have a major impact on the revenues of the "have-not" provinces. It surely did. However, it is also the case that what triggered the ceiling related more to what was happening in Ontario (rapidly rising revenues from the boom as well as from increases in tax rates) than what was happening in the "have-not" provinces.

Sharing the Pain?

One could mount an interesting case that the federal approach in all of this was to "balance" the pain across all provinces. EPF affected all provinces equally.[1] The equalization ceiling was obviously binding only on the seven "have-not" provinces, while the cap on CAP was restricted to the three "have" provinces. In this sense, Ottawa could presumably argue that any pain was distributed across *all* provinces. In turn, this lends support to one of Richard Simeon's

---

1 This statement assumes that the tax transfers are an integral part of the EPF program (as they are, in fact, under the legislation). The impact of *cash* transfers is not equal across the provinces.

earlier-mentioned trumps — namely, that regional distribution issues trump other distribution concerns.

Before rendering an assessment of the recent operations of fiscal federalism, it is instructive to devote attention to other areas of federal-provincial financial entanglement.

Federal-Provincial Financial Entanglement

While deficit shifting, à la Table 33, tends to make the headlines, there are other ways in which the federal government can offload onto the provinces. The best examples here relate to the 1989 federal initiative to clawback, beyond some threshold income level, family allowances and old age security payments. Under the regime in place prior to 1989, an elderly taxpayer who was subject to, say, a 50 percent marginal tax rate repaid in taxes one-half of his or her $3,928 OAS payment, or $1,964. Under the shared PIT system, about two-thirds of this tax revenue went to Ottawa and roughly one-third to the relevant province. The effect of the clawback was to deprive the provinces of their revenue from this source in the case of high-income individuals. The existing system remains in place for individuals whose net income is less than the designated income threshold.

In more detail, under the 1989 provisions, OAS will be taxed back fully when net income reaches $76,187[2] and, on the family allowance side, the allowances will be taxed back fully (for two children) when the net income of an earner in the family reaches $55,227. The amount of the clawback then will be deductible from net income for tax purposes — that is, the family allowances or the OAS would no longer enter into income. Hence, the provinces lose these tax revenues. In effect, the clawbacks are *federal* tax surcharges. As the elderly grow in number and their incomes increase, the loss of revenue to the provinces will become significant. To be sure, family allowances are now a thing of the past, but the new child tax benefit is also subject to a *federal* tax surcharge, and the disappearance of family allowances means that this income is no longer taxable by the provinces.

It is hard to argue against this provincial revenue loss in terms of principle. After all, family allowances and OAS payments are *federal* payments. Why should the provinces benefit from taxing them? Indeed, what may be anomalous is the pre-1989 system, which conferred this federal "gift" on the provinces. However, it was and is "sweeteners" of this kind that have provided much of the

---

2 This example is lifted from Courchene and Stewart (1991, 290), and the dollar values relate to the setting as of 1989.

glue that keeps the Tax Collection Agreements intact. If Ottawa keeps chipping away at the tax system and if it continues the fiscal squeeze on the provinces, before long some province or group of provinces will contemplate following Quebec's initiative and mount a separate PIT system. More likely, the provinces will insist on having the freedom to shift from a "tax on tax" approach to the shared PIT system (whereby the provinces levy a fixed tax rate — say, 55 percent — against federal basic tax) to a "tax on base" approach (whereby provinces can levy their own rate and bracket structure against the federally defined tax base).

Deficit Offloading: Reflections

Deficit offloading is a highly charged issue in both the social policy and federal-provincial relations arenas. As noted earlier, there is little to be gained by attempting to find some common ground or interpretation here, because there is none. My reflections with respect to this set of issues have already been offered in the introductory section. At this juncture, I shall elaborate on two general points. The first is that the provinces must have had their heads in the sand not to have seen this coming. Relatedly, I do not think it inappropriate that Ottawa has curtailed the rate of transfer growth. More assertively, I support, subject to a caveat to be elaborated later, the ongoing degree of fiscal stringency embodied in deficit offloading (although not necessarily the form that it has taken, especially in terms of CAP). After all, the provincial public sectors spent the 1980s believing themselves largely immune from the traumatic dislocations taking place in the private sector. How many huge corporations must be brought to their knees before the provinces (particularly Nova Scotia, with its dozen or so institutions) begin to question the effectiveness and efficiency of the university sector, or (for example, Ontario, where they exist as two solitudes) the interface between universities and community colleges, or the transition from school to work? Restructuring is inevitable and essential, and I view the pressure coming from the federal-provincial transfer system as both message and messenger in this process.

In the face of such a fiscal crunch, the obvious, indeed rational, response by the provinces will always be to appeal to Ottawa to ratchet up transfer payments. Were Ottawa to have caved in, the result would have been to forestall the beginnings of a meaningful process of social policy restructuring. I recognize fully that much of the federal offloading is a direct result of the inability of federal governments to put the federal house in order. However, to reiterate a theme introduced earlier, a substantial portion of the series of deficit overruns over the past decade related to Ottawa's adherence to an outmoded approach to Social Canada. In any event, by whichever route we arrived at the current impasse, the twin reality is that fiscal constraint is with us for some time and social restructuring is inevitable.

This being said, my second general comment is that it is nonetheless the case that the nature of the fiscal interface between the two levels of government leaves much to be desired. There are several issues. The first is that the most difficult job in the country must be that of a provincial treasurer or finance minister. It is surely inappropriate to have a system where the federal budget can, essentially without warning and adequate lead time, impose major restraint on the provincial budgetary processes. Relatedly, the very arbitrariness of these federal unilateral initiatives means that the "negotiated" agreements have little meaning and the provinces are essentially at the continuous mercy of Ottawa. There are no longer any "rules of the game," as it were. The former framework of formula-driven transfers has been reduced to a series of political decisions, which has sapped the integrity of fiscal federalism. To this, as a third point, one must add the cap on CAP, which has led to a profound questioning of the east-west fairness or equity of the transfers. Finally, a series of incentive or accountability issues have come to the fore. Would Ontario have embarked on its welfare enrichment had it known that 50 percent sharing would be terminated?

The implication I draw from all of this is that the time has come to rethink fiscal federalism. In any case, it is unlikely that the CAP can be resurrected, unless Ottawa wants to shell out an additional $2 billion or so to Ontario on an annual basis. Specifically, some disentanglement with respect to the federal-provincial financial interface is probably the preferred route to take. Indeed, proposals have already been floated for converting CAP into a low-income child tax credit, for converting the cash component of postsecondary education (PSE) into a student voucher, and for converting the cash component of health into a further PIT tax transfer. While this obviously would serve to disentangle the federal provincial financial interface (and leave equalization as the only major federal-provincial transfer), equally obviously it would be consistent with enhanced accountability and an appropriate move in the direction of ensuring fiscal coincidence.

In the next two sections, I shall explore some of the rationale for greater disentanglement both in terms of the major transfers and of the shared personal income tax system.

A Note on the Evolution of Shared-Cost Programs

In the days of fiscal plenty, Ottawa used its revenue-generating capacity and its spending power to inaugurate a series of shared-cost programs for medicare, health, PSE, and welfare. These were important milestones in the development of Social Canada and in the development of "national" programs. However, once these programs became "established" and cultivated a most appreciative constituency, Ottawa began not only to back off its funding commitments — that is, deficit shifting — but also to impose additional conditions on the remaining transfers (for example, the *Canada Health Act*). Given that the provinces are completely vulnerable in this process, especially after the Supreme Court upheld the right of Parliament to alter, mid-stream, the CAP agreements, it is clearly in their interests to disentangle or "lock in" these funds in various ways. This may not be in Ottawa's interest, unless it obtains some savings in the process, because the existing EPF legislation embodies long-term federal savings as the cash transfers head toward zero.

The above discussion may be more relevant than one might at first expect: all the evidence points in the direction of a major new federal initiative in the area of training and apprenticeship; there is no question that this is a high priority item for the federal Liberals. If, as a result of deficit shifting, among other things, future fiscal flexibility will reside more at the federal than the provincial level, the stage could be set for another major social policy initiative. Were Ottawa to attempt to pursue some version of the old shared-cost route, it is clear that the provinces would be reluctant to sign on without some way to protect themselves against future deficit shifting and arbitrary program reregulation. I have already expressed the view that, while there is an important leadership and regulatory (freeing the internal market for skills mobility) role for Ottawa, a federal attempt to pre-empt the area would likely trigger another major federal-provincial conflict. And I reiterate my view that the major part of the design and integration of training into our social infrastructure should probably occur at the provincial level.

My personal reflections aside, we need some new approaches to the federal-provincial financial interface.

A New Shared Personal Income Tax

The time has come for another type of disentanglement — a shift from a tax on tax to a tax on base approach to the shared personal income tax. The rationale for this initiative in the context of the present chapter has to do with eliminating Ottawa's ability to force changes on provincial revenues via unilateral changes in parameters relating to the shared PIT. In the more general context of this monograph, the further rationale is that the provinces will need greater rate and bracket freedom if they use the income tax system as an instrument for the design, integration, and reconciliation of their own social infrastructure.

Thematic Tableau 4, adapted from an Ontario Economic Council (1983b) position paper, presents a range of alternatives for the shared PIT. Panel 1 focuses on the status quo, where the provinces are limited to a single tax applied to federal basic tax. By definition, they have to accept (and magnify) the federal vision of the appropriate degree of progressivity in the PIT. However, the provinces are also allowed to mount a set of nondiscriminatory tax credits and surcharges that Ottawa will collect for them, for a fee. In 1988, Ottawa collected 47 of these surcharges and credits for the provinces, with Saskatchewan leading the way with nine such additional credits/taxes, including a flat tax (Courchene and Stewart 1991).

Panel 2 addresses the issue of unilateral federal changes to the tax system. The approach here would involve some approach to joint decision making with respect to the tax parameters. Not only does this address only one of the above problems relating to the status quo, but it may well be a recipe for PIT deadlock.

Panel 3 contains the tax on base proposal. The details in the tableau are self-explanatory. One might add that this is not that much of a break with the status quo since, with enough tax surcharges, credits, and reductions, a province can come close to reproducing its desired rate and bracket structure. As under the present system, Ottawa would still collect provincial taxes free of charge and, in turn, the provinces would be required to adhere to the nondiscriminatory provisions of the tax collection agreements.

Panel 4 presents an alternative to a tax on base, one that embodies an enhanced use of the tax credit route. This is a poor substitute for a tax on base.

Finally, Panel 5 presents the extreme solution: other provinces adopt the Quebec model and establish their own, separate, personal income tax systems. It would be a major system error if some of the large provinces were forced to go this route to protect themselves from federal initiatives or if Ottawa were to refuse to go along with a tax on base approach. Not only would compliance and collection costs rise, but the provinces would gain very little flexibility over what they would have under a tax on base.

Many provinces are pushing for a move to a tax on base and the most recent advocate is Ontario's Fair Tax Commission. While valuable in its own right, a shift to a tax on base may also serve to restore some confidence in the declining fortunes of fiscal federalism.

Conclusion

The analysis of, and implications deriving from, deficit shifting here ranged far afield. While readers may not agree with my assessment of the various issues, the central message of the chapter should not be in doubt: however one wishes

Thematic Tableau 4

Alternatives to the Shared Personal Income Tax

Alternatives	Characteristics	Elaboration
1. The status quo (tax on tax)	• Centralized federal collection. • Minimizes administrative and compliance costs. • Provincial flexibility limited to applying single tax rate to basic federal tax and to implementing a restricted set of nondiscriminatory tax credits. • Provinces required to accept all federal changes in underlying tax structure. • Consultation on such changes limited or nonexistent.	• Provinces are expressing increased concern over lack of consultation with respect to major and sudden federal changes. • Provinces also appear to be constrained in implementing development tax credits.
2. A federal-provincial committee on the structure of the shared tax base	• No changes in the current tax collection agreements. • Provinces would have equal status on the committee, reflecting the joint occupancy of the tax field and the constitutional rights of both parties to engage in direct taxation.	• Could run into problems relating to federal budget secrecy in spite of recent initiatives to open up the process. • Would not prevent federal action, since there would be plenty of scope for Ottawa to enact changes *after* the calculation of basic federal tax (for example, federal tax credits). After some period of notice (say, three years) these federal changes would become part of the shared tax structure, even if there were no agreement on the part of the provinces. • A stronger version of this option would require joint federal-provincial agreement prior to all changes in the shared structure. Hence, all controversial federal changes would have to be implemented "below the line," as it were.

3. Tax on base	• Provinces would tax the federal base instead of piggybacking on the federal tax.
	• Provinces would have control over their own rate and bracket structures.
	• Federal changes in tax rates would no longer affect provincial revenues.
	• Common structure for the base would still obtain.
	• A slight increase in compliance and administrative costs.
	• Federal government would still have the power to alter the base and thereby bind the provinces, since base changes would affect their revenues.
	• Federal government would lose some control over vertical equity in the tax system; but if the provinces utilized the currently allowable tax decreases and surcharges they could come close to duplicating a tax on base.
4. An extension of the tax credit system	• Would appear to fit easily within the tax collection agreements.
	• All regionally or provincially nondiscriminatory tax credits would be allowed. For example, savings and investment credits that did not discriminate against assets in other provinces would be allowed.
	• Compliance and administrative costs would rise somewhat.
	• Provinces could offset some federal changes so that lack of consultation is less of a problem.
	• Current federal collection fee for provincial tax credits would continue to apply.
	• Could be combined with a joint consultative process and/or a tax on base.
	• Would change the current structure more in terms of degree than of substance.
5. Separate provincial PITs	• No restrictions on provincial PIT flexibility.
	• Maximize compliance and administrative costs since provinces would have to set up their own collection agencies.
	• Minimize necessity for federal-provincial consultation on tax matters.
	• Would require substantial horizontal (interprovincial) harmonization in order to minimize efficiency losses.

Source: Ontario Economic Council 1983b, Table 14.

to view the recent past, the relevant fact is that the combination of the fiscal crisis and deficit shifting has launched Social Canada in a new direction. One aspect of this is that the deteriorating provincial fiscal positions, in tandem with the oversight of bond-rating agencies, have generated a degree of provincial restraint that has no parallel in the postwar period — Newfoundland trims its public sector, Ontario launches into a social contract, Saskatchewan closes or restructures 52 hospitals, Alberta eliminates parliamentary pensions and embarks on what critics depict as near-draconian expenditure cuts. Thus, in one fell swoop, these actions have overcome the "staying power" of the status quo elaborated in the previous chapter and have set in place a reform dynamic.

The other aspect relates to the emerging reform dynamic relating to fiscal federalism. Part of this has to do with the recognition that CAP probably cannot be reconstituted, with the result that alternative conceptions for CAP are surfacing from various quarters. More intriguing, however, is how the various provincial restraint programs will reverberate back on any new conceptions for fiscal federalism. Will the government or residents of Alberta or Ontario begin to argue that equalization-receiving provinces should, as a criterion of eligibility, undergo the same degree of fiscal or social policy reform as they have undergone? While the situation may never get quite this far, it is nonetheless the case that the rhetoric and processes of traditional east-west sharing will not escape scrutiny.

One final substantive point: given that the fiscal pressures on the provinces will surely continue, the issue becomes one of whether provincial responses will be directed largely to cost cutting or to fundamental restructuring. This comes to the fore because of the jurisdictional overlap in the social envelope. No amount of fiscal squeezing of the provinces can generate meaningful restructuring *unless Ottawa is also willing to commit itself to major structural initiatives.* To be sure, Ottawa has introduced some welcome changes on the family benefits and elderly benefits fronts, but thus far it has been singularly unwilling to make meaningful structural changes to the critical area — UI and its relationship to welfare, training, and labor force re-entry. If this continues to be the framework within which the federal government is exerting fiscal pressure on the provinces, then there *is* a danger that the result will be social policy erosion rather than social policy restructuring. Indeed, I will go much further here: this is unconscionable behavior on the federal government's part because pressuring the provinces on the fiscal front without at the same time recognizing that Ottawa itself holds the key to unlocking the system in a manner consistent with the dictates of a global/information society inevitably will lead to a grinding down of Social Canada and an acceptance, willy-nilly, of a US vision and version of social policy.

If the fiscal crisis has finally overwhelmed the status quo and launched social policy in the direction of restructuring, it then becomes critical that this restructuring be in tune with the challenges and opportunities relating to the social infrastructure arising from the forces of globalization and the information revolution. This is the purpose of the next chapter.

Chapter 8

The Political Economy of Social Policy Reform III:
Globalization and the Information Revolution

The earlier analyses relating to the reform imperative on several occasions anticipated the implications of the emerging global economic order. For the most part, they were motivated by traditional arguments, such as incentive incompatibility, transfer dependency, jurisdictional overlap, and the failure of Social Canada to adjust to altered needs on the social policy front. In effect, Canadians used the fiscal cushion arising from our resource-based economy to mount a comprehensive system of transfers to persons, to businesses, and to governments. Arguably, this system was appropriate for the Canada of the 1950s and 1960s, but as the world economy evolved, Social Canada became increasingly offside with our economic imperatives. The challenge articulated in the previous chapters was to reintegrate the social and economic spheres in order to rekindle the failing engines of economic growth. As we have seen, this is a formidable challenge in its own right.

But something every bit as remarkable as it is fundamental has inserted itself in this inevitable process of reforming and restructuring Social Canada. With globalization and the knowledge/information, the world is in the throes of one of its epic transformations. The information revolution will have impacts on the role of human capital not unlike the impact of the industrial revolution on the role of physical capital. Richard Harris (1993) notes that there has been a fundamental shift in Canada's wealth-generation process away from a reliance on resource capital and toward a reliance on physical and especially human capital. He then adds a critical insight: whereas we ran up debts and deficits within a framework where our "national capital" was resources, the national collateral that now has to service this indebtedness is increasingly our human capital base. As the earlier analysis indicates, we do well when it comes to the upper echelon of human capital formation but we fare poorly in terms of how we prepare other Canadians for this new global order.

In a sense, the perspective in this chapter fundamentally alters the nature of the mandate for social policy reform. To this point, one could mount an effective case that Social Canada was too inefficient and too inexpensive to enable us to regain our competitive edge. Under the existing paradigm, cost cutting on the social policy front was, of and by itself, arguably an appropriate policy. Not so under this new paradigm. Social policy re-emerges as an indispensable factor since, in an era where knowledge is at the cutting edge of competitiveness, social policy as it relates to human capital and skills formation becomes indistinguishable from economic policy.

The challenge could not be more stark: without a social envelope restructured in line with the dictates of globalization and the knowledge/information revolution, Canada will have little chance to maintain its historically elevated position in the international pecking order of nations. But there is more. The forces of globalization are also altering the fundamental economic reality of Canada. Policies that were obvious when trade flowed east-west in this country are far from obvious when trade begins to flow north-south.

The purpose of this chapter is, first, to focus on what globalization and the information revolution mean for Social Canada and, second, to focus on a few areas where these forces imply a wholesale rethinking and restructuring of Social Canada.

Globalization and the Information Revolution

Globalization is a catch-all term for the series of tumultuous recent and ongoing changes that, in combination, are ushering in one of the most significant transformations in socio-economic history. Indeed, Richard Lipsey (1994) speaks in terms of the dawning of a new techno-economic paradigm. At the most basic of levels, globalization is easy to define. It is the process of the increasing internationalization of manufacturing and, progressively, of services as well. Firms now compete with truly global strategies involving selling worldwide, sourcing components worldwide, and locating activities in various parts of the globe to seek out absolute advantage. Globalization in this sense decouples firms from the factor endowments of a region or country. Boundaries on a political map may be as clear as ever, but boundaries on an economic or competitive map have vanished (Ohmae 1990, 18–19). Hence, it is increasingly meaningless to speak in terms, say, of a US car. Even in the United States, favoring a "US" over a "Japanese" brand name may well *decrease* US value added. To quote Ohmae once again (ibid., viii), "nothing is overseas any longer" or, if one prefers, everything is!

Another view of globalization is to associate it with the information revolution. The implications arising from a world where knowledge or human capital, rather than physical capital, is on the cutting edge of competitiveness are obviously central to rethinking social and economic policy. Foremost among these is that much of the existing social policy environment was conceived and deployed in the era where resources were king, where trade flowed largely in an east-west direction, and where tariffs provided considerable protection for Canadian products (and east-west trade). None of these features remain. Globalization and free trade have reversed the last two while globalization in tandem with the information revolution have eroded the erstwhile rents from resources. As Peter Drucker has remarked (1986, 21), we are witnessing three fundamental uncouplings in the chain links of the global economy:

- the primary sector has become uncoupled from the industrial economy;
- in the industrial sector itself, production has become uncoupled from employment; and
- capital movements, rather than trade in goods and services, have become the engines and the driving force of the world economy. These two have not, perhaps, become uncoupled. But the link has become quite loose, and worse, quite unpredictable.

Not surprisingly, perhaps, all three of these uncouplings have been wreaking havoc in Canada over the past decade.

While adjustment and restructuring are apparent everywhere in the private sector, the social envelope has not made the transition from a resource-based mentality to a human-capital-based mentality. For example, apprenticeship and skills training were not viewed as essential to our prosperity in an era when high school dropouts could earn "middle-class" incomes in the forests, mines, or energy sector.

The impact of this information revolution, particularly in the context of an integrating world, is also altering aspects of the institutional fabric of domestic and international economic relationships. In terms of the latter, *The Economist* (July 21, 1990) posed the following intriguing question: who, in the future, should regulate an Australian firm that trades Japanese futures on Chicago's Globex out of London? What is developing in response to this and similar concerns across the entire integration spectrum, is a passing of powers upward from the nation state, whether in terms of enhanced integration (the European Union), or trade pacts (the North American Free Trade Agreement), or transferring aspects of regulatory powers or standards upward to supranational bodies (the Bank for International Settlements' capital adequacy rules for global banks). At the same time, among the most significant beneficiaries of the informatics revolution are individual citizens. One need not adhere to the claim that the advent and spread of the personal computer, and the inherent flexibility this represented, effectively brought down the Soviet empire in order to recognize that telecomputational advances have empowered citizens in a manner that was inconceivable only a decade or so ago. Citizens can now access, transmit, manipulate, and transform information in ways and quantities that governments of all stripes are increasingly powerless to prevent. It is this "democratization" of information that led Ohmae to define globalization as "consumer sovereignty": "performance standards are now set in the global market place by those that *buy* the products, not those who *make* or *regulate* them" (Ohmae 1990, dust jacket, [emphasis added]). As I shall argue, the implications go well beyond this, however, in that some of the powers that one typically associated with nation-states are being transferred downward.

A third view of globalization and the information revolution is that its essence is "ultra" mobility. This concept — or its counterpart, the resulting potential for "bypass" — also has significant implications for the social envelope. For example, consider the power to tax. We have long known that taxation falls on immobile factors, not mobile ones. If Canada attempts to levy taxes on capital that are higher than those elsewhere, capital will simply leave (or not contemplate entry) until the real returns rise sufficiently to offset the higher tax. The resulting lower capital/labor and capital/land ratios will ensure that labor and land will ultimately bear the burden of the higher tax on capital. But if, in this context, one considers the Robert Reich (1991) thesis that the top end of the labor market is becoming highly mobile and progressively linking itself to the global economy, then the burden will fall selectively on the less-mobile segments of the labor market.

Another important factor, the potential for bypass, is beginning to alter fundamentally the ways in which one can deliver social policy. Where bypass is nonexistent or minimal, the public sector can, by ownership or regulation, extract monopoly rents and engage in a variety of cross-subsidization schemes. Telecommunications comes to mind here — in particular, the tradition of using long-distance rates to subsidize local rates. The ubiquitousness of bypass means that this is no longer possible. In more general terms, it is becoming progressively more difficult to use the allocative system to deliver distributional objectives. Phrased differently, the distributive system (that is, the tax transfer system) is emerging as the only viable vehicle for achieving distributional goals. As an aside, this is to be welcomed because distribution now becomes up front and visible, unlike the case for cross-subsidization schemes, which tended to obliterate any potential statistical trail.

With these brief generalizations with respect to globalization and the information revolution as a backdrop, Thematic Tableaux 5 and 6 summarize their implications for the future of the social envelope. As will become apparent immediately, these summary points touch on issues well beyond the strict confines of the social envelope. However, this is both essential and inevitable, given that what is at stake is nothing less than the transformation of society and the environment in which social policy must operate.

Since these tableaux are reasonably self-contained, I shall focus only on areas that merit some elaboration. The first of these relates to the third bullet of Tableau 5 — namely, the implications that arise as a result of power being transferred downward from nation states to citizens and to international cities. In tandem with the earlier reflection that powers are also being passed upward from nation-states, this means that what remains in terms of "economic sovereignty" as we approach the millennium will likely have less and less to do with the role of nation-states and more and more to do with how a society decides to "live and work and play," as it were. In Canada, at least, the powers related to these functions rest more with the provinces than with Ottawa. Enter the potential for flourishing subnational "distinct societies." Thus, what might at first be an anomaly — namely, an integrating world economy and, in terms of these distinct societies, a splintering world polity — is in reality a rather direct consequence of the decline of the economic relevance of the nation-state or, alternatively, of an increase in the ability of subnational units to link themselves to the emerging global institutional arrangements. This brings to mind one of the slogans of the environmentalists — think globally, act locally. Elsewhere (Courchene 1994b), I have referred to this as the "glocalization" of economic life.

As Thematic Tableau 5 indicates, there is another way in which powers will be transferred downward. I have argued (ibid., chap. 5) that, to the extent that institutions are globalizing, this is taking place via the network of international cities — Montreal, Toronto, and Vancouver for Canada. The economies of scale and scope associated with the concentration of the information and services infrastructure means that these international cities become not only growth poles but the essential connectors outward toward the Londons and Tokyos and inward to their regional hinterlands. Already, Barcelona, Toulouse, and Montpelier are forging economic links that will take them out from under Madrid and Paris and into a European Union or Brussels framework. Transferred to Canada, this means that for a distinct society to have meaning in an economic sense it must evolve around an international city: without Montreal, there would be no Bloc Québécois!

On the surface, these observations may seem more interesting than relevant, at least as far as Social Canada is concerned. However, they do become relevant once one considers other aspects of globalization and, in particular, the observation that Canada is becoming less and less a single national economy and more and more a series of cross-border, north-south economies. Moreover, these series of economies are not only very different from each other (and as is clear from Figure 4 in Chapter 2 their business cycles are not synchronous), but the manner in which they are likely to integrate north-south (or, in British

Thematic Tableau 5

Globalization and Social Policy:
A Subjective "Tour d'horizon"

General Implications

- At its most basic level, globalization is the internationalization of production. Even at this level, it represents a severe challenge to social policy because welfare states in all countries were geared to their respective national production machines. What is the optimal nature of the social policy envelope when production is international?
- It is the international private sector that is globalizing, not the international public sector. Thus, economic space is transcending political space. In countervail fashion, some functions of the economic nation-state are being passed upward (free trade, the European Union, the Bank for International Settlements).
- Power is also flowing downward both to citizens and to international cities since it is largely via the latter that "institutions" are globalizing. The European regional science literature now focuses on the "regional/international" interface and not only the national/international interface — that is, economic regions are cutting across traditional political boundaries.
- Globalization as represented by free trade pacts has other social policy implications. With freer markets, delivering social policy via cross-subsidization is more difficult. Distributional (that is, tax transfer) instruments, not allocative instruments, must now deliver social policy. This is a welcome development.
- Relatedly, with the spread of free trade deals, whether in Europe or America, social policy issues are coming under the rubric of competition policy — hence, the increasing use of the term "social dumping."

Relevance for Canada

- As trade increasingly flows north-south, Canada will cease to be a single economy and become a series of north-south, cross-border economies. What will then bind us east-west is more of a social policy railway than an economic policy railway. The emerging challenge is how to mount an east-west transfer system over an increasing north-south trading system.
- In particular, the political economy of transfers will alter. When the second-round spending effects of equalization and interregional transfers tend to go south, rather than back to the "golden horseshoe", how will this alter Canadians' (or Ontarians') taste for transfers?
- In an increasing number of areas, a central vision emanating from the center will no longer be acceptable — the regions will be too economically diverse in that the requirements for a Great Lakes economy like Ontario will differ from those for a Pacific Rim economy like British Columbia. Part of the solution will likely be one or all of greater decentralization, greater asymmetry and greater east-west flexibility (including wage flexibility).

Columbia's case, north-south and Pacific Rim) is also likely to be quite different. This is the rationale for the last bullet of Thematic Tableau 5 — namely, that the dictates of a Great Lakes economy like Ontario in terms of how it might ideally structure its constellation of social programs (welfare, UI, training, apprenticeship) could be quite different from the way a Pacific Rim economy like British Columbia might wish to integrate its social infrastructure. As indicated, this suggests that a single vision emanating from the center may have to give way to one or more of greater decentralization, greater asymmetry, or greater east-west flexibility (including wage flexibility).

Asymmetry is also likely to increase because of the constitutional implications that arise from Thematic Tableau 6. With the heightened importance of human capital and the relatively diminished importance of goods flows, more of what binds Canadians together east-west will relate to social policy. As suggested in the second-to-last bullet of the tableau, this may alter the optimal distribution of powers in the federation: much of what Ottawa currently does in terms of forestry, mining, energy, and so on is no longer the "stuff" of national identity.

The central message from Thematic Tableau 6 is straightforward: despite its resource endowments, Canada has no choice but to make the transition from a resource-based economy and society to a human-capital/knowledge-based economy and society. We were able to become a high wage/high transfer economy largely because of our resource endowments and the protective tariff. With the various rounds of multilateral trade negotiations and the free trade agreement with the United States and Mexico, the tariff wall is basically history. And while one may not buy into Drucker's (1986) claim that resources are now peripheral to the economic success of the developed economies, the fact remains that the cushion of resource rents has largely evaporated. The only way back to a high-wage and, if we wish, high-transfer economy is to provide both citizen upward mobility in terms of skills enhancement and an industrial system geared to high-value-added production.

The unfortunate aspect of all this is that the challenge is much greater than it should have been. While I have used the term "revolution" to describe the new global economic order, there were plenty of signals that the old order was no longer sustainable. Thus, we had ample time and warning that we needed to make the transition. However, while we were quite willing to throw all sorts of money in the form of welfare, UI, and short-term job creation at low-income and low-skilled Canadians, we were singularly incapable of removing the anti-human-capital incentives from these social programs, let alone investing in the human capital of these Canadians.

By way of summary to this point, Thematic Tableaus 5 and 6, and the globalization and information revolutions that underpin them, speak directly to the thrust of this study in several ways:

Thematic Tableau 6

The Information Revolution and Social Policy: A Subjective "Tour d'Horizon"

- The information revolution is inherently decentralizing in that individuals can now access, transform, transmit and manipulate data and information in ways that governments are powerless to prevent. This will make old-style governance more difficult for governments of all stripes.
- With knowledge at the cutting edge of competitiveness, aspects of social policy become indistinguishable from economic policy. Regardless of what the Constitution may say, it is inconceivable that the federal government will be relegated to the sidelines of social policy if national competitiveness is at stake.
- Drucker's predictions (1986) are holding up well — the manufacturing sector is becoming uncoupled from the resource sector (that is, GNP is becoming less raw-materials intensive) and, within manufacturing, production is becoming uncoupled from employment. The latest version of the latter is the prediction for a low-employment-growth recovery.
- Despite its generous resource endowments, Canada cannot avoid making the transition from a resource-based economy and society to a knowledge-based economy and society. Further success in the resource areas will progressively require the application of knowledge and high-value-added techniques.
- The middle class in this new era will include versions of technologists and information analysts. But Canada remains a professional society. — hence, the disappearing middle class. Social policy has a critical role to play in this inevitable shift from boards and mortar to mortar boards.
- In tandem with globalization, the information revolution is altering much of the old order:
  - Interregional transfers will have to tilt from "place prosperity" to "people prosperity." To the extent that place prosperity remains important, it ought to be a provincial, not a federal, matter.
  - There is emerging the notion of a global "maximum wage" for certain activities. Wages beyond this maximum wage will shift the activity offshore. As Drucker (1993) notes, this is a powerful argument for "contracting out" — that is, to enhance the productivity of these activities.
- This is turning the original British North America Act on its head. Some of the line functions, such as forestry, fishing, mining, and, energy, can and probably should be devolved to the provinces (in any event, they will continue to be driven by global imperatives) and some of the traditional provincial areas, such as education and training, will have to take on national, if not federal, dimensions. Since not all provinces will be able or willing to take down these areas, asymmetry will likely increase.
- We will witness an exciting and perhaps bewildering set of provincial experiments across the full range of the social envelope. Ottawa's role is to provide the framework within which this experimentation can take place and to ensure that there is information with respect to the successes and failures. In the same way that Saskatchewan's experimentation led to medicare a quarter of a century ago, the ongoing process is, Schumpeterian-like, creating or re-creating key elements of our new social order.

- Implicitly, they sound the death knell for the old social policy order.
- Explicitly, however, they effectively raise social policy (in particular, as it relates to human capital and skills formation) level with economic policy in terms of our future competitiveness.
- Intriguingly, they buttress the earlier criticisms of the old social order — that is, the reform imperatives point generally in the same direction.
- They also buttress the earlier point that the social policy reform process should focus on designing a set of programs geared to ensure that individual Canadians have both access and opportunity to enhance their skills and human capital.
- Finally, but hardly exhaustively, they point in the direction of greater flexibility in terms of highly charged issues such as the division of powers and asymmetry. Relatedly, they lend support to the earlier point that the fiscal arrangements ought to be derivative rather than determining — that is, the critical issue for Canadians is that the social infrastructure be appropriate to the new global order. Who delivers these programs and how they are financed are obviously important, but they should not stand in the way of developing this appropriate social infrastructure.

All in all, globalization and the information revolution provide yet another reason the forces of inertia cited in Chapter 6 cannot and will not carry the day. The issue is no longer one of providing a social network acceptable to Canadians; rather, it is one of ensuring that our economy is poised to succeed in this emerging global economic order. As indicated in the Tableaux, social policy is progressively indistinguishable from economic policy.

The above emphasis has been on how globalization and the information society serve to advance the underlying thrust of the monograph. The danger in this way of viewing the new global order is that it is merely an extension of existing societal forces for change. This is not the case. Globalization and information are more akin to a revolution in terms of how Canadians will ultimately view their country and society. Some of the entries in the Tableaux refer to these fundamental societal changes. For example, the fact that we have to implement an east-west social system over a north-south trading system is surely a break, conceptually, from the perception of "old Canada." Moreover, the recommendation that the role of the federal government is to focus on "people prosperity" and to leave "place prosperity" to the provinces is also a break from Canadian tradition, although this was also a recommendation of the Macdonald Royal Commission. (As an important aside, I view the equalization program as a part of people prosperity rather than place prosperity.) More generally, I do not think that we can as yet appreciate the full ramifications for Social or Economic Canada that are likely to emerge as globalization and the information society proceeds. In order to highlight one example of what the future may harbor in terms of the evolution of Social Canada I will elaborate on the reference in Thematic Tableau 6 to the "global maximum wage."

Contracting Out and the Global Maximum Wage

Much of the discussion of social policy within the old paradigm focused on the role of minimum wages. Market-oriented economists typically zeroed in on the employment-reducing implications of minimum wages whereas social activists tended to argue for higher minimum wages in order that the resulting incomes were at least at the accepted "poverty line" levels. With globalization and the information revolution, an emerging issue will be what might be referred to as the "global maximum wage." This is the threshold beyond which domestic employment activities will be shifted offshore, out of province, or contracted out. The economic resurgence of Moncton, New Brunswick, as the telemarketing capital of Canada is a direct result of the application of the concept of a global maximum wage. However, the point I want to make here is that, following Drucker (1993), this provides yet another argument in favor of outsourcing or contracting out.

Now, contracting out is hardly new, but it is going to spread to new areas. After all, our much-loved medicare system really involves contracting out to individual physicians — so why not hospitals, social workers, correctional services, and so on? To begin the discussion, I want to draw on some evidence from a recent issue of *The Economist* (March 6–12, 1993, 14–15). In the late 1980s, Toyota produced roughly 4.5 million cars with 65,000 workers. General Motors produced about 8 million cars with 750,000 workers. That is, Toyota produced about 70 cars per worker and GM produced 11. This huge difference in output per worker is not primarily due to automation. Rather, it relates to the underlying differences in the two enterprises. GM is a full-function manufacturer while Toyota is principally a designer/assembler. Toyota depends twice as much as its nearest US competitor on a huge network of suppliers and subcontractors — 47,308 of them at last count. Governments may not know it or want it, but the fiscal crisis and the behavior of public sector unions means the contracting out is also the way of their future. It is already well under way in the private sector, so the focus here is on the public sector.

Until now, public sector unions have quite effectively argued that contracting out is simply a way to reduce the "social wage" (economizing on pensions and other benefits). In good economic times, this argument has largely carried the day. Less so now, particularly that something else is afoot. Every once in a while, a book comes out that is not only timely but effectively challenges the status quo. Drucker's *Post-Capitalist Society* (1993) is such a book. Drucker argues that the greatest need for outsourcing is found in government. Part of the reason relates to economics. But beyond this, Drucker argues that contracting out is necessary because it provides opportunities, dignity, and income for service workers, particularly in recognition of the march of globalization and the information society. I shall not repeat the examples that Drucker proffers, but I shall reproduce a few aspects of his analysis (ibid., 95):

- These contracting organizations offer career opportunities for people doing such [service]. Their executives take such work seriously; they are therefore willing to invest time and money in redesigning the work and its tools. They are willing, even eager, to do the hard work needed to improve productivity. Above all, they take the people who do such work seriously enough to challenge them to take the lead in improving their work and its productivity. Outsourcing is necessary not just because of the economics involved. It is necessary because it provides opportunities, income, and dignity for service workers....We should therefore expect within a fairly short period of years to find such work contracted out to independent organizations, which compete and get paid for their own effectiveness in making this kind of work more productive.
- This means a radical change in structure for the organizations of tomorrow. It means that the big business, the government agency, the large university will not be the one that employs a great many people. It *will* be the one that has substantial revenues and substantial results — achieved in large part because it itself does only work that is focused on its mission; work that is directly related to results; work that it recognizes, values, and rewards appropriately. The rest it contracts out.

There is a social policy issue in all of this:

- a rapid increase in the productivity of service workers is required to avert the danger of a new "class conflict" between the two dominant groups in the postcapitalist society: knowledge workers and service workers. To make service work productive is thus the first social priority of the postcapitalist society, in addition to being an economic priority. (Ibid,, 95–96).

I am realistic enough not to expect that governments will embrace contracting out with open arms, nor to expect that public sector unions will alter their stance toward contracting out. However, I do feel confident that some government, somewhere will "buy" this analysis and engage in innovative contracting out. If the results are positive, as I expect they will be, the flood gates will open. This will be Schumpeterian creative destruction in the full sense — the positive feedbacks will entrench and expand the new initiatives. I recognize that, over the short term, contracting out may well decrease wages/benefits for some workers. But this is the wrong comparison, since globalization will eventually ensure that service workers' wages will fall in line with productivity. Thus, contracting out will, by enhancing productivity, lead to an *increase* in wages a few years hence from what would otherwise be the case.

Cast in more traditional terms, the old paradigm, replete with minimum wages and income-support systems with confiscatory tax rates in the transition from welfare/UI to work, effectively forced people into rather exclusive "working" or "not working" categories where, all too frequently, the latter could be better off than the former. The new paradigm will cut through much of this. The emphasis will be on negative income tax arrangements, on-the-job training experiences, apprenticeship, and the full range of activities that fall under the rubric of what the Europeans call "active labor force" policies. If this constellation of programs is well designed, there will be no need for minimum wages and our production system will be flexible enough to prevent much of the offshore contracting out that poses a threat to the existing socio-economic order. This represents a sea change in the structure of our socio-economic policy, but as long as the emphasis in all of this is on the upgrading of Canadians' skills and human capital then we are well on our way to grappling successfully with the imperatives of the new global order. The difficulty in all of this is that aspects of the status quo look quite appealing in comparison with some of these proposals. Unfortunately, inherent in the process of globalization and the information society is that, in many areas, the status quo cannot hold.

Conclusion

In lieu of a formal conclusion, readers can refer back to the summary Thematic Tableaux 5 and 6. The larger message is that, under the twin pressures of the fiscal burden and the new global economic order, social policy reform and restructuring is not only inevitable but already under way. The remainder of the monograph is devoted to outlining and evaluating the alternative scenarios relating to this restructuring.

Part VI

Reform and Restructuring:
Initiatives and Options

Chapter 9

Embryonic Social Policy Restructuring:
Selected Provincial Initiatives
and the 1994 Federal Budget

Social policy restructuring is under way virtually across the entire social envelope. In this chapter, I shall focus primarily on one general area, the welfare/unemployment insurance (UI)/work subsystem, and I shall detail the initiatives or proposals arising from four provincial governments — Quebec, Ontario, New Brunswick, and Newfoundland — as well as the measures embodied in the 1994 federal budget. Except for the Quebec reform, which has been in place for several years now, the remaining provincial initiatives are in the form of either pilot projects or proposals. Nonetheless, all are interesting and all will be evaluated from the vantage point of the relevant aspects of the restructuring imperatives developed in the preceding chapters.

The role of the following chapter is to cast the net much wider and assemble a rather comprehensive menu of reform options relating to the full range of issues addressed in the monograph. Chapter 11 then presents my preferred blueprint for Social Canada in the millennium.

Implicit in these final chapters is the assumption that the reform imperatives in the previous chapter have carried the day and that the time has now come to focus on restructuring in terms both of options and principles.

Quebec's Parental Wage Assistance Program

Quebec has long been the most creative province on the social policy front (which is not quite the same as saying that it has the best approach). Its most novel approach in terms of the general thrust of this chapter is its Parental Wage Assistance (PWA) program (Aide aux parents pour leur revenus de travail) established in 1988. PWA contains three components: a supplement to employment income, the reimbursement of approximately 55 percent of eligible day care expenses, and a housing allowance. In addition, PWA is integrated into the

Quebec personal income tax system in a way that ensures that these payments fall to zero as families become eligible for provincial taxation.

Applicants meeting the PWA eligibility requirements come under the program for each month in which they have earned $150 in employment income and received not more than $300 in income from various government programs such as UI or workers' compensation. The assistance is calculated according to the applicants' estimated employment income for the year. It is paid in monthly installments of 75 percent of the expected annual benefit calculated on a monthly basis: these installments are paid only for those months in which the applicant earns employment income. The balance will be paid by the Ministry of Revenue at the end of the year, when a reconciliation is made between the installments paid and the benefits actually due. Any overpayments that might occur during the year are recovered at the time of the annual reconciliation.

The assistance paid takes the following factors into account: number of months worked during the benefit year; income from employment and other sources; assets; number of dependent children; family type (single parent or couple); day care expenses incurred; and housing costs. Here are two examples for 1990:

- The assistance given by PWA is $3,357 for a two-parent, one-child household, with one parent working through the entire year and earning $12,000 in employment income;
- A single-parent family with $4,200 in child care expenses for a young child and with employment income of $9,000 over 12 months is entitled to $5,151, of which $2,814 represents a partial reimbursement for child care expenses.

Thus, workers with modest incomes and with dependent children will be encouraged by PWA to remain in the workforce. Moreover, UI and welfare recipients with dependent children will have an incentive for joining the workforce. In effect, this is a version of a negative income tax. The wage supplementation takes account of family size/type and it is integrated with the Quebec personal income tax. All in all, it is an experiment worthy of close monitoring. (For more elaboration and a positive assessment of the PWA program, see Bouchard 1993.)

In terms of the analysis in previous chapters, there are a few general comments that deserve highlight. First, while there are doubtless several reasons Quebec has emerged as a leader in social policy reform, the fact that it has its own separate income tax is surely prominent among them. The income tax system is an obvious instrument around which to design, deliver, and reconcile an income-tested, negative income tax or wage supplementation program. Second, and related, there has always been a tension in the system in terms of how a *single* value for the minimum wage could at the same time accommodate or be appropriate for, say, individuals and families. Quebec has handled this by gearing wage supplementation not to income *per se*, but to family status (number of dependents) adjusted income. The break-even point where PWA falls to zero for a single person will be at a lower income level than for a family of four (with a single worker) because the latter has greater tax deductions or credits and, therefore, begins to pay *positive* Quebec income tax at a higher income level than is the case for an individual. Third, and again related, the wage supplementation system is integrated with the personal income tax system in such a way that the transition between the negative and positive side of the income tax system does not overlap — that is, persons in receipt of PWA are not at the same time paying positive Quebec income taxes.

More generally, it is not very surprising that Quebec is now in the forefront in terms of wanting all training to be devolved to the province. Again, there are special reasons for this (for example, language), but it is also true that it does have an infrastructure in place that can facilitate such a devolution. It seems to me that if other provinces wish to play a more prominent role in integrating the welfare to work transition, they ought to have the flexibility to use the personal income tax as a coordinating and delivery mechanism. As Thematic Tableau 4 indicated, this does not require that they follow Quebec's lead and establish a separate income tax system — a tax-on-base approach will suffice.

NB Works

The governments of Canada and New Brunswick have undertaken a joint demonstration project, referred to as "NB Works" (New Brunswick 1992). The goals of NB Works are threefold: to develop the human resource and employment potential of the social-assistance-recipient caseload; to begin to change the attitude that may exist that income assistance is an end in itself to an attitude that people can increase their employability and job-ready status; and to save social assistance costs by moving persons from caseload to work.

The target population is social assistance recipients who have been receiving assistance for at least six months, who have low educational achievement but at least grade 9, and who have little or no labor force attachment. After selection and the requisite testing, participants are assigned a case counselor who prepares a plan that lays out the work, education, and skills training path to be followed. The work phase constitutes up to 20 weeks of work, chosen to fit the participant's plan (and, as we shall see, to qualify applicants for UI!). This is followed by the education/training phase. When skills training is complete, job search training and possibly another job experience will follow in partnership with a private sector employer.

The funding is based on three "intakes" of 1000 a year for a total of 3,000 potential participants. The total cost of this pilot project is set at $176.8 million. Thus, the cost per participant is just under $60,000. If one assumes that each participant is in the program for three years, this works out to be in the neighborhood of $19,200 per year per participant. Ottawa's share is $119.4 million, with $81 million from UI and $32.4 million from Health and Welfare. New Brunswick will contribute $57.4 million, with $32.4 million from the Department of Income Assistance and $25 million from the Department of Advanced Education and Labour. In terms of New Brunswick's contribution, social assistance benefits that clients would have received had they not chosen to participate in this program are diverted to finance, among other things, the training phase. This is the $32.4 million total for both Health and Welfare and New Brunswick's welfare department (and it reflects the 50–50 sharing under the Canada Assistance Plan).

Essentially, the employment phase qualifies participants for UI benefits in the form of training allowances, child care and transportation allowances. (Under the provisions of the *Unemployment Insurance Act*, these benefits will continue for three and a half years). Participants will be at least as well off in terms of disposable income as they would have been under social assistance. Costs of child care and transportation are add-ons. Because of this, the $81 million UI component to overall funding is larger than the $64.8 million that would have come from welfare (the sums of the federal and provincial $32.4 million for welfare).

While the demonstration projection is not far enough along to attempt anything in the way of a definitive evaluation, it has nonetheless attracted much attention in policy circles, most of it favorable. To be sure, it has some attractive features — shifting the emphasis away from income support and toward skills development and labor market reintegration. It also provides an integration of sorts between UI and social assistance — an integration that is clearly long overdue in the social sphere. New Brunswick obviously benefits — the province spends $25 million of new money and Ottawa throws in $81 million, thanks to UI.

My initial reaction is that this is an extremely costly approach. It may well be appropriate for a pilot project, but it would "break the bank" if applied across the board. It seems to me that it is an expensive mop-up exercise to enhance the skills of persons who for some reason or other did not acquire skills in high school or technical college. It is to be hoped that the next move will be to introduce these counseling/training/education services and programs into high schools or postsecondary institutions when the students can still rely on their families for income support. Second, with this much money floating around, it will be interesting to see if some private sector training facilities are enticed to set up shop. In line with the earlier discussion of "procurement federalism," of which NB Works is really a variant, Ottawa must ensure that this is not another exercise to buttress provincial PSE institutions.

Nonetheless, NB Works merits close monitoring because the shift from "passive" to "active" labor is clearly the way of the future and we are in dire need of experiments to see what works and what does not.

A Military-Civilian Training Interface

New Brunswick probably has a legitimate claim to being Canada's most innovative province in the 1990s: Frank McKenna is the first premier to have his e-mail code on his "business" card, as part of his province's embracing the electronic superhighway. More relevant, for present purposes, is that New Brunswick recently struck a deal with the military to cooperate in a training pilot project. As noted in an earlier chapter, this is an area where the possibility exists for a constructive partnership.

On January 24, 1994, Premier McKenna and the Minister of National Defence inaugurated a pilot project to help young, unemployed New Brunswickers build new futures. Under this initiative, the first of its kind in the country, 30 young volunteers will be "fast tracked" into a 20-week package of military, life skills, and occupational training and job experience. In more detail, the training will consist of:

- five and a half weeks of basic military training;
- two to eight weeks of occupational training;
- two days of job search skills;
- the remainder of 20 weeks devoted to on-the-job experience.

Three occupations are available — basic stores person (three weeks of training); basic cook (eight weeks of training) and basic administrative clerk (two weeks of training). In terms of the range of training involved, the eight-weeks of basic cook training involves the following: prepare nutritionally balanced meals ranging from light lunches to formal banquets; prepare extra meals, snacks, and box lunches for personnel who work shifts; exposure to ordering and storing all food-related items; serve meals at steam-tables; prepare soups, salads, sauces, and vegetables; cut, prepare, and cook meat; produce cakes, pastries, and other baked goods including decorative; exposure to ration accounting; menu planning; sanitation and cleaning of kitchen/dining areas and equipment; and exposure to preparing special meals in hospitals and flight meals for aircraft. This is a scaled-down version of the training that the military provides for its noncommissioned members who opt for training as a cook. While this project is not directly associated with NB Works, it is nonetheless a complementary initiative and may hold considerable promise. (For more detail on the potential for accessing military expertise in training civilian Canada, and for an early assessment of this New Brunswick experiment, see Courchene and Campbell 1994.) Thus, both NB Works and this military pilot project merit close monitoring because they may serve as useful models for the rest of Canada.

Newfoundland's Income Supplementation Program

By far the most ambitious, comprehensive, and, in many areas, innovative proposal is that prepared by Newfoundland's Economic Recovery Commission (ERC) and made public by Premier Clyde Wells in a press conference in December 1993. The basis for the description and evaluation that follows is the Commission's Information Paper, "Proposal for a New Income Supplementation Program and Other Reforms to the Income Security System" (1993). Conceptually, and even in a direct sense, this document has its roots in Newfoundland's Royal Commission on Employment and Unemployment (which reported in 1986) since Douglas House was the Chair of the Royal Commission and is the head of the ERC.

While I shall argue that the ISP contains some severe incentive and financing problems (indeed, I think that they are fatal in terms of the viability of the specific proposal), the publication and proposal are to be welcomed. Rarely in a public document have I seen such a frank assessment of the status quo and rarely, as well, has such a comprehensive set of proposals been developed to address the weaknesses of the current environment. At the outset, it is important to note that the report describes itself as a "tentative, working document" (p. 3). In more detail: "It must be emphasized that this is a proposal for discussion purposes only at this stage, and the final parameters of the proposed changes will only be determined after federal input and full public consultation" (p. 4). Thus, while I do not believe that the current version can survive, the general approach has considerable virtue and, in some version, may well see the light of legislative day.

The Need for Reform

Before focusing on the restructuring details it is informative, in terms of both motivating the ISP proposal and the overall thrust of this study, to reproduce a few background tables from the Newfoundland proposal that detail the inade-

---

Box 1: *Weaknesses in the System*

1.   discourages self-employment and small-scale enterprise;

2.   undermines personal and community initiatives;

3.   undermines the importance of education;

4.   distorts the efforts of local development groups;

5.   creates disincentives to work;

6.   impedes productivity for employers.

Source: Newfoundland 1993, p. 2.

---

quacies of the status quo. While some of the points made in Box 1 were included as part of the analysis in Chapter 3, they merit reproduction because they now have the "imprimatur" of Premier Wells. Box 2, "Startling Facts," should not be nearly as startling to those who have followed Canada's many experiments in the general area of "place prosperity." Taken together, however, Boxes 1 and 2 probably make the case for social policy reform in a more cogent manner (and certainly in a more efficient manner) than I have managed to do in the previous chapters.

As a final piece of background, Table 34 presents a listing of federal and provincial transfers to Newfoundlanders in fiscal year 1991/92. The grand total, $2.352 billion, represents $4,100 per capita. Note that these are "gross benefits" — for example, offsetting the $1.041 billion of UI benefits are UI premiums paid by Newfoundlanders — roughly $180 million for 1988 from Chapter 3 — as well as any income taxes generated by these benefits.

Basically, the ISP program takes most, but not all, of this $2.352 billion in transfers and reworks them into a rather sophisticated combination of a negative income tax/wage supplementation scheme. To this I now turn.

The ISP Proposal

At base, the Newfoundland proposal recasts UI and welfare into an Income Supplementation Program comprising two main components — a basic income supplement (BIS) and a work supplement (WS). In more detail:

•   For most people, welfare (or social assistance) would cease to exist. It would be converted to a basic income supplement (BIS) of $3,000 per adult (25–64

Box 2:   *Startling Facts*

- In 1988, *48 percent* of those employed throughout the province received UI benefits at some point during the year.
- Dependency is highest in rural areas, where *70 percent* of individuals who had employment income also received UI.
- Between 1981 and 1989 seasonality in this province rose while for Canada as a whole it declined. In 1989 the seasonal variation in employment in this province was *three times* that for Canada.
- Over the period 1981 to 1989 employment income grew by *6.4 percent* per year while UI income grew by *13.5 percent* per year.
- The proportion of our working age population with a *university education has fallen* over the past ten years *relative to the rest of Canada*. The proportion with only elementary education is far above the rest of Canada. This situation has not improved in 15 years.
- *Lack of education* is most pronounced amongst UI recipients in our rural resource-based industries, particularly in fish harvesting and processing occupations, as well as in the construction trades.
- These *barriers to growth* reduce the effectiveness of government agencies such as Enterprise Newfoundland and Labrador, the Department of Industry, Trade and Technology and the Atlantic Canada Opportunities Agency.
- The pattern of attachment to UI and to occupations requiring little formal education is firmly entrenched amongst Newfoundlanders, often when they are as young as 19 years of age.
- Our young people are much more dependent on UI than is the case elsewhere in Canada, and those that become attached to the system have invested much less in their education.
- Between 1981 and 1985 provincial productivity growth was at about 30 percent of productivity growth for Canada as a whole. Between 1985 and 1989 the situation deteriorated and Newfoundland was the only province to record a negative productivity growth rate.
- This deterioration in the province's relative productivity growth could affect the competitive position of our industries and, thus, our standard of living over the long term.
- Declining productivity could be felt through reductions in employment, real per capita incomes, and governments' ability to maintain an adequate level of public services.
- Given the current income security system, there is little reason to expect that provincial income disparities with other provinces would disappear or that unemployment levels would fall significantly through employment growth.

Source: Newfoundland 1993, 5–6.

Table 34:   *Estimated Income Security Programs and Expenditures, Newfoundland, fiscal year 1991/92*

	Value of Benefits
	($ millions)
Unemployment insurance	1,041
Old age security	248
Canada Pension Plan	233
Guaranteed Income Supplement	140
Job creation[a]	76
Estimated costs of program delivery	150
Social assistance	152
Refundable sales tax credit[b]	65
Family allowance	66
Workers' compensation[b]	90
War allowances	28
Spouses' allowance	23
Veterans' disability[b]	12
Refundable sales tax credit[c]	28
Total[d]	2,352

[a] Includes those projects in which participants receive government sponsored (or subsidized) wages and/or obtain UI insurable weeks of employment. UI section 25 program expenditures are excluded from this total and added as a component of unemployment insurance benefits.

[b] 1991 calendar year.

[c] 1990 calendar year.

[d] These data are the most recent available. It is unlikely that yearly variations in most of the categories would change the total significantly.

Source: Newfoundland 1993, 7.

years old). Persons 65 years of age and older would continue to be covered by the existing range of social programs.

- Children under 18 would qualify for a BIS of $1,500. This would be paid to the parent or guardian. This would be merged with the federal child tax benefit, which means that Ottawa would finance most of this, given that the federal credit is $1,020 for each child over six years of age and $1,233 for each child under six. Note that the first child in a single-parent household would receive an "adult" BIS, again payable to the single parent.
- Youths between 18 and 20 who reside at home would receive the $1,500 BIS, but payable to them directly. This category would not be eligible for work supplementation (see below), but would be eligible for educational

supplementation. Youths aged between 21–24 would receive a BIS of $2,000 per year, wherever they reside. They would be eligible for WS.

- After the first $500 of earned income, there would be a 20 percent work supplementation, to a maximum of $2,000. Thus, $10,500 of earned income (even for the self-employed) would generate the maximum WS — that is, $3,000.

- Now come the "tax-back" arrangements, which the proposal refers to as "benefit reduction" (BR). BR would not begin until *family* earned income (not individual income) reaches $15,000. Thereafter, there is a 40 percent clawback rate on additional earned income until all the provincial benefits (BIS and WS) are repaid.

These are the basics of the ISP proposal. They are summarized in Table 35.

Before focusing on how the system will operate for a family of four, it is useful to detail some of the other important complementary features of the proposal:

- UI for Newfoundlanders would be altered. The minimum entry level of weeks would rise from 10 to 20, and each week of contributions would lead to one week of benefits, up to a maximum of 35 weeks. Self-employed persons would not be eligible for UI. In addition, UI benefits would be part of "family income" for tax-back or benefit-reduction purposes.

- For persons or families who are not able to find work or who cannot work, social assistance (welfare) would still be there to top up income where needs dictate — this could include housing subsidies, medical (drug) expenses, and so on.

- There would be an educational supplement (ES) to complement the ISP. Participants would be able to access a yearly ES supplement to offset the direct costs of postsecondary education for up to four years. There would appear to be no age restriction in terms of accessing this ES.

The ISP in Action

To its credit, the proposal conducts a rather comprehensive "sensitivity analysis" — it compares the pre- and post-ISP situations for different family sizes and for different employment categories (no work, part-time work, full-time work, as well as the 10/42 syndrome). I shall limit attention here to the impacts on a family of four — two adults, two children, with one wage earner.

Figure 20 presents the operations of the ISP for our family of four. The vertical axis is total income (earned income plus BIS plus WS). The horizontal axis is earned income, which, as already noted, would include UI income/bene-

Table 35: *Proposed Parameters of Newfoundland's Income Supplementation Program*

Parameters	Description	Level of Support
Basic income supplement	Adult	$3,000
	Young adult (21 to 24 years)	$2,000
	Youth (18 to 20 years)	$1,500
	Child	$1,500
Work supplementation	Range	$500 to $10,500
	Rate	20%
	None for under 21 years of age	
Benefit reduction	Trigger amount	$15,000
	Rate	40%

Note: First child of single-parent family equivalent to adult benefit ($3,000).
Source: Newfoundland 1993, 17.

fits. The BIS for a family of four is $9,000. The first $500 of earned income is ineligible for a work supplement. Thereafter, total income increases by 120 percent of earned income until the maximum WS of $2,000 is reached. This occurs at an earned income level of $10,500 in Figure 20. At this point, the family is in receipt of the maximum ISP — $11,000, composed of $9,000 of BIS and $2,000 of WS. Between earned income levels of $10,500 and $15,000, the family is allowed to pocket all earned income — there is no clawback of benefits until earned income reaches $15,000.

Beyond $15,000, earned income is clawed back at a 40 percent tax rate. Simple mathematics dictates that to pay back $11,000 at a 40 percent tax rate requires $27,500. Thus, the break-even level, where the family has paid back its $11,000 of ISP benefits, occurs at an earned income level of $42,500.

In terms of Figure 20, the lower line represents the value of ISP benefits at different levels of earned income. As indicated, it falls from its $11,000 level at an earned income level of $15,000 to a zero level at an earned income level of $42,500.

The upper line in the figure depicts the relationship between total income and earned income. From $500 of earned income to $10,500, this upper line has an effective gradient of 1.2 — that is, each dollar of earned income leads to $1.20 of total income. Between $10,500 and $15,000 the gradient is unity — an extra dollar of earned income leads to an extra dollar of total income (zero taxation). If income were measured identically on both axes (which, for some reason, it does not in the original), this would be represented by a 45° line segment.

Figure 20: *Newfoundland's Income Supplementation Program*
(family of four — two adults, two children — with one wage earner)

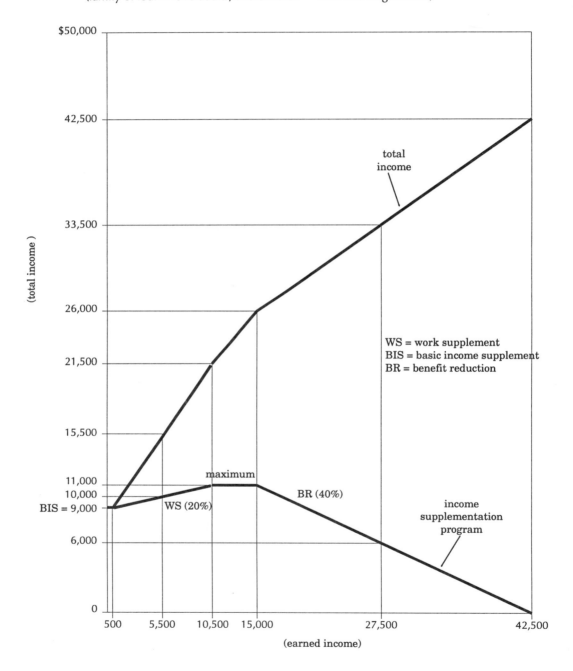

Source: Newfoundland 1993, 18.

Beyond $15,000, total income increases by 60 cents for each dollar of earned income. This reflects the 40 percent clawback.

Design Flaw #1:
Confiscatory Tax Rates

Figure 20 is a faithful representation of the ISP model as it relates to the *internal* operations of the system. Incredibly, however, it does not incorporate the operations of the personal income tax system. The federal-plus-Newfoundland marginal tax rates up to a taxable income level of $29,590 (for 1992) are 28.73 percent (that is, the 17 percent federal rate multiplied by 1.69, where the Newfoundland rate is 69 percent of federal basic tax). From $29,591 to $59,180, the combined marginal rate is 43.94 percent. Beyond this taxable income level, the marginal rate is 49.01 percent.

The value of personal tax credits for a family of four is such that this family unit will pay no income tax until earned income exceeds $12,670. To facilitate the analysis, let us assume that pension deductions and the like mean that the 28.73 percent marginal rate does not kick in until the $15,000 earned income level. However, beyond this point the marginal tax rate on earned income is 68.73 percent — 40 percent from the ISP and 28.73 percent from income tax. This rate applies to levels of taxable income up to $29,590. Again, for simplicity, let us assume that a taxable income level of $29,590 corresponds to an earned income level of, say, $32,500. This means that, for the last $10,000 of earned income in Figure 20 (that is, from $32,500 to $42,500), earnings will be subject to an *overall* (ISP and income tax) marginal tax rate of 83.94 percent!

But this is not all. The ISP incorporates the federal child tax credit as part of the BIS for the children in the family. Beyond a *net* income level in the range of $26,000, Ottawa taxes this back at a 5 percent rate on each dollar of earned income in the case of two children. This means that the effective marginal tax rate beyond $15,000 is 73.73 percent, up to $32,000 or so of earning income, and then it rises to 88.94 percent until the federal tax credit is clawed back, after which (about $40,000) it falls to 83.94 percent.[1]

Because the ISP benefit reductions are based on *family* income, a wide variety of anomalies can arise. For example, were one of the children to earn $1,000 from a paper route (if children do this anymore), this will be subject to a 40 percent clawback under the ISP, assuming that it is reported. And so on.

---

1 Actually, because the Newfoundland proposal incorporates the federal child tax credit into its basic allowance for children, it may be that one should assume that this 5 percent clawback is already embedded in the 40 percent benefit reduction rate. This is not clear from the documentation.

The general point must be clear by now. The overall marginal tax rates under the ISP are dramatic — indeed, *they are virtually confiscatory over significant segments of income.* This may well render the program nonviable, economically and fiscally, because the incentives to go underground with marginal tax rates in the range of 84–89 percent will be well-nigh irresistible.

The problem obviously lies in the design of the ISP. To be sure, there is also an incentive problem with respect to the status quo, in that each dollar of earned income on welfare is typically taxed at 100 percent, and the same is true for UI (after the zero tax threshold of 25 percent of benefits is reached). While 100 percent is obviously too high, *minus 20 percent* is equally obviously far too low because it eventually gets one into the near-confiscatory clawbacks under the ISP.

There are many viable percentages between plus 100 percent and minus 20 percent. Why not a tax-back rate of 50 percent on each dollar of earned income, which would generate a break-even level of $18,000? This would be close enough to the earned income range where this family would begin to pay income tax that some sort of integration between this version of the ISP and income taxation could easily be worked out. This would still provide an incentive to work, and it would obviate the need for the confiscatory taxes embodied in the ISP. The obvious comparison here is with the Quebec PWA program, which *is* integrated with the income taxation system.

Why did Newfoundland, by some measures the poorest province in the country, opt for an ISP scheme with a break-even level (for a family of four) of $42,500? I think I know part of the answer. The existing set of UI arrangements is such that one needs break-even levels in this high range in order to dominate what people can receive within the present system. The modified ISP version that I outlined above ($9,000 basic income with a 50 percent tax-back rate on earned income until the break-even level of $18,000) would fare poorly in terms of what now exists. But how sustainable is the status quo? This leads rather directly to the second major problem with the ISP — the nature of the financing.

Design Flaw #2: Financing

Table 36 presents the financing details of the ISP. From the final column, the cost to Newfoundland is $630.1 million, with an additional federal increase in training of $150 million. (I assume that buried somewhere in here is the cost of the educational supplement, since it is not identified separately.) Note also that Newfoundland only saves $77 million of its current $180.1 million expenditures on social assistance. Readers of the document are not informed as to whether Ottawa would continue its full CAP payments to Newfoundland.

Table 36:   *Income Supplementation and Related Programs, Newfoundland:*
            Current and Proposed Expenditures

	Current	Proposed[a]	Difference
	($ millions)		
Income supplementation program	—	630.1	+630.1
Unemployment insurance benefits (1992/93)[c]	968.0	279.8	− 688.2
Social assistance (1992/93)	180.1	103.1	− 77.0
Child tax benefit (1993 projected)	132.3	132.3	0.0
Job creation, federal (1991/92)[d]	38.4	27.0	− 11.4
Job creation, provincial (1991/92)	37.3	27.3	− 10.0
Training, federal (1992/93)[e]	133.0	283.0	+150.0[b]
Training, provincial (1991/92)	1.0	1.0	0.0
Total	*1,490.1*	*1,483.6*	*− 6.5*

[a] These are preliminary cost estimates, therefore the differences in the current and proposed costs are also estimates. Total costs would be expected to change when final data are available.

[b] Alternatively, the income supplementation program could be made more generous. For example, the adult grant and/or the work supplementation rate could be increased.

[c] Excludes UI training.

[d] Excludes section 25 expenditures. Section 25 is included as a component of UI.

[e] Includes UI training and other federal training expenditures. Total was estimated using 1992/93 Employment and Immigration budget figures for job creation and training minus 1991/92 job creation expenditures.

Source: Newfoundland 1993, 48.

However, the key source of funds — $688.2 million — comes from UI "savings" in Newfoundland. While, as noted earlier, one has to compliment Newfoundland for being so open about its proposal, this borders on the incredible because it implies that Newfoundland's generous, but incentive-ridden, ISP proposal will be financed by a UI "payroll" tax on the rest of Canadian workers and employers! Thorsell (1994) made this point earlier.

Moreover, this is only the financing related to the ISP. There is a special transitional program related to the fishery, called the Fisheries Transition Payments. The document estimates the value of the Northern Cod Adjustment and Recovery Program (NCARP) to be $587.6 million for 1993 (or roughly $1,000 per capita). Under NCARP, fish harvesters are eligible for $18,000 per year, processors receive $14,000, and, as the report points out, there can be more than one recipient in a family. NCARP is up for renegotiation or phase out in the spring of 1994. The proposal recommends that this transfer of $587.6 million be reduced to zero over a six-year period, after which the estimated $150 million cost for the remaining fish harvesters and fish processors would be financed via the ISP. These costs are in addition to the cost estimates contained in Table 36.

Some perspective is needed here. One hopes that Canadians will be generous in terms of some transition funding if and when (and surely the issue is only "when") the status quo no longer obtains. After all, Newfoundlanders reacted rationally to a set of inappropriate incentives in the overall transfer system. It literally took decades for transfer dependency to develop. Even apart from the fact that Ottawa must bear some (much?) of the blame for the disappearance of the cod, one cannot expect individual Newfoundlanders to bear the full cost of massive readjustment.

This being said, however, the financial principles underlying the ISP are unacceptable. What the scheme does is effectively "lock in" *all* the existing transfers and redirect *some* of them to a new program — one that embodies disincentives every bit as perverse as those it is designed to replace. The document is quite clear about this: "the reforms we propose would make better use of the millions of dollars already being spent on income security each year, and would not require large amounts of new money from Ottawa" (pp. 6–7). Among the many difficulties with this approach is that it gives priority once again to "place" rather than to "people." If Newfoundland feels that it has "property rights" over all transfers currently being spent in the province, the same is no doubt true for the rest of the Atlantic region, the Gaspésie, and Northern Ontario. This would spell the end of meaningful restructuring and, with it, Social Canada as well. What this proposal does do, however, is highlight the fact that restructuring will be difficult politically and that the ultimate catalyst will not be the arguments by mere scribblers such as I but the fiscal crisis and the long-overdue realization that the status quo is no longer viable economically.

I want to end the present discussion with a quite different concern related to the ISP. How can Newfoundland, even with Ottawa's approval, modify the UI program over its territory? I can see how, under the NB Works pilot project, one can suspend the operations of the national social system because the 3,000 people will voluntarily "sign on" to the program. But who is a Newfoundlander under the proposed UI modifications as part of the ISP? If a Gaspésian works for ten weeks in Newfoundland and then goes back to the Gaspésie to file for UI, will he qualify? What about a Newfoundlander who loses her job in Calgary after ten weeks and goes back to file in St. John's? Will she be denied benefits? She could get them if she filed in the Gaspésie! I could detail more complicated examples, but the point should be clear: modifying an individually based national program on the basis of territory will probably not work in a society as mobile as is Canada. It could work if UI were converted to a series of ten provincial programs. But this is a quite different conception of UI, since interprovincial transfers would no longer exist. More on this, too, later.

Ottawa cannot possibly (or, since everything is possible, should not) give a green light to Newfoundland's proposed ISP. But the proposal itself is instructive. First of all, it sends an embarrassing signal to Ottawa that the province that is the chief financial beneficiary of UI no longer feels that the program is serving its residents well. Second, and as important, it also signals that the provinces have come to the realization that major structural changes in Social Canada are now inevitable, so that the time has come for them to design appealing alternatives that attempt to "lock in" the existing money flows. To a degree, this is also true of NB Works, although the scale is much smaller.

Perhaps the best way to view the Newfoundland proposal is that it is the opening salvo in the restructuring process. One should not expect that in an initial, unsolicited proposal, Newfoundland would voluntarily offer to forgo any of its existing transfers. But the proposal may constitute an effective opening position in what will likely be a prolonged set of negotiations.

But now that various "have-not" provinces have joined other Canadians in calling for restructuring Social Canada, where is Ontario?

Ontario's *Turning Point*

In mid-1993, Ontario's Department of Community and Social Services released its position paper, *Turning Point* (Ontario 1993b), which is a general blueprint for a wholesale revamping of Ontario's welfare system. While what Ontario eventually does on the welfare or social assistance front obviously will have a major impact on the entire system, I shall not devote nearly as much space to *Turning Point* as I did to Newfoundland's ISP, largely because the former does not constitute a formal proposal — that is, the specific legislation has not yet been tabled. This is not in any way meant to downgrade either the importance or impact of Ontario's restructuring.

Box 3 contains the essence of the position paper's proposals. In its words (ibid., 15):

> The Ontario Government intends to dismantle the welfare system as we know it. Social assistance will be replaced by two new income programs: the Ontario Child Income Program [OCIP] and the Ontario Adult Benefit [OAB]. In order to help adults make the transition to independence, an employment planning system — Job Link — will convert them to training education and jobs.

Box 3:   *The Details of Ontario's* Turning Point

Integrated Supports for People with Low Incomes

Unlike the current welfare system, Ontario's new approach will have a clear philosophy and set of goals with programs designed to produce results.

Philosophy

- promote independence by encouraging job preparation;
- provide fair treatment to all low-income families, including those with parents working full time.

Programs

- Ontario Child Income Program
  - provides a simple monthly cheque to all low-income families;
  - amount of cheque depends on family income, number of children;
  - removes children's benefits from welfare system; serves as an incentive to work, since unemployed adults can take full-time jobs and keep children's benefits.
- Ontario Adult Benefit (OAB)
  - provides a simple monthly cheque to adults in transition to meet basic needs for food, clothing, shelter, and personal needs;
  - benefit levels will ensure that people are always better off working full-time;
  - provides extra financial assistance to persons with disabilities, long-term income to people who cannot work.
- Job Link
  - available to OAB recipients;
  - connects people to education, training, and job placement programs;
  - replaces OAB cheque with an Education and Training Allowance that takes into account both basic needs and cost of job preparation and job search activities.

Goals

- help people move quickly back to work;
- provide long-term support to people who cannot work;
- address child poverty.

Results

- all families will be able to meet their children's basic needs without welfare;
- families with parents working full time at low incomes will receive fair support;
- unemployed adults will learn new skills and find jobs;
- persons with disabilities will receive the support they need to train and work;
- persons who cannot work will receive adequate and secure financial support.

Source: Ontario 1993b, 3.

Both of these issues — the treatment of children under welfare and the shift from a passive to an active labor market approach for adults — are obviously key elements in any reform package.

While there are no doubt many motivations underlying this position paper (and some are listed under "philosophy" and "goals" in Box 3), high on the list must be the related facts that one in nine Ontarians was on welfare in 1993 and that Ontario has finally realized that the incentives in the existing program are perverse.

In terms of the latter, the most significant initiative is OCIP. This is a version of a guaranteed annual income for children. It addresses, head on, one of the key incentive problems of the status quo — namely, that income from work at the minimum wage dominates welfare for a single adult but not for a family unit with children. *Turning Point* gets around this incentive issue because OCIP payments will no longer be linked to welfare. Henceforth, payments to children will depend on family income (and, obviously, on the number of children) and not on whether the adults are on welfare. *Turning Point* does not indicate how Ontario will tailor these payments to income — the income level at which these payments will begin to decrease; the effective clawback rate and, therefore, the break-even level; and whether or not these will be run through the tax system or through a special program.

Earlier in this study, I argued that one attractive option for replacing the Canada Assistance Plan was to convert it into a new refundable child tax credit. The existing child tax credit begins to be clawed back when family net income reaches $26,000. However, the existing credit is not primarily an antipoverty measure: it also has to do with maintaining aspects of horizontal equity (up to some threshold level) in the tax system between families with children and those without children. If the new tax credit were to be primary an antipoverty measure (as it should be if the monies are coming from CAP), it would make sense for the break-even or phaseout level to be at the $26,000 family net income level, or even lower. Thus, there may be opportunities for cooperation here between Ottawa and Ontario and, by extension, the rest of the provinces.

In any event, OCIP is both innovative and, as far as I can tell, conceptually appropriate.

With children looked after by OCIP, there will be incentives for adults to enter the labor force, no matter how many children there are in their family. Moreover, *Turning Point* is intent on heightening this incentive further by proposing that the minimum wage be moved up from its current 48 percent of the average industrial wage to 60 percent. My view is that this would be a mistake: this is the old "binary" model — either welfare or work — albeit with a greater incentive to make the transition than under the existing model. Far better, it seems to me, to have a negative income tax approach to this transition whereby the wage earner will pocket a certain percentage of any earned income. The legislation should incorporate some version of this model rather than an all or nothing approach where one either is or is not on welfare.

The Job Link component converts the system into an "active" labor force policy. Indeed, as Box 3 indicates, adults who become involved in Job Link will not receive an OAB but a more comprehensive Education and Training Allowance (ETA). Assuming that this feature carries over to the legislation, it will be interesting to see what sorts of incentives will exist here. Will they be largely financial in that the benefits under ETA will exceed those under OAB by a margin sufficient to entice adults into Job Link? Or will there be a presumption that the able-to-work will move into Job Link? That is, will this be more like "workfare" or, perhaps more appropriately, "training-fare"? As an intriguing aside, there are some constraints under CAP funding that limit the ability of a province to convert welfare into versions of workfare. However, Ontario has a great deal of freedom here because the 50 percent CAP sharing covers only about 60 percent of its overall welfare spending, so that this excess spending amounts to 100 cent Ontario dollars and it is not obvious that Ottawa can put much in the way of a constraint on how Ontario spends 100 cent dollars.

In more general terms, the concepts embodied in *Turning Point*, if they resurface in legislation, are likely to have a major impact on social assistance spending in Canada. Specifically:

- the provision for a separate benefit for low-income children effectively takes children's benefits out of welfare as we know it;
- the incentives to work for adults in family units with children will be enhanced significantly, especially so if these OAB are also income tested; and
- Ontario appears to be integrating welfare and education/training/placement — that is, it is integrating the welfare-to-work transition.

The combination will pose problems for the continuance of the Canada Assistance Plan because Ontario's approaches to funding do not square well with the existing features of CAP. Thus, Ontario presumably will be pressing for some alternative CAP arrangement that will not only accommodate this new policy but remove the current feature where it is spending 28 cent dollars and most of the other provinces are spending 50 cent dollars. Some equal per capita block funding, especially if it comes in terms of a set equalized tax point transfer might appeal to Ontario. So might the earlier suggestion that Ottawa convert CAP into a low-income benefit for children. Equity would result because *all* children would be treated identically in terms of their family income irrespective of where they may reside. In any event, this represents a major change in

Ontario's approach to welfare, which will likely also have significant implications for fiscal federalism.

Beyond this, if one combined *Turning Point* with the Ontario Training and Adjustment Board, Ontario would be in a position to contemplate taking over the responsibility for *all* training in the province. Were this to materialize, it would only be a matter of time before Ontario looked closely at ensuring that UI was also integrated or at least coordinated with this overall approach to the entire income support/education/training/work subsystem. If Ontario joined Quebec in having a comprehensive design and delivery program for this subsystem, it might well be difficult for Ottawa not to respond to the wishes of the two provinces. Under such a scenario, Ottawa's role could be reduced further if some of the existing cash dollars got translated into tax point transfers or even if Ontario requested access to the additional 16.5 personal income tax points currently assigned to Quebec.

All in all, then, the proposals embodied in *Turning Point* could, if implemented, generate quite fundamental changes in Social Canada. (As this monograph was going to press, Ontario announced that the ongoing fiscal reality will likely delay the introduction of at least the child benefits component of *Turning Point*. This does not detract from the appealing features of the proposal. And it does open up the area for Ottawa to embark on an antipoverty refundable tax credit to replace CAP.)

The 1994 Federal Budget

The final set of reform proposals relates to the initiatives associated with the February 1994 federal budget. Following the details of these changes, I shall present a brief assessment.

Equalization

In a move that predated the budget by a week or two, the federal government extended the existing formula for equalization payments for five years, from April 1, 1994, to April 1, 1999. Action was required at this time because in 1992, the program was extended for only two years. However, the ceiling will be calculated from fiscal year 1992/93 rather than 1994/95. This means that the cumulative growth of equalization from the 1992/93 base for any given year, say 1997/98, cannot exceed the cumulative growth in gross national product (GNP) over the 1992/93 to 1997/98 period.

There were two "sweeteners" in the deal for the recipient provinces. The first related to several tax base changes that were designed to update and improve the measurement of fiscal capacity. The estimated annual benefit to the recipient provinces is $165 million in fiscal year 1994/95 and about $900 million over the five-year renewal period. The ceiling will operate in a way that ensures that these benefits are not cut off by the ceiling, should it apply.

Second, measures have been taken to alleviate excessive equalization reductions with specific and exceptional natural resource concentrations. Again the ceiling will be adjusted to accommodate this.

Established Programs Financing and the Canada Assistance Plan

From *The Budget Plan* (Martin 1994a, 38–39):

> In 1994/95 no new restraint measures will be applied to either CAP or EPF [Established Programs Financing] transfers. As a result, CAP transfers will grow by a projected 5.4 percent in 1994–95, while EPF will grow by a projected 1.3 percent [note that EPF is frozen in per capita terms, so that this reflects population growth — TJC].
>
> In 1995/96 and beyond, existing legislation provides for EPF entitlements to grow in line with the growth in gross national product (GNP) minus three percentage points. No further changes will be made to the formula governing EPF transfers, pending social security reform in 1996/97. As a result, EPF entitlements are projected to grow by an additional 1.4 percent in 1995/96.
>
> Starting in 1995/96, CAP transfers to each province and territory will be kept to 1994/95 levels until superseded by social security reform in 1996/97.

All of this is by way of prelude to the social security reform. The document notes (ibid., 38) that the "federal government will require that entitlements under the social security transfers to provinces and territories (CAP and the postsecondary education component of EPF, or any successors to these transfers) be no higher after reform in 1996–97 than they are now, in 1993/94." This will allow Ottawa to secure a minimum of $1.5 billion in savings in 1996/97 (relative to what these transfers would otherwise have been in this year). A related document (Martin 1994b, 25) states that "if social security reform fails to achieve these savings by 1996/97, other measures will be taken by the government to secure them."

Unemployment Insurance

The 1994 federal budget contained two related UI measures that are estimated to reduce UI expenditures by $725 million in fiscal year 1994/95 and $2.4 billion per year thereafter:

- Effective April 1994, there will be a restructuring of unemployment insurance benefit entitlements for new beneficiaries such that the maximum duration of unemployment insurance claims will be reduced. The amount of the reduction for the individuals will be in part determined by the employee's work history.
- Effective July 1994, the minimum entrance requirement will be increased to twelve weeks from the current ten weeks. The benefit rate for new beneficiaries will be adjusted from the current 57 percent of insurable earnings to a new two-part rate structure. Claimants with dependents and insurable earnings below one-half the maximum insurable earnings will receive 60 percent of their insured earnings and other claimants will receive 55 percent. Maximum insurance earnings currently stand at $780 per week. The method of determining maximum insurable earnings will not be changed.

Assessment

Turning first to UI, Table 37 contains the new UI benefit schedule. The old benefit entitlements appear in Table 6. As noted, the entry weeks have been altered from 10–20 weeks to 12–20 weeks. And most of the benefit weeks in Table 37 are lower than their counterparts in Table 6. Indeed, the only exception to this appears to be the benefits for working for 52 weeks in a region with less than 6 percent unemployment — 36 weeks from Table 37 and 35 weeks from Table 6. Basically, the new entitlements scale down benefits without addressing any of the anomalies. For example, 12 weeks of work in a region with more than 16 percent unemployment yields 32 benefit weeks. This length of benefit in a region with less than 6 percent unemployment requires 48 weeks of work. One trusts that these changes were dictated by the need to get the 1994 deficit beneath the desired target and that they are but a prelude to meaningful UI reform in the context of the ongoing social policy review.

Ottawa has come down much harder on EPF and CAP than on equalization. In terms of CAP, in particular, the budget recognizes that the above measures will not address the differences in federal financial support for social assistance arising from the cap on CAP, but then hints that the social security reform will strive for greater fairness.

On the equalization front, the initiatives go some considerable way toward assuaging the concerns of the recipient provinces, but they run counter to the thrust of much of the forgoing analysis, which suggests that we already over-equalize. Not surprising, the push to alter the definition of specific tax bases within equalization generally comes from the recipient provinces and not from the "have" provinces. I am sure I could find other equally appropriate tax-base

Table 37: Proposed New Unemployment Insurance Benefit Entitlement Schedule
(length of UI claim depending on weeks of work and regional unemployment rate)

Weeks of Work	6% and under	6% to 7%	7% to 8%	8% to 9%	9% to 10%	10% to 11%	11% to 12%	12% to 13%	13% to 14%	14% to 15%	15% to 16%	over 16%	Weeks of Work
12									26	28	30	32	12
13								24	26	28	30	32	13
14							23	25	27	29	31	33	14
15						21	23	25	27	29	31	33	15
16					20	22	24	26	28	30	32	34	16
17				18	20	22	24	26	28	30	32	34	17
18			17	19	21	23	25	27	29	31	33	35	18
19		15	17	19	21	23	25	27	29	31	33	35	19
20	14	16	18	20	22	24	26	28	30	32	34	36	20
21	14	16	18	20	22	24	26	28	30	32	34	36	21
22	15	17	19	21	23	25	27	29	31	33	35	37	22
23	15	17	19	21	23	25	27	29	31	33	35	37	23
24	16	18	20	22	24	26	28	30	32	34	36	38	24
25	16	18	20	22	24	26	28	30	32	34	36	38	25
26	17	19	21	23	25	27	29	31	33	35	37	39	26
27	17	19	21	23	25	27	29	31	33	35	37	39	27
28	18	20	22	24	26	28	30	32	34	36	38	40	28
29	18	20	22	24	26	28	30	32	34	36	38	40	29
30	19	21	23	25	27	29	31	33	35	37	39	41	30
31	19	21	23	25	27	29	31	33	35	37	39	41	31
32	20	22	24	26	28	30	32	34	36	38	40	42	32

Table 37: *Proposed New Unemployment Insurance Benefit Entitlement Schedule* - cont'd.

Weeks of Work	6% and under	6% to 7%	7% to 8%	8% to 9%	9% to 10%	10% to 11%	11% to 12%	12% to 13%	13% to 14%	14% to 15%	15% to 16%	over 16%	Weeks of Work
33	20	22	24	26	28	30	32	34	36	38	40	42	33
34	21	23	25	27	29	31	33	35	37	39	41	43	34
35	21	23	25	27	29	31	33	35	37	39	41	43	35
36	22	24	26	28	30	32	34	36	38	40	42	44	36
37	22	24	26	28	30	32	34	36	38	40	42	44	37
38	23	25	27	29	31	33	35	37	39	41	43	45	38
39	23	25	27	29	31	33	35	37	39	41	43	45	39
40	24	26	28	30	32	34	36	38	40	42	44	46	40
41	25	27	29	31	33	35	37	39	41	43	45	47	41
42	26	28	30	32	34	36	38	40	42	44	46	48	42
43	27	29	31	33	35	37	39	41	43	45	47	49	43
44	28	30	32	34	36	38	40	42	44	46	48	50	44
45	29	31	33	35	37	39	41	43	45	47	49	50	45
46	30	32	34	36	38	40	42	44	46	48	50	50	46
47	31	33	35	37	39	41	43	45	47	49	50	50	47
48	32	34	36	38	40	42	44	46	48	50	50	50	48
49	33	35	37	39	41	43	45	47	49	50	50	50	49
50	34	36	38	40	42	44	46	48	50	50	50	50	50
51	35	37	39	41	43	45	47	49	50	50	50	50	51
52	36	38	40	42	44	46	48	50	50	50	50	50	52

Source: Axworthy 1994, Annex 1.

changes — such as those relating to the treatment of hydro rents under the equalization program — that would serve to *decrease* equalization. This comment aside, the net result of these tax base changes will be to complicate further the equalization program. Provinces will have a special incentive to pour money into these "privileged" bases (some of which are in the resource sector) because the equalization ceiling will not be binding for these specified bases. Privileging the development of specific tax bases is surely not the role for the equalization program. It is a redistributive instrument and it should not be distorted to impinge on allocative efficiency.

What has to be addressed is the fact that equalization is a confiscatory tax in terms of any improvement in provincial tax bases. It is fully confiscatory for the Atlantic provinces because they are not part of the five-province standard; it is effectively confiscatory for Saskatchewan and Manitoba because they have such a small weight in the standard; and it is only partially confiscatory for Quebec because the province has a substantial weight in the standard. Under this framework, provinces can increase their revenues if they raise their tax rates, but in the current environment this route is politically difficult. This leaves two other avenues. One is to hope that the "have" provinces prosper or, more precisely, that the five-province standard increases. The other is to devote resources to research and lobbying designed to persuade the equalization authorities to make "appropriate" changes in the program. While I am not privy to the internal workings of equalization, my guess is that the have-provinces play little role here. I do recall that Saskatchewan effectively shut down its equalization unit when the energy price hikes in the 1970s pushed it temporarily into the "have" province group. This is entirely rational behavior on the part of the recipient provinces. But it is also rent-seeking behavior. It would be far better to alter the conception of the program to ensure that there are rewards to provinces that engage in policies that serve to increase their tax bases.

Overall, therefore, the budget does not represent much in the way of social policy reform. It does, however, signal some future reform in terms of EPF and CAP. The optimistic view is that the role of the 1994 budget was, in terms of its social policy content, not to constrain the range of options open to the reform process, although it has apparently locked in and further distorted equalization for another five-year period.

Conclusion

Social policy reform is now under way. This chapter has focused in detail on selected initiatives by several provinces as well as those embodied in the 1994 federal budget. The role of the next chapter is to present a full menu of reform options across the range of subject areas addressed in the previous chapters.

Chapter 10

Options for Reform

As documented in the previous chapter, various Canadian governments are becoming actively engaged in rethinking and reworking Social Canada. Indeed, the social policy scene is changing so rapidly that by the time this monograph appears several other provincial governments will, via their budgets or other initiatives, have embarked on significant aspects of social policy reform. And the federal government will likely have released its promised White Paper on options for social policy or human resource restructuring.

In order to facilitate coming to grips with both the nature and scope of social policy reform, the role of the present chapter is to assemble in one place the various reform options. Accordingly, Tables 38 through 41 compile a range of options relating to the retirement income subsystem (Table 38), unemployment insurance (UI) reform options (Table 39), proposals for reworking welfare (Table 40), and alternatives for reworking federal-provincial transfers (Table 41). Proposals relating to other reform measures (for example, minimum wage reform and approaches to training) will be dealt with in the text rather than in tabular form.

While these reform proposals are wide ranging and fairly comprehensive, they make no claim to being exhaustive. In general, most of them have been mentioned in the previous chapters. Because of this, many of the entries in the tables will not be elaborated in the text. There are a few exceptions. In Table 39, for example, one of the UI options cited is the reform proposed by the Forget Commission (Canada 1986). Since this option was not discussed earlier in the monograph, some elaboration is warranted. Similarly, innovative proposals from a recent monograph by Hobson and St-Hilaire (1994) on reforming the fiscal arrangements are recorded in the tables and amplified in the text.

These reform options serve several roles. First, they reflect well on the Canadian policy community, in terms of both the broad range of options and the creative nature of many of them. Second, by including several options relating to a given reform area, the pros and cons of each option become more evident. Third, the combining in one place of the options for several subsystems forces an "integrative discipline" on would-be social reformers. One cannot pick an "ideal" reform option from each of Tables 38 through 41 without at the same time ensuring that these individual programs form a consistent social policy *system*. Finally, and related, this tabulation of reform options provides a convenient backdrop to the final substantive chapter of the monograph — articulating a framework and a set of principles for selecting options that will remake our social infrastructure for the turn of the century. As a bridge between this menu of reform options and my preferred future for Social Canada, the present chapter concludes with an alternative assessment of the status quo — namely, that most of Canada's social policy problems relate to its social insurance programs.

I now briefly overview these reform options, beginning with the retirement income subsystem.

Options for the Retirement Income Subsystem

Table 38 presents a series of reform options for the retirement income subsystem. Since all of these options have been addressed, in one way or another, in the proceeding chapters, much of the analysis of the proposals is left to the reader.

Several principles underpin the table. One is that Canada's population is aging and that a significant portion of the elderly will have high incomes. This raises the joint issues of affordability and fairness. We have made some progress in this direction: old age security (OAS) benefits are now taxed back for high-income golden agers, and the 1994 federal budget has initiated the tax-back of the age credit. Saskatchewan has led the way in treating high-income elderly in the same way as high-income nonelderly in terms of the province's drug plan. Alberta, in its 1994 budget, is now following suit. These initiatives make eminent sense on both affordability and equity grounds. For example, were I to retire in Ontario on my university pension, I would have access to free drugs, whereas persons working at the minimum wage would not. Not only is this patently unfair, it is also eroding support for the intergenerational aspect of our implicit social contract. In the prosperous 1960s, the intergenerational transfer was clearly and appropriately from the young to the old. The shoe is now on the other foot, and the rich elderly — rich largely through tax-assisted savings instruments such as Registered Retirement Savings Plans (RRSPs) and Registered Pension Plans (RPPs) — must be prepared to engage in reverse transfers.

This leads directly to the second principle underlying Table 38 — namely, the enormity of the emerging intergenerational income chasm. Our policy framework privileges future income (retirement income) at the expense of current income. Apart from the debt burden that the young will have to shoulder, not only do we not provide them with the skills needed to compete in the millennium, but we also saddle them with a range of payroll taxes that reduce their employment prospects and, if they are employed, their take-home pay. The future they face under the status quo is a threefold increase in Canada Pension Plan/Quebec Pension Plan (CPP/QPP) premiums, for example, without any increase in real benefits at the retirement end. This is a ticking societal time bomb.

Accordingly, Table 38 contains proposals that would ameliorate this situation — spreading CPP/QPP premiums over the entire wage spectrum (at lower rates) so that the payroll tax does not focus largely on the low-income segment of the workforce; altering RRSPs so that there is also an incentive for lower-income Canadians to save for retirement; and contemplating rolling the two retirement income subsystems into a single super "Guaranteed Income Supplement" (GIS) for all Canadians. As noted in Chapter 3's analysis of the philosophy underpinning the personal income tax system, those who espouse an expenditure approach to personal income taxation will be adamantly opposed to converting RRSPs and RPPs from a deduction to a credit. I repeat my earlier view that for RPPs and RRSPs to remain as they are will probably require a set of reforms that will take some of the burden off lower-income savers. Although not included as a formal option in Table 38, one alternative could be to convert the CPP into an RRSP-type scheme that would be eligible for full deductibility.

I have no illusions that reform will be easy here. The elderly lobby is incredibly powerful (and they all vote!), and successive federal governments have allowed them to harbor some very mistaken notions, such as that they have fully "paid for" their CPP/QPP pensions. On the technical side, major reform is also difficult because tax and retirement planning is very long term and it typically assumes the existence of many of the current programs. Transitional periods become important here.

As a way of proceeding, I have long held the view that the preferred route is for the federal government to issue a White Paper containing a full range of options, then turn it over to the elderly themselves to sort out the options. It is one thing for this lobby to rail against some unilateral federal or provincial initiatives. It is quite another for the elderly to reconcile a set of options where the tradeoffs are not only between the elderly and nonelderly, but also *within the elderly cohort*. For this to work, however, Ottawa will probably have to detail a credible failsafe position. Nonetheless, I would be surprised if this approach did not yield very creative proposals.

One final word with respect to this issue. I am no doubt guilty in much of the above analysis of viewing the social infrastructure as it pertains to the elderly largely in terms of issues relating to affordability and equity. But there is another and perhaps much more important perspective. With life expectancy rates rising, the golden agers represent one of the most important and unrecognized of our society's assets. We have been negligent in public policy terms in that we appear to be unable to design frameworks that would use their

Table 38: Reform Options — The Retirement Income Subsystem

Reform Options	Elaboration	Implications/Comments
A. *Current Status*	Generally, a success story in that we have reduced poverty among the elderly. Remaining issues relate to distribution within the subsystem and, much more important, the intergenerational transfer issues, including both the amount of the transfer (as the elderly grow in number) and the form of financing the transfer (that is, frequently a tax on "jobs").	Degree of subsidy is masked by (mistaken) perception that programs such as CPP/QPP are fully funded. The young generation is facing sharp increases in CPP/QPP contribution rates without any increase in real (constant dollar) benefits.
B. *General Reforms* 1. Raise age for eligibility for social programs	Could be justified in terms of increasing life expectancy. Savings from increasing qualifying age to, say, 67 would be very significant. the United States is doing this. So is Sweden. Would ease the inter-generational transfer issue.	Need adequate lead times because long-term plans and contracts are built around current retirement age. Could be a partial substitute for major program reform.
2. Income test access for range of ancillary benefits	Best example is free drugs in some provinces to all seniors regardless of income. Seems inappropriate in era where an increasing number of seniors will have high incomes. Pertains largely to provincial not federal programs.	Enhance equity (based on ability to pay). This is especially true since much of the high income relates to tax-assisted savings. Saskatchewan is a leader here.
3. Eliminate age and pension deduction/credits under income tax	No reason for special tax concessions for elderly. Could use some of the savings to increase value of super-GIS in reforms C.1 and D.3 below.	Appropriate to have some phase in, say, over three years. In 1994 federal budget, Ottawa declared intention to tax back the age exemption.
C. *OAS/GIS* 1. Convert to enhanced GIS	Roll OAS into a larger GIS. Would be a negative income tax for elderly. Would replace clawback of OAS — that is, break-even point would occur at lower income level. Would incorporate reform B.3.	Provinces could top this up, but should not involve con-fiscatory tax rates as exists now in Ontario (GAINS-A and the GIS).

Table 38: *Reform Options — The Retirement Income Subsystem* - cont'd.

Reform Options	Elaboration	Implications/Comments
D. CPP/QPP 1. Status quo	Implies rising payroll tax (perhaps to 16%) for lower income employees. (See relevant text above.) And this is just to maintain existing level of real benefits. Reflects initial decision (1966) for plan to only be partially funded.	Major intergenerational inequity. Transfer from young to old *and* diminishes job opportunities for young. Unsustainable.
2. Invest CPP/QPP funds at market rates	Offers some relief, but not all that much since the "fund" does not really exist, except as a liability of provinces to the plan.	QPP does this in the Caisse de dépôt et placement du Québec.
3. Roll into super GIS (incorporating reform C.1)	Would combine OAS/GIS and CPP/QPP into a single overarching program for the elderly. Would have to be phased in gradually. CPP/QPP contribution rates could be maintained temporarily at a reduced level and spread over *all* wages. Would be a full-blown negative income tax for elderly financed by ability to pay.	Should allow low-income workers more access to RRSPs — for example, remove the 20% of income limit, but maintain the overall limits. Perhaps allow the RRSP credits or deductions to be refundable to encourage low-income persons to save. Present system is geared far too much to high incomes. Applies to reforms E.1 and E.2 as well.
E. RPPs and RRSPs 1. Reimpose limits on RRSPs	Popular in many circles because tax-assisted savings viewed as too generous for the rich. Basically, this is a societal equity decision. I prefer reform E.2 as an equity measure.	Important not to drive a wedge between RRSPs and RPPs because latter are not available for self-employed. Might reduce savings rates, but major savings shortfall comes from government deficits.
2. Convert contributions from deductions to a tax credit at 17% (lowest federal bracket)	Benefits from RPPs and RRSPs come from (a) tax deduction, which is worth more to the rich; (b) interest income from tax deferral; and (c) potential income splitting on retirement (spousal RRSPs). Converting (a) to a tax credit would tend to equalize incentives for saving across income classes especially if it is refundable. Overall tax advantage would still be substantial because of (b) above.	Current system can be viewed as a move toward expenditure taxation, which many analysts prefer. (Applies to reform E.1 as well). But why should CPP/QPP be a tax credit and RPPs and RRSPs a tax deduction?

expertise, experience, and, indeed, their willingness to continue in their retirement years to make contributions to our economy and society.

To be sure, this does not mean that we should abandon the earlier issues of affordability and equity in terms of social infrastructure redesign for the elderly, but it probably does mean that the "options paper" should be broad enough to allow the elderly to propose creative ways of reintegrating their expertise and experience fully into the Canadian society and economy.

Options for UI Reform

Table 39 contains a range of options for reforming UI. I have little trouble in rejecting outright the two "tinkering" proposals, whether that in the 1994 federal budget or the Newfoundland version referred to in Chapter 9. There can be no meaningful restructuring of Social Canada without a complete rethinking and overhaul of UI. And what this has to mean is taking UI out of the income support matrix for persons with short-term or marginal labor force attachment. Phrased differently, UI has to be directed to insuring against job loss for long-term labor force attachment. Assuming that UI remains a national program, reform option 3 is, from my perspective, the minimum acceptable version — 30 weeks (uniform across the country) for entry and three weeks of work to generate each week of benefits. Now that Newfoundland has suggested a *uniform* entry level (albeit at 20 weeks) and now that Ottawa has inaugurated a special program for fishers, the time is ripe to abandon the concept of variable entry requirements. Obviously, however, one cannot simply opt for this version of UI without important changes elsewhere in the system and, in particular, in the design and funding of welfare. More on this overlap later, as well as some elaboration on the nature of the incentives within UI.

The Forget Commission Proposal

Option 4, the Forget Commission proposal, merits elaboration because it has not featured in the analysis earlier in the monograph. Under this proposal, benefits would be "annualized" — each claimant would be entitled automatically to a full year of benefits (50 weeks of benefits plus the two-week waiting period). Unlike the present system, however, benefits would be based on earnings *over the full year* prior to the claim. In more detail (Canada 1986, 183):

- There would be a uniform entry requirement of 350 hours of work (roughly equivalent to ten weeks), which would apply to all workers, including those applying for sickness and maternity benefits, as well as to new entrants to the labor force, re-entrants, and repeaters.

- Benefits, after a transition period, would be based on average weekly earnings in the preceding 52 weeks and not, as now, on earnings in the preceding 10 to 20 weeks.

- Benefits would be paid in 50 weekly installments, after a two-week waiting period. This would eliminate the current practice of varying the duration of benefits according to weeks worked and regional rates of unemployment.

Thus, all benefit periods would be set uniformly at one year regardless of previous work experience, provided only that the minimum requirement of ten weeks was met.[1] Note that these ten weeks need not be consecutive: ten weeks worked over the past year would satisfy the requirement. In one sense, while this compulsory 52-week benefit period represents a change in principle, it was not that major a change from the status quo that existed at the time of the Forget Commission, since the combination of high unemployment rates and regionally extended benefits implied that many claimants qualified for close to a year of benefits.

The major innovation occurs in the method of benefit payout. All claimants are eligible to receive in benefits two-thirds of their insurable earnings over the past year, but these must be paid out in *equal installments over 50 weeks*. Consider two individuals, both of whom earn $500 per week — essentially the maximum weekly insurable earnings level in the time frame of the Forget Commission. Assume both file a UI claim, but one individual has worked for 50 weeks over the past year and the other for ten. The longer-term worker qualifies for two-thirds of his or her annual earnings of $25,000 (50 × 500) to be paid out over 50 weeks. Because that claimant also worked 50 weeks, however, the benefit payment is equal to two-thirds of his or her insurable earnings — that is, $333.32. This would not differ much from the current payout to a long-term worker except that, under the Forget Commission's proposal, the replacement rate would be increased from (the then) 60 percent to 66⅔ percent.

The situation is quite different for the second claimant, who has worked for only ten weeks. The shorter-term worker's annual earnings are one-fifth those of the longer-term worker, so the weekly benefit rate will also be one-fifth, or $66.67. Under the existing (1986) arrangements, the second claimant would qualify for a weekly benefit of $300 — that is, 60 percent of $500 — for a period that could be as long as 42 weeks if the regional unemployment rate exceeded 9 percent. In other words, the then-existing system allowed the worker to qualify

---

1 The next few paragraphs are from Courchene 1987, 110–111. They are written from the perspective of 1986, when the Forget Commission's report was published.

Table 39:   Reform Options — Unemployment Insurance

Reform Options	Elaboration	Implications/Comments
1. Tinkering (the 1994 federal budget)	As outlined in Chapter 9, these changes move the entry requirement up from 10 weeks to 12 weeks, but still retain the differentiated entry. The maximum number of weeks of benefits has been reduced, which further penalizes long-term labor force attachment. The shift in benefits from 57% of earnings to 55% and 60% (depending on family status) introduces yet further social policy measures into what ought to be a social insurance policy.	It is to be hoped that this is a prelude to some meaningful reform. If not, then social policy reform will probably come to naught.
2. More tinkering (for example, the Newfoundland proposal — 20 weeks entry requirement and one week of benefits for each week of work to a maximum 35 weeks)	Treats Canadians identically independent of residence. This feature is desirable. But it is hardly insurance in the sense that it is still geared to short-term labor attachment and, therefore, will continue to interfere with and complicate the income support subsystem.	More generous than current program in some instances (for example, in low-unemployment areas, 20 weeks of work does not now generate 20 weeks of UI).
3. Reward longer-term labor force attachment (for example, 30 weeks entry requirement and one week of benefits for every three weeks of work to a maximum of 52 weeks)	Removes UI from short-term income support. Full benefits (52 weeks) requires three years of work. This is more in line with insurance principles and would significantly reduce the overall cost as well as the "tax on jobs" because of the payroll tax.	Would require rethinking and refinancing provincial welfare program because UI would no longer be able to be used as a vehicle for income support for temporary attachment to the labor force.
4. Forget Commission	Described in the text of this chapter.	See the text of this chapter.

Table 39: *Reform Options — Unemplyment Insurance* - cont'd.

Reform Options	Elaboration	Implications/Comments
5. Provincialize UI	Provinces would be free to design UI to suit their economic and social needs. Would require portability arrangements. Benefits would be paid by province of work, regardless of residence of beneficiary. Contributions would be equalized to allow affordability for all provinces. More details in the text.	Would require a constitutional amendment or else enabling legislation on Ottawa's part since UI is a federal competence. Would likely have implications for welfare (see text).
6. Abolish UI	Would presume the existence of a comprehensive welfare program or guaranteed annual income (perhaps with a larger federal presence). As noted in Chapter 2, Australia has achieved relative income equality across its states *without* a UI program.	This policy change may be too radical for Canadians. But it is important that the proposal be on the table because it forces us to ask ourselves why we have a UI program in the first place.
7. Altering UI incentives: • tax-back rates • financing • experience rating	These are generic issues and are relevant to all options (except option 6). These are elaborated in the text.	The incentives in UI are every bit as troublesome as its overall design (that is, entry weeks and the relationship between weeks worked and benefit weeks).

for benefits of $12,600, based on earnings of $5,000. By contrast, annualization would ensure that maximum benefits will be two-thirds of insurable earnings for all claimants.

Note that, by limiting the maximum payout to $3,333.33 — that is, two-thirds of the annual earnings of $5,000 — rather than $12,600 as under the current system, annualization indirectly eliminates regional benefits.

Obviously, annualization would have a major impact on those workers who, for one reason or another, are part of the 10/42 system. The prospect of giving up a $500 per week job after ten weeks to collect $66.67 per week on UI is not very appealing. Hence, for this class of worker, annualization presumably will induce longer labor force attachment.

This is an intriguing proposal in that, while short-term labor force attachment triggers the maximum benefit weeks, the benefits themselves are a function of contributions over the previous year. Thus, the concern mentioned earlier that UI be geared to longer term labor force attachment is reflected under the Forget Commission proposals on the benefit side, not on the length of benefits nor on the entry requirement. What made this proposal unappealing when it was first enunciated, and what still makes it difficult to implement, is that it *presumes* that some version of a guaranteed annual income is already in place or else that there is some alternative financing mechanism for welfare (since many of the ten-week workers will need some income support other than UI). On the other hand what makes the proposal intriguing from a public policy perspective is that it addresses the issue from a completely novel perspective. We need these "novel perspective" approaches to long-standing policy issues, even if they end up not being feasible at the time they are introduced onto the policy agenda. Given that almost all of the social envelope is currently up for grabs, theoretically if not practically, the Forget Commission proposal may make considerable sense in the context of the renewal of Social Canada.

The Macdonald Commission Proposal

In roughly the same time frame, the Macdonald Commission (Canada 1985) also came out with a proposal for revamping UI. Among its recommendations were:

- reducing benefits to 50 percent of eligible earnings;
- raising entrance requirements to 15 or 20 weeks of insured work;
- tightening the link between the maximum benefit period and the minimum employment period: for example, establish a ratio of two or three weeks of work to qualify for one week of benefits; and
- eliminating the regional differentiation within the UI program (ibid., 611).

Table 39 does not incorporate this proposal as an option. It would fall somewhere between option 2 and 3 were it included. In my view, it is now dominated by option 3.

Provincializing UI

Another option would be to provincialize UI, in much the same way as workers' compensation is provincialized. The outline of such a proposal appears as option 5 in Table 38. One obvious advantage is that this approach would allow provinces to experiment with UI and its relationship to welfare, education, and training. One disadvantage is that, on the surface at least, this approach would put an end to the interprovincial transfers arising from UI. The way around this, as suggested in conversations with University of Western Ontario political scientist Bob Young, is to have UI *contributions* enter equalization, either via the existing formula or a special equalization formula. This means that all provinces would have access to the five-province per capita average of UI contributions (or perhaps the national average level).

Many provinces, particularly in Atlantic Canada, have expressed a desire to alter UI so as to make it more consistent with their overall human resource policy. Provincializing UI and equalizing contributions is the obvious way to allow greater provincial control over UI and yet ensure that it remains a "national program" (in the same way that welfare or medicare are national programs).

One might note that, while workers' compensation is run at the provincial level, there is no equalization of workers' compensation premiums or contributions. Since a UI program run along the lines of option 3 would be a dramatically reduced version of the status quo, perhaps there would be no need to equalize UI premiums. But this option is probably too far removed from the status quo to be in the choice set this time around.

The Incentives in UI

The final option listed in Table 39 highlights, without elaboration, a range of issues associated with the incentives in the UI system. I shall elaborate on them in turn.

Tax-Back Rates

Under the status quo, UI beneficiaries can earn up to 25 percent of their benefits without any benefit loss. Beyond this, the tax-back rate is confiscatory —

100 percent — until benefits are exhausted. This is an open invitation to participate in the underground economy. Is there a better approach?

To address this issue, it is instructive to note that income support payments such as GIS and the child tax credit are typically not taxable, *per se*, but are subject to clawbacks from earned income. Social insurance payments such as UI (and as workers' compensation ought to be, as will be detailed later in the chapter) are deemed to be part of earned income and are, therefore, taxable and trigger clawbacks in terms of income support transfers. The challenge is to introduce incentives to encourage a transition from UI to work. (Note that here I am assuming that some version of option 3 of Table 39 is the relevant UI program, so that we are talking about persons who have had some longer-term attachment to the labor market.) The option of using UI benefits to finance further training should always be open. However, in terms of the transition back to work, why not make the tax-back rate equal to the benefit rate? For example, if benefits are 50 percent of average eligible UI earnings, then the tax-back rate on a new job should also be 50 percent. This means that a person's UI benefits will fall to zero if he or she finds a new job that pays the same as the one just lost. If the person's earnings on the new job are only at 80 percent of the previous one, UI payments will bring them up to 90 percent; if earnings are at 70 percent, UI will bring them up to 85 percent. In other words, under a 50 percent benefit rate and a 50 percent tax-back rate, UI would ensure that accepting a lower paying job than the one lost will bring total earnings half-way between the new and old jobs for the duration of UI benefit eligibility. Were the benefit rate and tax-back rate set at 55 percent, then UI would also fall to zero for a new job with the same earnings as the old one, and UI would ensure that any difference between new and old earnings is narrowed by 45 percent of the difference. And so on for different tax-back and benefit rates.

Note that the rationale here is not to encourage people to accept a lower-paying job, although this may occur. Rather, the incentive is to temporarily cushion earnings in the new job, with prospects that, by the time the benefits run out, the employee will have worked his or her way up to the former earnings level.

There are likely even more novel ways of approaching this back-to-work incentive, but in the interim this option is clearly superior to the status quo.

Financing UI

Unemployment insurance is financed by a payroll tax payable by both employees and employers. As outlined in the 1994 federal budget, the employee rate will be $3.00 per $100 of insurable earnings up to the weekly maximum insurable earnings of $780. Employers' contribution rates are 1.4 times those of the employees, or $4.20 per $100 of insurable earnings. Were Canada to adopt some version of option 3 from Table 39, this payroll tax would fall considerably, even given the existing UI deficit.

However, the existing UI deficit is, I think, substantially exaggerated. Not only are UI benefits taxable but, at income levels above 1.5 times the level of maximum insurable earnings, these benefits are effectively fully clawed back. The income tax revenues associated with these taxes and clawbacks are *not* factored into UI financing. Why should the equilibrium UI contribution rates be set so as to match *gross* (before-tax) UI benefits? Why not equilibrate contribution rates with *net* (after-tax) UI benefits? Surely the constellation of payroll taxes is already way too high now without raising them further because of inappropriate accounting procedures. This issue will loom even longer if we move toward income-testing UI benefits, as argued in the previous section.

Experience Rating

Economists have long argued that one of the fundamental problems with UI was the lack of experience rating — that is, not tying premiums to the likelihood of, or experience relating to, layoffs. Under such a system, contribution rates would be much higher for seasonal industries, for example. However, experience rating was never taken seriously in the policymaking corridors, in part because of some of the technical issues that it would give rise to but, in part as well, because UI was *designed* to favor certain industries and regions. In terms of reform options, it would be much better to opt for a proposal like option 3 of Table 39 and only then to address the issue of whether experience rating in the new system would enhance the efficacy of the program. This is but another way of saying that much of the industry cross-subsidization (which triggers arguments for experience rating) is due to the nature of the *existing* UI structure, and would be ameliorated substantially under a program that embodied longer-term labor force attachment. If this prediction proves to be wrong, then the experience-rating issues should resurface. Note that the thrust of this paragraph is not to argue against experience rating. Rather, it is to suggest that the problems associated with UI go much beyond experience rating, and it is important to address the fundamentals first.

No UI for Under-25-Year-Olds

Influenced in part by the observations that the presence of UI serves as a disincentive toward further education, some policy analysts have suggested that persons under 25 should not be eligible for UI. Rather, they would receive education or training vouchers and/or income support to upgrade their skills. While one can sympathize with the intent of this proposal, it is not obvious that it would survive a challenge under the Charter of Rights and Freedoms. But, as is the case with experience rating, this issue looms large, in part at least, because of the nature of the existing program. A program embodying much longer labor force attachment to qualify for UI would alter the incentives for young people to abandon formal education.

Nonetheless, I would support an "active" labor market strategy for young persons. The point I want to emphasize, though, is that a policy that shifts under-25-year-olds from passive to active income support under UI is *not* a substitute for meaningful UI reform.

An International Perspective on UI

As *The Economist* (February 26, 1994, 71) notes, different countries approach unemployment benefits from quite different perspectives. Most European governments encourage long-term unemployment by paying generous benefits for long periods. In the United States, benefits are less generous and benefits run out after six months so that there is a strong incentive to find a job. *The Economist* then points out that Sweden may offer a less harsh solution — active labor market policies:

> Instead of just handing out dole money to the long-term unemployed, the Swedish government keeps them in touch with the labor market — through placement services, training schemes, recruitment subsidies and temporary public sector jobs. This carrot comes with a stick: if an unemployed person refuses a job or a place on a training scheme, his benefits may stop. By ensuring that the long-term unemployed compete for jobs, this helps to restrain wages and hold down the NAIRU [nonaccelerating-inflation rate of unemployment]. (Ibid.)

Canada's UI system has the advantage of neither the US nor the Swedish system. Consequently, we resemble the continental Europeans and are in danger of embracing their labor market rigidities and sclerosis. However, if we want to introduce the Swedish system, then we probably have to go some way toward option 5 — namely, provincializing UI — since an attempt by the federal government to take over training would trigger a massive battle with the provinces. In addition, training should not be the privilege of UI beneficiaries at the expense, say, of those on welfare. Perhaps a version of Dupré's "procurement federalism" approach (see Chapter 5) might forge the needed link here. Nonetheless, this would still not rule out the desirability of embracing a reformed UI system that rewards longer-term labor force attachment.

Welfare Options

Table 40 details a variety of options for reworking welfare. In most cases, these options are, again, either straightforward or have been dealt with at length earlier in the monograph. It should be noted that options relating to reforming the Canada Assistance Plan (CAP) itself appear in the relevant panel of Table 41. The only CAP reform touched on in Table 40 relates to converting CAP into a refundable, low-income child tax credit (option 2c).

While the options relating to welfare reform in Table 40 may be evident enough, they do not address directly the manner in which the welfare-to-work transition ought to be managed. This is a sufficient challenge in its own right: it becomes a larger challenge if the revised UI program rewards longer-term labor force attachment since this will put greater pressure on welfare, at least initially. There is no one answer in terms of how to manage this interface, but the next section explores a few key issues.

The Welfare-to-Work Transition

The welfare-to-work transition is caught up in what economists might refer to as a "low-level equilibrium." On the supply side, particularly where children are involved, the "binary" approach to welfare (that is, you are either on welfare or you are not) serves to trap many individuals and families into a life of welfare dependence. On the demand side, minimum wages and the constellation of rising payroll taxes decrease the demand for low-skilled labor. The result is the low-level equilibrium already alluded to.

One aspect of this equilibrium is the shift toward part-time work. Employers recognize the advantages of part-time work since it allows them to avoid some of the payroll taxes. But unless a person can find two such part-time jobs, there will be little incentive for individuals to exit or leave welfare. To be sure, much of the recent mushrooming of welfare rolls reflects the coincidence of major industrial restructuring and the recession. However, even if aggregate demand picks up and sorts out the cyclical aspect of the increase in welfare, the structural (restructuring) component will remain. Thus, any meaningful policy approach must address both the demand and supply sides of this welfare-to-work nexus.

Most provinces have now come to the realization that passive income support does not work. In terms of shifting toward active labor market policies, Canada is a laggard among the developed countries. According to statistics from the Organisation for Economic Co-operation and Development (OECD), Canada allocated only 23 percent of its labor market program expenditures to active uses, ranking eighteenth out of 22 countries (OECD 1989). By 1992–93, this

Table 40: Reform Options — Welfare

Proposal	Elaboration	Implications/Comments
1. Maintain the status quo	This incorporates a multitude of approaches and proposals. All provinces are engaged in a variety of experiments — workfare, training fare, wage supplementation, pilot projects.	These experiments will continue and are critically important. The remaining proposals in this table focus on various aspects of welfare reform that are being considered in the various provincial capitals.
2. A separate program for children in welfare families:	For a single parent with, say, three children, it is virtually impossible for labor force attachment to dominate welfare unless the parent has skills that can command a middle-class salary.	Some new design features are necessary.
(a) Ontario's *Turning Point* proposal	Would provide support for children independent of whether parent or parents are on welfare or are working. Presumably, this child support would be income tested.	Were Ontario to follow through on this proposal, it may need to have the flexibility associated with a "tax-on-base" approach to the shared personal income tax (Thematic Tableau 4).
(b) Quebec's Parental Wage Assistance program	Wage assistance is geared to family size and falls to zero when the family qualifies for positive taxation under Quebec's income tax. This is a partial solution to the children issue by focusing not on the wage (allocation) front but on the supplementation (tax transfer) front. Has considerable merit.	Easier for Quebec to implement because it has its own personal income tax system. For other provinces to follow this route would require, at a minimum, a tax on base approach to the shared personal income tax.

Table 40:   Reform Options — Welfare - cont'd.

Proposal	Elaboration	Implications/Comments
(c) Convert CAP to a low-income refundable tax credit	The existing refundable tax credit begins to be offset at income levels in the mid-$20,000 area. This would be a new low-income tax credit and would be *fully taxed back* at this mid-$20,000 level. This implies that Ottawa would look after the needs of the elderly and children and would leave the provinces to focus on welfare for adults and to integrate this with training, education, and the transition to the labor market.	Some provinces may object to this. But if done through the income tax system, it is within Ottawa's constitutional power. The existing per capita CAP payments are indefensible on equity grounds. This system would treat all children identically across provinces. In one fell swoop, as it were, this would assuage the concerns of the "have" provinces with respect to the cap on CAP.
3. Ensuring that the tax rate in the transition from welfare to work is not confiscatory	Most welfare systems in Canada are "binary": you are either on welfare or you are not. This naturally focuses emphasis on ensuring that the minimum wage is high enough to dominate welfare benefits. But this is creating welfare traps because of the changing nature of the labor market and, in particular, the proliferation of part-time jobs. Some version of a negative income tax is appropriate here — any and all work will generate an increase in take-home income.	This negative income tax approach is an obvious solution that has thus far not made any inroads at the provincial level (except in Quebec). Perhaps this is because the provinces do not have control over the rate and bracket structure of their portion of income taxes. There has to be a revolution in thinking here.
4. A full-blown income-tested guaranteed annual income, with some federal role, at least for funding	In principle, this is the way to go. In practice, several problems arise. To make economic sense, such an approach would have to be geared to what is appropriate in rural Canada and to let provinces top this up for urban areas. A second problem is that provinces might want to engage in some version of workfare or training-fare that might be offside with a national program.	Newfoundland's proposal for a negative income tax (elaborated in Chapter 9) is an example of what can go wrong with this sort of thing. There will be a tendency for such a proposal to dominate *all* existing programs, including UI, which probably ensures that any such proposals will be too generous. We are slowly but surely moving in the direction of a negative income tax, and perhaps we should continue with this evolution rather than opting for "big bang" restructuring.

proportion had risen to 30 percent, but we still only placed fifteenth out of the 22 countries (OECD 1993). Sweden is the leader here.

One encouraging note is that "training-fare" and even aspects of workfare are now high on the agendas of several provinces. To a degree, this is a corrective operation — compensating for the failure of school-to-work transition. The longer-term approach must be one of instilling a training and skills culture at the secondary and postsecondary levels of education, replete with close contacts with industry. To the extent that skills are upgraded, then exiting welfare becomes easier since labor force income may dominate welfare income (especially in the context of a separate program for children as in Table 40).

But more is needed on the supply side. In particular, the role of minimum wages probably has to be rethought in the context of reforming welfare. Quoting once again from *The Economist* (February 26, 1994, 70):

> Many countries set minimum wages, with the intention of protecting the living standards of workers in low-paid jobs. But it is misguided for governments to try to protect the poor by forcing up wages. Minimum wages eliminate the jobs of too many of those they are supposed to help....Minimum wages are especially likely to damage the job prospects of the young, who start out in low-wage jobs. In France, the minimum wage rose from around 40 percent of the average wage in the early 1970s to 50 percent by the mid-1980s. The jobless rate among those aged 24 or under rose from 4 percent to more than 20 percent. America's federal minimum wage, in contrast, fell from 40 percent to 30 percent of the average wage in the 1980s; its youth unemployment rate is barely half that in France.

Beyond these considerations, the conception of the role of minimum wages as one of providing income above the poverty line does not mesh well with income testing. Emphasis under the latter shifts to the concept of *total* income — from work *and* income-tested welfare. Under income testing, work, whether at $4.00 per hour or $8.00 per hour and whether part-time or full-time increases total income. Thus, as the system moves toward income testing, provinces ought to become more flexible in terms of minimum wage legislation and allow greater opportunities for people to enter the labor market and increase their overall income. There is, I think, already a recognition that this is appropriate when it comes to wages related to apprenticeship and/or certification. If work is contributing to certification, then the rationale for minimum wages disappears — either the relevant minimum wages should be set aside or an "education/training" voucher could be used to compensate the firm sponsoring the training or apprenticeship. This recognition should be extended further to become more consistent with an income-tested approach to welfare. It seems to me that this will be the next major area where the various provinces will undertake initiatives and experimentation. Among the many issues that will have to be addressed are the length of the reconciliation period (three months, six months, annually?) and the further incentives that may be needed to ensure that these earnings are reported. Here again, provincial experimentation will likely hold the key in terms of what approaches are effective.

In the larger context of overall social policy reform, another set of welfare-related issues arises. The reworking of Social Canada is being undertaken within a framework of generating significant savings. Much of this of necessity must come from UI reform. But some of these UI savings presumably will be earmarked for training and some will be "federal" savings as erstwhile UI claimants fall back on provincial welfare, at least in the first instance. I suspect that there will be a natural tendency to attempt to rely on UI premiums to finance some of these former UI functions. Except as a transition measure, this is surely inappropriate since enhancing employment prospects must also be part of the solution. What this means, and what Ottawa appears to recognize, at least as it enters the social policy reform process, is that everything in Tables 38 to 41 must be on the reform table if the multiple goals of the reform process are to be achieved and, more important, if Canada's social infrastructure is to be consistent with the emerging social and economic imperatives.

Options for Fiscal Federalism

Table 41 presents a range of options for reforming Established Programs Financing (EPF), CAP, and equalization. That these proposals for reworking fiscal federalism should follow the reform options for welfare, UI, and the retirement income subsystem in this chapter is entirely by design. One of the premises of this monograph, enunciated earlier, is that the fiscal arrangements ought to be derivative, not determining. Without even glancing at the details of Table 41, it should already be clear that the choices one makes among the options in the earlier tables will constrain what will be possible or appropriate in terms of Table 41. Were we to follow this bottom-up approach and attempt to design programs from the vantage point of Canadians, this would represent a sea change in recent social policy evolution. The concern always remains that, in the final analysis, the two levels of government will strike a deal on the future of the fiscal arrangements (that is, on the items in Table 41) that, once again, will straightjacket the evolution of individual programs.

Notwithstanding this concern, Table 41 canvasses a wide range of innovative proposals for reforming the three major federal transfers to the provinces. The task of forging some link between program reform options and reforming

Table 41: Reform Options — Established Programs Financing, the Canada Assistance Plan, and Equalization

Reform Option	Elaboration	Implication/Comments
1. *EPF* (a) The status quo	In 1995/96, the ceiling expires and EPF reverts to a GNP minus 3% ceiling. As the economy picks up and personal income taxes increase, the residual cash transfers will fall eventually to zero (see Chapter 4). Ottawa also notes in its 1994 budget that CAP and the PSE component of EPF will have entitlements after reforms in 1996/97 no higher than they are in 1993/94.	The budget anticipates some savings in these transfers as a result of reform. If, for some reason, the reform process does not realize these savings, then alternative measures will be undertaken to generate the savings. Relative to current projections, the savings in 1996/97 from CAP and PSE transfers will be $1.5 billion.
(b) Convert cash component of PSE into a portable PSE voucher	Would complement the interest in the income-contingent-repayment proposal for financing PSE. Would be portable across provinces as well as across PSE alternatives (university, college, training). Would enhance Ottawa's visibility and also lead to needed competition in PSE sector.	Some provinces might object. But the alternative may be that the cash component of PSE eventually falls to zero.
(c) Convert cash component of health transfer to a tax transfer	Would decentralize health care in terms of funding (although the tax transfer would be equalized). Would have to be accompanied by some commitment on the part of the provinces to abide by national health care guidelines.	Would not sit well with those who view Ottawa as the architect and defender of medicare. But this is hard to square with the fact that, under existing arrangements, the cash portion of the transfer will fall to zero.
(d) Convert cash component of EPF to a standalone, block-funded transfer	Would recognize formally that tax point transfers are really part of provinces' own revenues. This would be a very messy transfer program because the per capita cash transfers would vary from province to province if one wished to preserve the equality of the overall (tax plus cash) entitlement.	No reason to have overall equality in per capita terms since, as noted in earlier chapters, the provinces do not spend equal per capita. Alterative is (a) let tax point transfers be equalized under formula and (b) have cash set at equal per capita levels.
(e) The Hobson and St-Hilaire proposal	This is a superequalized tax transfer (see text for elaboration).	See text.

Table 41: Reform Options — Established Programs Financing, the Canada Assistance Plan, and Equalization - cont'd.

Reform Option	Elaboration	Implication/Comments
2. CAP		
(a) Business as usual	CAP will group in line with formula for 1994/95 (including cap on CAP). Will then freeze CAP at 1994/95 levels, until new social security reforms are in place.	This sidesteps major problems with cap on CAP — 28 cent dollars for Ontario and 50 cent dollars for Quebec, for example.
(b) Convert CAP to an equalized tax point transfer	This could be part of a package that would convert both CAP and EPF to additional tax points and then leave an (expanded) equalization program as the only federal transfer.	Norrie (1994) argues that this degree of devolution without any federal strings related to minimum standards would eventually erode support for the expanded equalization programs. Nonetheless, it has the virtue of streamlining the federal-provincial transfer system and it would be welcomed by several provinces. Not much in it for Ottawa, though.
(c) CAP as is, but introduce "needs" related to welfare into the equalization formula	This proposal has long been a favorite of the "have-not" provinces. The idea is that the poorer provinces have a higher welfare burden (that is, greater unemployment) and, therefore, they deserve extra support. This would come from an equalization program that incorporates provincial "needs" on the welfare side.	There are at least two problems with this approach. First, Ontario has the largest welfare "need" and this province is clearly being discriminated against now, so this takes the wind out of the sails of the proposal from the vantage point of the "have-not" provinces. Second, this approach does not make sense unless one also takes UI benefits into account. Beyond this, if one introduces "need" into the equalization formula, why not "costs" and/or capitalization, as articulated earlier in the text?
(d) The Hobson and St-Hilaire proposal	Introduces equalization into CAP. See text for details.	See text. But comments for 2(c) apply here as well.
(e) Convert CAP to a refundable low-income tax credit for children	See Table 40, option 2(c).	See Table 40, option 2(c).
(f) Move to an income-tested guaranteed annual income (GAI) or negative income tax	We would be part way there if we implemented option 2(e). A viable option if UI became a program that required longer-term labor force attachment. Could involve Ottawa in greater income support role. If so, would probably require some minimum level appropriate to rural Canada and leave provinces to top up benefits for urban areas.	Would involve complete rethinking of federal-provincial transfers. As long as the GAI is delivered through the tax system, there should be no constitutional problems. But it may be difficult to implement politically, particularly in Quebec. See Chapter 11 for alternative ways to work around these constitutional issues.

Table 41: Reform Options — Established Programs Financing, the Canada Assistance Plan, and Equalization - cont'd.

Reform Option	Elaboration	Implication/Comments
3. Equalization (a) Business as usual	The recent equalization agreement (for five years beginning April 1, 1994) will retain the ceiling provision, which will be based on 1992/93 rather than on 1994/95 — see Chapter 4 for details relating to the ceiling.	While this is a five-year agreement, it will be influenced by changes elsewhere in the social envelope. For example, if the result of the social policy review is to increase tax point transfers, then these will enter the equalization formula, which means that the ceiling provisions must be altered.
(b) Remove "bells and whistles" — equalize to "national average" standard without a ceiling	This is a return to the pre-1974 era. The ceiling did hit hard in the late 1980s, largely because of the Ontario boom. But some provinces were in a different cyclical phase than was Ontario. The shift to a national average standard from the five-province standard is not a big dollar item in the current time frame. But it could be if resource prices were to increase.	This approach would be acceptable if there were no other specific regional aspects to other programs. But the presence of superequalization under EPF, the cap on CAP, and the regional aspects of UI spill over to the equalization program. Also see my comment in the note to this table.
(c) "Net" schemes (i): two-tiered equalization schemes	First proposal by Courchene and Copplestone (1980). Ottawa would equalize shared revenues or revenues that have a "base" in all provinces. Resource revenues would be equalized via an interprovincial revenue-sharing pool — resource-rich provinces would put funds in and resource-poor provinces would draw benefits. Scheme would be self-financing.	The note to the table focuses on one advantage of this proposal. The downside could be, among other things, that it is difficult to bind the provinces to maintain this interprovincial revenue-sharing pool over time. The Germans have a version of this, but it is enshrined in their Basic Law (that is, constitution).
(d) "Net" schemes (ii): a federally run "net" scheme that would fully equalize net fiscal benefits by bringing revenues of rich provinces down (Boadway and Hobson 1993)	Ottawa would equalize provincial revenues to the national average level. Then those provinces with revenues above the national average would have their *cash transfers in other programs* reduced in order to bring their revenues down to the national average.	In my view, this is a redistribution run wild. Essentially, Ottawa's role is to convert the federation on the revenue side to the equivalent of a unitary state. Alberta would lose transfers because it decides not to introduce a sales tax!
(e) Introduce costs and needs into equalization	Allow equalization to reflect special needs of provinces and the fact that different revenues raising capacities of provinces are capitalized in land, rents, wages, and so on.	I have not done the empirical work here, but surely "capitalization" would dominate "needs." Indeed, the United States does not even have revenue equalization, on the assumption that capitalization, of and by itself, will obviate the need for equalization. As a compromise, one might equalize to, say, 90 percent of the national average standard. This approach allows "dynamic efficiency" issues to run parallel with redistributive issues in designing equalization.

Table 41: Reform Options — *Established Programs Financing, the Canada Assistance Plan, and Equalization* - cont'd.

Reform Option	Elaboration	Implication/Comments
(f) Negative income tax-type equalization • provinces get 70 percent of differences between own fiscal capacity and the equalization standard	A province with a fiscal capacity of 80 percent of the national average would receive 70 percent of the gap, that is, equalization would bring revenues up to 94 percent of the national average.	Revenues in recipient provinces would increase by 30 percent with respect to any improvement in their economic base. Under the existing framework, the increase is zero. Provinces also partially insulated from swings (up or down) in the equalization standard.

Note: In the resource boom era with the national average standard, energy revenues were mushrooming, which, in turn, was driving up equalization. The problem was that Ottawa did not have much access to revenues from resources. Hence, Alberta's resource revenues would increase equalization and yet 40 percent or so of Ottawa's revenues to pay for the increased equalization would come from Ontario. This let to the abandonment of full equalization of resource revenues from 1974 onward until 1982 when the five-province standard was introduced. An interprovincial revenue sharing pool would "solve" this in the sense that the resource-rich provinces would contribute funds directly into this tier of the equalization scheme. For more detail, consult Courchene and Copplestone 1980.

the major federal transfers is left to the conclusion of this section and to the final substantive chapter of the monograph.

EPF Options

The EPF status quo is anything but static. In fiscal year 1995/96, the EPF ceiling freeze runs out and returns to a regime of gross national product growth minus 3 percent. However, the 1994 federal budget foresees a $1.5 billion savings for 1996/97 from the combination of CAP and the postsecondary education (PSE) component of EPF. No matter how one slices this, the recent past as well as the already-legislated future of EPF involves substantial deficit offloading to the provinces. As noted in Chapter 7, one way to view EPF is to recognize that what began essentially as an equivalent to a transfer of roughly 27 tax points will, once the cash component falls to zero, effectively become a transfer of roughly 13.5 tax points. Hence, Ottawa is in the driver's seat here. Innovative as the remaining proposals may be, all of them attempt in one way or another to lock in the existing level of cash transfers before they dwindle to zero.

Two implications flow from this. First, the provinces may well be willing to accept some options (for example, converting the cash component of PSE into a portable student voucher) that in other circumstances they would not countenance, since the alternative could be that these cash transfers fall to zero. Second, to the extent that allowing the cash component to fall to zero is part of the current reality, it appears that there is precious little for Ottawa in any of these reform proposals. Hence, proposals such as 1(b) that convert the PSE cash transfer into a portable voucher must be sold to Ottawa in terms of visibility, accountability, and the fact that knowledge is critical to overall competitiveness. To be sure, these are attractive arguments for the federal government, which has long bemoaned the lack of visibility and accountability associated with federal-provincial transfers. Moreover, there is a cost to Ottawa if it lets EPF cash fall to zero — the system will dramatically decentralize in terms of taxing power, in terms of a federal say in program design and evolution and, likely, in terms of the degree to which these provincial programs will respect the principles of an internal common market.

The Hobson and St-Hilaire Proposal

The most novel EPF proposal is that just recently published by Hobson and St-Hilaire (1994). In order to motivate this proposal, it is instructive to devote some attention initially to option 1(d) — namely, to block fund the cash component of EPF. This approach would recognize that the equalized tax point transfer is notional and that the cash component (including the Quebec abatement) is the only real transfer. However, because of superequalization (see Chapter 4), this cash component is not equal across provinces in per capita terms. For the Atlantic provinces, it is something on the order of $360 per person and more like $300 per person in Ontario. Were one to opt for block funding, should the payments incorporate these existing per capita differences across provinces or should any cash payments be equal per capita? The problem with the former route is that these transfers (embodying differences in per capita funding) would be highly visible and would likely become politicized — for example, another "hit" on Ontario. Ottawa could, of course, reply that, if one were to combine these cash transfers with the tax transfers, the overall result would be equal per capita transfers. But this is a tough sell in this era of 30-second clips. A second problem attending this approach to block funding is that, over time, the values per province of the former tax transfer would alter, which, in turn, would require periodic (annual?) adjustment of the cash transfers. In other words, this approach to block funding is probably unworkable and unsalable.

On the other hand, equal per capita block funding of the cash component is not only workable but easy to comprehend. But the result would no longer be equal per capita *overall* transfers. If forced to choose between these two approaches, it should come as no surprise that I would opt for the latter since, on average, the "have" provinces spend more per capita on EPF.

There is an important lesson for policy analysts here. While Boothe (1992) and Dupré (1994) argue that Ottawa should stop the masquerade and jettison the tax transfer component of EPF, this does not take account of the politics of the status quo. Presumably, Ottawa recognizes the masquerade as well. But including the tax transfer component in the transfer is essential, *politically*, in order to maintain the per capita equality of the overall EPF transfer. That is, an *equal per capita overall ceiling*, even though this embodies an inequality in terms of per capita cash transfers, is relatively easy to sell politically.

What the Hobson and St-Hilaire proposal does in this context is to rework EPF in a novel way, but one that still embodies the overall equal per capita feature of the status quo. In their words (1994, 38–39):

> In order to achieve complete fiscal disentanglement, tax room should be devolved to the provinces once and for all with respect to the established programs. One way of achieving this within the existing EPF framework would be for the federal government to cede the value of the cash component of EPF to the provinces as an explicit tax abatement rather than actually transfer further tax room. That is, a fixed percentage of federal income tax revenues would be earmarked for the established programs. These revenues would not, however, be distributed according to collections by province; rather,

they would be pooled for purposes of "topping up" the per-capita value of the existing EPF tax transfer by province to its fully equalized value with any surplus being distributed on an equal per-capita basis. The federal role in funding social programs, then, would simply be to coordinate revenue pooling through centralized collection and redistribution. The number of tax points to be abated under EPF would need to be negotiated. It could be set at the effective number of tax points associated with EPF had the original block-funding amounts been escalated in accordance with GDP [gross domestic product] to the present time, less the total equalized value of the EPF tax transfer. Alternatively, it could be the number of tax points associated with the current level of total cash transfers under EPF. No doubt, other reference points might be explored. What is important is that, once set, there would be no further erosion of the effective number of tax points transferred under EPF.

In other words, Ottawa would, in lieu of cash transfers, transfer some new tax points not to the provinces but to an earmarked "pool." These funds would then be distributed to the provinces so as to ensure that all provinces would have equal per capita EPF funding — that is, the sum of the existing equalized tax point transfers plus the distributions from the pool would be equal in per capita terms. There would no longer be a ceiling — the total EPF pot would be the sum of the existing equalized tax point transfers and the new tax points (abatements, in their terms) allocated to the pool. This sum would grow along with the growth of incomes.

This is a very clever proposal. It effectively converts EPF into a full tax point transfer, but does so in a way that guarantees the equal per capita result that characterizes the status quo. While recognizing its ingenuity, I remain unimpressed. First, some special provisions would have to be put in place to ensure that this "tax abatement" is irrevocable. How does one do this, in light of the recent Supreme Court ruling with respect to the cap on CAP? Second, how will one prevent Ottawa from putting conditions on the distribution of the pool's revenues? Are we not right back to the old EPF problems? Even if one were to assume that concerns could be managed, there is a third problem: superequalization, whereby all provinces are brought up to the level of the top province. How long will it be before the poorer provinces mount a case that the *existing* equalization program should be consistent with the new EPF arrangements and also embody the top province as the standard. Actually, in the context of the second-to-last sentence of the above quote (that is, "other reference points might be explored"), the authors offer the following footnote (ibid., 80):

> Boadway and Hobson (1993) go further than this. They argue that one way of attaining fully equalized fiscal capacities [identical across provinces — TJC] would be to compute EPF entitlements as a net entitlement, that is

actual entitlement plus equalization entitlement. For those provinces with negative equalization entitlements (the have provinces), then, the net EPF entitlement would be less than for the have-not provinces. Under such a scheme, the net effect would be to equalize fully the per capita revenues of the provinces. While this would be consistent with the equity and efficiency arguments present in the Economic Council of Canada (1982)...it would involve a significantly expanded federal presence in cash transfers. Certainly the levels of cash transfers under EPF at present would be insufficient to achieve this goal.

This means that those provinces with revenues *above* the equalization standard (that is, the "have" provinces), will see their cash transfers from this new EPF pool and cash transfers from other federal-provincial programs decreased until an overall equality in per capita provincial revenues is achieved. Alberta would not transfer revenues directly to the poorer provinces, but Ottawa would effectively accomplish this by diverting Alberta's cash transfers to the "have-not" provinces. The constraint, as noted by Boadway and Hobson (1993), is that there may not be sufficient cash transfers in the system to accomplish this. This constraint aside, under this system, Alberta would end up with the lowest per capita revenues in the system, since its EPF cash would be reduced because equalization *assumes* that it has a sales tax even though it does not.

I grant that I may be reading far too much into the Hobson and St-Hilaire proposal. The above quote is from a footnote and not from the text. (However, option 3[d] of Table 41 contains this Boadway and Hobson [1994] equalization option.) While it may appear inappropriate to link the Hobson and St-Hilaire EPF option with the Boadway and Hobson equalization option, my rationale for this linkage is that it is critical to recognize the underlying logic or dynamic in any reform proposal. And the underlying dynamic of the Hobson and St-Hilaire proposal is clearly in the direction of reworking all federal transfers in order to ensure absolute equality across provinces of per capital revenues.

The problem with this genre of proposals is that they elevate redistributional concerns to be the *only* federal concern. As was implicit, if not explicit, in earlier chapters, this approach assumes that federations are inherently dysfunctional societal structures on the distribution side and that the role of federal-provincial transfers is to convert federations into virtual unitary states in terms of distribution. Thus, irrespective of how wages and capitalization might vary across the provinces, the amount of total money available to be spent on Albertans (from Alberta and from Canada) must be identical on a per capita basis with the total amount of money able to be spent on Newfoundlanders (from Newfoundland and from Canada). This conception of horizontal equity ignores the dynamic efficiency and competitive-federalism rationales, among others, for opting for federal states.

Thus, while recognizing the ingenuity of this proposal, I shall recommend (in Chapter 11) other options for reforming EPF as well as for reforming equalization.

CAP Options

No federal-provincial transfer program is in as much trouble as CAP. The integrity and, therefore, the future of the entire federal-provincial transfer system is in the balance if the "have-not" provinces have access to 50 percent federal sharing for welfare while Ontario has 28 percent sharing (with Alberta and British Columbia somewhere in between). But even if one focuses only on the "have-not" provinces, the per capita differentials are progressively more difficult to justify.

However, every bit as problematical for CAP is the likely evolution of provincial welfare schemes. For example, Ontario's proposal for funding children of low-income families (under *Turning Point*) would not fall within CAP guidelines. Nor would an "active" human resource strategy (training-fare, workfare). Phrased differently, CAP as we know it is almost certainly dead and probably the sooner the better, since it is now reining in the ability of the provinces to respond creatively to their welfare challenge.

In this light, the options for CAP in Table 41 take on added significance because the status quo is probably not in the reform set. As is by now obvious, my preference is option (e), converting CAP into a low-income tax credit for children. This will automatically direct federal funds to those provinces where need is greatest.

There are two proposals in Table 41 that do attempt to incorporate need directly. The more common of the two is option 2(c), which would introduce a needs component relating to welfare into the equalization formula. In addition to the elaboration and comments with respect to this proposal in Table 41, it seems a bit peculiar to introduce a needs component relating to a specific expenditure proposal into a transfer that is unconditional (that is, can be spent where the provinces please).

A needs component makes more sense in the context of a conditional transfer. The United States used to run these sorts of transfers. For example, for highway construction the subsidy to the various states depended on, among other factors, its per capita income and the cost of a mile of road in the state. Thus low-income states with, say, mountainous terrain would receive more-than-national-average subsidization on both counts. The Hobson and St-Hilaire (1994) proposal for CAP runs along these lines. There would be a standardized national benefit per capita (somehow calculated) and the overall federal commitment would be 50 percent of this standardized national benefit. However, provinces with needs greater than the national average (that is, a number of provincial "standardized beneficiaries" per capita proportionally larger than the number of national average "standardized beneficiaries" per capita) would receive more than 50 percent cost sharing. If the measures of needs were the number of social assistance recipients per capita, then, in the current time frame, Ontario would receive more than 50 percent funding, while some of the "have-not" provinces would receive less than 50 percent sharing. This is exactly how such a system *ought* to work. However, it would be a tough sell, especially to the "have-not" provinces that have always looked on a needs-related CAP as a way to increase their transfers.

Note that this is not the same as adding a needs factor to the existing CAP program. The difference is that the definition of a beneficiary, under the Hobson and St-Hilaire proposal, would be *standardized across all provinces*. Under the current system, the province essentially defines who is or is not a beneficiary and the definitions can and do vary across provinces. Standardization is important because it reduces the ability of provinces to influence the number of beneficiaries for formula purposes.

Readers desiring more detail (including a specific formula) relating to this proposal should consult Hobson/St-Hilaire (1994, Chapter 4).

In a sense, this proposal has arrived too late. It should have been in place over the past couple of decades. The problem with introducing it now is that provincial welfare systems are likely to evolve in ways in which any attempt at defining a "standardized" welfare beneficiary will be very difficult. For example, under income testing, is a person in Quebec who receives a wage supplement under the Parental Wage Assistance program a full beneficiary? What about a person who works part time while still receiving some welfare in a province that introduces income testing? And how does one treat the children in each of these two cases — as full beneficiaries or only as part beneficiaries? Standardization made eminent sense when welfare was "binary" (you are either on welfare or not on welfare). Not only will it be more complicated to define a standard in this new era, but the very attempt at a definition could well skew provincial programs in a transfer-maximizing direction. Intriguingly, therefore, under the old system, standardization would have reduced moral hazard. Given the way in which welfare systems are now evolving, it may well increase moral hazard.

Equalization Options

There are three principles (not mutually consistent) underpinning the various reform options for equalization in Table 41. First, equalization is not sufficiently redistributive; second, there is a mismatch between the provincial distribution of revenues that trigger equalization and the provincial distribution of revenues that are used to pay equalization; and third, equalization is too large in that it neglects the dynamic efficiency issues. I shall deal with each, beginning with the revenue mismatch under the heading of two-tier equalization schemes.

Two-Tier Schemes

As indicated in the note to Table 41, equalization payments can increase because of the differences across provinces in fiscal capacity relating to broad-based tax sources such as income or sales. Payments can also increase because of increases in province-specific revenues such as those from fossil energy. The distribution of Ottawa's consolidated revenue across the provinces is such that there would be a serious mismatch with respect to equalization triggered by increases in provincial resource revenues. Ottawa's solution to this has been to downplay the role of resource revenues in the equalization formula, via either partial equalization (1976–82) or the five-province standard, which excludes Alberta (1982 to the present).

An alternative way of addressing this issue is a two-tiered equalization program. This is the Courchene and Copplestone (1980) proposal (option 3[c] in Table 41). The first tier, run by Ottawa, would include all broad-based revenues. The second tier would be an interprovincial revenue-sharing pool related to resource revenues. Provinces with a share of per capita resource revenues above the national (all-province) average would contribute a portion of this excess (say 20 percent or 30 percent) into the resource revenue-sharing pool and low-resource provinces would draw down an equivalent portion for any deficiency. The pool would be run by the provinces and be self-financing. (More details on this proposal and several other variants, including the inter-*Länder* sharing pool in the German federation, are available in Courchene 1984, chap. 8.)

There are several advantages to this approach. First, there would be a closer match across provinces between what triggers equalization and who pays for it. Second, while these schemes are not confiscatory (20 percent to 30 percent of average resource revenues beyond the all-province average, not 100 percent) they would be an efficient way of bringing greater equality in net fiscal benefits across provinces — that is, a dollar of equalization flowing through a revenue sharing pool reduces the difference in net fiscal benefits much more than a dollar of equalization moving through the existing system or through tier one. While there are some concerns relating to resource-sharing pools (see Table 41), I still recall a comment made by economist John Helliwell of the University of British Columbia (himself an author, with Anthony Scott, of an interprovincial revenue-sharing proposal for equalization) — if interprovincial revenue sharing pools do not make sense, neither does the United Way.

To facilitate the discussion of the other "net" schemes in Table 41 (that is, option 3[d]), it is useful to introduce it by focusing initially on the second of the principles underlying the equalization options — namely enhancing redistribution.

Enhancing Redistribution

Option 3(b) proposes to allow the existing formula to work "as it should," so to speak — move to a national average standard and eliminate any ceilings. The implications/comments column of 3(b) highlights some concerns.

Much more redistributive is option 3(d), which essentially argues for fully equalizing provincial per capita revenues. The concept of "net" here is that this full equalization would include bringing the revenues of the rich provinces down. This would not be done directly, but rather indirectly — provinces with negative equalization entitlements would have their federal cash transfers *from other programs* reduced accordingly. For this to be feasible, there must be other transfer programs that involve cash transfers. Transferring further tax points to the provinces runs counter to this general approach because they restrict the ability of the federal government to pursue full redistribution. As the reader will note, this scheme has already been discussed and evaluated in the earlier context of the Hobson and St-Hilaire proposal for reforming EPF. Note that it is included in Table 41 as a variant of an interprovincial revenue-sharing pool. What it does have in common with an interprovincial revenue-sharing pool is that the rich provinces do pay for the equalization, although this is not through a formal pool but through a federal decrease, from other programs, in cash transfers otherwise owed to the rich provinces.

Dynamic Efficiency

Option 3(e) implicitly, perhaps explicitly, argues that we overequalize in Canada because we miscalculate net fiscal benefits and we place redistribution on a pedestal to the exclusion of the dynamic-efficiency/growth concerns.

In terms of the former, the issue is straightforward. By ignoring the fact that Toronto is becoming more and more like Tokyo and New York and less and less like Kingston or Dartmouth (that is, by ignoring capitalization factors that affect property values, rents, wages, and so on), we run the risk of substantial overequalization. The fact that many Canadians argue for *full* equalization of revenue per capita for provincial revenues when the United States has opted for *zero* equalization of revenue differentials is surely not all due to our different value systems. On the US side, the decision not to engage in comprehensive revenue equalization is presumably due to their view that the capitalization will take care of this, their view of the appropriate nature of the process of interregional or interstate adjustment, and, of course, their view of the notion of sharing under their federation. Boadway and Flatters (1994) argue against bringing "costs" (that is, capitalization) into equalization because this might remove an incentive on the part of rich provinces to keep their costs in line. But the rich provinces would not get equalization — the impact of introducing costs would be to decrease the equalization of provinces with lower costs. In analytical terms, once costs are introduced, net fiscal benefits are no longer so disparate. Indeed, one can turn the Boadway and Flatters observation on its head: by not introducing costs, we are overequalizing[2] and, indeed, this overequalization is likely capitalized into wages and prices in "have-not" provinces! Not to put too fine a point on it, this is part of the transfer-dependency syndrome.

This argument carries even more weight in an increasingly integrated economy. As noted in the first bullet of Thematic Tableau 5 above, we have to rethink the nature of the optimal social contract in the context of production as being international. It was one thing to argue for a generous (or more generous) approach to equalization when trade was east-west and our economy was operating behind tariff walls. Equalization payments would offset any tendency for firms and people in Halifax, for example, to relocate to Toronto on fiscal grounds. It is quite another when tariffs are effectively gone and trade flows north-south and where firms and persons leave Toronto or Vancouver for venues south, especially when some of Canada's lack of north-south competitiveness relates to the tax cost of the existing system of east-west distribution.

The dynamic efficiency concern is related, but it shifts the focus from "too much redistribution" to "too little adjustment." One of the most surprising aspects of the European Union's (EU) move toward a single currency is that it does not contemplate much in the way of an equalization program. The earlier MacDougall Report (1977), after surveying the various equalization schemes in other nations, recommended the eventual establishment of an equalization program that would guarantee member states 65 percent of the EU average fiscal capacity. To be sure, the EU is confederal rather than federal, so that comparisons may be somewhat beside the point. However, it is important to recognize aspects of the rationale for this limited equalization. Part relates to the changing perception of the role of government in modern economies and, in

---

2 In a working paper, Shah (1994) develops and estimates a comprehensive approach to equalization, one that embodies both revenue means and expenditure needs. His results indicate that we do indeed overequalize in Canada..

particular, the movement from a Keynesian to a neo-conservative paradigm. Part also relates to the fear that too much equalization will sap dynamic efficiency and growth. In the jargon of the EU, the fear is "wage demonstration" effects — wages would rise well beyond what productivity would dictate and this would lead to divergent growth. Canadians might term this transfer dependency.

It should hardly come as a surprise that I believe that Canada's equalization program has to incorporate both redistributional and dynamic efficiency features. To adopt such a position need not reflect a change in underlying values or the role one assigns to equalization in the federation. Rather, a case can be made that the perspective through which these values must be filtered has, of necessity, shifted from a domestic (east-west) to an international (north-south) perspective.

Toward this end, the final option (3f) in Table 41 attempts to incorporate some dynamic-efficiency elements into equalization. The option is referred to as an negative income tax-type equalization scheme. Provinces would be eligible to receive in equalization 70 percent of the gap between their own standardized fiscal capacities and, say, the national average standard. As noted in the table, a province with a fiscal capacity of 80 percent of the national average would receive 70 percent of this gap in terms of equalization — that is, its per capita revenues would be brought up to 94 percent of the national average. And a province with 90 percent of the national average would be brought up to 97 percent. In negative income tax terms, the tax-back rate is 70 percent. Thus, if a province increases its tax bases, it will pocket 30 cents on each additional dollar of own revenues. Setting aside the issue of how an increase in a province's tax base affects the standard itself,[3] under the existing system the tax-back rate is 100 percent for the "have-not" provinces.

There is another advantage of this negative income tax approach to equalization. One of the characteristics of the five-province standard over the past decade was its vulnerability to marked swings triggered largely, but not solely, by the boom and bust of the Ontario economy. In turn, this led to wide swings in the level of equalization payments. Under this 70-percent-of-gap proposal, these swings would be tempered — a province's equalization would increase by only 70 percent of any increase in the standard and it would fall by only 70 percent of any decrease in the standard.

Two final points merit highlight. First, this scheme would not affect the rate of growth of equalization — it would grow at the same rate as the standard; rather, the impact would be to temper the variations. Second, this 70-percent-

---

3 This caveat would apply to all equalization programs, so that it should not enter into the comparisons.

of-gap approach need not mean lower equalization; this would depend on the definition of the equalization standard.

These issues pertaining to the potential stabilizing properties of option 3(f) of Table 41 aside, the underlying principle is that if confiscatory taxes do not make sense for individuals, why should they for provinces?

Other Reform Options

The list of reform areas runs well beyond those captured in Tables 38 to 41 — for example, day care, payroll taxation, and curriculum reform as well as a series of reforms in associated areas such as tax assignment, tax harmonization, and even macro policy. Rather than address these issues in the present context, I shall focus on two other areas — workers' compensation and training.

Workers' Compensation

The analysis of workers' compensation in Chapter 5 focused largely on some overview financial statistics. In order to address reform options, however, it is necessary to delve into the benefit structure in more detail. Since there are ten benefit structures, one for each province, some corners need to be cut. Accordingly, what follows will deal only with the Ontario benefit structure.

Apart from survivors' benefits, Ontario has a dual-award system. One of these awards relates to "noneconomic loss" (NEL) — the loss of enjoyment of life caused by permanent impairment. This is a once-and-for-all payment based on age, not income. The base amount is $45,000 (indexed to inflation as of January 1990) which increases by $1,000 for each year that the person is less than 45 years of age at the time of the accident, to a maximum of $65,000 for persons 25 years of age and under. This base amount also decreases by $1,000 for each year that the claimant is over 45 years of age, to a minimum of $25,000. Thus, if a 25-year-old incurs a liability that is deemed, by the adjudication process, to result in a 30 percent impairment, the once-and-for-all, tax-exempt NEL benefit will be $19,500 — that is, 30 percent of $65,000. And so on for the various degrees of impairment, many of which are determined by the regulations pursuant to the legislation.

The second type of benefit relates to "future economic loss" (FEL). This component is ongoing and relates to the worker's future loss of earnings resulting from the disability. Compensation is based on 90 percent of the difference between pre-injury net earnings — where "net" refers to income after taxes and payroll contributions — and what the legislation refers to as "likely post-injury net earnings." In turn, "likely post-injury net earnings" will be based on what a worker is likely to be able to earn from suitable and available employment. Under the Ontario legislation, employers with more than 20 employees have an obligation either to offer re-employment to claimants, perhaps in a less demanding job, or to continue to look for a job that the worker can perform. Thus, if a person's net income prior to the injury was $2,000 per month and is $1,000 per month, post-injury, the FEL benefit will be $900 per month —that is, 90 percent of the $1,000 differential. This benefit is tax free and is escalated by the rate of inflation. The benefit is reviewed after two years and again after five years, after which it is locked in until age 65. At this point, the FEL benefit is converted to a workers' compensation retirement pension, which is financed by a workers' compensation contribution of 10 percent of the FEL benefit annually to a pension pool. In other words, the claimant receives 100 percent of the pre- and post-earnings differential, except that 10 percent of this is allocated to a pension fund. Since workers' compensation benefits are not taxable, this pension fund is not eligible for offset against the Guaranteed Income Supplement, for example.

Complications arise in assessing "likely post-injury net earnings" because it refers to suitable and available employment. Suitability has both an occupational dimension (finding suitable employment) and a personal dimension (vocational rehabilitation, including training, to ensure that the claimant's skills are more suitable to re-employment). Claimants have a right to these vocational rehabilitation services (which cover a broad range of ways to help workers return to the workforce) at full compensation. It is far from clear, however, what happens if there is no work "available." At this point, significant discretion enters the system and presumably the caseworker has a major input into the decision, which could encompass more training, compensated job search in other locations, deeming the worker to be unemployable and therefore eligible for 90 percent of his or her pre-injury earnings, or holding firm on the theoretical post-injury earnings potential and allowing welfare to top up any FEL benefit.

This, then, is a brief overview of the Ontario workers' compensation program as it relates to the benefit structure. Even more than is the case for welfare, no two provinces approach workers' compensation in the same manner. Indeed, the provincial schemes differ markedly, as is clear from Tables 24, 25, and 26. This makes it difficult to frame reform proposals. Even more difficult is the fact that claimants are "victims" of the economic system, as it were, and therefore merit special efforts to ensure that they are treated equitably. Nonetheless, with some trepidation, I offer the following observations and recommendations based largely, but not wholly, on the Ontario model.

First, I reiterate the recommendation I made in Chapter 5 that, henceforth, workers' compensation benefits, at least the FEL component, become taxable. This can be done with minimum lead time for those who are now contributing to workers' compensation. Presumably this will imply higher overall, but henceforth taxable, benefit payments in terms of any future claims. For those currently on workers' compensation benefits, this becomes more difficult and will have to involve greater lead times and/or transitions (or these benefits can be "grandfathered"). In another sense, the degree of difficulty may be exaggerated, since workers' compensation benefits are adjusted annually for inflation and/or the evolution of average wages. Given that Ottawa has moved to partial indexation and even freezes of its social programs, the provinces surely will follow suit. Thus, in terms of the final column of Table 24, I expect that more provinces will opt for partial indexation of workers' compensation benefits. (As this monograph was going to press, Ontario had signaled its intention to move toward partial indexation.) In the context of any such partial indexation, it may be possible to move gradually toward full taxation of benefits, even for existing beneficiaries.

Intriguingly, the decision to make workers' compensation benefits taxable lies with Ottawa, not with the provinces. All Ottawa has to do is declare them as income for tax purposes since it controls the parameters of the personal income tax system. (This would not apply to the Quebec personal income tax.) While I have not researched the issue, I would guess that the reason workers' compensation benefits are defined in "net" terms was to avoid the situation where provincial benefits are taxed by Ottawa. This was a more serious problem a few decades ago, when the provincial share of the personal income tax was much lower than it is today. The way to handle this problem now is either to earmark taxes related to workers' compensation to be returned to the provinces or to allow the provinces to mount special tax credits to collect any workers' compensation taxes owing.

At first blush, the advantage of taxing workers' compensation benefits may appear illusory. Benefits will go up initially (to allow for taxation), but contribution rates would not since the additional benefits would be taxed back (and allocated to the workers' compensation account). With workers' compensation benefits taxable, however, they could be fully integrated into the overall system of income support and social insurance. In turn, this would allow much greater flexibility in terms of social policy evolution since all social policy benefits will be either taxable or eligible for offset. Relatedly, workers' compensation beneficiaries would be free to engage in labor market activities but they would be taxed on their total income. Under the Ontario system, there is no incentive for a workers' compensation claimant to improve his or her labor market status because the tax rate, at 90 percent, essentially will be confiscatory. Indeed, the opposite is true: there is very little incentive for recipients to maximize their FEL benefit since this will, after five years, lock in tax-free income until retirement. Once this income is locked in, the claimant will then have an incentive to maximize labor market income. This is fully rational behavior on the part of claimants. The problem lies in the design of the system, which should not place claimants in a position where they are encouraged to play the system rather than the labor markets. It would be much better if the benefits were taxable or issued in the form of a negative income tax so that the claimant is rewarded for market income (and the costs of workers' compensation would fall apace).

A second potential problem with Ontario's benefit system is its focus on the "availability" of employment. It is probably not unreasonable to take availability into account at the outset and even at the time of the two-year review. But availability should not play a role in the five-year review — the benefit should relate only to the earnings potential of the claimant. This means that, after two years, the claimant will know that any availability premium will disappear so that enhancing earnings will not prejudice this component of the benefit — it will disappear anyway.

A final comment relates to the workers' compensation pension. We may well have a situation where a claimant has access to OAS/GIS, CPP/QPP, an occupational pension, and now a nontaxable workers' compensation pension. Surely, the latter, too, should be taxable.

The more relevant issue here is that there are ten systems of workers' compensation, each of which is searching for ways to trade off equity and efficiency. As in other areas, we will surely witness a substantial degree of experimenting in design and delivery, which, in my view, is not only desirable but essential if we are to regain control of the workers' compensation system.

A second general reform of workers' compensation would be to adopt the recommendation by Vaillancourt (1994, 277) to move from employer-only contributions to joint employer-employee contributions. This would ensure that employees have a financial interest in all aspects of job safety and would give them more power at the bargaining table with respect to safety issues.

Finally, some enhanced societal accountability must be brought to bear on workers' compensation boards. They have operated largely as unaccountable provincial fiefdoms at the same time that workers' compensation was recording the highest social policy expenditure growth. To be sure, a large part of this problem relates to the fact that the Canadian policy community has ignored the operations of these boards. This is about to change. It is anomalous that, with all the emphasis on health and safety in the workplace, workers' compensation benefits appear to be uncontrollable.

Training

A set of reform options for training appears in Chapter 5 and a selected subset will be reproduced in the final chapter. For present purposes, attention is directed to what is probably the key issue relating to training: who should control it?

As part of the analysis in Chapter 8, I argued that, since knowledge is at the cutting edge of competitiveness, it is only natural that Ottawa will want to play a role here. But what role? Ottawa cannot deliver training — this is the responsibility of the provinces (for secondary, university, and community college training) and the private sector. Hence, we are talking about a potential federal leadership/coordination role and/or a funding role.

The leadership side is obvious. Ottawa must ensure that the foot-dragging on establishing occupation standards stops (as Maxwell 1994 notes) and that the internal economic union as it applies to labor mobility is full and free. Indeed, any funding role on Ottawa's part should be predicated on these conditions being in place.

In terms of funding, were Ottawa to bite the bullet on UI reform and adopt option 3 from Table 39, the UI "savings" would be dramatic; — perhaps as high as $10 billion. This is obviously an uneducated guess, but relatively harmless because a $6 billion or $12 billion figure will do just as well in terms of what follows. The word "savings" has been put in quotes because it is not evident that these are federal government savings. Once the UI deficit is wiped out (which *would* represent federal savings), the UI fund would start to move into substantial surplus. Then the fun begins. Much of the analysis in this monograph would suggest that UI contribution rates should fall in tandem so as to reduce the "silent killer" of jobs. But despite the fact that UI has been "privatized" in the sense of breaking even, except for temporary periods, it is still a federal competence under the Constitution. If Ottawa were to maintain UI contribution rates at existing levels and then attempt to divert the surplus to training according to federal priorities, the stage could be set, depending on the process, for a massive federal-provincial confrontation. We have enough experience in these matters to know that the losers in such a process will be individual Canadians.

I think that the Charlottetown Accord got it right. For those provinces that want to integrate training/education/welfare and the transition to the labor market, Ottawa should yield the field, subject to the earlier caveats and some further ones. Specifically, Ottawa must use its leverage to ensure (*à la* Dupré in Chapter 5) that the provinces do not discriminate against the private sector in the provision of training and apprenticeship. Finally, the Canadian Labour Force Development Board may be the ideal way to devolve training, given that it incorporates representatives from, among other interests, labor, business, Ottawa, and the relevant province (or provinces if some provinces decide to integrate their approach). The end result should be a single "window" for the welfare, unemployment insurance, training, and education constellation. While the federal government must be "in the neighborhood," as it were, this has to be a provincial window, at least for those provinces that want to exercise this right.

Postscript:
Social Insurance as the Problem Area

As I indicated in the acknowledgments, this monograph was completed while I was an adjunct professor at the Federalism Research Centre of Australian National University (ANU), Canberra. As part of my research on Australia, I had the privilege of presenting a defense of Australian federalism at a constitutional conference in Melbourne (Courchene 1994d).

Among other points, I noted that Australia appears to have accomplished something quite unique and, indeed, quite remarkable — an egalitarian society financed at US tax rates. My colleagues at ANU quickly pointed out that this was due largely to the fact that Australia had little in the way of social insurance — no UI, no equivalent of the CPP/QPP, and private-sector-influenced workers' compensation whereby employers in some states can choose among alternative insurers — and that its income support system was highly targeted. In the process of rereading this chapter, the relevance of this observation for Canada became increasingly apparent. UI, has, by virtually all indicators, lost its way. CPP/QPP is woefully underfunded, to the point where contribution rates eventually will have to increase threefold to achieve "pay-as-you-go" equilibrium. And workers' compensation is not only the fastest-growing social program in terms of benefit payouts, but its unfunded liabilities are spiraling upward as well. As a result, social insurance contributions are likely to climb to rates in the 25 percent range in the next century, with such rates falling hardest on low- and middle-income Canadians — precisely those whose employment prospects are under siege from the forces of globalization.

Some of the reasons Canada's experience with social insurance has been so disappointing, both fiscally and in terms of constraining the future of Social Canada, are as follows:

- a tendency to extend benefits beyond pure insurance to incorporate distributional goals — this is obvious for UI; a recent example from the CPP/QPP front is the 1992 increase in benefits (from $113.14 per month to $154.70 per month) for children of dead or disabled CPP contributors;
- weak fiscal accountability, in that not only are these programs typically off budget, but the incentives for increasing benefits are quite distinct from the process of increasing contribution rates (for the CPP/QPP, for example);

- poor financial accountability, especially for the CPP/QPP and worker's compensation, in that focus is directed to the immediate term ("pay-as-you-go") and the accumulating unfunded liabilities are ignored;
- in the case of the CPP/QPP, the apparent diversion by the combined federal and provincial governments of pensioners' assets to their own purposes; as Lam, Prince, and Cutt (1993, 70) point out, had the excess of contributions over benefits been invested at market rates (rather than turned over to the provinces at federal government bond rates), the equilibrium steady-state contribution rate would be 8 percent rather than the estimated 16 percent.
- poor societal accountability in the case of the CPP/QPP, since governments allowed people to believe that their contributions were "fully buying" their CPP/QPP, whereas the facts are clearly otherwise;
- in the case of workers' compensation boards, a lack of political accountability in that boards functioned largely as a "state within a state;" and, finally, but not exhaustively
- the lack of targeting of these social insurance programs, even to the point where the CPP/QPP probably could be labeled as regressive.

With this as backdrop, one approach to social policy reform would be to phase out both UI and the CPP/QPP and to replace them with targeted income support programs — say, some version of a negative income tax. For workers' compensation, a solution would be to introduce the recommendations I proposed earlier in this chapter. Together with sorting out some of the incentive problems that exist elsewhere in the system, this proposal would, in one fell swoop, put Social Canada on a viable fiscal footing. The system would be equitable in the sense that it would apply universally to those in need of income support. It would reduce the existing high degree of moral hazard in the current system. And the elimination of payroll taxes for UI and the CPP/QPP and their likely reduction for workers' compensation would do more for employment — particularly of younger and less-skilled Canadians — than almost any conceivable job-creation package.

As I noted, this is in the nature of a postscript or addendum to the analysis. My preferred blueprint for the future of Social Canada will proceed along different lines. There can be little doubt, however, that we have mismanaged our social insurance programs, and I could easily be persuaded that a frontal attack on social insurance would constitute an appropriate alternative route for restructuring Social Canada.

Conclusion

This has been an overview of the range of options pertaining to remaking Canada's social policy infrastructure. The last chapter will represent my attempt to bring the analysis from this and the previous chapters to bear on the design of a blueprint for Social Canada in the millennium. However, one of the features of the above analysis is that there is sufficient discussion and evaluation of the options for readers to design their own social policy blueprints.

Part VII

Social Canada in the Millennium

Chapter 11

A Blueprint for Social Canada

There is no single best way to rework Canada's social infrastructure. And if, by some chance, there were a first-best way to restructure the system for Ontario, it does not follow that this would also be the first-best way for Nova Scotia or British Columbia. Part of this may have to do with the preferences of British Columbians as distinct from, say, the preferences of Quebecers, in terms of how their social infrastructure ought to evolve. This is what a federal system is all about. Part also may result from the fact that the dictates of a Great Lakes economy may differ from those of a Pacific Rim economy. For example, in "communitarian capitalist" countries (to use the term popularized by Lester Thurow [1992]) such as Japan and Germany, firms tend to play a larger role in training than in "individualistic capitalist" countries (for example, the English-speaking countries). Quebec tends to imitate aspects of the former and it may be the case that British Columbia will also be influenced by the Asian approach to the employee-firm relationship. This could lead to quite different approaches to integrating and coordinating the welfare, unemployment, training, and education (WUTE) interface.

Accepting this need for flexibility, it is nonetheless the case that some approaches to restructuring appear to be preferable to others. The purpose of this final chapter is to draw on the previous analysis and evaluation of Social Canada in order to provide a blueprint or framework for our social infrastructure in the millennium.

The chapter proceeds by presenting, in summary fashion, the range of social and economic *imperatives* that must inform any restructuring. This is followed by a series of restructuring *principles* that ought to guide the reform process. With these as backdrop, the analysis then develops a preferred blueprint for the new Social Canada. However, this blueprint probably cannot be applied identically across provinces because of, among other items, the presence of the 16.5 tax abatement points currently allocated to Quebec. Attention will be directed toward alternative ways of finessing this issue. Beyond this, there are other implications arising from the blueprint that merit attention — the impact on the division of powers, the impact on internal migration, and the cost implications of the reform. A concluding section completes the chapter and the book.

Restructuring Imperatives

Social Canada cannot be reworked in isolation from forces or imperatives that have dramatically altered our political economy environment. They include the following:

- The socio-economic needs of Canadians in the 1990s are markedly different than the needs of the prosperous 1950s and 1960s, when much of the existing social policy infrastructure was put in place.
- Canada's fiscal predicament is nothing short of staggering. All policy areas, social policy included, must make their contribution to restoring Canada's fiscal integrity.
- In tandem, the above two imperatives represent a tremendous challenge to Social Canada in the millennium. Not only must the social envelope be restructured and reoriented to the new socio-economic needs and goals, but this restructuring must be accomplished within an environment of fiscal constraint, unlike the era of fiscal surpluses when the existing infrastructure was implemented.
- We are entering an era where knowledge is increasingly on the cutting edge of competitiveness. Not only does this call for a knowledge-enhancing social infrastructure, but social policy has a critical "bridging" role to play in the transition from a resource-based mentality and society to a knowledge-based mentality and society.
- With economic links increasingly north-south rather than east-west, a restructured Social Canada must ensure that the east-west (interprovincial or federal-provincial) transfer system is consistent with a north-south trading system.
- Almost of necessity, the previous two imperatives imply that the new Social Canada must focus more on "people" than on "place."
- Compounding much or all of this is that the process of globalization is generating a polarization of incomes — increased returns to human capital and a reduction in one or both of jobs and incomes of the less skilled. This will influence not only social policy goals but also the nature of the appropriate instruments for delivering social policy.
- Canada is the world's largest mature federation. It is also among the world's most economically diverse nations. But our economic diversity coincides with a geographical/regional diversity. Hence, uniform and inflexible policy frameworks (for economic policy, social policy, and so on) emanating from the center are likely to be inappropriate and unworkable.

- With the North American Free Trade Agreement constraining what we can do on the allocative front, social policy goals will have to be pursued via tax transfer instruments rather than allocative instruments.

Restructuring Principles

All of the above imperatives are more or less external or "exogenous" to the social envelope and, therefore, to social policy restructuring — "more or less," to allow for some interaction between social policy and these restructuring imperatives. For example, the relationship between social policy and the debt/deficit over-hang is clearly not one of exogeneity — governments' adherence to the outmoded social paradigm led to much of the fiscal excess over the past decade. Cruelly, perhaps, the resulting fiscal burden is now reverberating powerfully back on Social Canada. Nonetheless, from the perspective of 1994, the fiscal crisis is appropriately viewed as an exogenous force that serves to rein in the reworking of our social infrastructure.

Corresponding to these exogenous forces is an equally important set of forces that are largely or entirely internal or "endogenous" to the reworking of Social Canada. As the title of this section indicates, I am referring to these as "restructuring principles."

Largely for presentation purposes, I adopt a three-tiered approach to these principles. The first tier relates to those principles that must inform any social policy restructuring because they are embodied in the *Constitution Act, 1982.* The second tier draws from the analyses in the previous chapters. Here the definition of principles relates primarily to a series of operating or process lessons that have been gleaned from the foregoing review and assessment of our existing social policy framework. The third tier relates to some personal views, or perhaps biases, that underpin the entire monograph and, by extension, underpin my reworking of Social Canada.

Constitutional Principles

Foremost among the constitutional principles are those embodied in section 36 of the *Constitution Act, 1982.* In effect, sections 36(1) and 36(2) articulate, respectively, the underlying nature of the Canadian social contract as it applies both to individual citizens and to the provinces:

> Equality of opportunity (from section 36(1)). Without altering the legislative authority of Parliament or of the provincial legislatures, or the rights of any of them with respect to the exercise of their legislative authority, Parliament

and the legislatures, together with the government of Canada and the provincial governments, are committed to promoting equal opportunities for the well-being of Canadians; furthering economic development to reduce disparity in opportunities; and providing essential public services of reasonable quality to all Canadians.

Equalization (from section 36(2)). "Parliament and the government of Canada are committed to the principle of making equalization payments to ensure that provincial governments have sufficient revenues to provide reasonably comparable levels of public services at reasonably comparable levels of taxation."

These principles may not be justiciable, at least not to the degree that applies to other provisions of the Constitution. Nonetheless, they represent important beacons that will illuminate the way in terms of social policy restructuring.

The Constitution informs other aspects of Social Canada as well. The federal power over trade and commerce (section 91(2)), the "free trade clause" (section 121), and the mobility provisions of the Charter of Rights and Freedoms provide the basis for an economic and social union. In my view, these provisions do not go far enough, so that they will be amplified in the context of the second-tier set of principles. Finally, and most obviously, given the large number of constitutional challenges, the principles of the Charter will play a key role in the reworking of Social Canada — principles such as the equality provisions of section 15 and the various nondiscrimination provisions.

Operational Principles

As noted, the second tier of principles is operational in nature and derives from the various conclusions and implications arising from the analysis in the foregoing chapters. Among these operational principles are the following:

- Social policy reform must begin from the "bottom up" — that is, by focusing on individual Canadians and their social infrastructure needs. The critical first task is to ensure that the structure and incentives within individual programs as well as within the system of programs are consistent, socio-economically, with the needs and aspirations of Canadians. Then, and only then, should we address the issues of which level of government should deliver these various programs and how they should be financed.
- By way of further elaboration, two corollaries flow from this. First, the structure of federal-provincial transfers should be derivative, not determining. That is, they should accommodate, not frustrate, the development of a social infrastructure appropriate for and sensitive to the needs of

Canadians. Second, jurisdictional in-fighting cannot be allowed to stand in the way of designing a system appropriate to the needs of Canadians. Far better to allow some asymmetries in design and delivery to arise if the alternative is to compromise the nature of the programs themselves.

- In terms of making sections 36(1) and 36(2) of the *Constitution Act, 1982* operational, both equality of opportunity and equalization must be informed by the realities of globalization and the information revolution. For example, with respect to equalization, dynamic efficiency concerns as well as redistributive equity concerns both have a role to play. The role of the former has to do not only with the new global order but also with the "policy equilibrium" aspects of transfer dependency that have now become entrenched, as documented in Chapter 2.

- The system must be able to evolve or recreate itself from within. Were one to put in place the ideal social infrastructure for 1994, it would likely be outmoded early in the millennium. Design features that facilitate flexibility and evolution are clearly to be preferred. In this context, ensuring that *all* benefits are either taxable or eligible for offset is critical. Specifically, this means that workers' compensation benefits must be taxable.

- Provincial experimentation over a wide range of the social envelope should be encouraged. This is essential for two reasons. First, what is appropriate for one province or economic region may not be appropriate for all. Second, and more important, innovative approaches to design or delivery developed in one province are sure to spread to other provinces given the nature of the fiscal constraint. This is critical because in many social policy areas there is no single best approach, so that "learning by doing" can become the optimal societal strategy.

- The federal role in terms of this experimentation is to establish the appropriate framework within which it can proceed. Indeed, the required nature of the social and economic union in this context goes beyond the provisions referred to under the tier-one principles. In the language of the Charlottetown Accord, we need to embrace "positive integration" — for example, extending the Red Seal program to ensure that skills acquired in one jurisdiction are transferable to all other jurisdictions.

- We should aim to limit "interprovincial gaming" and moral hazard. Decisions made in the ten provincial capitals should not be able to trigger open-ended contributions from Ottawa (and vice versa). In the fiscal federalism literature, this is frequently referred to as the principle of "fiscal coincidence" — the jurisdiction responsible for spending should also be responsible, on the margin at least, for raising the associated taxes. Another way of stating this is that provinces ought to bear the full financial responsibility for their policy decisions. While this is not an argument against equalization, it is also the case that equalization can be subjected to some of these precepts as well. In short, accountability matters and, where possible, should infuse all transfers, whether individual or federal-provincial. In terms of the moral hazard issue — namely, the ability of individuals to influence their social policy benefits — the problem lies in the program incentives. As with intergovernmental gaming, it is essential that opportunities for moral hazard be reduced. This is important in its own right, and also in the broader social policy context: social policy becomes an easy target for straightforward cost cutting if there is a widespread perception that the system is open to abuse.

• Visibility and transparency are also characteristics that should be integral to any policy area, including social policy.

• Social policy should be consistent with enhancing individual self-reliance. Among other things, this means that marginal tax rates in the transition back to market income must be kept within acceptable ranges.

• Transition measures are important. Many Canadians have, by acting rationally, become hostage to the inappropriate set of incentives within the existing social infrastructure. They cannot be made to bear the full adjustment costs of a restructured Social Canada.

Subjective Principles

This third tier of principles is, as the section head indicates, really more in the way of personal reflections of someone who has been a student of the evolution of Social Canada over the past two decades. I do not insist that these reflections be embraced by others. However, in the context of this chapter, they become important because they will play a role in the manner in which I shall approach reworking Social Canada:

• Canada, in the millennium, will be largely defined by its social infrastructure. As a working "mission statement," as it were, I adhere to the notion that Social Canada's role is to provide full opportunity for Canadians to develop and enhance their skills and human capital to enable them to become full participants in the emerging global/information society.

• Accomplishing this means, however, that fundamental restructuring of the social envelope is in order in terms of both programs and goals. Mere tinkering or half-way measures will not allow social policy to exit from the current perception that it is an unnecessary cost hindering our international competitiveness. Phrased differently, such tinkering will lead inevitably to the Americanization of Social Canada because we will fall short of the challenge on all of the fiscal, economic, and social policy fronts.

The latter point needs elaboration. Canadians have made impressive postwar gains in social policy, all the more impressive because while we were integrating with the Americans economically we were diverging from them in terms of our social contract. However, under the onslaught of what I have referred to as "restructuring imperatives," our postwar achievements now hang in the balance. In order to maintain a distinctive, made-in-Canada social infrastructure, we have little option but to filter our long-standing values of fairness, sharing, and equity through the new realities of fiscal restraint, globalization, and the information revolution. Actually, we have precious little in the way of alternatives here. If we do not opt for a made-in-Canada social policy, we will likely end up with a made-in-international-capital-markets social policy.

With this as backdrop, the challenge now is to convert these largely exogenous restructuring imperatives and largely internal restructuring principles into a blueprint for the new Social Canada.

Toward a New Social Canada

At one level, reconstituting Social Canada for the millennium is now relatively straightforward: select program options from Chapter 10 that will "work" individually and as an integrated system and that will also be consistent with the restructuring imperatives and principles. Not surprisingly, however, complications arise because there will always be alternative, yet consistent, ways to integrate such a wide range of programs. Some of these alternatives will be addressed in the context of presenting the basic framework. Others, such as the asymmetries that may arise for Quebec, will be discussed in a separate section.

What follows, therefore, is a 12-point blueprint that reflects the manner in which I believe the sets of restructuring imperatives and principles interact with the range of available options. The blueprint proceeds on a program-by-program basis, beginning with unemployment insurance (UI).

UI Reform

UI must be taken out of the short-term, first-resort, income assistance system. Without this, social policy reform effectively will come to naught. Short of jettisoning UI entirely (along the lines of the postscript in Chapter 10), my clear preference is to adopt option 3 from Table 39: a *uniform* 30-week entry period with each week of benefits requiring three weeks of previous work. The real test for Ottawa in this renewal process is whether it will rethink UI in the context of the combination of insurance principles and longer-term labor force attachment. The fact that the federal government is now developing separate programs for problem industries, such as the fisheries, should make it easier to redesign UI along the lines of longer-term labor force attachment.

Beyond this change in the structure of UI, the UI-to-work transition must embody a set of new and more appropriate incentives. The proposal in Chapter 10 — that the benefit rate be set equal to the tax-back rate, is my preferred approach. This should generate further UI savings since the incentive would exist to re-enter the labor force while on UI benefits.

The proposal that UI take the form of training and education benefits for persons under 25 is, despite its apparent public appeal, likely to be difficult to implement. Assuming that it would not violate Charter principles, how would it operate? Would it be a separate "training fund" financed by contributions? Would it be administered by Ottawa? That is, would Ottawa look after the training of these young UI beneficiaries and the provinces look after the training of other young Canadians? This is a recipe for bureaucratic layering. My perspective on this is the following: first, all UI beneficiaries should be encouraged to upgrade their skills; second, if there is a special training/education program for young Canadians on UI, this should be integrated into the overall welfare, unemployment insurance, training, and education network and coordinated by the provinces. More on this issue later. Experience rating of industries should be set aside until it is obvious that it is a serious issue under this new approach to UI.

Finally, now that UI is essentially a self-financing contributory scheme, the management of the program should be transferred to a business/labor executive with room for some government representation on the board. This should ensure that UI sticks to its knitting, as it were, and does not become diverted once again to political goals.

Welfare

Children

The philosophy underpinning Ontario's *Turning Point* has got it right. The major welfare trap relates to the presence of children. Children should be covered under a separate negative income tax that would not depend on whether the parent(s) were on welfare or working, but where the benefits would be offset against other income (except welfare payments to the parent(s)). This has to be a *low-income*, antipoverty, refundable tax credit (unlike the existing tax credit for children, which is middle income). The preferred approach here is for Ottawa to convert the Canada Assistance Plan (CAP) into such a low-income, refundable tax credit where the tax-back process would begin from the first dollar of earned income and the break-even point would be roughly at the income level where the existing tax credit now begins to be taxed back (mid-$20,000) or perhaps even lower.

Actually, I would go somewhat further afield here. The income threshold triggering the clawback of the *existing* child tax credit is too high. Depending on how wide a net Ottawa is prepared to cast over the social policy review process, I would recommend that this existing child credit income threshold be reduced by several thousand dollars in order to mesh with the new antipoverty child credit. While this approach has considerable conceptual merit, it is not without its operational difficulties. Prior to focusing on the latter, allow me to indicate some of the benefits.

First, it would solve the 28 cents versus 50 cents controversy in CAP that is currently undermining the very integrity of the federal-provincial transfer system. Second, the income distribution impacts across the provinces would be very equitable in the sense that children of low-income families would benefit no matter where they live. Third, this gives Ottawa both accountability and visibility. It is, of course, true that the former CAP payments would now be going to some low-income families who are not now on welfare. But this will occur in any event as the provincial welfare systems evolve. Fourth, the changes in UI are likely to increase the welfare burden differentially across provinces. This new approach to CAP would automatically compensate for such differential burdens — henceforth, the provinces would be responsible only for the adults.

On the operational side, while the 28 cents versus 50 cents issue would no longer exist, the rich provinces might not welcome this initiative because the value of the tax credit would be identical across provinces — in the same way that old age security (OAS) and Guaranteed Income Supplement (GIS) are identical. Presumably, the tax credit will be set so that it is appropriate for, say, Saskatchewan. Ontario may feel that it has to top this up for Toronto. So be it. Alternatively, and probably appropriately, Ontario could structure its welfare incentives so that the unemployables on welfare are not concentrated in Toronto.

A second operational issue is that the income effect of this tax credit could tilt the preferences of family heads toward fewer hours of work. This issue was highlighted by David Brown (1994) in his appearance before the Parliamentary Committee on social policy reform.[1] This would be offset by the incentives for those currently on welfare to enter the labor force. Obviously, the issue is which will dominate. I think that the latter effect will dominate, for two reasons. First, people can now withdraw from the labor force and collect welfare. Second, the provinces will make this behavior more difficult by engaging in a variety of "active" labor market policies, including workfare and training-fare. Nonetheless, this is an important caveat.

---

1 One way to quantify the potential impact is to attempt to ascertain the impact of the introduction of the *existing* child tax credit on work effort. See Brown 1994.

The third operational issue relates to delivery — the value of the tax credit, the requirement for monthly delivery (like the GIS) with, say, quarterly reconciliation, and so on. In terms of the cost of the program, Ottawa would have a fair degree of flexibility. Indeed, the 1994 federal budget already signaled a decrease in CAP payments. This would be incorporated in the tax credit. Nor does it follow that the tax credits for three children need be three times the value of the credit for a single child. This is not the standard practice under provincial welfare schemes, so it should likewise not constrain Ottawa.

One final point: there has been much discussion in policy circles to the effect that Ottawa wants to play a more direct role in some of these areas. One popular proposal is that the provinces would "look after" the unemployable unemployed whereas Ottawa would focus on the employable unemployed. This would result in a bureaucratic quagmire, not all that different conceptually from the earlier issue relating to the under-25 population. It would be much better to cut through all of this by having Ottawa focus on the children and leave to the provinces the adults, to whom I now turn.

Adults

With children covered under a separate, income-tested, federally run program, the provinces could focus welfare on adults and make critical strides toward an active labor force policy. Training-fare should be in and some provinces might opt for workfare as well. Provincial flexibility should obviously be encouraged, but there should also be a set of all-province minimum standards. For example, provinces should not be allowed to pursue workfare or training-fare that would lead to a substantial reduction in the family income (say, for example, by insisting on training that saddles the adult with significant day care expenses). But such an interprovincial or federal-provincial pact should strive to free up the system dramatically in comparison with the status quo. Canadian social reformers have long waxed eloquent about the virtues of the Swedish social infrastructure. As noted in the previous chapter, Sweden leads the way in the percentage of overall labor market expenditures devoted to "active" labor market policies. Education, retraining, migration, and so on are old hat to the Swedes. We should incorporate provisions that, at a minimum, ensure that the provinces have the freedom to maneuver on the training/workfare/location front at least to the same degree that the Swedes permit.

Minimum Wages

Since children would be looked after under a separate program, it is likely that work at the minimum wage would dominate the welfare benefit for a single adult (and *all* adults are, by economic definition under this proposal, single). In its 1993 policy document, *Turning Point*, Ontario proposes to increase its minimum wage from 48 percent to 60 percent of the industrial wage. This would be a major social and economic policy error. In the previous chapter, the quote from *The Economist* (February 26, 1994) scolded France for raising its minimum wage from 40 percent of the average wage to 50 percent and, in the process, seeing the youth unemployment rate rise from 4 percent to 20 percent. The minimum wage can hardly take all the flak for this, nor can the fact that the US minimum wage fell from 40 percent to 30 percent of the average wage take all the credit for the much lower unemployment rate in the United States than in Canada. Nonetheless, were Ontario to follow through with this minimum wage philosophy, the costs would be very significant, including the loss of jobs by many of the now "working poor."

The more significant analytical and, I think, social policy point as well is that moving in the direction of income testing marginalizes the role of high minimum wages. What counts now is *total income*. Under an income-tested approach to welfare, the way to increase total income is to increase work income, at whatever wage and whether part time or full time. People with adequate skills will command adequate wages. The problem lies at the low end. These people probably could never command a job at a wage equal to 60 percent of the average industrial wage, probably not even one equal to 48 percent. But many of them do work now, in the underground economy, for wages that are much lower. It is important that this work be brought above ground.

The way for the provinces to go here is to income test adult welfare so as to encourage labor force attachment. There are many alternatives available: normal income testing, a wage supplement (à la Quebec) so as to encourage labor force attachment, employment vouchers for persons on welfare without work for, say, 6 months. High minimum wages would stifle all of this.

Analytically, the basic point at issue here can be expressed as follows. Wage rates are one of the key allocative devices in a mixed economy. However, in a "binary" approach to welfare, minimum wages take on a redistributive as well as an allocative role — namely, that work at the minimum wage is expected to deliver above-poverty income. Whether they help more than hurt in alleviating poverty is not at issue here. At issue is that, under the above proposals, the "social" or "redistributive" aspect of minimum wages is being transferred to the child tax credit and (it is hoped) incentive-related welfare system for adults. In this new environment, wages can assume their allocative role.[2] In the final analysis, the provinces will decide what to do with their minimum wages, but my guess is that some province, somewhere, will experiment in this area.

---

2 I am indebted to Andrew Coyne for pointing this out in the context of the C.D. Howe Institute's Roundtable for Journalists on Social Policy, Toronto, May 27, 1994.

Postsecondary Education

The recommendation relating to the cash component of postsecondary education (PSE) is to convert it into a portable student voucher that can be applied to universities, to provincially run community colleges (or their equivalent), to private sector training institutes, and to accredited industry-run apprenticeship or certification programs. The values for the voucher would differ by end use and would be tailored to the number of users and the funds available. In terms of the funding, one should note that the federal government is insisting on reductions in total PSE cash payments as part of the social security review (see the discussion of the 1994 federal budget in Chapter 9), so that there presumably are fewer dollars in this envelope.

The net result of this proposal would be to divert some erstwhile funds away from university and community college financing and toward nongovernment training and/or apprenticeship. This would be appropriate given the present structure of subsidies in the system. Moreover, it would be consistent with the federal government's taking a more active financial interest in the skills formation of Canadians.

Beyond this, some provinces may wish to move toward an income-contingent repayment system for financing PSE. The federal voucher proposal is fully consistent with such a scheme.

Other Education Reforms

There is a host of needed reforms in the education sector: altering curricula for a knowledge/information society, allowing more community input or choice in the public school system (that is, downplaying the role of teachers' unions and bureaucrats), facilitating greater industry and/or professional linkages in both high schools and PSE institutions (especially community colleges), enhancing access to university courses for students in community colleges and vice versa, and so on. But there are no "levers" in the social security review to ensure that these and similar measures can be implemented. The way that such reform will come about is via experimentation in the various provinces. This experimentation is already under way. Readers interested in a vision in terms of what primary and secondary schooling ought to mean in an information era can consult Drucker (1993) — in particular, his chapter on "The Accountable School." We have a long way to go here.

Training

If they wish, the provinces should have the responsibility for integrating training into the rest of the "active" labor force strategy — welfare, secondary education, PSE, and the linkages forged with business and labor. One way to accomplish this is for training to fall under what I have elsewhere (Courchene 1991) referred to as "concurrency with provincial paramountcy." This would allow both levels of government to play a role in the training area but, if a province wished, it could exercise "paramountcy" in terms of legislation and integration. The incentives, under concurrency with provincial paramountcy, would be for Ottawa to legislate flexible framework policies and strategies so that there would be no need for the provinces to exercise their paramountcy (although, Quebec would probably do so on principle).

As alluded to in earlier chapters, one promising approach would be to have provincial training boards with representation on the board from Ottawa, provincial business and labor groups, as well as other stakeholders involved in an "active" labor force strategy.

The essential point is that the system should move toward a "single window" in terms of the overall labor market strategy and, for those provinces that so desire, this should be a provincially coordinated window.

One final point: Canada's training deficit is not primarily related to funding. Indeed, embarking on a series of expensive training programs is almost surely not the way to go. Of the industrialized countries, Canada is already among the high spenders on education. Instead, the challenge is to develop a training culture and society. In other words, we need a fresh "state of mind" when it comes to training, and our governments need to adopt a corresponding "mind of state" with respect to this issue. This has to be a coordinated effort among governments, citizens, business, labor, and the entire schooling/training system. Lester Thurow (1993) has expressed the challenge in its starkest form: "If capital is borrowable, raw materials are buyable and technology is copyable, what are you left with if you want to run a high-wage economy? Only skills, there isn't anything else." This is what making the transition from a resource-based to human-capital-based economy and society has to mean. Our existing funding must be refocused to this end. This does not preclude devoting some social policy savings to training, but it would be a serious mistake to think we can "buy" a training culture: we must first aspire to a skills-enhancing culture, then "learn" our way to achieving it. Governments at all levels have a leadership and facilitating role to play here. Canadians will respond if given the opportunity to do so.

Workers' Compensation

In terms of workers' compensation, I reiterate the proposal I made in the previous chapter: taxation of benefits, a move toward joint employer-employee contributions, design features that eliminate much of the moral hazard and encourage claimants to maximize post-injury earnings, and an enhanced degree of accountability. I am confident that competitive federalism will play a critical role in the rethinking and redirecting of workers' compensation.

Health

The cash component of Established Programs Financing (EPF) should be converted into a further personal income tax point transfer, which would be equalized under the formal equalization formula. Transitional measures would be appropriate here. For example, the existing (fiscal year 1995/96) level of the overall EPF transfer could be allowed to apply until the value of the equalized transfer under this new proposal exceeds this value, after which the new proposal would determine the flows.

Provincial experimentation and restructuring in the health area is in full bloom. Ottawa should encourage this experimentation and should ensure that there is in place an interprovincial accord that recognizes the basic principles underpinning medicare. The 1994 *Canada Health Act* is too draconian a model for this purpose. The federal authorities must recognize that, in spite of their deficit shifting, medicare remains a sacred trust because the provinces and their citizens deem it to be so.

Allow me to inject a personal observation. The medicare system that Canadians hold near and dear no longer exists. To be sure, the high-profile aspects are still around — zero user fees, accessibility, and so on. But beneath the surface, health care is undergoing a veritable revolution. At the local level, there is a shift toward holistic treatment and at the conceptual level the emphasis is shifting away from sickness and toward well-being. These developments are truly exciting and they will eventually restructure the health care subsector. There may need to be some national (federal or preferably federal-provincial) oversight in just how far afield aspects of this provincial experimentation should be allowed to go. The problem with the *Canada Health Act* is that it is focused on what the *last generation's* version of health ought to have been about. I think that the climate is right for Ottawa and the provinces to work toward a "Canada Well-Being Act" that would reflect the new realities and incorporate some guidelines and incentives that would restore the general health area as one of the cornerstones of Canadian social policy in the millennium.

Social Services

The area of social services has been, by and large, neglected in this study. This omission is not related to any perceived lack of importance but, rather, to my total lack of expertise with respect to this area.

Nonetheless, the conversion of welfare from needs testing to income testing would free up an enormous bureaucracy. My guess is that the provinces will begin to redeploy these social workers in a more holistic context. Specifically, I expect that the provinces would begin to move toward the Quebec single-window model, where social services, nutritional counselling, prenatal care, legal services, substance-abuse counseling, and so on are integrated progressively into a one-stop "well-being" center. Expect rather dramatic moves in this direction in several of the provinces. My earlier comments on the future of health (or well-being) are relevant here.

The Retirement Income Subsystem

We need a negative income tax for the elderly. At a minimum, the OAS and the GIS should be rolled into a single GIS, with no age or pension credits. Ideally, we should strive toward incorporating the Canada Pension Plan (CPP) into this negative income tax as well. The issue here relates to the dramatic burden placed on today's low-income Canadians — namely, facing a progressively increasing CPP payroll tax with little in the way of expected future benefits (see Chapter 3). Phasing out the CPP, or incorporating it into a "super GIS" is difficult because of the long horizons involved in retirement planning and the fact that the CPP/QPP has been integrated into some occupational pension plans. However, given that so many young Canadians apparently believe that there will be no CPP when they retire, the way is open for the government to make some critical moves here. The "baby boomers" will not retire for two decades. This ought to be adequate lead time provided that we act now. Beyond these concerns with respect to program structure, several other reforms may be appropriate. One would be to follow the United States and Sweden by increasing the elderly age threshold from 65 to 67 years. At the provincial level, the provinces should follow Saskatchewan's example and treat the high-income group of the elderly in the same manner as the high-income component of the nonelderly when it comes to issues such as drug programs.

Equalization

Given that the above proposals have eliminated both EPF and CAP from the federal-provincial financial interface, this leaves equalization as the only remaining major federal-provincial transfer. By now, it should be evident that the equalization system falls short of the mark when it comes to incentives relating to dynamic efficiency. For six of the "have-not" provinces (and to a lesser degree for Quebec as well), there are virtually *no* financial rewards if they increase the value of their own revenue bases. Phrased differently, there are no aggregate revenue penalties on these provinces from legislative measures that may serve to *decrease* their own tax bases. We are talking about policies that influence nearly half of Canada's gross national product. This is no longer acceptable.

Accordingly, my recommendation is to convert equalization into a version of a negative income tax for provinces. One acceptable option would comprise: moving from the five-province standard to the national-average standard; removing all ceilings and floors; and equalizing 70 percent of the difference between the national average standard and the province's own standardized fiscal capacity. This recommendation is embodied in the last row of Table 41.

Actually, I would prefer a program that embodied an even greater incentive than 30 cents on the dollar. For example, a graduated negative income tax could be implemented — 90 percent of the fiscal capacity gap up to 75 percent of the national average; 75 percent of the gap between 75 percent and 90 percent of the national average; and 50 percent of the gap between 90 percent and 100 percent of the national average.

Once again, transitional measures would be needed. One could freeze equalization at the fiscal year 1995/96 levels (but incorporating any social-security-review-related tax point transfers such as those related to medicare) and allow provinces to receive these levels until the equalization associated with this new proposal breaks through this level.

This new approach (say, the 70 percent version) to equalization is absolutely critical to the remaking of both Social and Economic Canada. The fact that we have allowed redistributive goals to dominate totally any concerns related to dynamic efficiency means that internal equity or equality considerations are compromising internal and external comparative advantage considerations.

A Tax on Base Approach

The personal income tax (PIT) system is a powerful integrating and reconciling device for the social envelope. Provinces should be allowed the flexibility of opting for a tax on base approach instead of the existing tax on tax approach (see Thematic Tableau 4). This is neither a major technical issue nor, necessarily, a change in overall income taxation. What it does mean is that the provinces can impose their own income-distribution preferences on their own part of the tax system. But they can come pretty close to this under the current system by means of a series of tax credits, surcharges, flat taxes, and so on. More to the point, it will allow freedom for the provinces to use their share of the PIT as an integration device for income testing welfare, for embarking on a wage-supplementation scheme, for embarking on an income-contingent repayment approach to university financing, and so on. This is an idea whose time has come.

A Social and Economic Union

All of the above recommendations have to be embedded within an overarching approach to the social and economic union. This union would incorporate both "negative" and "positive" integration, to use the jargon of the Charlottetown Accord. In terms of negative integration, neither Ottawa nor the provinces should be allowed to impede the free flow of goods, services, labor, and capital across the country. The tax collection agreements would be part of this negative integration, in the sense that the provinces would continue to be prohibited from mounting discriminatory tax credits within the shared PIT.

But positive integration must also be pursued. Among other things, this must mean well-defined and transparent skills-accreditation procedures as well as fair and open processes for transferring skills accreditation across the country. The fact that we have failed so miserably in this area ought to be viewed as a national tragedy, let alone a national outrage. For more than two decades now, Germany has had occupational standards and full national accreditation for over 400 occupations. Even Switzerland, which by some measures qualifies as the world's most decentralized federal systems, does the same for over 200 skill categories. This is just one more example of our tendency to favor place over people. More to the point, it raises the basic issue of whether our federation exists to satisfy the desire of governments or to pursue the interests of individual Canadians. Surely, as we embrace the information era, these barriers to skills mobility must come to an end. One approach to all of this, alluded to earlier, is that Ottawa should not transfer a single training dollar to the provinces until there is an iron commitment on the part of the provinces to fall into line. Ideally, we should follow the Germans and Swiss by having business and labor be full partners with governments (and citizens) in designing a free internal market for occupational skills.

Finally, an underlying goal of the social and economic union must be to convert the various provincial programs into national ones, via such principles as portability, no residency requirements, and nondiscriminatory access for all Canadians to provincial programs and services. Actually, thanks to the federal spending power, we do rather well here. "More of the same" is the operative message.

Recapitulation

This, then, is my approach to reworking Social Canada for the millennium. To say that there are holes or gaps in this overview is surely an understatement. No doubt the financial and conceptual "gap filling" will be a challenging task.

Nonetheless, the primary goal of the exercise was to design the overall blueprint and framework in line with the descriptive and analytical framework of the previous ten chapters. The remainder of this chapter is devoted to assessing aspects of the viability of this blueprint, beginning with the special challenge posed by the Quebec tax abatement.

Quebec and Asymmetry

As part of the federal-provincial financial interface, Quebec receives 16.5 additional PIT tax points — 8.5 PIT points for EPF, 5 PIT points for CAP, and 3 points for other programs. These tax points are already included in Quebec's tax rates as part of its separate personal income tax system. It receives a correspondingly smaller amount of cash transfers than do the other provinces.

The challenge is as follows. How does Ottawa convert CAP into an antipoverty refundable tax credit for children for Quebec or effectively eliminate EPF when this province "receives" much of CAP and EPF in terms of tax credits?

The first general point to make is that this is not special treatment for Quebec. All provinces had the choice in the 1960s of opting for tax points in lieu of cash. Only Quebec did so. The only way of "removing" these tax points is for Ottawa simultaneously to increase cash transfers to Quebec, increase by a similar amount the rates of federal taxation on Quebecers, and then assume that the province will reduce its tax rates accordingly under the Quebec PIT. But *Ottawa* cannot reduce the Quebec tax rates under this province's separate PIT. This approach surely would trigger political fireworks for many reasons, not least because it would attempt to unwind an agreement that is nearly 30 years old. Therefore, I deem this option to be wholly inoperative — Quebec's 16.5 additional PIT points are part of the Canadian landscape and will almost assuredly remain so.

The second general point is that the presence of these additional tax points for Quebec has the potential for wreaking havoc with *any* thorough reworking of Social Canada. Indeed, they pose enormous problems for the status quo, because Quebec's cash transfers under EPF will fall to zero well before those of any other province. Ottawa has legislation on its books to the effect that, if this occurs and if the value of Quebec's tax abatement under EPF grows through the EPF ceiling, Ottawa will *decrease* Quebec's cash transfers from other programs. This is a political minefield. Thus, asymmetry is probably an inevitable aspect of social policy arrangements under any scenario, including the status quo.

The real issue is whether we wish somehow to accommodate this inevitable asymmetry or prefer to abort the social policy review because it will embody asymmetry. I want to address various scenarios in this context.

Put All Provinces on the Level of Quebec

One obvious solution would be to grant these 16.5 additional PIT points to all provinces. This is clearly the "clean" solution, especially in the context where the provinces have the right to opt for a tax on base approach to the PIT. The new value of an equalized tax point is roughly $800 million. To be sure, Quebec's 16.5 additional tax points are not equalized, but a generalized 16.5 tax point transfer surely would be. Thus, the value of such an additional equalized tax transfer would be $13.2 billion (including the amount now going to Quebec). This represents roughly three-quarters of the current amount of the cash transfer under EPF and CAP combined. Given that the Minister of Finance wants $1.5 billion in saving from EPF and CAP, and given that the cash component of EPF is heading downward, Ottawa could embark on this 16.5 across-the-board tax point transfer and then declare the end of EPF and CAP. The decentralist in me cries "hurrah," but on reflection this solution would be inferior to that contained in the blueprint.

The issue thus becomes the following: do we want symmetry to drive Social Canada or do we want a coherent approach to our socio-economic challenges to underlie the remaking of our social infrastructure. My preference is to accept the asymmetry. But are there not ways to finesse this asymmetry?

Finessing the Asymmetry

Consider the following multifaceted scenario. First, Ottawa declares EPF null and void and introduces the alternatives elaborated in the above blueprint. While the value of Quebec's 8.5 PIT tax abatement is, for internal EPF calculations, allocated somehow between PSE and health, the fact of the matter is that EPF is an *unconditional* transfer and the Quebec tax abatements are, in effect, also *unconditional* abatements. Fortuitously, it turns out, from Table 14, that the value of the cash component of the EPF health transfer to Quebec is $1.37 billion, while the value of its unequalized tax abatement is $1.1 billion. This means that converting Quebec's 8.5 unequalized tax abatement into an equalized tax transfer would probably still leave the value within the $1.37 billion cash transfer. In other words, it appears that the proposal in the blueprint to convert the cash component of the EPF health transfer into an equalized transfer would require roughly a transfer of 8.5 tax points (assuming that Ottawa wants to maintain the existing level of health transfers). This being the case, all provinces would get an additional 8.5 tax points and Quebec's 8.5 unequalized tax abatement would be converted into an equalized tax transfer. There is no sleight of hand here: this solution is entirely above board and fully consistent with the reality that EPF is an unconditional transfer. Thus, there is no problem with respect to the blueprint's proposals for EPF — Quebec's treatment is full and fair. And the asymmetry has been removed!

Finessing the CAP proposal (that is, converting CAP into an antipoverty refundable tax credit) is, admittedly, a bit more difficult. Ottawa would have no alternative but to take the constitutional route here and simply assert that it has the authority to inaugurate the antipoverty tax credit. It would then tell Quebec that its 5 unequalized PIT points for CAP, already incorporated in Quebec's tax system, will not be challenged but henceforth be incorporated as an offset in the equalization problem. In other words, in lieu of cash transfers under equalization, Quebec would receive some of its equalization in the form of an unequalized tax abatement. Thus, the abatement would be shifted from CAP to equalization because CAP would no longer exist.

There is precedent for this. The remaining 3 points of the Quebec tax abatement were initially associated with the old youth allowance program. When this program was terminated, Quebec was allowed to keep these 3 unequalized tax points, but it transferred an equivalent amount of cash to Ottawa. Effectively, therefore, Quebec was renting these 3 tax points from Ottawa. For all practical purposes, these tax points can be viewed as an offset to the equalization program. The CAP proposal would just add 5 more tax points for offset under equalization.

Thus, there is a way to apply the preferred blueprint to Quebec as well as to the other provinces. The EPF aspect of this would involve no compromise at all. The CAP conversion would, but there appear to be acceptable ways around this, as noted in the previous paragraph. Nonetheless, some asymmetries with respect to provincial treatment would remain, although these would now be buried in the equalization program. Yet these are *not* asymmetries in the sense of unequal treatment of the provinces on Ottawa's part. As noted, they have arisen because the rest of the provinces decided in the 1960s *not* to follow Quebec in opting for tax point transfers rather than cash transfers. Intriguingly, this proposed solution would serve to *decrease* the asymmetry across provinces.

I now turn to the old chestnut of Canadian federalism — the centralization/decentralization issue.

Centralization/Decentralization and the Division of Powers

The design of the social policy blueprint was driven by the desire that the resulting social policy infrastructure reflect the needs and challenges facing individual Canadians. Nonetheless, the end result is an intriguing mixture of both greater centralization in some places and greater decentralization in others. Since this or any other blueprint has to be "sold" both to Canadians and to their governments, it is instructive to focus on the above proposal from the vantage point of intergovernmental relations or the division of powers.

The Blueprint and the Division of Powers

From the intergovernmental perspective, it is convenient to view the blueprint as resting on four pillars.[3]

The first of these is that there would be a much clearer delineation of roles within the federal system. Gone would be the fiscal and financial entanglement associated with EPF and CAP. The blueprint would be a substantial improvement on the status quo in terms of political and financial accountability, visibility/transparency, and efficiency.

The second pillar relates to the federal role. In the social policy field, Ottawa would now take care of children and seniors. Via vouchers to PSE students, it would play a *funding* role related to higher education and to skills formation, but little in the way of a regulatory or legislative role. In terms of the old federal-provincial transfer system, Ottawa's role would be confined to equalization, which at the same time would be larger (because of the health tax point transfer) and more incentive-compatible with the new economic order (the negative income tax approach). Finally, Ottawa would take the lead in restructuring UI.

The third pillar relates to the provinces, which would gain, via the additional transfer of tax points, financial control over medicare and health. Even more important, perhaps, the provinces would acquire paramountcy in terms of training and thus the flexibility to forge an integrated and "active" labor force policy across welfare, PSE, labor, industry, and the transition from school to work. A "single window" for an active labor-market strategy would now be a reality. Beyond this, the provinces would have rate and bracket flexibility in terms of their share of the personal income tax, so that they would now have an additional valuable instrument for integrating the welfare-to-work subsystem.

The fourth pillar is the economic and social union. In the jargon of the 1980–82 constitutional debates, this may well be part of the "people's package," but governments must take the lead here. And not just the federal government, since I have long held the view that for programs to be national they need not be federal.

Thus, while the blueprint was constructed from the bottom up, it does have some appealing features when viewed from the top down.

---

3 I am grateful to Fred Gorbet (1994) for suggesting that I recast the blueprint in the context of the division of powers.

Cost and Affordability

I have by design shied away from any estimates of the cost of the blueprint. There are two reasons for this. The first is that I was principally interested in the design and delivery features of a new Social Canada. That is, the focus has been on structure, incentives, efficiency, accountability, and so on, and on the nature of interactions among Canadians, the provinces, and Ottawa. The second reason is the more relevant in this context — namely, that the blueprint is consistent with a rather wide range of costs. If affordability is a determining issue, then one simply scales the blueprint down to meet the allocated budget. And vice versa.

To be sure, one theme that has carried throughout the analysis is that all policy areas, social policy included, must make their contribution to putting our fiscal houses in order. There is nothing in the blueprint that is inconsistent with this. Indeed, it would be far better to derive an appropriate infrastructure and then scale it to affordability concerns than to approach the restructuring process from the other end of the spectrum by letting fiscal criteria drive the restructuring.

Other Issues

The blueprint is really a series of building blocks. As such, the devil may well be in the details. Each area will have its own set of conceptual and operational problems. It could not be otherwise for this or any other restructuring of Social Canada.

Moreover, the blueprint will interact with other policy issues. Consider just one — internal migration. Will the above proposal trigger an increase in internal migration? And if so, compared to what? Canada may be in for considerable internal migration when the economic recovery finally embodies employment recovery. Canadians have always moved in search of work, and they will continue to do so. More worrisome on the internal migration front is what will happen if the northern cod do not come back. In this case, we had better ensure that our immigration policy is sufficiently flexible to anticipate this reality.

In terms of any additional impact on internal immigration arising from the blueprint, one could argue that the restructuring of UI might have some consequences. On the other hand, the new child tax credit, while identical across the country in dollar terms, would probably act as a buffer because it would be worth more in relation to average incomes in regions that are potentially vulnerable to UI changes.

Over the longer term, the distribution of population will probably have more to do with the economic viability of the various provinces (for example, the manner in which they integrate both east-west and north-south) and with external forces such as the impact of the information revolution on the location of industries and employees. There may be some short-term challenges to certain regions arising from the blueprint, but that is why transitional measures are needed. Over the longer term, however, the blueprint is a recipe for economic viability.

Conclusion

This, then, is my preferred blueprint for reworking Canada's social infrastructure. As noted earlier, readers are free to design their own blueprints in terms of the preceding analysis and options contained in Chapter 10. My goal in this chapter was to design a social policy system that was informed by the restructuring imperatives, by the restructuring principles, and by the need, at long last, to put individual Canadians front and center in the program design.

By way of a concluding comment, I believe that Canada will, in the millennium, be largely defined by its social infrastructure both in its own right and because an appropriate social infrastructure will be an integral part of competitiveness in the new global economic order. Obviously, getting the rest of the policy framework in place will also be critical. But this is much less of a challenge. I do not know what the optimal structure will be for the banking sector or for the telecommunications industry in the year 2000. What I do know, however, is that market forces will ensure that our policies in these areas will be appropriate. In this important sense, social policy restructuring is far more difficult and challenging. Markets may provide some signals, but they cannot do the restructuring. Hence, we must rely on ourselves, on our collective will, and on our political "entrepreneurs." To be a Canadian in the next century must, among other things, mean that all citizens have access to a social infrastructure that allows them full opportunity to develop and enhance their skills and human capital in order that they be full participants in the Canadian and global societies. This is what the social policy blueprint is all about. And this is why we have to succeed in rethinking and reworking Social Canada in the millennium.

Appendix

Changes to Federal Social Programs and Taxes, 1985–93

Child Benefits

1986

- Partial indexation of family allowances (benefits adjusted each year to the amount of inflation over three percent).
- Refundable child tax credit increased from $384 per child in 1985 to $454 per child in 1986.
- Prepayment of refundable child tax credit introduced for families with net incomes of $15,000 or less ($300 per child in November 1986 and the remaining $154 after 1986 income taxes are filed early in 1987).
- Family income threshold for maximum refundable child tax credit lowered from $26,330 to $23,500 and partially indexed (to the amount of inflation over three percent).
- Children's tax exemption kept at $710 per child.

1987

- Refundable child tax credit increased from $454 per child in 1986 to $489 per child in 1987.
- Children's tax exemption reduced from $710 per child in 1986 to $560 per child in 1987.

1988

- Refundable child tax credit increased from $489 in 1987 to $559 per child in 1988; increased by an additional $100 for each child age 6 and under (less 25 percent of any child care expense deduction claimed for the child),

---

This appendix is reproduced, with permission, from Battle and Torjman 1993a.

bringing the total maximum credit to $659 for each child age 6 and under and $559 for each child age 7 to 17.

- Family income threshold for prepayment of the refundable child tax credit ($16,060) set at two-thirds of threshold for the refundable child tax credit ($24,090).
- Children's tax exemption converted to nonrefundable child tax credit worth $66 in federal income tax savings for each of the first two children and $132 for each additional child in a family.

1989

- Nonrefundable child tax credit partially indexed from $66 in 1988 to $67 in 1989.
- Refundable child tax credit adjusted by partial indexation from $559 in 1988 to $565 per child in 1989; increased by an additional $200 for each child age 6 and under (less 25 percent of any child care expense deduction claimed for the child), bringing the total maximum credit to $765 for each child age 6 and under and $565 for each child age 7 to 17.
- Family income threshold for maximum refundable child tax credit adjusted by partial indexation from $24,090 in 1987 to $24,355 in 1989.
- Clawback imposed on family allowances (benefits reduced by 15 cents for every dollar of the higher-income parent's net income over $50,000); phased in by one-third in 1989, two-thirds in 1990 and fully from 1991 on, so families affected by the clawback required to repay only one-third of amount for 1989.

1991

- Canada ratified the United Nations Convention on the Rights of the Child.

1992

- "Brighter Futures Initiative" announced: new child tax benefit proposed (see 1993); $500 million Child Development Initiative to promote the health and well-being of children at risk.

1993

- Child tax benefit introduced: replaced family allowances, nonrefundable child tax credit and refundable child tax credit with single refundable monthly credit worth maximum $1,233 a year for each child age 6 and under and $1,020 a year for each child age 7 to 17; larger families get an extra $75 a year for third and each additional child. Maximum credits paid to families with net family incomes under $25,921, above which the credits are reduced by 2.5 cents for every additional dollar or net family income for families with one child and five cents for every additional dollar for families with two or more children. Working poor families get up to $500 more per household per year from an "earned-income supplement" payable to those with employment earnings of $3,750 or more; the supplement phases in at a rate of eight percent, so the maximum $500 begins once employment earnings reach $10,000 and continues until net family income of $25,921, above which the earned-income supplement is reduced by 10 cents for every additional dollar of net family income. The new child tax benefit (including the earned-income supplement) and the income thresholds are partially indexed (to the amount of inflation over three percent).

Child Care

1987

- "National Strategy on Child Care" announced, but its centerpiece — a new Child Care Act to replace day care provisions of the Canada Assistance Plan (CAP) — failed to become law before the November 1988 election.

1988

- Child care expense deduction raised from $2,000 to $4,000 for each child age 6 and under and for children with special needs; remained $2,000 for children ages 7 to 14.
- Maximum family limit of $8,000 for child care expense deductions eliminated.
- Child Care Special Initiatives Fund, part of the National Strategy on Child Care, began on April 1, 1988 ($100 million over seven years).

1993

- Child care expense deduction increased from $4,000 to $5,000 for each child age 6 and under and from $2,000 to $3,000 for each child age 7 to 14.

Pensions

1985

- Spouse's Allowance extended to all widows and widowers 60 through 64 years of age who are in need, regardless of their spouse's age at death (before, the deceased spouse had to be 65 or older).
- Proposal in 1985 budget to partially index old age security benefits (to the amount of inflation over three percent) abandoned in face of widespread criticism from seniors' organizations and other groups.

1986

- Limit on income tax deduction for Registered Pension Plan contributions ($3,500) abolished.
- Limit on income tax deduction for Registered Retirement Savings Plan contributions for taxpayers without Registered Pension Plans (lesser of $5,500 or 20 percent of earnings) raised to the lesser of $7,500 or 20 percent of earnings.

1987

- Canada Pension Plan (CPP) amendments include:
  - flexible retirement benefits payable as early as age 60 and up to age 70 (with actuarial adjustment downward of 0.5 percent for each month between 60 and 65 and upward of 0.5 percent for each month between 65 and 70);
  - increased disability benefits (monthly flat-rate portion went from $91.06 in 1986 to $242.95 in 1987) raising total maximum monthly benefit from $455.64 in 1986 to $634.09 in 1987;
  - in the event of divorce after 1987, time limit of three years lifted for applying for credit-splitting (that is, equal division of all Canada Pension Plan credits earned by both spouses during their life together); requirement of formal application replaced by Minister of National Health and Welfare being informed of the divorce and receiving information necessary to effect the division; and credit-splitting made mandatory except where a spousal agreement entered into after June 4, 1986, expressly mentions the spouses' intention not to divide CPP credits and

where such a spousal agreement is permitted under provincial family law (only Quebec and Alberta currently permit this exception);

- extension of current credit-splitting provisions to cover marital separations and the breakdown of common-law relationships (formal application for credit-splitting is still required);
- married spouses permitted to share in retirement pensions earned by both partners during their marriage;
- more equitable calculation of combined benefits (that is, combined survivor and retirement, combined survivor and disability);
- survivor benefits to continue for survivors who remarry;
- payment of two children's benefits if both partners die or become disabled.

- Schedule of long-term increases in Canada Pension Plan contribution rates for employees and employers agreed to by Ottawa and the provinces: rates increased by 0.20 percentage points annually from 1987 through 1992 and 0.15 percentage points annually from 1993 through 2011; every five years, federal and provincial finance ministers to review contribution rates, making any required changes and extending schedule for five more years.
- Canada Pension Plan contribution rate increased from 3.6 percent (1.8 percent for employees, 1.8 percent for employers and 3.6 percent for self-employed) of contributory earnings (earnings between \$2,500 and \$25,800) in 1986 to 3.8 percent (1.9 percent for employees and employers, 3.8 percent for self-employed) of contributory earnings (earnings between \$2,500 and \$25,900) in 1987.
- Improvements to *Federal Pension Benefits Standards Act* governing occupational pension plans for employees under federal jurisdiction (federal and territorial government and Crown corporation workers, workers in federally-regulated industries such as banks, interprovincial transportation, radio and television broadcasting) include:

- all full-time employees in an occupational group covered by a pension plan must be eligible to join the plan after two continuous years on the job;
- part-time employees earning at least 35 percent of the Year's Maximum Pensionable Earnings under the Canada or Quebec Pension Plan for two consecutive years have the right after two continuous years on the job to join pension plans available to full-time workers in the same occupational group;
- pension contributions must be vested (that is, employees are entitled to contributions made on their behalf by their employer) and locked in (that is, employee and employer contributions are not accessible to the employee

until retirement) after a worker has belonged to a pension plan for two years (applies to pension benefits earned after January 1, 1987);

- better portability provisions (plan members who change jobs can transfer vested pension benefits to the plan of their new employer, if that plan so permits, or to an individual locked-in RRSP or to an annuity that pays pension benefits upon retirement);
- plans subject to the *Pension Benefits Standards Act* must provide the option of a lifetime survivor pension equal to 60 percent of the pension of a deceased plan member who was eligible for retirement at the time of death (the survivor pension can be waived if both spouses so declare in writing); survivors whose deceased spouses were not eligible to retire at the time of death must receive a benefit worth the value of the vested pension that has accrued after 1986; survivor benefits can no longer be terminated if the survivor remarries.

1988

- Pensioners allowed to deduct Canada/Quebec Pension Plan contributions, unemployment insurance premiums and employment expense deduction when calculating their income for purposes of determining their eligibility for and benefits from the Guaranteed Income Supplement or Spouse's Allowance.
- Canada Pension Plan contribution rate increased to 4.0 percent of contributory earnings (2.0 percent for employees and employers, 4.0 percent for self-employed) of contributory earnings (earnings between $2,600 and $26,500).

1989

- Clawback imposed on old age security program: old age pension reduced by 15 cents for every dollar of the senior's net individual income over $50,000; partial clawback applies to pensioners with net incomes between $50,000 and $76,333 (that is, they keep a portion of their old age pension after paying income taxes and clawback) and full clawback affects those with net incomes over $76,333 (that is, they must repay all of their old age pension); clawback phased in over three years, so clawed-back pensioners had to repay one-third of clawback in 1989, two-thirds in 1990 and the full amount from 1991 on.
- Canada Pension Plan contribution rate increased to 4.2 percent (2.1 percent for employees and employers, 4.2 percent for self-employed) of contributory earnings (earnings between $2,700 and $27,700).

1990

- Canada Pension Plan contribution rate increased to 4.4 percent (2.2 percent for employees and employers, 4.4 percent for self-employed) of contributory earnings (earnings between $2,900 and $29,000).

1991

- Canada Pension Plan contribution rate increased to 4.6 percent (2.3 percent for employees and employers, 4.6 percent for self-employed) of contributory earnings (earnings between $3,000 and $30,500).
- Limit on income tax deduction for RRSP contributions for taxpayers who belong to Registered Pension Plans set at the amount of any unused RRSP contribution room at the end of the preceding taxation year plus the lesser of $11,500 or 18 percent of the previous year's earnings minus the taxpayer's Pension Adjustment (a measure of the value of Registered Pension Plan benefits accrued the previous year).
- Limit on income tax deduction for RRSP contributions for taxpayers without Registered Pension Plans raised from the lesser of $7,500 or 20 percent of earnings to the lesser of $11,500 or 18 percent of earnings for the previous year.

1992

- Increase in benefits for children of CPP contributors who die or are disabled (from $113.14 a month in 1991 to $154.70 a month in 1992).
- Revised schedule of long-term increases in Canada Pension Plan contribution rates for employees and employers agreed to by Ottawa and the provinces: 0.20 percentage points annually from 1987 through 1996, 0.25 percentage points annually from 1997 through 2006 and 0.20 percentage points annually from 2006 through 2016; as a result, combined employee-employer contribution rate for 2011 will be 9.10 percent under revised schedule as opposed to 7.60 percent under previous schedule.
- Canada Pension Plan contribution rate increased to 4.8 percent (2.4 percent for employees and employers, 4.8 percent for self-employed) of contributory earnings (earnings between $3,200 and $32,200).
- Limit on income tax deduction for RRSP contributions for taxpayers without Registered Pension Plans raised from the lesser of $11,500 or 18 percent of earnings for the previous year to the lesser of $12,500 or 18 percent of earnings for the previous year.

1993

- Canada Pension Plan contribution rate increased to 5.0 percent (2.5 percent for employees and employers, 5.0 percent for self-employed) of contributory earnings (earnings between $3,300 and $33,400).
- Planned increase on limit on income tax deduction for RRSP contributions for taxpayers without Registered Pension Plan (to the lesser of $13,500 or 18 percent of previous year's earnings) delayed until 1994, so 1993 limit remained at 1992 level (lesser of $12,500 or 18 percent of earnings).

Unemployment Insurance

1985

- Severance payments included as employment earnings for establishing unemployment insurance (UI) benefits.

1986

- Pension income included as employment earnings for establishing UI benefits.
- UI premiums for 1986 kept to 1985 rates — $2.35 per $100 of insurable earnings for employees and $3.29 per $100 of insurable earnings for employers — instead of increasing under existing rules to $2.60 per $100 of insurable earnings for employees and $3.64 per $100 of insurable earnings for employers.

1987

- Pension income not to affect UI entitlement if claim established on the basis of insurable employment accumulated after the pension commenced or if the UI claim started before January 5, 1986.

1988

- Mothers who are not able to take their newborns home immediately after birth may defer their 15 weeks of maternity leave until baby is released from hospital (retroactive to March 23, 1987).
- Extended maternity benefits to father who, due to death or disability of mother, becomes primary caregiver.

1989

- UI premiums ($2.35 for every $100 of insurable earnings for employees and $3.29 per $100 of insurable earnings for employers, in effect from 1985 through 1988) lowered to $1.96 per $100 of insurable earnings for employees and $2.73 per $100 of insurable earnings for employers.

1990

- Full cost of UI shifted to employers and employees (Ottawa's share was $2.9 billion out of a total of $12.6 billion in 1989).
- UI premiums increased to $2.25 per $100 insurable earnings for employees and $3.15 per $100 of insurable earnings for employers for 1990 through 1992.
- Qualifying period for UI increased from 10–14 weeks to 10–20 weeks depending on regional unemployment rate.
- Maximum duration of UI benefits reduced from 46–50 weeks to 35–50 weeks.
- In addition to 15 weeks of existing UI maternity benefits, ten weeks of parental benefits made available to mother or father (or shared between them) of newborn or adopted child; parental benefits may be extended to 15 weeks where the child is six months or older upon arrival at the claimant's home and suffers from a physical, psychological or emotional condition.
- UI sickness benefits remain unchanged at 15 weeks but may be combined with maternity and parental benefits; maximum of 30 weeks in special benefit entitlements.
- UI retirement benefits payable when insured person reached age 65 (three-week lump sum) eliminated; aged workers continue to contribute but eligible only for regular UI benefits.
- UI penalties increased for quitting employment without just cause, refusing to accept suitable employment or being fired for misconduct: waiting period for benefits increased to between 7 and 12 weeks, and benefits for recipients in these categories reduced from 60 to 50 percent of average weekly insurable earnings.

1991

- UI premiums increased to $2.80 per $100 of insurable earnings for employees and $3.92 per $100 of insurable earnings for employers, effective July 1, 1991.

1992

- UI premiums increased to $3.00 per $100 of insurable earnings for employees and to $4.20 per $100 of insurable earnings for employers.

1993

- UI premiums amended to encourage expansion of small business; federal government to pay any increase in UI employer premiums in 1993 to maximum of $30,000 per enterprise.
- UI benefits reduced from 60 to 57 percent of insurable earnings for new beneficiaries effective April 4, 1993.
- UI benefits denied to workers who quit jobs without just cause.

Federal Social Transfers to the Provinces

1985

- Federal-Provincial Agreement on Enhancement of Employment Opportunities for Social Assistance Recipients ("four-corner" agreement) announced to encourage employability enhancement measures (for example, training) for welfare recipients.

1986

- Higher earnings exemptions permitted for welfare recipients (pursuant to the "four-corner" agreement).
- Federal transfers to provinces and territories for health and postsecondary education under the *Established Programs Financing (EPF) Act* partially indexed to increase in GNP less two percentage points (before, federal payments were adjusted by the full increase in GNP).

1990

- Federal transfer payments to the provinces and territories for health and postsecondary education under EPF frozen at their 1989/90 level for 1990/91 and 1991/92, after which partial indexation formula of GNP less three percentage points to apply.

- "Cap on CAP" — federal transfer payments to Ontario, Alberta and British Columbia for cost-sharing welfare and social services under the Canada Assistance Plan (CAP) limited to increase of five percent a year for 1990/91 and 1991/92.

1991

- Freeze on federal transfer payments to the provinces and territories for health and postsecondary education under EPF for 1990/91 and 1991/92 extended through the end of 1994/95, after which partial indexation formula of GNP less three percentage points to apply.
- "Cap on CAP" extended through 1994/95, so in effect from 1990/91 through 1994/95.

Taxes

1985

- Temporary high-income surtax imposed on upper-income taxpayers from July 1985 to December 1986 (five percent of basic federal tax between $6,000 and $15,000 and 10 percent of basic federal tax above $15,000).
- Capital gains exemption introduced (up to a lifetime limit of $500,000, later reduced to $100,000 for capital gains other than qualifying farm property and small business corporation shares, which remain $500,000); phased in between 1985 and 1990.
- Registered Home Ownership Savings Plan (RHOSP) eliminated (introduced in 1974, the program had allowed taxpayers who are not home owners to deduct from taxable income contributions up to $1,000 a year, to a lifetime maximum $10,000, to save for a home).

1986

- Partial indexation introduced for income tax exemptions and tax brackets (to the amount of inflation over three percent); personal exemptions and brackets were fully indexed before.
- Federal tax reduction eliminated (the program, in place from 1973 through 1985, had eased federal income tax for low and middle-income taxpayers; in 1985, it cut federal income tax by up to $100 for taxpayers with basic federal tax of $6,000 or less, above which the credit was reduced by 10 percent to disappear at basic federal tax of $7,000).

- General surtax of three percent of basic federal tax imposed on all taxpayers effective July 1, 1986.
- Disability tax deduction increased from $2,590 to $2,860 and extended from persons who are blind or confined to a bed or wheelchair to cover all persons who are severely disabled; Department of National Health and Welfare must certify applicants to be markedly restricted in activities of daily living.
- Refundable sales tax credit introduced for low-income families and individuals (maximum $50 per adult and $25 per child for households with net family income $15,000 or less, above which benefits are reduced by five percent of additional income).

1988

- Personal exemptions and most deductions in the personal income tax system converted to nonrefundable credits: $1,020 for basic personal credit, $850 for married and equivalent-to-married credit, $550 for aged credit; $550 for disability credit; $66 for each of the first two dependent children 17 and under and $132 for the third and each subsequent child 17 and under, $250 for dependents over 18 who are physically or mentally infirm; 17 percent of Canada/Quebec Pension Plan contributions, unemployment insurance premiums, private pension income up to $1,000, disability amount for dependant other than a spouse, tuition fees and education amount transferred from child, amounts transferred from spouse; 17 percent of charitable donations up to $250 and 29 percent of charitable donations above $250.
- Number of tax brackets reduced from ten to three (17 percent on taxable income up to $27,500, 26 percent on taxable income between $27,501 and $54,999, and 29 percent on taxable income of $55,000 and above); top marginal tax rate lowered from 34 to 29 percent.
- Refundable sales tax credit increased from $50 to $70 per adult and from $25 to $35 per child for households with net family income $16,000 or less.

1989

- Refundable sales tax credit increased from $70 to $100 per adult and from $35 to $50 per child for households with net family income $16,000 or less.
- General surtax on all taxpayers increased from three to five percent, effective July 1, 1989.
- High-income surtax reimposed on upper-income taxpayers (three percent of basic federal tax exceeding $15,000) effective July 1, 1989.

- Medical expenses credit expanded to include part-time attendant care expenses required to enable severely disabled persons to work (taxpayer can deduct the costs of care provided by a part-time attendant; deduction is limited to two-thirds of eligible income -that is, income from employment, training allowance under the *National Training Act* or a grant for research or similar work — up to a maximum of $5,000).

1990

- Refundable sales tax credit increased from $100 to $140 per adult and from $50 to $70 per child for households with net family income $18,000 or less.

1991

- Goods and services tax (GST) introduced: 7 percent on broad range of goods and services, with the exception of certain items such as basic groceries, prescription drugs, medical devices, health care services, educational services, child and personal care, and legal aid services.
- Refundable GST credit introduced to partially offset burden of GST on lower-income Canadians: maximum benefits for 1991 were $190 per adult, $100 per child and a "living alone" supplement of up to $100 for single adults and single parents with net incomes between $6,175 and $25,215; maximum credits paid to households with net family income $25,215 or less, and benefits are reduced by five cents for every dollar above the threshold; both credits and threshold partially indexed to the amount of inflation over 3 percent.
- Disability tax credit increased from $575 to $700; administrative guidelines defining eligibility for the credit (regarding the terms "activities of daily living" and "markedly restricted" (incorporated in the *Income Tax Act* to ensure uniformity in their interpretation.
- Medical expenses tax credit expanded to include: up to $5,000 of part-time attendant care expenses (provided by nonrelatives) which are not otherwise deductible (formerly restricted to severely disabled Canadians who work); specially trained service animals to assist individuals with severe and prolonged impairments; home modifications to reduce mobility restrictions for persons with severe and permanent disabilities; and incontinence products.
- Tax provisions amended to allow businesses to deduct fully the expense of modifications to accommodate persons with disabilities (for example, interior and exterior ramps, alterations to bathrooms, widening of doorways) in the year these costs are incurred.

- Allowances paid to disabled employees for taxi, paratransport and parking no longer considered taxable for those eligible for the disability credit by reason of severe mobility or sight impairment; employer allowances paid to employees for attendant care required to perform employment duties (for example, readers for blind persons, coaches for persons with mental handicaps) no longer considered a taxable benefit.

- Tax liability of lump-sum payments of Canada/Quebec Pension Plan disability pensions to be reduced by spreading the amount over the years in respect of which they are paid.

- Limit on tax deduction for RRSP and Registered Pension Plans contributions modified (see "Pensions").

1992

- Education tax credit increased from 17 percent of $60 for each whole or part month taxfiler was enrolled as full-time student to 17 percent of $80 for each whole or part month taxfiler was enrolled as full-time student.

- Total amount of tuition fee and education credits that a student can transfer to a supporting taxpayer increased from $600 to $680.

- General surtax on all taxpayers lowered from 5 percent of basic federal tax to four percent, effective July 1, 1992.

- Medical expenses tax credit expanded to include visual or vibratory signalling devices for persons with hearing impairments; payment for rehabilitative therapies to adjust for hearing or speech loss.

- List of devices eligible for immediate tax write-off for businesses expanded to include: elevator car position indicators for persons with visual impairments; visual fire alarm indicators, telephone devices and listening devices for persons with hearing impairments; and disability-specific computer attachments.

- Education tax credit made available to persons with disabilities who attend a qualifying postsecondary educational institution on a part-time basis.

- Definition of "earned income" for purposes of RRSP contributions expanded to include disability pensions paid under the Canada/Quebec Pension Plans.

- In addition to tax measures to assist persons who disabilities, "National Strategy for the Integration of Persons with Disabilities" ($158 million over five years) announced to promote their economic integration.

1993

- Couples living in common-law relationships to be treated as married spouses for tax purposes: one-earner common-law couples now will be able to claim the married credit and will be allowed to contribute to a spousal RRSP; they will no longer be able to claim the equivalent-to-married credit (that is, to pretend they are single parents) and must (as in the case of married couples) combine their incomes for determining eligibility for the GST credit and the new child tax benefit.

- General surtax on all taxpayers lowered from four percent of basic federal tax to three percent, effective January 1, 1993.
- Home Buyers' Plan introduced: home buyers can withdraw up to $20,000 from their RRSPs for down payment on a new or existing home without having to pay income tax on the withdrawal; the RRSP withdrawal must be repaid to the RRSP in equal instalments over a 15-year period (amounts not repaid to be treated as a permanent withdrawal from the RRSP and subject to income tax).
- GST credit, formerly paid every three months (January, April, July, and October), to be paid once every six months (April and October), though the total annual benefit will not change.

Social Housing

1990

- Social housing budget ($1.695 billion in 1989/90) limited to $1.785 billion in 1990/91 (15 percent less than planed, for a $16 million cut) and $1.871 million in 1991/92 (15 percent less than planned, for a cut of $35 million).

1991

- Fifteen percent reduction in planned funds for new social housing, announced in 1990 budget, extended through 1995/96.

1992

- Social housing budget restricted to an average 3 percent annual increase from 1992/93 through 1996/97.
- Cooperative Housing Program terminated.

1993

- Social housing budget frozen at $2 billion ($600 million cut for 1993/94 through 1997/98).

References

Axworthy, Lloyd. 1994. *Proposed Changes to the Unemployment Insurance Program*, Budget Backgrounder. Ottawa: Department of Human Resources Development.

Banting, Keith G. 1992. "Neoconservatism in an Open Economy: The Social Role of the Canadian State." *International Political Science Review* 13: 149–170.

Battle, Ken, and Sherri Torjman. 1993a. *Federal Social Programs: Setting the Record Straight*. Ottawa: Caledon Institute of Social Policy.

———. 1993b. *Opening the Books on Social Spending*. Ottawa: Caledon Institute of Social Policy.

Beach, Charles M., and George A. Slotsve. 1994. "Polarization of Earnings in the Canadian Labour Market." In *Stabilization, Growth and Distribution: Linkages in the Knowledge Era*, The Bell Canada Papers on Economic and Public Policy 2. Kingston, Ont.: Queen's University, John Deutsch Institute for the Study of Economic Policy.

Blomqvist, Åke. 1989. "Health Care in the 1990s: An Economist's View." In *Healthy Populace, Healthy Policy*, edited by S.M. Davis. Kingston, Ont.: Queen's University, School of Policy Studies.

Boadway, Robin W., and Frank Flatters. 1994. "Fiscal Federalism: Is the System in Crisis?" In *The Future of Fiscal Federalism*, edited by Keith Banting, Douglas Brown, and Thomas J. Courchene. Kingston, Ont.: Queen's University, School of Policy Studies.

———, and Paul A.R. Hobson. 1993. *Intergovernmental Fiscal Relations in Canada*. Toronto: Canadian Tax Foundation.

Boothe, Paul. 1992. "Federal Budgeting in the 1990s: The End of Fiscal Federalism." In *The Federal 1992 Budget*, edited by T.J. Courchene and M.F.J. Prachowny. Kingston, Ont.: Queen's University, John Deutsch Institute for the Study of Economic Policy.

———, and Barbara Johnston. 1993. *Stealing the Emperor's Clothes: Deficit Offloading and National Standards in Health Care*, C.D. Howe Institute Commentary 41. Toronto: C.D. Howe Institute, March.

Bouchard, Geneviève. 1993. "Provincial Perspective: Quebec." In *Income Security in Canada: Changing Needs, Changing Means*, edited by Elisabeth Reynolds. Montreal: Institute for Research on Public Policy.

Brown, David. 1994. Presentation to the House of Commons Standing Committee on Human Resources Development. Ottawa, March 10.

Canada. 1985. Royal Commission on the Economic Union and Development Prospects for Canada [chaired by Donald Macdonald]. *Report*, 3v. Ottawa: Supply and Services Canada.

———. 1986. Commission of Inquiry on Unemployment Insurance [chaired by Claude Forget]. *Report*. Ottawa: Supply and Services Canada.

————. 1990. Department of National Health and Welfare. *Payment Schedule Comparison Rates Effective July 1990*. Ottawa.

————. 1991. Department of National Health and Welfare. *Inventory of Income Security Programs in Canada*. Ottawa.

————. 1992a. Department of Finance. *Federal Provincial Study on the Cost of Government and Expenditure Management*. Ottawa.

————. 1992b. Department of Finance. *Federal Transfers to the Provinces*. Ottawa: Department of Finance, Federal-Provincial Relations Division.

————. 1993. Task Force on Income and Adjustment in the Atlantic Fishery [chaired by Richard Cashin]. *Charting a New Course: Towards the Fishery of the Future*. Ottawa: Supply and Services Canada.

————. 1994. Department of National Health and Welfare. *Preliminary Estimates of Health Expenditures in Canada: 1987–1991*. Ottawa.

Canadian Federation of Independent Business. 1993. *Wage Watch: Measurement of the Public Sector / Private Sector Wage Gap*. Toronto.

Canadian Labour Market and Productivity Centre. 1990. "A Review of Regional Economic Development Policy in Canada." *Quarterly Labour Market Productivity Review* (Spring/ Summer), pp. 23–34.

Canadian Teachers' Federation. 1993. "Background Material for a Seminar on 'The Impact of Federal Economic Policies on Public Education and Teachers'," Ottawa, Delta Hotel, June 20–22.

Cashin Report. *See* Canada. 1993. Task Force on Income and Adjustment in the Atlantic Fishery.

Chandler, Teresa. 1993. "Restructuring: The New 'R' Word." *CABE News* (Canadian Association of Business Economists) (Fall).

Chaykowski, Richard P., and Terry Thomason. 1994. "Canadian Workers' Compensation: Institutions and Economics." In *Research in Canadian Workers' Compensation*, edited by T. Thomason and R. Chaykowski. Kingston, Ont.: Queen's University, School of Industrial Relations.

Commission of the European Communities. 1993. "Stable Money — Sound Finances." *European Economy* 53.

Courchene, Thomas J. 1978. "Avenues of Adjustment: The Transfer System and Regional Disparities." In *Canadian Confederation at the Crossroads: The Search for a Federal-Provincial Balance*, edited by Michael Walker et al. Vancouver: Fraser Institute.

————. 1979. *Refinancing the Canadian Federation: A Survey of the 1977 Fiscal Arrangements Act*. Montreal: C.D. Howe Research Institute.

————. 1980. "Towards a Protected Society: The Politicization of Economic Life." *Canadian Journal of Economics* 13 (November): 556–577.

————. 1984. *Equalization Payments: Past, Present and Future*. Toronto: Ontario Economic Council.

————. 1987. *Social Policy in the 1990s: Agenda for Reform*, Policy Study 3. Toronto: C.D. Howe Institute.

———. 1989. "Summing Up: A Public Policy Perspective." In *Healthy Populace, Healthy Policy*, edited by S.M. Davis. Kingston, Ont.: Queen's University, School of Policy Studies.

———. 1991. *The Community of the Canadas*, Reflections 8. Kingston, Ont.: Queen's University, Institute of Intergovernmental Relations.

———. 1992a. "Mon pays, c'est l'hiver: Reflections of a Market Populist." *Canadian Journal of Economics* 25 (November): 759–791.

———. 1992b. *Rearrangements: The Courchene Papers*. Oakville: Mosaic Press.

———. 1993. "Path-Dependency, Positive Feedback and Paradigm Warp: A Schumpeterian Approach to the Social Order." In *Income Security in Canada: Changing Needs, Changing Means*, edited by Elisabeth Reynolds. Montreal: Institute for Research on Public Policy.

———. 1994a. "Canada's Social Policy Deficit: Implications for Fiscal Federalism." In Keith Banting, Douglas Brown and Thomas Courchene (eds.) *The Future of Fiscal Federalism*, edited by Keith Banting, Douglas Brown, and Thomas J. Courchene. Kingston, Ont.: Queen's University, School of Policy Studies.

———. 1994b. "Glocalization, Institutional Evolution and the Australian Federation." In a forthcoming conference volume. Canberra: Australian National University, Federalism Research Centre.

———. 1994c. "Reflections on Canadian Federalism: Are There Implications for the European Economic Union?" *European Economy*.

———. 1994d. "Two Cheers for Australian Federalism." In *Australian Federalism: Future Directions,* edited by Cheryl Saunders. Melbourne: University of Melbourne, Centre for Comparative Constitutional Studies, forthcoming.

———, and Robert G. Campbell. 1994. "Marching to a Different Drummer: A Role for the Military in Civilian Training?" Kingston, Ont., Queen's University, School of Policy Studies. Mimeographed.

———, and Glen H. Copplestone. 1980. "Alternative Equalization Programs: Two-tier Systems." In *Fiscal Dimensions of Canadian Federalism*, edited by Richard M. Bird. Toronto: The Canadian Tax Foundation.

———, and Lisa M. Powell. 1992. *A First Nations Province*. Kingston, Ont.: Queen's University, Institute of Intergovernmental Relations.

———, and Arthur E. Stewart. 1991. "Provincial Personal Income Taxation and the Future of the Tax Collection Agreements." In *Provincial Finances vol. 2: Plaudits, Problems and Prospects*, edited by Melville McMillan. Toronto: Canadian Tax Foundation.

Drucker, Peter F. 1986. "The Changed World Economy." *Foreign Affairs* 64 (Spring): 3–17.

———. 1993. *Post-Capitalist Society*. New York: Harper Business.

Dupré, Stefan. 1994. "The Promise of Procurement Federalism." In *The Future of Fiscal Federalism*, edited by Keith Banting, Douglas Brown, and Thomas J. Courchene. Kingston, Ont.: Queen's University, School of Policy Studies.

Economic Council of Canada. 1992a. *A Lot To Learn: Education and Training in Canada*. Ottawa: Supply and Services Canada.

———. 1992b. *The New Face of Poverty: Income Security Needs of Canadian Families*. Ottawa: Supply and Services Canada.

Forget Commission. *See* Canada. 1986. Commission of Inquiry on Unemployment Insurance.

Gaylin, Willard. 1993. "Faulty Diagnosis: Why Clinton's Health Care Plan Won't Cure What Ails Us." *Harper's Magazine* (October), pp. 57–64.

Gorbet, Fred. 1994. "Comment on 'Social Canada in the Millennium.'" Toronto, C.D. Howe Institute. Mimeographed.

Hamilton, Colleen, and John Whalley. 1984. "Reforming Public Pensions in Canada: Issues and Options." In *Pensions Today and Tomorrow: Background Studies*, edited by David W. Conklin, Jalynn H. Bennett, and Thomas J. Courchene. Toronto: Ontario Economic Council.

Harris, Richard G. 1993. *Trade, Money, and Wealth in the Canadian Economy*, Benefactors Lecture, 1993. Toronto: C.D. Howe Institute.

Hay, Alan. 1976. "Is Ontario Paying Too Much?" *Hospital Administration in Canada*, pp. 19–29.

Heclo, Hugh. 1984. "Toward a New Welfare State." In *The Development of Welfare States in Europe and America*, edited by Peter Flora and H.J. Heidenheimer. London: Transactions Books.

Helliwell, John F. 1994. "Convergence and Migration among Provinces." Policy Study 94-2. Toronto: University of Toronto, Institute for Policy Analysis.

Hobson, Paul A., and France St-Hilaire. 1993. "The Financing and Delivery of Social Policy: Fiscal Transfers for Social Assistance and Social Services." In *Income Security in Canada: Changing Needs, Changing Means*, edited by Elisabeth Reynolds. Montreal: Institute for Research on Public Policy.

———, and France St-Hilaire. 1994. *Reforming Federal-Provincial Fiscal Arrangements: Toward Sustainable Federalism*. Montreal: Institute for Research on Public Policy.

House Report. *See* Newfoundland. 1986. Royal Commission on Employment and Unemployment.

Hurley, Jeremiah, Jonathan Lomas, and Vandna Bhatia. 1993. "Is the Wolf Finally at the Door? Provincial Reform to Manage Health-Care Resources," Centre for Health Economics and Policy Analysis Working Paper 93-12. Hamilton: McMaster University.

IRPP. 1993. "The State of Canadian Public Finances: Lessons from Abroad and Directions for the Future," Montreal, Institute for Research on Public Policy Working Paper, May 27.

Jenness, R.A., and M.C. McCracken. 1993a. *Ontario and the Canada Assistance Plan*. Ottawa: Informetrica.

———, and M.C. McCracken. 1993b. *Review of Established Program Financing Systems*. Ottawa: Informetrica.

Jérôme-Forget, Monique. 1993. "Workers' Compensation in Crisis." *Policy Options* (July/August, pp. 54–59).

Kroeger, Arthur. 1994. "Government and the 'Jobs' Issue." *Canadian Business Economics* 2 (2): 42–53.

Lam, Newman, Michael Prince, and James Cutt. 1993. *Reforming the Public Pension System in Canada: Retrospect and Prospect*. Victoria, BC: University of Victoria, Centre for Public Sector Studies.

Leslie, Peter M. 1993. "The Fiscal Crisis of Canadian Federalism." In *A Partnership in Trouble: Renegotiating Fiscal Federalism*, Policy Study 18, by Peter M. Leslie, Kenneth Norrie, and Irene K. Ip. Toronto: C.D. Howe Institute.

Lindbeck, Assar. 1993. "Overshooting, Reform and Retreat of the Welfare State," The Seventh Tinbergen Lecture delivered on October 1, 1993, at de Nederlandsche Bank, Amsterdam. Stockholm: Institute For International Economic Studies.

Lipsey, Richard G. 1993. "Wanted: A New Social Contract." *Policy Options* 14 (July/August): 5–9.

———. 1994. "Markets, Technological Change and Economic Growth." Presentation to the 10th Annual General Meeting of the Pakistan Society of Development Economics. Burnaby, BC, Simon Fraser University, Department of Economics. Mimeographed.

McCracken, M.C., and R.A. Jenness. 1993. *Labour Market Development and Training*. Ottawa: Informetrica.

Macdonald Commission. *See* Canada. 1985. Royal Commission on the Economic Union and Development Prospects for Canada.

MacDougall, D., et al. 1977. *Report of the Study Group on the Role of Public Finance in European Integration*. Luxembourg: Office for Official Publications of the European Communities.

McKenna, Frank. 1993. Speech on Education to the Annual Couchiching Conference, August 5. Mimeographed.

Makin, Kirk. 1994. "Newfoundland is hitting rock bottom." *Globe and Mail* (Toronto), January 6, p. A1.

Martin, Paul. 1994a. *The Budget Plan*. Ottawa: Department of Finance.

———. 1994b. *Facing Choices Together: A Response to the Pre-Budget Consultations*. Ottawa: Department of Finance.

Maxwell, Judith. 1993. "Legacies." Lakehead University Convocation Address, Thunder Bay, Ont., May 29.

———. 1994. "More Carrots, Please: Education, Training and Fiscal Federalism." In *The Future of Fiscal Federalism*, edited by Keith Banting, Douglas Brown, and Thomas J. Courchene. Kingston, Ont.: Queen's University, School of Policy Studies.

National Council of Welfare. 1989. *A Pension Primer*. Ottawa: Supply and Services Canada.

———. 1992. *Welfare Incomes: 1991*. Ottawa: National Council of Welfare.

New Brunswick. 1992. *NB Works: A Joint Pilot/Demonstration Program between New Brunswick and Canada*. Fredericton, NB: Department of Advanced Education and Labour and Department of Income Assistance.

Newfoundland. 1986. Royal Commission on Employment and Unemployment [chaired by Douglas House]. *Building on Our Strengths*. St. John's: Queen's Printer.

———. 1993. Economic Recovery Commission. *Proposals for a New Income Supplementation Program and Other Reforms to the Income Security System*. St. John's: Queen's Printer.

Norrie, Kenneth. 1993. "Intergovernmental Transfers in Canada: An Historical Perspective on Some Current Policy Issues." In *A Partnership in Trouble: Renegotiating Fiscal Federalism*, Policy Study 18, by Peter M. Leslie, Kenneth Norrie, and Irene K. Ip. Toronto: C.D. Howe Institute.

———. 1994. "Social Policy and Equalization: New Ways to Meet an Old Objective." In *The Future of Fiscal Federalism*, edited by Keith Banting, Douglas Brown, and Thomas J. Courchene. Kingston, Ont.: Queen's University, School of Policy Studies.

Oates, Wallace. 1972. *Fiscal Federalism*. New York: Harcourt, Brace, Jovanovich.

OECD. 1989. *Employment Outlook 1989*. Paris: Organisation for Economic Co-operation and Development.

———. 1993. *Employment Outlook 1993*. Paris: Organisation for Economic Co-operation and Development.

Ohmae, Kenichi. 1990. *The Borderless Economy: Power and Strategy in the Interlinked Economy*. New York: Harper Business.

Ontario. 1992. "Financing Canada's National Social Programs: The Need for Reform." Paper presented to the First Ministers' Conference, Toronto, March.

———. 1993a. Fair Tax Commission. *Fair Taxation in a Changing World*. Toronto: Publications Ontario.

———. 1993b. Ministry of Community and Social Services. *Turning Point: New Support Programs for People with Low Incomes*. Toronto: Queen's Printer for Onatrio.

Ontario Economic Council. 1983a. *Pensions Today and Tomorrow: An Ontario Economic Council Position Paper*. Toronto.

———. 1983b. *A Separate Personal Income Tax for Ontario: An Ontario Economic Council Position Paper*. Toronto.

Powell, Lisa M. 1992. "Toward Child-Care Policy Development in Canada." In *Social Policy in the Global Economy*, edited by Terrance Hunsley. Kingston, Ont.: Queen's University, School of Policy Studies.

Proulx, Pierre-Paul. 1991. "Un examin des échanges commerciaux du Québec avec les autres provinces canadiennes, les États-Unis et le reste du monde." In Quebec. Commission on the Political and Constitutional Future of Quebec [Bélanger-Campeau Commission]. *Éléments d'analyse économique pertinents à la révision du statut politique et constitutionnel du Québec* [Background papers], vol. 1. Quebec.

Queen's University. 1992. Faculty of Medicine. "Dean's Letter." Kingston, Ont.

Reich, Robert. 1991. *The Work of Nations*. New York: Alfred A. Knopf.

Richards, John. 1994. "Big Bang or Quiet Tinkering: A Round Table." In *The Future of Fiscal Federalism*, edited by Keith Banting, Douglas Brown, and Thomas J. Courchene. Kingston, Ont.: Queen's University, School of Policy Studies.

Sarlo, Christopher A. 1992. *Poverty in Canada*. Vancouver: Fraser Institute.

————. 1993. "Income Equivalencies of Social Assistance Benefits (Ontario)." Unpublished.

Shah, Anwar. 1994. "A Fiscal Needs Approach to Equalization Transfers in a Decentralized Federation," Policy Research Working Paper 1289. Washington, DC: World Bank, Public Economics Division, Policy Research Department.

Simeon, Richard. 1994. "The Political Context for Renegotiating Fiscal Federalism." In *The Future of Fiscal Federalism*, edited by Keith Banting, Douglas Brown, and Thomas J. Courchene. Kingston, Ont.: Queen's University, School of Policy Studies.

Springate, David. 1973. *Regional Incentives and Private Investment*, HRI Commentary 6. Montreal: C.D. Howe Research Institute.

Thomason, T., and R. Chaykowski, eds. 1994. *Research In Canadian Workers' Compensation*. Kingston, Ont.: Queen's University, School of Industrial Relations, forthcoming.

Thomson, David. 1991. *Selfish Generations? The Aging of New Zealand's Welfare State*. Wellington: Bridget Williams Books.

Thorsell, William. 1994. "Newfoundland's proposed 'reform' a shrewd way to postpone real change." *Globe and Mail* (Toronto), January 1, p. D6.

Thurow, Lester. 1992. *Head to Head*. New York: William Morrow.

————. 1993. "Six Revolutions, Six Economic Challenges." *Toronto Star*, January 28, p. A21.

Tuohy, Carolyn. 1994. "Health Policy and Fiscal Federalism." In *The Future of Fiscal Federalism*, edited by Keith Banting, Douglas Brown, and Thomas J. Courchene. Kingston, Ont.: Queen's University, School of Policy Studies.

Vaillancourt, François. 1994. "Income Distribution, Income Security, and Fiscal Federalism." In *The Future of Fiscal Federalism*, edited by Keith Banting, Douglas Brown, and Thomas J. Courchene. Kingston, Ont.: Queen's University, School of Policy Studies.

Members of the
C.D. Howe Institute[*]

[*] The views expressed in this publication are those of the author and do not necessarily reflect the opinions of the Institute's members.

Gérard Limoges
London Life Insurance Company
J.W. (Wes) MacAleer
McCallum Hill Companies
McCarthy Tétrault
W.A. Macdonald
MacDonald, Dettwiler & Associates Ltd.
McKinsey & Company
Maclab Enterprises
James Maclaren Industries Inc.
Maclean Hunter Limited
Jack M. MacLeod
McMillan Binch
MacMillan Bloedel Limited
William Mackness
Mannville Oil & Gas Ltd.
The Manufacturers Life Insurance Company
Maple Leaf Foods Inc.
Maritime Telegraph & Telephone Company, Limited
Marsh & McLennan Limited
Master Equity Investments Inc.
James Mauldin
The Mercantile and General Reinsurance Group
William M. Mercer Limited
Merck Frosst Canada Inc.
Ronald H. Meredith-Jones
Methanex Corporation
Micmac Maliseet Development Corporation Inc.
Miles Canada Inc.
Robert Mitchell Inc.
The Molson Companies Limited
Monsanto Canada Inc.
Montreal Trust
Moore Corporation Limited
The Mutual Life Assurance Company of Canada
National Trust
National Westminster Bank of Canada
Nesbitt Thomson Deacon
E.P. Neufeld
Noma Industries Limited
Noranda Forest Inc.

Noranda Inc.
North American Life Assurance Company
Northwood Pulp and Timber Limited
NOVA Corporation of Alberta
Ontario Hydro
The Oshawa Group Limited
James S. Palmer
PanCanadian Petroleum Limited
Pembina Corporation
Petro-Canada
Philips, Hager & North Ltd.
Les Placements T.A.L. Ltée.
Placer Dome Inc.
David A. Potts
Power Corporation of Canada
PowerWest Financial Ltd.
Pratt & Whitney Canada Inc.
Price Waterhouse
J. Robert S. Prichard
Procor Limited
ProGas Limited
QUNO Corporation
RBC Dominion Securities Inc.
Redpath Industries Limited
Henri Remmer
Retail Council of Canada
Richardson Greenshields of Canada Limited
R.T. Riley
Robin Hood Multifoods Inc.
Rogers Communications Inc.
Rothschild Canada Limited
Royal Bank of Canada
ROYCO Hotels & Resorts
St. Lawrence Cement Inc.
Samuel, Son & Co., Limited
Sandwell Inc.
Sanpalo Investments Corporation
Guylaine Saucier
André Saumier
Sceptre Investment Counsel
Sceptre Resources Limited
Dick Schmeelk
ScotiaMcLeod Inc.

Sierra Systems Consultants Inc.
Sharwood and Company
Shell Canada Limited
Sherritt Inc.
Sidbec-Dosco Inc.
Southam Inc.
Spar Aerospace Limited
Speirs Consultants Inc.
Philip Spencer, Q.C.
The Standard Life Assurance Company
Strategico Inc.
Sun Life Assurance Company of Canada
Suncor Inc.
Swiss Bank Corporation (Canada)
TELUS Corporation
Laurent Thibault
3M Canada Inc.
The Toronto Dominion Bank
Toronto Star Newspaper Limited
The Toronto Stock Exchange
TransAlta Utilities Corporation
TransCanada PipeLines Limited
Trimac Limited
Trizec Corporation Ltd.
Robert J. Turner

Unilever Canada Limited
Urgel Bourgie Limitée
Vancouver Stock Exchange
Gustavo Vega Cánovas
Manon Vennat
VIA Rail Canada Inc.
J.H. Warren
West Fraser Timber Co. Ltd.
Westcoast Energy Inc.
George Weston Limited
Weston Road Wholesale Lumber Ltd.
Alfred G. Wirth
M.K. Wong & Associates Ltd.
Wood Gundy Inc.
Fred R. Wright
Xerox Canada Inc.
Paul H. Ziff

Honorary Members

G. Arnold Hart
David Kirk
Paul H. Leman
A.M. Runciman
J. Ross Tolmie, Q.C.